1/06

kahn

THE U.S. SUPREME COURT
AND MEDICAL ETHICS

D1059766

PARAGON ISSUES IN PHILOSOPHY

THE U.S. SUPREME COURT AND MEDICAL ETHICS

FROM CONTRACEPTION TO MANAGED HEALTH CARE

BRYAN HILLIARD

St. Louis Community College
at Meramec
LIBRARY

First Edition 2004

Published in the United States by
Paragon House
2285 University Avenue West
St. Paul, MN 55114

Copyright © 2004 by Paragon House

All rights reserved. No part of this book may be reproduced, in any form, without written permission from the publisher, unless by a reviewer who wishes to quote brief passages.

Library of Congress Cataloging-in-Publication Data

Hilliard, Bryan, 1957-
    The U.S. Supreme Court and medical ethics : from contraception to managed health care / Bryan Hilliard.
        p. cm. -- (Paragon issues in philosophy)
    Includes bibliographical references.
    ISBN 1-55778-831-6 (pbk. : alk. paper)
    1. Medical laws and legislation--United States. 2. Civil rights--United States. 3. Medical ethics--United States. 4. Medical care--Moral and ethical aspects. I. Title. II. Series.

    KF3821.H55 2004
    344.7304'1--dc22
                                    2004000289

Manufactured in the United States of America

The paper used in this publication meets the minimum requirements of American National Standard for Information Sciences—Permanence of Paper for Printed Library Materials, ANSIZ39.48-1984.

10 9 8 7 6 5 4 3 2 1

For current information about all releases from Paragon House, visit the web site at http://www.paragonhouse.com

For Brenda,

with all my love and affection

Contents

PREFACE

The idea for this book was generated by a question: "Does the United States Supreme Court do medical ethics?" An elderly woman posed this question after listening to a presentation I had given on ethical and legal issues in death and dying. Several months earlier the United States Supreme Court had handed down its two decisions on the constitutionality of state laws prohibiting assistance from physicians in hastening the deaths of terminally ill patients. For the past hour I had been talking with this group, comprised mainly of nurses and social workers from a nearby hospital, patients, and their family members. Two physicians practicing in family medicine also were in attendance and had contributed to the discussion.

I confess I was surprised by the question. Up to this point in the presentation we had discussed such matters as the distinction between euthanasia and physician-assisted suicide, ethical arguments favoring and opposing each, the concept of double effect, professional obligations to ease suffering, advantages and disadvantages of advance directives, reasons a state might wish to explicitly prohibit physician-aided death, and so on. The discussion had been lively and, I hoped, beneficial for everyone in attendance. But then came this question.

I resisted the temptation to launch into a lengthy lecture on what it might mean to "do" medical ethics, whether by Supreme Court justices or anyone else. My next inclination was to inform her that throughout the history of the Supreme Court, several justices (Byron White and Antonin Scalia came immediately to mind) had openly resisted appeals to moral commitments or normative ethical insights, either those of the justices or of the larger community, in judicial decision-making. Instead, I responded by providing more detail on the recent Court decisions and on what various justices had said on the topic of physician-assisted suicide. I dutifully recounted conceptual matters surrounding constitutional issues such as substantive due process, liberty interest, and equal protection. I even presented some of the justices' concerns and observations surrounding death with dignity, suicide, the integrity of the medical profession, sanctity of life, double effect, and the nature of suffering.

Much to my surprise, my questioner was satisfied with these observations. As a matter of fact, my comments generated enthusiastic and sometimes heated discussion over whether the justices had properly understood the issues at stake. If my memory serves, the presentation and discussion ended without consensus regarding how well the Supreme Court understood and applied the relevant issues and concepts. But the discussion did result in all the participants, myself included, having a deeper understanding of the complex ethical, constitutional, professional, and even public policy concerns surrounding whether physicians should be allowed to help patients end their lives.

I left the presentation still not knowing how to answer the question of whether the Supreme Court does medical ethics. However, I could not help but wonder if examining decisions of the High Court might facilitate a deeper understanding of a wide range of concerns and dilemmas that are the mainstay of medical ethics. Might studying Supreme Court decisions serve as an effective teaching tool for those new to the study of ethical problems in health care? Might health care professionals and members of hospital ethics committees gain practical benefit through exposure to Court decisions? Might we learn more about the moral commitments of the justices and how those commitments influence constitutional law?

Of course, pondering the usefulness of Supreme Court decisions is not exactly revolutionary, and this is so for at least two reasons. First, anyone teaching medical ethics courses, or working as an ethics consultant in hospitals, or giving talks on health care dilemmas to the general public knows full well the immense interest in and fascination with how the law handles ethical issues in medicine. In fact, many people associate medical ethics with the law; discussion of abortion, refusal of life-sustaining treatment, and managed care attest to that. Practically everyone is affected by health care—those who deliver it, those who receive it, and those who study it—and we desire to know and understand the moral and legal context in which health care is delivered. When ethical issues in medicine are the center of attention, Americans are drawn to the law in all its variations: state and federal court decisions, state and federal regulations, and national legislation.

In addition to widespread interest in the law in and of itself, specific Supreme Court decisions have received a great deal of scrutiny within medical ethics. Several high-profile opinions of the Court have attracted the attention of those interested in medical ethics, whether they be teachers, scholars, practicing physicians, or students. Excerpts from majority opinions of the Court's contraception, abortion, and physician-assisted suicide cases appear in many books and articles. These cases have inspired thousands of pages of commentary and analysis, most of it insightful and thought-provoking. Although some of this effort has examined the impact of medical ethics on the Court, and that of the Court on medical ethics, analysis is limited to majority opinions or becomes bogged down with technical discussions of constitutional interpretation. In addition, students, health care professionals, and lay readers do not easily understand much of this material.

This book—using as its starting point "Does the Supreme Court do medical ethics?"—introduces students, health care professionals, and lay readers to an innovative and exciting approach to engaging in and thinking about issues and dilemmas central to medical ethics. The tragedies, dilemmas, and issues that play an intricate role in health care come to life in the decisions of the Supreme Court. The decisions excerpted in this book have much to teach students, professionals, and the lay public about the basics of ethical reasoning in medicine and how the justices reason when they consider issues in bioethics law. This knowledge and understanding can be very valuable not only in evaluating decisions and individual opinions of the Court, but also in addressing the ethical dilemmas and moral problems that confront us every day as patients, family members of patients, students, and professionals. We develop a deeper understanding and appreciation for the relevance of medical ethics by reading these cases. We understand the political, social, economic, and public policy challenges more fully by reading these cases. Ultimately we come to an understanding of what it means for the Court to "do" medical ethics.

Without the assistance, encouragement, and inspiration of students, friends, and colleagues this book would not have been possible. The enthusiasm for the project shown by the staff at Paragon House is greatly appreciated. Gordon Anderson and Rosemary Yokoi were immensely supportive, and I enjoyed working with them. Hugh Hindman, Bill Hutchins, Tom Lansford, Jerry Menikoff, Tom Smith, and Bruce Waller offered inspiration. I am especially indebted to Patrick Hayden and John Roth, who were always willing to offer ideas and encouragement. Their patience went above and beyond the call of duty. In addition, several nurses, social workers, and hospital chaplains introduced me to the real-world challenges and dilemmas occurring every day in clinical medicine and in health care facilities. Their dedication to ethically sound, high-quality patient care informs all my thinking and writing in bioethics. Finally, and most important, I owe an immense debt of gratitude to my wife, Brenda. Not only did she believe in the project, she spent countless hours listening, contributing ideas, and proofreading the manuscript. Only through her efforts was this book possible.

INTRODUCTION

Every Supreme Court case that involves a claim of individual rights is brought by a real person, who has sought legal redress for some kind of oppression. American constitutional history is the history of real people with real grievances. Judges—who are also real people—do not always uphold these claims, but their decisions affect many lives: first, of the individuals who brought the case, and second, of those whose rights are determined by the Court's ruling.

—Peter Irons, *A People's History of the Supreme Court*

When the concerns and dilemmas of medical ethics intersect with the standards and principles of constitutional law, the impact on Americans is often profound and long-lasting. Much of medical ethics is concerned with articulating and justifying values and rules that ground morally permissible medical practice and patient care. Much of constitutional law focuses on articulating and justifying standards of constitutional interpretation that in turn guide decisions by courts on the proper limits of federal and state power. In cases involving bioethics law the concepts and principles so common in medical ethics and the various methods of constitutional interpretation and application that are staples of constitutional adjudication come together in such a way as to be confusing for students of both bioethics and health law, medical professionals, and policy makers. This intersection of distinctive practices, languages, and concepts, often involving a collision of disciplines, occurs more often than one might think and directly impacts how patients and their families experience medical care. Anyone concerned with health, illness, life, and death must pay attention.

Consider, for example, how medical ethics and constitutional law might interact with one another in the following scenario. A young man in the final stage of a painful, terminal illness asks his physician to assist him in ending his life. The physician is well aware of her professional obligations and values: on the one hand she is bound never to kill patients, yet she also has a duty to alleviate suffering. If the physician seeks a consultation from a medical ethicist, she may be informed of various principles and theories that alternately find permissible and impermissible the assistance of a physician in hastening the death of terminally ill patients. Respect for patient autonomy might require granting the patient his wish, yet duties stemming from the principle of nonmaleficence (to do no harm) may counsel against such a practice. Suppose further that the physician discovers she is practicing in a state that explicitly prohibits assistance in suicide. When she turns to consult sources in an effort to determine if her state's laws violate the Federal Constitution she discovers differing views of the matter. One such view holds that the United States Constitution grants specific rights to individuals against the state, but that such rights arise only as part of recognized traditions of society. Thus the patient has no right against the state such that the state must permit the physician to assist in his death, since preservation of life is a traditionally recognized value held by society. An alternative view stresses that the Constitution recognizes as rights those actions that are fundamental to liberty, such as those implicating privacy and self-determination. On this view, no right is more fundamental than the right to escape the indignities and suffering that accompany the end stages of a disease, thus the state's ban is unconstitutional. What is the physician to do? What options, if any, does her terminally ill and suffering patient have? We discover that interactions between medical ethics and constitutional law have real implications for real people.

The above scenario, while certainly oversimplified, highlights the reasons many Americans view dilemmas in medical ethics through the practices and authority of the law. Indeed, this perspective is understandable given that so many dilemmas find their way into American courtrooms. Many Americans view issues and dilemmas in medical ethics as proper for the law to address and resolve. Although most court cases involving disputes between physicians and patients or between physicians and the state do not require the attention of constitutional law, many cases in fact do raise constitutional questions and have implications for constitutional law. The conflicts within and between medical ethics and constitutional law range over many issues and policies of great concern to Americans: abortion, sterilization, treatment options for people suffering from diminished capacity, refusal of treatment for religious reasons, public health regulations, physician-assisted suicide, and managed care. Physicians, other health care professionals, patients, families, and government all are profoundly affected by this interaction between the moral and the legal as well as by subsequent conflicts between the two. Nowhere are these conflicts more visible, and nowhere are the results more influential, than in the rulings of the United States Supreme Court.

The High Court, through the opinions of the justices, encapsulates the nuance and import of both law and ethics. One of the tasks of the Supreme Court is to interpret the Constitution of the United States, and both the manner in which the Constitution is interpreted and the conclusions the justices reach have immense significance for the study of the moral dimensions of medicine. Studying the reasoning behind and implications of particular constitutional concepts and interpretations deepens and makes more relevant the study of medical ethics in both its theoretical and practical applications. A careful examination of the justices' opinions on controversial health care issues demonstrates that not only are constitutional principles employed and interpreted, but ethical principles and concepts are as well. Too often those interested in health care and the ethics of health care ignore ethical reasoning, concepts, and principles underlying what the justices have to say. I contend that significant insight is to be gained by considering the opinions of the justices within the context of a medical ethics framework. Often the justices themselves, either explicitly or implicitly, provide the framework when deciding cases; that is, their reasons for finding a particular policy or law constitutional rests at least in part on considerations of an ethical or moral nature.

The purpose of this book is threefold. First, the relationship between medical ethics and constitutional law is illustrated in detail. Exploring how the justices interpret and apply certain provisions of the Constitution instructs us on how certain theories and principles in medical ethics are interpreted and applied. Second, readers are provided with a real sense of how ethical reasoning and moral commitments have found their way into the arguments of the justices. Identifying the use and sometimes misuse of ethical reasoning by the justices as well as by the disputing parties bringing cases to the Court highlights how medical ethics has impacted constitutional adjudication and public policy. Third, and perhaps most important, this book provides readers with a deeper, richer, and more comprehensive understanding of ethical issues in health care than they might otherwise receive from conventional books on medical ethics. The Supreme Court cases represented in these pages exemplify some of the most difficult decisions the justices have ever had to make. Studying their arguments creates a new dimension in our understanding of the practical and theoretical implications of medical ethics. This method will succeed if we pay close attention to what the justices actually say. As we familiarize ourselves with how the justices understand and employ ethical reasoning, we may discover there is a great deal to learn by noticing what the justices do not say as well.

Perhaps a brief but nonetheless instructive example will best illustrate the purposes of the book. In *Stenberg v. Carhart*, the U.S. Supreme Court ruled that states may not prohibit D&X procedures, commonly known as partial-birth abortion. In his opinion disagreeing with the Court's ruling, Justice Kennedy observes in part, "A state may take measures to ensure the medical profession and its members are viewed as healers…." This is a fascinating statement in that there exists in medical ethics a long tradition of discussing and debating the responsibilities of physicians and the proper goals of medicine. Healing is no doubt a worthy goal of medicine, but is it the only worthy goal? Reflection on the ethical and professional responsibilities of medicine may reveal additional duties of physicians that hold equal or even greater significance. The issue here is not so much whether Justice Kennedy is right or wrong in asserting that the primary responsibility of physicians is to heal and that the state should foster that responsibility. Rather, his assertion provides us with an opportunity to consider the ideal model for understanding the duties of physicians and for articulating the goals of medicine. We certainly then may assess whether Justice Kennedy has a superficial understanding of what medicine and medical professionals should be doing. The presence or absence of in-depth ethical reflection by Supreme Court justices regarding the moral responsibilities of physicians has real consequences for physicians and their patients.

Prior to reading and analyzing the Supreme Court decisions excerpted in the following chapters, readers are encouraged to study carefully the following sections that outline some of the basic concepts and principles relevant to constitutional law and medical ethics. Reading legal decisions for the first time can be confusing and frustrating; however, the material included below should prepare you for understanding and evaluating the justices' arguments. My goal is to make reading the opinions of the justices as enjoyable, thought-provoking, and beneficial as possible. Each section below, while brief, is designed with that goal in mind. As you read the opinions of the Court and consider the accompanying questions for discussion and ethical reflection, you should refer back to this material as often as necessary. I sincerely believe that not only will you gain a deeper understanding of medical ethics by reading these decisions, you also will become genuinely excited over how medical ethics has impacted and influenced the nation's highest court.

Medical Ethics and the Law

A great deal has been written regarding the relationship between medical ethics and the law.[1] Students in medical ethics courses, members of hospital ethics committees, ethics consultants, and health care professionals quickly realize that law has been a force and an influence on medical ethics and that medical ethics has been a force and an influence on the law. Whether this influence has positively or negatively affected either discipline is open to debate. Not open to debate is the realization that any definitive progress in addressing the problems and dilemmas in medical care, whether they exist at the public policy level or at the level of individual patients and physicians, requires an understanding of the relationship. Below we briefly consider, first, how medical ethics and law differ, and second, how they in actuality have a dramatic impact on one another.

On first appearance, medical ethics and law have very little in common. Most everyone knows that judging an action to be morally permissible or obligatory does not automatically translate into a moral judgment that the same action should be legal. For example, we may be willing to judge that the state is morally permitted to provide adequate training for mentally retarded persons under its care, but unwilling to argue that the state acts immorally if it refuses to pass the relevant laws or to implement the policies that will ensure such training. A judgment that an action is immoral does not allow us to confidently assert that the state or federal government is acting immorally if it refuses to designate the action as illegal. One can consistently hold that abortion or contraception is immoral, yet refuse to conclude that the state acts immorally when it refuses to prohibit such activities. To be clear, I may think it morally permissible for the state to pay for abortions for poor women who need these procedures in order to protect their health. I may even be willing to provide justification for my moral judgment; such a justification might rest on appeals to the bad or negative consequences for women and society as a whole if abortions for medically necessary reasons are not financed. At the same time, however, I can consistently hold that the U.S. Supreme Court does not act immorally when it refuses to require states to pay for medically necessary abortions. Again, I can offer moral justification for my judgment; such a justification could rely on my contention that the state is permitted (morally and constitutionally) to determine what activities it will and will not fund so long as no constitutional rights are directly violated. No doubt, the connection between judging actions as moral or immoral and judging laws and policies as moral or immoral is complex.

This complexity speaks directly to the notion that medical ethics and law share very little in common and do not impact one another. Medical ethics (or bioethics, or health care ethics) is the critical and systematic study of the moral dimensions of medicine and the life sciences. Medical ethicists are concerned with explaining, evaluating, and analyzing relevant moral norms, concepts, principles, and theories in order to guide decision making and policy formation in health care. Medical ethics recognizes that dilemmas and problems in medicine are complex, and that perhaps more than one approach or answer is morally justified. But medical ethics is also aspirational in that it articulates and recommends moral ideals toward which we can all strive. On the other hand, law—generally understood to include regulations, administrative orders, legislative actions and statutes, common law and constitutional law principles, and court decisions—is concerned with the proper understanding and application of facts and experiences through which it can order society and individual arrangements within society. Law tends to break down dilemmas or problems into two opposing sides. Law employs tools such as proper procedures and inductive reasoning to reach and enforce its conclusions. Law shies away from being aspirational, focusing instead on practical solutions that can be supported by custom, process, and the facts at hand. On first appearance, then, medical ethics and law are different, so how do we understand and explain their relationship to each other?

Carl E. Schneider has made the observation that law has had

a dramatic impact on the moral life of America.[2] Perhaps one of the best examples of law's impact on morality comes in the area of civil rights. Courts, including the Supreme Court, were able to deal with issues of race and segregation in a way that was disinterested and principled. Schneider notes that the Supreme Court in particular was able to perceive that "…the country had failed to deal honestly and decently with a great moral crisis of its history. Calling on the deepest moral lessons of the Constitution, the Court compelled the country to confront that crisis."[3] At this point in our history, we face several crises in health care, and the U. S. Supreme Court has played and will continue to play a strong role in addressing these crises.

Another way that the law and medical ethics are related to each other is obvious and has already been alluded to in this introduction: people think and talk about ethical dilemmas in the language of the law. Our physician who struggles over the proper course of action for her terminally ill patient may well wonder what course of action is morally justifiable, but she considers her moral responsibilities in terms of legal rights and proper procedures. Indeed, the public at large tends to frame ethical debates about abortion, euthanasia, treatment of vulnerable populations, and the practices of managed care organizations in terms of rights and legal procedures. This reliance on rights and proper procedures demonstrates another way in which medical ethics and the law are related. Alexander Morgan Capron says it best:

> While much of law is concerned with commerce and institutions, both public and private, bioethics is essentially about people and about the fundamental choices that determine and even define their lives. If the law has brought to bioethical cases an attention to rights and procedure, bioethics has enriched legal analysis with life-and-death dramas.[4]

In both the common law and in constitutional law we witness the force of medical ethics. At the level of common law, we are familiar with a myriad of lower court decisions where judges have been influenced by such concepts as self-determination and best interests. The common law doctrine of informed consent, for example, has evolved over the years to include considerations of medical ethics. At the level of constitutional adjudication, we are aware of several famous cases (included in this book) where the deliberations of at least some of the justices seem heavily influenced by such concepts as dignity, best interests, and autonomy. Cases involving homosexuality, forced medication of people with mental illness, and physician-assisted suicide come immediately to mind.

In the final analysis, discerning exactly where law has influenced medical ethics and where medical ethics has influenced law may be impossible. Is our understanding of informed consent influenced more by the common law principle of bodily integrity or that mainstay of medical ethics, the principle of autonomy? Does our understanding of the meaning and proper scope of privacy rest in a specific interpretation of the Due Process Clause of the Fourteenth Amendment, or does our conception of privacy derive from an appeal to the language of rights? But then again, the law, not just medical ethics, appeals to autonomy and rights to justify its decisions. As you read through the cases in this book, you will have an opportunity to recognize and evaluate the impact that medical ethics and the law have had on each other. Do not be surprised, however, if the lines between the two are blurred at times.

Functions and Purpose of the U.S. Supreme Court

Understanding the arguments and rulings of the justices of the U.S. Supreme Court requires some familiarity with the functions and purpose of the High Court itself. Alexander Bickel's description of the Court is at once enlightening and intriguing. "The least dangerous branch of the American government is the most extraordinarily powerful court of law the world has ever known. The power which distinguishes the Supreme Court of the United States is that of constitutional review of actions of the other branches of government, federal and state."[5] This short passage is enlightening in that it informs us that the Supreme Court has the power to examine and even overturn actions of the individual states, of Congress, and of the President of the United States. We are intrigued by the fact that this power is exercised by an institution described as "the least dangerous" of the three branches of government, yet we are told the Supreme Court has power over the other branches. How is this possible? To answer this question, we turn to a brief examination of the concepts of federalism and judicial review.

Article III, Section 1 of the U.S. Constitution reads in part, "The judicial power of the United States shall be vested in one Supreme Court, and in such inferior Courts as the Congress may from time to time ordain and establish." Among the responsibilities of the Supreme Court is the interpretation of the Constitution. Since the Constitution allocates power to three groups—the federal government, the states, and the people—the Supreme Court has the task of determining the proper allocation of power and authority among the three. Federalism is the form of government the United States has adopted whereby there is a sharing and a balancing of power.[6] When cases involving bioethical issues come before the Court, they often involve struggles over the proper allocation of power or authority. For example, an individual state and the federal government may disagree over whether the state may permit physicians to prescribe marijuana to terminally ill cancer patients. The federal government believes it has the power to regulate dangerous substances and to prohibit their use even by terminally ill patients. The state, on the other hand, although perhaps recognizing that the federal government may legitimately regulate dangerous drugs, believes it has the power and authority to make exceptions for terminally ill patients. Here we have a struggle over the proper uses and limits of power. These same kinds of struggles can occur between the people and either a state or the federal government. Physician-assisted suicide and the right of families to refuse life-sustaining treatment for their loved ones are two recent examples. The Supreme Court, through interpreting the Constitution, is charged with resolving these struggles.

Closely associated with federalism is the concept of judicial review. At its simplest, judicial review means the Supreme Court has the power to say what the law is. In an early case, *Marbury v. Madison* (1803), Chief Justice John Marshall declared that the Supreme Court has the authority to review, and overturn if necessary, acts of Congress. Marshall strongly believed that even though the Constitution does not grant it explicit authority to review congressional acts, the Supreme Court is the final arbiter of what the Constitution means. Part of Justice Marshall's rationale was that the Constitution is the written law, and not even a majority of the people can enact statutes that violate the written law. In addition, Marshall believed, and many have since come to agree, that the justices have a special capacity and responsibility to interpret the Constitution. Not only may the Court review actions of the legislative and executive branches, it also may review and overturn the actions of state legislatures and lower courts. The Court will invalidate state and federal laws, statutes, and regulations if the justices determine that the statute or law violates one or more provisions of the Constitution.

That the Court has taken upon itself the discretion to overturn the actions and laws of democratically elected officials (state and federal) has immense import. Many people find such power disturbing and believe it poses a substantial threat to a viable republic. In invalidating laws and statutes, the Court may appear to be acting as a "super legislature," imposing its own values and its own sense of right and wrong on the nation. Others find judicial review of state and federal actions a natural function of the High Court, a function the Constitution intended it to have. The justices are free to interpret the provisions and intent of the Constitution without direct pressure from either the people or the other branches of government. This independence allows the justices to be fair and impartial. Whether judicial review is a proper function of the U.S. Supreme Court is in large measure irrelevant; judicial review is here to stay. Nowhere is the significance of judicial review more evident than in cases of bioethics law. As you read through the cases in this book, you will have ample opportunity to evaluate the process of judicial review.

Outline of Relevant Constitutional Principles and Concepts

In Supreme Court cases dealing with bioethics law, certain constitutional principles and concepts appear with regularity. Familiarity with these concepts and principles is tremendously important in understanding many of the arguments and approaches the Justices employ in determining whether to uphold a particular law. Acquiring a basic understanding of select concepts will aid you not only in drawing connections between constitutional and ethical argumentation but also in recognizing the influence medical ethics has had on the justices' reasoning.

Many cases implicating bioethical issues under consideration by the Court involve the Fourteenth Amendment. After the Civil War, many in Congress were determined to grant full citizenship for African-Americans; even after the war, Southern states continued to pass laws restricting the rights of African-Americans. In 1866, Congress drafted and proposed the Fourteenth Amendment, and it was ratified by the states in 1868. The Fourteenth Amendment reads in part, "...nor shall any State deprive any person of life, liberty, or property, without due process of law; nor deny to any person within its jurisdiction the equal protection of the laws." The first half of this passage is known as the Due Process Clause, and the second half is referred to as the Equal Protection Clause. Over the course of many years and through multiple Supreme Court decisions, the Fourteenth Amendment has evolved into a means by which many of the values and rights outlined in the Bill of Rights are applied to the states. Due in part to this expansion of rights, and in part to various interpretations of due process and equal protection, many of the Court's decisions in the area of medical ethics center on interpretation and application of these two clauses.

The Due Process Clause has two meanings or applications—procedural and substantive. By procedural due process we usually mean that the Constitution requires fair procedures be in place and enforced whenever the government threatens to restrict the freedom or liberty of individuals. Examples of proper and fair procedures include being present at one's trial and the opportunity to present an adequate defense. The substantive meaning or application of due process has had much more impact on medical ethics. The High Court has determined that the Constitution recognizes and guarantees certain rights to individuals against government interference. These substantive rights include rights to privacy, self-determination, travel, and so on. These rights are substantive in that they are necessary for achieving and maintaining life, liberty, and happiness. Government may limit these rights, but, according to the justices, government may do so only with very good reason.

The second part of the Fourteenth Amendment—state and local governments may not deny individuals equal protection of the law—is called the Equal Protection Clause. In actuality, the terms of the clause do not apply to actions of the federal government, but the Supreme Court has determined that if the federal government classifies individuals in a way that violates equal protection, such violations will fall under provisions of the Fifth Amendment.[7] Government constantly classifies people and then imposes limits on what distinct classes of people are allowed to do. Some people, for example, are classified as visually impaired and as a result are not allowed to drive cars.[8] Of course, one hopes that government has good reason both to classify people and to limit their activities or rights. On those occasions when one or more of an individual's fundamental rights are denied based on classification, then the Supreme Court will examine both the reason for the classification and the interest government asserts as cause for limiting individual rights. The stronger or more fundamental the right that government is infringing, the stronger will be its burden in demonstrating that the classification was necessary and that the violation of rights stemming from the classification meets legitimate state interests. As you can imagine, equal protection analysis by the Supreme Court can be somewhat complicated. For our purposes the following summary of the three types of analysis should be sufficient.[9]

The first level of equal protection analysis is the rational or minimum level of review, in which the Court examines whether a rational basis exists for government's classification of persons and its subsequent imposition of limitations on their actions.[10] An example of where the Court applies this minimal level of review is in the area of legislative actions based on economic status. Any legislation affecting persons based on economic status has to bear only a rational relationship to a governmental interest not prohibited by the Constitution. The intermediate or heightened review level is applied when the Court seeks to determine if the government's classification has a substantial relationship to an important government interest, for example. The Court will apply an intermediate level of review in cases involving gender classifications. Strict scrutiny is the third type of review under equal protection. When the Court reviews legislation under this standard, it independently evaluates the purpose of the legislation. For a law to pass strict scrutiny, the justices have to be persuaded not only that the state is pursuing a constitutionally compelling interest, but also that the classification is necessary to meet that interest. Strict scrutiny is generally applied in cases involving racial classifications.

Whether the Supreme Court chooses to employ minimum, heightened, or strict scrutiny to specific instances of government classifications clearly has tremendous ethical significance. This ethical significance is magnified by the fact that the Court will apply the strict scrutiny test in reviewing legislation that limits fundamental constitutional rights under substantive due process as well. What the justices consider a fundamental constitutional right and what they consider an illegitimate violation of that right constitute questions of great concern for medical ethics and health policy. Unfortunately, great confusion and dispute also exist with regard to how the justices decide which level of scrutiny to apply. Do underlying ethical values and moral commitments influence the justices in determining not only which level or test to use but also the final conclusions they reach upon employing that level?

As you read through the cases in this book you will note that the distinction between due process and equal protection clauses, as well as the distinction between procedural and substantive due process, plays an important role in the justices' reasoning regarding laws and regulations impacting dilemmas in medical ethics. The following brief description of the difference between the two clauses clarifies these distinctions.

> If a law burdens all persons equally when they exercise a specific right, then the courts will test the law under the due process clause. If, however, the law distinguishes between who may and who may not exercise a right, then judicial review of the law falls under the equal protection guarantee because the issue now becomes whether the distinction between these persons is legitimate.[11]

Readers will notice that almost all the Supreme Court cases in this book are concerned with whether a specific law violates one or more fundamental rights protected by the Constitution. Obviously, medical ethics is also concerned with fundamental rights. Keep in mind that the federal government or a state typically does not attempt to take away a fundamental right from all citizens, but rather from a specific group of persons. What this means is that the Court will normally employ substantive due process analysis to determine whether a right is fundamental, but it will appeal to equal protection analysis to conclude whether a particular law unjustifiably infringes the rights of particular groups of individuals.[12] Again, the justices disagree over what constitutes a fundamental right and over whether a particular class of individuals is being unjustifiably discriminated against by government regulation of the fundamental right.

One last pair of concepts in constitutional law stands in

need of explication. When the Court considers the constitutionality of legislation, it may review the law "on its face" or "as applied." Understanding the difference between these two types of review is extremely important.[13] If a law is found unconstitutional on its face, the state may not enforce the law under any circumstances. On the other hand, if the Supreme Court holds a law unconstitutional as applied to the facts of a particular case, the law may be enforced by the state in different circumstances. Several cases in the upcoming chapters highlight this distinction between the two types of challenges.

Perhaps the place where we most easily recognize the significance of an as-applied versus facial challenge is the physician-assisted suicide cases. Consider a statute that prohibits aiding another person to commit suicide. Anyone challenging the statute—for example, terminally ill, suffering patients and their physicians—would challenge the statute as applied. That is, they would want the Court to hold that the law is unconstitutional in circumstances where physicians wish to aid patients in dying. Justice Rehnquist, however, seemed determined to view the challenge to the law as a facial challenge. That is, he viewed the prohibition against any person aiding another to commit suicide at its most general level and hence found the statute to be constitutional. Viewing the constitutional challenge to the prohibition against assistance in suicide as a facial one, and then ruling against the terminally ill patients and their doctors, was a major setback for advocates of a constitutional right to assistance in suicide. Keep this distinction between the two types of challenges in mind as you read and consider the justices' arguments. This distinction and how the justices employ it contribute to our assessment of the moral commitments of the justices. We now turn to a brief discussion of important theories and principles in medical ethics.

Outline of Relevant Theories and Principles in Medical Ethics

As you read the opinions of the justices, you are attempting to draw connections between judicial reasoning and moral reflection. In addition, you are making judgments regarding the influence of medical ethics on the Court's decisions, and the impact of the Court's decisions on decision-making in medical ethics. Is it possible to detect the moral commitments of a particular justice or of the parties who brought the case to the Court? Is it possible to detect, either in the justices or in the parties to the suit, a particular understanding (or misunderstanding) of a specific moral theory or principle? Of course, some knowledge of ethical theories and principles is required to engage in these exercises. Below is a brief outline of the more influential theories and principles utilized in much of medical ethics.[14]

Moral theories are frameworks in which justifications for one's actions, or inactions, can be articulated and defended. We might think of ethical theories as resources toward which we can turn for help and guidance in making moral judgments. We constantly make moral judgments regarding our own actions, those of other persons, and those of government and institutions. A particular moral theory can serve as a defense of those judgments, both to ourselves and to others. Sketched below are four of the most popular moral theories; they are popular not only in the sense that they are commonly used, but also because each has been the recipient of decades of philosophical evaluation and refinement. In addition, as you read the excerpts from the Supreme Court cases, you will discover that the justices often appeal to one or more of these theories.

Utilitarianism. Developed by Jeremy Bentham (1748–1832) and John Stuart Mill (1806–73), this theory may well be the most commonly used justification for decisions, practices, and policies in the moral realm. Utilitarianism is a type of consequentialist ethics in which the rightness or wrongness of an action or rule is determined by the balance of good and bad consequences of that action or rule for all parties concerned. Actions or rules are right if they produce more utility than disutility, and they are wrong if they produce more disutility than utility. As a result, we are obligated always to produce the greatest balance of positive over disvalue. Much disagreement exists over which values should be maximized, but values such as happiness, freedom, and health are considered very important by most utilitarians. Utilitarianism requires an "…objective assessment of everyone's interests and an impartial choice to maximize good outcomes for all affected parties…."[15]

Kantianism. Developed by Immanuel Kant (1724–1804), this theory is in many respects the opposite of Utilitarianism. Kantianism does not assess the rightness or wrongness of actions in terms of their consequences but instead insists that determining an action or policy to be right or wrong depends on an intrinsic property of the action or policy itself. Two principles guide decisions on whether actions are morally right or wrong. The first, the universalization principle, asserts that an action will be right if everyone is able to consent to adopting and following the rule presupposed by the action. The second, the means-ends principle, asserts that actions will be right if they treat all human beings as ends in themselves and not merely as means. These two principles require us to act out of a sense of duty and obligation, both to ourselves and to others. Kantianism, by imposing categorical rules, inserts a degree of certainty and comfort into our attempts to solve moral dilemmas.

Natural Law Theory. This moral theory emerges from Roman Catholic tradition and was given its most influential formulation by St. Thomas Aquinas (1225–74). This theory asserts that an objective standard for moral truth exists and that this standard is human nature. That is, people are morally obligated to act in ways that promote the fulfillment of human nature. When people or institutions or governments act in ways that run counter to the dictates of the natural inclinations of human beings, then they are acting immorally. Human nature is described in terms of goals that human beings generally tend to seek or fulfill. Determining the goals in turn provides us with the values all humans should seek to honor and fulfill. Natural law theory identifies four values that we are naturally inclined to promote. These are biological life, procreation, knowledge of the world and God, and the realization of relationships with other human beings. We should point out that natural law theory imposes a hierarchy of values in which biological life ranks first and relationships last.

Rights-Based Theory. A theory based on rights views morality in terms of liberty, fundamental human rights, and the best interests of individuals. The language of rights is obviously important to the moral life; some have even suggested that an appeal to rights is more effective than traditional moral theories in fostering moral consideration of individual freedom and expression. Consideration of rights and rights talk are especially prominent in democratic societies. Beauchamp and Childress explain: "Rights are *justified claims* that individuals and groups can make upon other individuals or upon society; to have a right is to be in a position to determine, by one's choices, what others should do or need not do."[16] Rights obviously play an important role in formulation of public policy and in judicial decision-making. In addition, most people would agree that rights are not absolute; that is, occasions exist when even the strongest right can be overridden by other considerations such as the advancement of great utility.

This outline of ethical theories should give you a starting point from which to identify moral commitments found in many of the arguments presented by the justices. In addition to these ethical theories, it will also be helpful to have some background on some of the most important principles in medical ethics. Ethical theories and most professional codes of ethics in health care recognize certain moral principles from which to determine morally appropriate rules of action. At its simplest, a moral principle is a norm that guides actions in the moral context.[17] Below we outline five basic moral principles in medical ethics.[18] As you read through the cases in this book you will notice the justices referencing and discussing these principles.

Autonomy. The concept of autonomy plays an important role in medicine, bioethics, and constitutional law. It is quite possible that no other principle has received as much attention in medical ethics discussions and at the U.S. Supreme Court than autonomy. At its simplest, autonomy means acting for oneself from one's own desires. That is, doing what one in fact wants to do. By autonomy we generally mean the ability to form carefully considered goals and desires as well as the ability to fulfill those goals and desires. Autonomy implies control, self-determination, self-rule, liberty, privacy, and freedom. Autonomy is closely associated with rationality, moral agency, and personhood. An autonomous person is a person who is free from controlling influences and at the same time has the ability to understand alternative courses of actions and the implications of those alternatives. The degree to which obligations to promote and respect autonomy are stronger and more stringent than obligations to promote other values is a matter of great debate in both law and ethics.

Nonmaleficence. All theories of morality recognize and require that we not intentionally inflict unnecessary harm or injury on other people. That physicians must "do no harm" is the admonition of one of the earliest codes of professional ethics, the Hippocratic Oath. Duties of nonmaleficence arise from the special skill, training, and responsibilities of physicians and the relative vulnerability and dependence of patients and clients. Duties not to cause intentional injury or harm to others are usually considered stronger and more stringent than duties to help or promote the welfare of others. However, the distinction between not harming and helping others may not be as sharp as one would like. In addition, determining when the principle of nonmaleficence has been violated requires a definition of "harm." Many commonly construe "harm" to mean "thwarting, defeating, or setting back some party's interest."[19] This understanding of harm allows us to construct rules such as "Do not cause suffering" or "Do not kill" that flow from the principle of nonmaleficence.

Beneficence. Most people probably believe we should help others when we are able to do so. This belief acquires special significance in the context of the health care professional–layperson relationship; physicians have a duty to help or benefit their patients. This is the principle of beneficence: to have a moral obligation to act for the benefit of others. Where the principle of nonmaleficence implicates duties to do no harm, the principle of beneficence implies that we have at least a limited duty to help others. That is, nonmaleficence requires us to refrain from doing something that will cause harm, but beneficence requires that we take positive steps to help other people. Determining just how strong is the duty of health care professionals, or anyone for that matter, to promote the welfare of others is in much dispute. Many commentators have argued, for example, that taking steps to help others is morally ideal, but that no one is obligated to promote anyone's welfare. In medicine, however, we tend to defend a principle of beneficence that requires at least a limited duty on the part of physicians to benefit individuals and society as a whole.

Justice. When we debate the fairness of a particular health care policy or the way an individual has been treated at the hands of a physician or insurance company we often find ourselves speaking in terms of justice. Is justice served when Congress refuses to pay for medically necessary abortions for indigent women? Is it just when a physician spends only five minutes with a patient? Does justice allow insurance companies to deny payment for experimental medical treatment when such treatment is the patient's only hope for survival? The terms "justice" and "distributive justice" play an important rule in medical ethics. By justice we usually mean fairness, desert, or entitlement. By distributive justice we usually mean the just distribution of social burdens and benefits such as taxes, military service, and medical care. Theories of justice are concerned with articulating and defending principles that will justify making distinctions with regard to how we distribute benefits and burdens. Principles of equality, need, contribution, and effort are evaluated and applied in articulating and defending what constitutes distributive justice.

Organization of the Book

Unlike other books exploring the connections between law and bioethics, the focus here is explicitly on theories, concepts, principles, and problems central to medical ethics; that is, this is first and foremost a medical ethics book. Most books covering bio-ethics and law are designed for students in law school or practi-tioners of health law. Their focus is typically the examination of principles and concepts in the common law and in constitutional law, with exploration of the implications for medical ethics oc-cupying a place of secondary importance. This text is designed to be accessible to students, hospital ethics committee members, and health care professionals with no background in ethics or constitutional law as well as beneficial to those with much more experience in working and studying in these disciplines.

Each chapter is organized to maximize both reading en-joyment of the excerpts and understanding of the relevance of Court decisions for medical ethics. Each chapter opens with a brief explanation of the importance of the cases included in that chapter. Next, a description of the constitutional issues and fac-tual background of all the cases is provided. A brief outline of some of the more relevant concepts and arguments in medical ethics found in the cases follows. Each case is introduced by its name and citation from *United States Reports* (the official record that contains the full text of all U.S. Supreme Court decisions). Information regarding how each justice ruled in the case also is provided. Next, you will find a list of questions and items for ethical reflection, which is followed by excerpts from the actual case. Many of these excerpts include concurring and dissenting opinions (not typically found in other books on bioethics and law). Excerpts are edited, using ellipses and brackets, to enhance understanding. Finally, a list of additional readings relevant to understanding the relationship between ethics and law or to ana-lyzing and evaluating various rulings of the Court for medical ethics is provided at the end of the chapter. Most of these sources should be easy to locate, and they provide much more in-depth explanation and analysis of ethical concepts than is found here.

The first two chapters examine issues of privacy and au-tonomy as these relate to sexual activity, reproductive freedom, parental freedom, and the conflicts that may arise between preg-nant women and their fetuses. Different interpretations of the meaning of privacy and autonomy are at the heart of many disputes both in medical ethics and constitutional jurisprudence. Of special note is the interplay between these concepts and the distinction between procedural and substantive due process as well as the analysis of equal protection. The four cases covered in chapter 1 are especially instructive. The opinions of the justices—majority, concurring, and dissenting—in the seven cases under consideration in these first two chapters have influenced later discussions of the connections between ethical and constitutional reasoning in the area of medical ethics.

Abortion is the focus of concern in chapters 3 and 4. No other issue in medical ethics has occupied so much of the Court's time and exacted so much of the Court's energy than the problem of when, if ever, women may terminate their pregnancies. Ethical and constitutional issues surrounding the concept of privacy are once again considered. A distinction is made between early abortion cases and later abortion cases. In the former, the right to abortion in and of itself as well as the concept of personhood is examined. In the latter, we examine specific state-imposed regulations designed to discourage abortion and the ethical and constitutional foundations for such regulations. The opinions of the justices provide an excellent opportunity for students of medical ethics to consider the meaning and scope of the "undue burden" concept.

Two rather famous cases are the focus of chapter 5. Here we examine the role religion has played in medical treatment. Examining the ethical and constitutional justifications for infringing upon religious freedom informs much important discussion in medical ethics. The implications for such areas as public health and refusal of life-sustaining treatment are significant. Again, we have an opportunity to examine the link between autonomy and interpretations of specific constitutional provisions. In addition, we are concerned with justifiable limitations on the freedom of parents to decide medical treatment for their children. How the justices balance the rights of individuals with the interests of the state is quite revealing. What the justices have to say in these cases impacts future ethical problems and policy concerns regarding end-of-life care and public health.

The duties and obligations of health care professionals come under ethical scrutiny in chapters 6 and 7. Here we are interested in such principles as confidentiality, informed consent, beneficence, and professional integrity. Cases in these chapters provide the reader with a good idea of how the Court views the physician-patient relationship and the validity and scope of physician independence to prescribe treatments. One important focus of these chapters is the exploration of the ethical and constitutional boundaries of federal government involvement in the relationship between patients and their doctors. Of particular interest is the issue of when and to what extent doctors can act on behalf of the state. These cases help us address and evaluate future problems related to physician-assisted suicide and partial birth abortion, considered in later chapters.

In chapter 8 we examine to what extent, if any, the Constitution provides protection for and mandates treatment of people suffering from mental illness and mental retardation. In addition to revisiting the moral and constitutional issues surrounding sterilization in chapter 2, we examine what, if any, obligations the state has with regard to treating and restraining people with mental illness. Again, we witness the justices struggle with the importance of the distinction between substantive and procedural due process, and we gain insight into the ethical significance individual justices attach to the distinction. Of particular interest is the issue of whether, and under what circumstances, the state may force psychotropic medication on individuals in mental health facilities or prisons.

Three of the most famous decisions in U.S. Supreme Court history are examined in chapter 9. These decisions highlight what are perhaps the most significant dilemmas and problems discussed in medical ethics at the current time. Every day, physicians, patients, and families struggle with moral and constitutional issues surrounding termination of life support for incompetent patients and physician-assisted suicide. These cases allow us to explore and debate the ethical distinctions between actions that kill and actions that let patients die. At the heart of this debate are the concepts of liberty, privacy, and autonomy. We will discover that the justices cannot escape the realization, already known by medical ethicists and many policy analysts, that dying does not come easy in America.

Nothing has challenged both medical ethics and constitutional jurisprudence more than the phenomenon of managed care. Concerns over access, quality, trust, and cost of medical treatment raise not only ethical issues but constitutional ones as well. Politicians, policy makers, ethicists, and now the justices of the Supreme Court realize that the American health care system is in trouble. Issues surrounding medical negligence, the practice of medicine by managed care organizations, and the rewarding of physicians for delaying or denying care have dramatic implications for patients and society. Chapter 10 explores issues surrounding the importance of health, the right to health care, and conflicts of interest. We realize the impact of Supreme Court decisions on medical ethics as the justices struggle to comprehend and resolve these relatively new and perplexing dilemmas in health care.

Through the use of select excerpts, readers discover that the justices employ ethical argumentation, moral reflection, and value judgments in reaching their decisions. Such appeals to ethics and values are often explicit, but sometimes constitutional concepts and principles obscure moral commitments. To what extent justices purposely "hide" their moral judgments is not certain. What is certain is that the justices often have interesting, intriguing, creative, and even perplexing observations and arguments to make regarding the ethical aspects and the moral impact of specific policies, laws, and constitutional issues brought before them. This book exposes students and professionals interested in health care services and patient care to the ways in which ethical argumentation comes alive and is used in judicial reasoning.

Notes

1.   For those new to the study of the relationship between medical ethics and law, three excellent sources are worth consulting. See Alexander Morgan Capron, "Law and Bioethics," in *The Encyclopedia of Bioethics*, 2nd ed., Warren T. Reich (New York: Simon & Schuster and Macmillan, 1995), pp. 1329–35; Howard Brody, "Law and Morality," in the *Encyclopedia of Bioethics*, pp. 1335–40; Carl E. Schneider, "Moral Discourse, Bioethics, and the Law," *Hastings Center Report* 26 (1996): 37–39. The material in this section is heavily influenced by these three sources.

2.   Schneider, "Moral Discourse, Bioethics, and the Law," pp. 37–39.

3.   Ibid., p. 37.

4.   Capron, "Law and Bioethics," p. 1329.

5.   Alexander M. Bickel, *The Least Dangerous Branch: The Supreme Court at the Bar of Politics*, 2nd ed. (New Haven: Yale University Press, 1986).

6.   The best discussion of federalism as it relates to bioethics law can be found in Jerry Menikoff, *Law and Bioethics: An Introduction* (Washington, DC: Georgetown University Press, 2001), pp. 9–14.

7.   John E. Nowak and Ronald D. Rotunda, *Constitutional Law*, 6th ed. (St. Paul, MN: West Group, 2000), p. 633.

8.   J. W. Peltason and Sue Davis, *Understanding the Constitution*, 15th ed. (Belmont, CA: Wadsworth, 2000), p. 387.

9.   Menikoff, *Law and Bioethics,* p. 25.

10.   This discussion of the three standards of equal protection analysis is indebted to Menikoff, *Law and Bioethics,*and Nowak and Rotunda, *Constitutional Law*.

11.   Nowak and Rotunda, *Constitutional Law,* p. 395.

12.   Ibid., p. 396.

13.   Sonia M. Suter, "Ambivalent Unanimity: An Analysis of the Supreme Court's Holding," in *Law at the End of Life: The Supreme Court and Assisted Suicide* (Ann Arbor: University of Michigan Press, 2000), p. 29.

14.   Three of the best sources for description, evaluation, and analysis of ethical theories in medical ethics are Tom L. Beauchamp and James F. Childress, *Principles of Biomedical Ethics*, 5th ed. (New York: Oxford University Press, 2001), pp. 337–83; C. E. Harris, Jr., *Applying Moral Theories*, 3rd ed. (Belmont, CA: Wadsworth, 1997), pp. 97–190; and Ronald Munson, ed., *Intervention and Reflection: Basic Issues in Medical Ethics*, 6th ed. (Belmont,

CA: Wadsworth, 2000), pp. 3–31. These sources are well worth consulting, and they heavily influence the discussion of ethical theories below.

15. Beauchamp and Childress, *Principles of Biomedical Ethics*, p. 348.

16. Ibid., p. 357.

17. Ibid., pp. 12–13.

18. This discussion is based on material found in Beauchamp and Childress, *Principles of Biomedical Ethics*, pp. 57–231; and Munson, *Intervention and Reflection*, pp. 31–45.

19. Beauchamp and Childress, *Principles of Biomedical Ethics*, p. 117.

For Further Reading

Beauchamp, Tom L., and James F. Childress. *Principles of Biomedical Ethics*, 5th edition. New York: Oxford University Press, 2001.

Bobbitt, Philip. "Constitutional Interpretation." In *The Oxford Companion to the Supreme Court of the United States*, Kermit L. Hall, ed. New York: Oxford University Press, 1992.

Brody, Baruch A. "Law and Morality." In *The Encyclopedia of Bioethics*, 2nd edition, Warren Reich, ed. New York: Simon & Schuster and Macmillan, 1995.

Capron, Alexander Morgan. "Law and Bioethics." In *The Encyclopedia of Bioethics*.

——— "Morality and the State, Law and Legalism." *Hastings Center Report* 26 (1996): 35–37.

Harris, Jr., C.E. *Applying Moral Theories*, 3rd edition. Belmont, CA: Wadsworth, 1997.

Meilaender, Gilbert. "Less Law? Or Different Law?" *Hastings Center Report* 26 (1996): 39–40.

Menikoff, Jerry. *Law and Bioethics: An Introduction*. Washington, DC: Georgetown University Press, 2001.

Schneider, Carl E. "Moral Discourse, Bioethics, and the Law." *Hastings Center Report* 26 (1996): 37–39.

Shapiro, Michael H., et al. *Bioethics and Law: Cases, Materials, and Problems*, 2nd edition. St. Paul, MN: West Group, 2003.

Veatch, Robert M. *The Basics of Bioethics.* Upper Saddle River, NJ: Prentice
     Hall, 2000.

CHAPTER ONE

THE CONTRACEPTION AND SEXUAL AUTONOMY CASES

...[T]he law has always been involved with health in one way or another. From earliest times the law—taking that to mean the disparate miscellany of statutes, judicial decisions and administrative regulations, rulings, pronouncements, orders and doctrines—has a posture that at once encourages, inhibits and is indifferent to health care.

—Eric W. Springer, "Law and Medicine: Reflections on a
Metaphysical Misalliance"

Beginning a book that explores the significance and impact of United States Supreme Court decisions for the study and application of medical ethics with a chapter on sex may seem rather strange. If indeed students of medical ethics—and health care professionals and their patients—can learn a great deal from the rulings and arguments of the Court, why begin, to put it bluntly, with sex? After all, physicians, ethicists, and judges surely have much more pressing issues to debate and problems to solve than whether people may take steps to prevent childbirth or who may have sex with whom. Although the four cases covered in this chapter do not directly impact ethical issues encountered by patients and physicians, three of the decisions have had significant influence on theoretical and practical bioethics. The best example of this influence can be found in discussions of the concept of privacy and the accompanying values and obligations resulting from a constitutionally recognized right to privacy. (The impact of the fourth case covered in this chapter remains to be seen.) The reasoning and analysis of both constitutional and ethical principles and concepts articulated in these cases set the stage for future decisions by the Court (as our fourth case amply demonstrates). Both the claim that Supreme Court decisions have ethical significance and the claim that those interested in medical ethics should pay attention to these decisions are supported by examining these four cases related to sexual autonomy.

Constitutional Issues and Background

Our first case, *Griswold v. Connecticut,* may have had more impact on the theory and practice of bioethics than any other Supreme Court decision. The state of Connecticut, in 1879, passed a law making it illegal for any person to use any drug, article, or instrument for the purpose of preventing pregnancy. Interestingly enough, the law had been challenged twice before the Supreme Court prior to 1965, but for various reasons the statute was still in force. Under scrutiny in this case were specific statutes, §§53-32 and 54-196 of the General Statutes of Connecticut. Estelle Griswold, executive director of the Planned Parenthood League, and Lee Buxton, a physician and professor at Yale Medical School who served as the medical director for the league, gave information and medical advice to married couples regarding the proper use of contraception. Both were charged in 1961 with violating Connecticut law and both were found guilty in Connecticut's Supreme Court of Errors and fined one hundred dollars each.

At issue in *Griswold* is the Due Process Clause of the Fourteenth Amendment, which reads in part, "…nor shall any State deprive any person of life, liberty, or property, without due process of law." Justice Douglas, in writing for the majority, begins by noting that individual guarantees in the Bill of Rights have penumbras, areas of additional implied rights, that give "life and substance" to the enumerated guarantees in the Bill of Rights. One such penumbra is the right to privacy, or a zone of privacy, which is a part of liberty. If privacy is a part of liberty, then Connecticut's ban on contraceptive use by married couples is a substantial violation of that liberty. This right to privacy, or zone of privacy, is found in several provisions of the Bill of Rights. Finding, or discovering, a right to privacy in any of the guarantees explicitly mentioned in the Bill of Rights is certainly controversial, as you will see when reading the dissents.

The second case in this chapter, *Eisenstadt v. Baird*, involved a Massachusetts law banning the use of contraceptives by unmarried couples. At the end of his lecture on contraception to a group of students at Boston University, William Baird gave a woman a can of contraceptive foam. He was arrested, charged, and convicted of a felony under Massachusetts law. The Court of Appeals overturned Baird's conviction, holding that the statute was a ban on contraception per se and therefore in conflict with the Supreme Court's earlier ruling in *Griswold*. The Massachusetts law under consideration by the Supreme Court prohibited a person from giving a drug, medicine, instrument, or article for the prevention of contraception except in the case of 1) a physician prescribing it to married persons, or 2) a pharmacist furnishing it to a married person presenting a physician's prescription.

Equal protection concerns are at the center of *Eisenstadt*. The Equal Protection Clause of the Fourteenth Amendment asserts that no state shall "deny to any person within its jurisdiction the equal protection of the laws." This clause requires both the federal and state government to treat similarly situated people in a similar way, unless the government has compelling reasons not to do so. In other words, any legislation or policy that burdens one group of people but not another group will raise equal protection questions. Justice Brennan, in writing for the majority, concluded that the Massachusetts law prohibiting use of any birth control method by unmarried people could not be defended on the grounds that the state desired to deter premarital sex and regulate the use of harmful substances.

Until the end of June 2003 the decision handed down in our next case was the law of the land. While the holding in *Bowers v. Hardwick* has been overruled, it continues to be well worth studying. In August 1982, police officers entered the home of Michael Hardwick and found him in bed with another man. They arrested Hardwick under Georgia's sodomy statute. In part, 16-6-2 of the Georgia Code states, "a) A person commits the offense of sodomy when he performs or submits to any sexual act involving the sex organs of one person and the mouth or anus of another…" b) A person convicted of the offense of sodomy shall be punished by imprisonment for not less than one nor more than twenty years…." Hardwick brought suit in Federal District Court challenging the constitutionality of the statute. The court dismissed the case, but the Court of Appeals for the Eleventh Circuit reversed stating that the Georgia law violated the fundamental rights of homosexuals. The Court of Appeals found that, given prior decisions of the U.S. Supreme Court, homosexual activity would have to be considered as a private and intimate association beyond the reach of state regulation. Interestingly, Justice Powell, two years after his retirement from the Court, stated that he made a mistake by deciding with the majority in *Bowers*.

Justice White, in writing for a 5-4 Court, framed the issue as whether "the Federal Constitution confers a fundamental right upon homosexuals to engage in sodomy." Not only did Justice White dismiss as unimportant privacy issues, he also questioned whether the Supreme Court should even be involved in such controversies that clearly are the province of the states. The four dissenters in this case were quite vigorous in their disagreement with the Court. The issue for some of the dissenters was not whether homosexual sodomy was a fundamental right, but rather the issue was determining a right to privacy which homosexuals and heterosexuals were entitled to enjoy.

In June 2003, on the last day of its 2002 term, the Court handed down what everyone agreed would be a landmark decision. One news outlet reported that Justice Kennedy's voice was shaking as he read the decision from the bench. Justice Scalia, in a practice rarely engaged in by justices, read his dissent to the packed courtroom. The decision, *Lawrence et al. v. Texas*, was the culmination of events that began in 1998, when police officers in Houston, Texas, responding to a call of an armed intruder, entered the home of John Lawrence and discovered him and Tyron Garner "engaging in a sexual act." The armed intruder call proved false, and no one questioned the propriety of officers entering the home. Both men were charged with violating Texas's law against homosexual conduct and spent the night in jail. At trial, each man entered a plea of "no contest." Each was fined two hundred dollars and required to pay court costs. The Court of Appeals for Texas's Fourteenth District considered the two men's claim that the statute violated the Equal Protection and Due Process Clauses of the Fourteenth Amendment. The Court of Appeals, applying *Bowers v. Hardwick*, rejected the constitutional claims and affirmed the convictions.

In a 6-3 decision, the Supreme Court overturned the Texas antisodomy law and in so doing overturned the decision in *Bowers* from seventeen years earlier. A majority of the justices found that the liberty guarantee in the Due Process Clause "presumes an autonomy of self that includes freedom of thought, belief, expression, and certain intimate conduct." That is, homosexuals have the freedom to engage in sodomy, which in turn constitutes intimate conduct. Unlike the majority in *Bowers*, Justice Kennedy found support for the constitutional protection of liberty and privacy interests for homosexuals in the Court's prior cases, especially *Griswold* and *Eisenstadt*. Only one justice, Justice O'Connor, would have invalidated the Texas law on equal protection grounds.

Ethical Issues and Background

The ethical principles and conceptual issues directly relevant to these four cases are autonomy and privacy. As we consider and evaluate the arguments of the justices relating to contraception and homosexuality, we can compare and contrast how they define and determine the scope of autonomy and privacy. For example, Justice White's understanding of autonomy and privacy in *Bowers* is certainly not as expansive as Justice Kennedy's understanding in *Lawrence*. Obviously, how a justice views and applies a particular principle has immense implications for medical ethics.

To be autonomous, or to possess autonomy, generally means to have the ability to form carefully considered goals and desires as well as the ability to fulfill those goals and desires.[1] Autonomy implies control, self-determination, self-rule, liberty, privacy, and freedom. An autonomous person is a person who is free from controlling influences (or at least free to a substantial degree) and who, at the same time, has the ability to understand alternatives and the implications of those alternatives. To have diminished autonomy is to be controlled by outside influences and/or not to understand choices and their implications. Although autonomy is a difficult concept to fully explain, almost all theories of autonomy agree that the concept must involve liberty and agency. Liberty is usually considered to mean freedom from causal influences, and agency usually means the ability to act intentionally. We must keep in mind, however, that acting free of controlling influences and acting with understanding are matters of degree. People can still act autonomously even if they do not totally understand relevant aspects of their decision and even if they are not totally free of controlling influences.

Central to discussions of autonomy in both medical ethics and constitutional law are issues associated with what it means to have a right to autonomy and delineating the justifiable limits on this right. All of us can readily agree that people have a right to act in ways that promote their freedom and self-determination, but respecting and acquiescing in an individual's choices is another matter; we often think we "know better" than others when they are considering courses of action with which we disagree. In addition, we normally do not think the right to self-determination is absolute; individuals do not have an unlimited right to require either physicians or the state to meet their needs. Determining and then justifying morally acceptable limits on autonomy in a society with many different value and ethical commitments is a central concern of both medical ethics and law.

Directly related to autonomy is the concept of privacy.[2] The meaning and scope of privacy can be as difficult to determine as that of autonomy. Making the distinction between privacy as control over access to one's person and privacy as the right to control that access helps clarify how the concept is used in both ethics and law. According to the first meaning, privacy is a state or condition of limited access. That is, a person may have privacy in her/his own home such that being in the home provides some control over what others may access about that person. According to the second meaning, privacy is the freedom or the right to limit access to personal information by others; in this context, individuals possess power to control access to their personal selves.

As with autonomy, much remains to be said regarding privacy. Specifically, and within the context of medical ethics and Supreme Court decisions, we are interested in the scope of privacy. That is, what types of activities and information does the right to privacy cover? We are also interested in justifications for a right to privacy. Our first case provides an opportunity to begin these discussions. As we move through other cases we will have a chance to elaborate on the meaning and justification of privacy.

Even these brief introductory remarks on autonomy and privacy provide background for determining and assessing the justices' positions on contraception and homosexuality. Freedom to engage in sexual activity while minimizing the threat of disease or pregnancy implicates issues of personal liberty and privacy. Exercising one's personal sexual preferences with other consenting adults also speaks to personal fulfillment and intimacy. But, as the justices realized, claiming a right to autonomy or asserting a right to privacy does not end the discussion. Reasons exist for limiting or even prohibiting contraceptive practices and homosexual activity. To what extent these reasons are convincing is, of course, a matter of dispute.

Reasons for finding contraception immoral can include the promotion of fidelity, the advancement of a moral society, and the protection of women. That widespread use of contraceptive devices will promote marital infidelity, or produce a society on the verge of total moral collapse, or result in the objectification of women is debatable. The justices certainly disagree over how much weight these moral considerations should carry against moral and constitutional recognition of a right to autonomy and privacy.

Much more controversial than contraception, especially since the early 1980s, is the moral and legal status of homosexuality. Several objections can be raised against the moral permissibility of homosexuality and, as we will see in the excerpts from *Bowers* and *Lawrence*, many of these moral arguments have been translated into reasons for finding homosexuality not deserving of constitutional protection. Three of these objections are briefly presented below.[3]

Religious objections usually rely on an appeal to a religious text or on a religious tradition for support. Examination of specific texts may reveal explicit or implicit condemnations of homosexuality, which, if considered the word of God, must be strictly followed. Or one might consider the history and traditions of religious communities, which over time have determined which practices are to be condoned and which practices are to be condemned.

Another type of argument appeals to the intrinsic immorality of homosexual sodomy. From this viewpoint, homosexuality is viewed as wrong in and of itself. Usually this type of argument appeals to a specific definition of "natural" and "unnatural" by which heterosexual sex is natural and homosexual sex is not. Obviously, the proponents of this position must further claim that what is natural is moral and what is unnatural is immoral.

There are those who would argue that specific institutions and society as a whole would be harmed if homosexuality were to be considered morally permissible. Only one kind of sexual behavior can be and should be tolerated by decent society. On this view, marriage and family are important institutions, and society has an obligation not only to protect them but also to ensure that they flourish. Moreover, any behavior, sexual or otherwise, that might threaten these institutions must be prohibited.

One final consideration, relating to both homosexuality

and contraception, is worth noting. Attention, both by the Court and in the wider society, has focused on the meaning and scope of marriage. Any exploration of the morality of gay and lesbian marriage raises the question, "What is marriage?" Two answers to this question are common: marriage is an institution and marriage is a practice.[4] To view marriage as an institution is to acknowledge that marriage is sacred, something to be respected as it is for all time. Marriage as a practice implies imperfection and change. Because the stakes are so high in this society, critical evaluation of this distinction is certainly in order. That individual justices subscribe to one or the other description of marriage is certain. What is not certain is the degree to which a particular justice subjects his/her evaluation to critical scrutiny.

As you read the excerpts below, consider how individual justices conceptualize autonomy and privacy. In addition, try to determine how persuasive they find certain arguments in support or against contraception and homosexuality.

Griswold v. Connecticut
381 U.S. 479 (1965)

Justice Douglas delivered the opinion of the Court, in which Chief Justice Warren and Justices Goldberg and Brennan joined. Justices Harlan and White concurred in the judgment. Justices Black and Stewart each filed dissents.

Areas for Discussion and Ethical Reflection

1. Recall the four ethical theories outlined in the introduction. Keep these theories in mind as you read the opinions below in *Griswold*. Of course, you will want to refer to these theories often as you read all the cases in the book. Justice Douglas expresses disbelief that the Constitution would offer no protection to a right of privacy in marriage. As a purely ethical matter, what moral framework offers the best rationale for Justice Douglas's position? Certainly, a rights-based theory seems appropriate. Is it the most appropriate?

2.   Much of medical ethics is concerned with laws and policies and the evaluation of those laws and policies. Obviously, some differences exist between ethical evaluations and constitutional evaluations of a particular law. The significance of those differences is, of course, a matter of debate. As you read *Griswold*, you will note Justice Stewart's characterization of the Connecticut statute as an "uncommonly silly law." How would you characterize the difference between an "offensive" or "silly" law and one that is unethical? How do you think Justice Stewart would make the distinction? You may wish to return to this question as you consider our last case in this chapter, *Lawrence et al. v. Texas*.

3.   How would you characterize the moral significance of the relationship between a husband and wife, or for that matter, the physician's role in that relationship? Surely both relationships have moral significance, but determining the meaning and scope of this significance can be quite difficult. Where does the right of association fit into your analysis?

4.   Justice Douglas begins his majority opinion by stating that the Court should not determine "the wisdom, need, and propriety of laws that touch economic problems, business affairs, or social conditions." And in his dissenting opinion, Justice Stewart seems to agree when he writes, "It is the essence of judicial duty to subordinate our own personal views, our own ideas of what legislation is wise and what is not." How is it then that each justice arrives at a radically different conclusion regarding the Connecticut law? Is one justice more sincere in his claim than the other? Is it possible to distinguish between what ought to be the case according to personal beliefs and what ought to be the case according to the best available ethical theory?

5.   If either or both Justice Douglas and Justice Stewart firmly held to the assertion that the Court should not determine the wisdom of policies, would that not imply that there would be little if anything for a student of medical ethics to analyze and evaluate in a Supreme Court opinion? Given that many ethical issues in medicine and biomedical research in the twenty-first

century involve economic, business, and social concerns, what relevance would the Supreme Court have for medical ethics?

6.   Justice Goldberg attaches a great deal of importance to the Ninth Amendment, which states, "The enumeration in the Constitution of certain rights shall not be construed to deny or disparage others retained by the people." Is he right to appeal to the Ninth Amendment in this case? Might the Ninth Amendment be employed to address many legal disputes in medical ethics?

7.   Justice Goldberg's argument for considering the right to privacy a fundamental right seems to result from an appeal to tradition. He notes that just because the Constitution does not expressly forbid the national or state government from interfering with marriage, the conclusion that such interference is constitutional is unjustified. Indeed, there does seem to be a long history of acknowledgment and respect for marital privacy. Evaluate Justice Goldberg's argument. You might return to this item after reading *Bowers* and *Lawrence*.

8.   Justice Black describes privacy as a "broad, abstract, and ambiguous concept." He concludes that almost any meaning can be derived from the concept. Is this true? Could other concepts in medical ethics, such as autonomy, informed consent, nonmaleficence, and truthfulness be described as broad, abstract, and ambiguous?

9.   The *Griswold* decision has had a dramatic impact on medical ethics, and that impact is still being felt forty years later. For example, one commentator has noted the effort to justify parental consent for the donation of organs by minor children to other family members.[5] That is, since *Griswold* is about the right to make intimate decisions, then such a right would extend to parents who wish to make the organ donation decision for their children. As you read the decision, ask yourself what are its implications. That is, are there indeed other areas and problems in medical ethics to which the case could be applied?

JUSTICE DOUGLAS:

...Coming to the merits, we are met with a wide range of questions that implicate the Due Process Clause of the Fourteenth Amendment....We do not sit as a super-legislature to determine the wisdom, need, and propriety of laws that touch economic problems, business affairs, or social conditions. This law, however, operates directly on an intimate relation of husband and wife and their physician's role in one aspect of that relation.

The association of people is not mentioned in the Constitution nor in the Bill of Rights. The right to educate a child in a school of the parents' choice—whether public or private or parochial—is also not mentioned. Nor is the right to study any particular subject or any foreign language. Yet the First Amendment has been construed to include certain of those rights.

...[S]pecific guarantees in the Bill of Rights have penumbras, formed by emanations from those guarantees that help give them life and substance. Various guarantees create zones of privacy. The right of association contained in the penumbra of the First Amendment is one, as we have seen. The Third Amendment in its prohibition against the quartering of soldiers "in any house" in time of peace without the consent of the owner is another facet of that privacy. The Fourth Amendment explicitly affirms the "right of the people to be secure in their persons, houses, papers, and effects, against unreasonable searches and seizures." The Fifth Amendment in its Self-Incrimination Clause enables the citizen to create a zone of privacy which government may not force him to surrender to his detriment. The Ninth Amendment provides: "The enumeration in the Constitution, of certain rights, shall not be construed to deny or disparage others retained by the people."

The Fourth and Fifth Amendments were described...as protection against all governmental invasions "of the sanctity of a man's home and the privacies of life." We recently referred...to the Fourth Amendment as creating a "right to privacy, no less important than any other right carefully and particularly reserved to the people."

We have had many controversies over these penumbral rights of "privacy and repose."....[T]he right of privacy which presses for recognition here is a legitimate one....

The present case, then, concerns a relationship lying within the zone of privacy created by several fundamental constitutional guarantees. And it concerns a law which, in forbidding the use of contraceptives rather than regulating their manufacture or sale, seeks to achieve its goals by means having a maximum destructive impact upon that relationship. Such a law cannot stand in light of the familiar principle, so often applied by this Court, that a "governmental purpose to control or prevent activities constitutionally subject to state regulation may not be achieved by means which sweep unnecessarily broadly and thereby invade the area of protected freedoms. Would we allow the police to search the sacred precincts of marital bedrooms for telltale signs of the use of contraceptives? The very idea is repulsive to the notions of privacy surrounding the marriage relationship.

We deal with a right of privacy older than the Bill of Rights—older than our political parties, older than our school system. Marriage is a coming together for better or for worse, hopefully enduring, and intimate to the degree of being sacred. It is an association that promotes a way of life, not causes; a harmony in living, not political faiths; a bilateral loyalty, not commercial or social projects. Yet it is an association for as noble a purpose as any involved in our prior decisions.

Reversed.

Justice Goldberg:

I agree with the Court that Connecticut's birth-control law unconstitutionally intrudes upon the right of marital privacy, and I join in its opinion and judgment. Although I have not accepted the view that "due process" as used in the Fourteenth Amendment incorporates all of the first eight Amendments, I do agree that the concept of liberty protects those personal rights that are fundamental, and is not confined to the specific terms of the Bill of Rights. My conclusion that the concept of liberty is not so restricted and that it embraces the right of marital privacy though that right is not mentioned explicitly in the Constitution is supported both by numerous decisions of this Court, referred to in the Court's opinion, and by the language and history of the Ninth Amendment. In reaching the conclusion that the right of marital privacy is protected, as being within the protected penumbra of specific guarantees of the Bill of Rights, the Court refers to the Ninth Amendment. I add these words to emphasize the relevance of that Amendment to the Court's holding....

This Court, in a series of decisions, has held that the Fourteenth Amendment absorbs and applies to the States those specifics of the first eight amendments which express fundamental personal rights. The language and history of the Ninth Amendment reveal that the Framers of the Constitution believed that there are additional fundamental rights, protected from governmental infringement, which exist alongside those fundamental rights specifically mentioned in the first eight constitutional amendments.

The Ninth Amendment reads, "The enumeration in the Constitution, of certain rights, shall not be construed to deny or disparage others retained by the people." The Amendment is almost entirely the work of James Madison. It was introduced in Congress by him and passed the House and Senate with little or no debate and virtually no change in language. It was proffered to quiet expressed fears that a bill of specifically enumerated rights could not be sufficiently broad to cover all essential rights and that the specific mention of certain rights would be interpreted as a denial that others were protected....

While this Court has had little occasion to interpret the Ninth Amendment, "[i]t cannot be presumed that any clause in the Constitution is intended to be without effect." In interpreting the Constitution, "real effect should be given to all the words it uses." The Ninth Amendment to the Constitution may be regarded by some as a recent discovery and may be forgotten by others, but since 1791 it has been a basic part of the Constitution which we are sworn to uphold. To hold that a right so basic and fundamental and so deep-rooted in our society as the right of privacy in marriage may be infringed because that right is not guaranteed in so many words by the first eight amendments to the Constitution is to ignore the Ninth Amendment and to give it no effect whatsoever. Moreover, a judicial construction that this fundamental right is not protected by the Constitution because it is not mentioned in explicit terms by one of the first eight amendments or elsewhere in the Constitution would violate the Ninth Amendment, which specifically states that "[t]he enumeration in the Constitution, of certain rights, shall not be construed to deny or disparage others retained by the people."

...In determining which rights are fundamental, judges are not left at large to decide cases in light of their personal and private notions. Rather, they must look to the "traditions and [collective] conscience of our people" to determine whether a principle is "so rooted [there]...as to be ranked as fundamental."...

Although the Constitution does not speak in so many words of the right of privacy in marriage, I cannot believe that it offers these fundamental rights no protection. The fact that no particular provision of the Constitution explicitly forbids the State from disrupting the traditional relation of the family—a relation as old and as fundamental as our entire civilization—sure does not show that the Government was meant to have the power to do so. Rather, as the Ninth Amendment expressly recognizes, there are fundamental personal rights such as this one, which are protected from abridgment by the Government though not specifically mentioned in the Constitution.

JUSTICE BLACK:

...In order that there may be no room at all to doubt why I vote as I do, I feel constrained to add that the law is every bit as offensive to me as it is to my Brethren of the majority and my Brothers Harlan, White and Goldberg who, reciting reasons why it is offensive to them, hold it unconstitutional. There is no single one of the graphic and eloquent strictures and criticisms fired at the policy of this Connecticut law either by the Court's opinion or by those of my concurring Brethren to which I cannot subscribe—except their conclusion that the evil qualities they see in the law make it unconstitutional....

The Court talks about a constitutional "right of privacy" as though there is some constitutional provision or provisions forbidding any law ever to be passed which might abridge the "privacy" of individuals. But there is not. There are, of course, guarantees in certain specific constitutional provisions which are designed in part to protect privacy at certain times and places with respect to certain activities. Such, for example, is the Fourth Amendment's guarantee against "unreasonable searches and seizures." But I think it belittles that Amendment to talk about it as though it protects nothing but "privacy." To treat it that way is to give it a niggardly interpretation, not the kind of liberal reading I think any Bill of Rights provision should be given. The average man would very likely not have his feelings soothed any more by having his property seized openly than by having it seized privately and by stealth. He simply wants his property left alone. And a person can be just as much, if not more, irritated, annoyed and injured by an unceremonious public arrest by a policeman as he is by a seizure in the privacy of his office or home.

One of the most effective ways of diluting or expanding a constitutionally guaranteed right is to substitute for the crucial word or words of a constitutional guarantee another word or words, more or less flexible and more or less restricted in meaning. This fact is well illustrated by the use of the term "right of privacy" as a comprehensive substitute for the Fourth Amendment's guarantee against "unreasonable searches and seizures." "Privacy" is a broad, abstract and ambiguous concept which can easily be shrunken in meaning but which can also, on the other hand, easily be interpreted as a constitutional ban against many things other than searches and seizures…. I like my privacy as well as the next one, but I am nevertheless compelled to admit that government has a right to invade it unless prohibited by some specific constitutional provision. For these reasons I cannot agree with the Court's judgment and the reasons it gives for holding this Connecticut law unconstitutional….

Justice Stewart:

Since 1879 Connecticut has had on its books a law which forbids the use of contraceptives by anyone. I think this is an uncommonly silly law. As a practical matter, the law is obviously unenforceable, except in the oblique context of the present case. As a philosophical matter, I believe the use of contraceptives in the relationship of marriage should be left to personal and private choice, based upon each individual's moral, ethical, and religious beliefs. As a matter of social policy, I think professional counsel about methods of birth control should be available to all, so that each individual's choice can be meaningfully made. But we are not asked in this case to say whether we think this law is unwise, or even asinine. We are asked to hold that it violates the United States Constitution. And that I cannot do.

In the course of its opinion the Court refers to no less than six Amendments to the Constitution: the First, the Third, the Fourth, the Fifth, the Ninth, and the Fourteenth. But the Court does not say which of these Amendments, if any, it thinks is infringed by this Connecticut law.

We are told that the Due Process Clause of the Fourteenth Amendment is not, as such, the "guide" in this case. With that much I agree. There is no claim that this law, duly enacted by the Connecticut Legislature, is unconstitutionally vague. There is no claim that the appellants were denied any of the elements of procedural due process at their trial, so as to make their convictions constitutionally invalid. And, as the Court says, the day has long passed since the Due Process Clause was regarded as a proper instrument for determining "the wisdom, need, and propriety" of state laws. My Brothers Harlan and White to the contrary, "[w]e have returned to the original constitutional proposition that courts do not substitute their social and economic beliefs for the judgment of legislative bodies, who are elected to pass laws."

[Justice Stewart next explains why the Connecticut law cannot be found invalid under the First, Third, Fourth, and Fifth Amendments.]

The Court also quotes the Ninth Amendment. But to say that the Ninth Amendment has anything to do with this case is to turn somersaults with history. The Ninth Amendment, like its companion the Tenth, which this Court held "states but a truism that all is retained which has not been surrendered," was framed by James Madison and adopted by the States simply to make clear that the adoption of the Bill of Rights did not alter the plan that the Federal Government was to be a government of express and limited powers, and that all rights and powers not delegated to it were retained by the people and the individual States. Until today no member of this Court has ever suggested that the Ninth Amendment meant anything else....

What provision of the Constitution, then, does make this state law invalid? The Court says it is the right of privacy "created by several fundamental constitutional guarantees." With all deference, I can find no such general right of privacy in the Bill of Rights, in any other part of the Constitution, or in any case ever before decided by this Court.

Eisenstadt v. Baird
405 U.S. 438 (1972)

Justice Brennan delivered the opinion of the Court, in which Justices Douglas, Stewart, and Marshall joined. Justice Douglas filed a concurring opinion. Justice White concurred in the result, which Justice Blackmun joined. Chief Justice Burger filed a dissenting opinion. Justices Powell and Rehnquist took no part in the case.

Areas for Discussion and Ethical Reflection

1.   This case is very similar to *Griswold* such that much of the ethical and legal significance is identical; however, *Eisenstadt* is important in its own right. One area of interest surrounds the distinction between due process and equal protection. The majority contends that the Massachusetts ban on contraceptives for unmarried people is a violation of the equal protection clause, yet there are references to substantive due process as well. From a moral perspective, does it matter which is used?

2.   Outline and evaluate Justice Brennan's arguments for striking down the Massachusetts law. Do these arguments have any relevance for medical ethics, specifically the physician-patient relationship? Or are his arguments simply an instance of technical interpretations of equal protection?

3.   Do you think single persons should be allowed to enjoy the same right to privacy as married couples with regard to sex and contraception? Why shouldn't we say that some relationships are more deserving of constitutional protection and ethical significance than others are? In fact, of course, we do. Undoubtedly we could think of morally significant reasons for the state to interfere with sexual interactions between unmarried couples as opposed to married persons. What interests might the state propose?

4.   A lower court contended that limiting contraception in and of itself would constitute infringement of fundamental human rights. How do you think a rule utilitarian would respond to this assertion? Natural law ethics would probably provide a much different answer. Which do you find the most convincing?

5.   Justice Brennan dismisses one possible argument Massachusetts might give for criminalizing contraception. He notes that Massachusetts might decide that forced pregnancy and giving birth to unwanted children should be a proper punishment for engaging in sex outside of marriage. What are Justice Brennan's reasons for dismissing as illegitimate this reasoning? From a moral perspective, why should a state not be allowed to decide to "punish" such "immoral behavior" in this way? As a matter of fact, ethics teachers often hear their students proclaim, especially in discussions of abortion, that people (usually women) should take responsibility for their actions. That is, students assert that people who engage in premarital sex should be forced to give birth and raise children as a means of extolling the virtues associated with responsibility.

6.   As you are reading *Eisenstadt v. Baird* consider the following observation regarding the connection between bioethics and law:

> "...[T]he legal analysis of bioethical issues is heavily involved with constitutional law (however much some may complain about this) and so with the operation of standards of review (however much some may complain about

that too). Moreover, bioethics illuminates constitutional law by pushing its categories to and beyond their previously understood borders."[6]

Indeed, this book assumes there is a great deal of truth in this passage. What might it mean to say that bioethics pushes constitutional law beyond previous borders? Why does *Eisenstadt* present the perfect opportunity to ask this question?

7.   Five years after its ruling in *Eisenstadt,* the Court had an opportunity to consider the constitutionality of laws prohibiting minors access to contraceptives. In *Carey v. Population Services International*, 431 U.S. 678 (1977), the Court invalidated a law allowing only pharmacists to sell contraceptives to people over sixteen and that prohibited altogether the sale of contraceptives to people under sixteen. With regard to minors, four justices implied that children have a right to freedom in matters relating to sexual intercourse. Three other justices voted to strike the law on grounds that it was arbitrary since the state was forcing minors to run the risk of becoming pregnant or contracting disease.[7] What ethical arguments would you provide in support of laws prohibiting minors access to contraceptives? What ethical arguments would you employ against such laws? Everyone can agree that minors need protection, but disagreement exists over who best should assume this duty, parents or the state.

JUSTICE BRENNAN:

...We agree [with the court of appeals] that the goals of deterring premarital sex and regulating the distribution of potentially harmful articles cannot reasonably be regarded as legislative aims of §§21 and 21A. And we hold that the statute, viewed as a prohibition on contraception per se, violates the rights of single persons under the Equal Protection Clause of the Fourteenth Amendment....

[The Court goes on to discuss why Baird should be allowed standing in this case, and to explain the principles governing application of the Equal Protection Clause.]

The question for our determination in this case is whether there is some ground of difference that rationally explains the different treatment accorded married and unmarried persons under [the Massachusetts law]. For the reasons that follow, we conclude that no such ground exists.

First. §21 stems from [an earlier statute], which prohibited, without exception, distribution of articles intended to be used as contraceptives. In *Commonwealth v. Allison*, the Massachusetts Supreme Judicial Court explained that the law's "plain purpose is to protect purity, to preserve chastity, to encourage continence and self restraint, to defend the sanctity of the home, and thus to engender in the State and nation a virile and virtuous race of men and women." Although the State clearly abandoned that purpose with the enactment of 21A, at least insofar as the illicit sexual activities of married persons are concerned, the court reiterated in Sturgis v. Attorney General, supra, that the object of the legislation is to discourage premarital sexual intercourse. Conceding that the State could, consistently with the Equal Protection Clause, regard the problems of extramarital and premarital sexual relations as "[e]vils...of different dimensions and proportions, requiring different remedies," we cannot agree that the deterrence of premarital sex may reasonably be regarded as the purpose of the Massachusetts law.

It would be plainly unreasonable to assume that Massachusetts has prescribed pregnancy and the birth of an unwanted child as punishment for fornication, which is a misdemeanor under Massachusetts [law]. Aside from the scheme of values that assumption would attribute to the State, it is abundantly clear that the effect of the ban on distribution of contraceptives to unmarried persons has at best a marginal relation to the proffered objective....Like Connecticut's laws, §§21 and 21A do not at all regulate the distribution of contraceptives when they are to be used to prevent, not pregnancy, but the spread of disease. Nor, in making contraceptives available to married persons without regard to their intended use, does Massachusetts attempt to deter married persons from engaging in illicit sexual relations with unmarried persons. Even on the assumption that the fear of pregnancy operates as a deterrent to fornication, the Massachusetts statute is thus so riddled with exceptions that deterrence of premarital sex cannot reasonably be regarded as its aim.

Moreover, §§21 and 21A on their face have a dubious relation to the State's criminal prohibition on fornication. As the Court of Appeals explained, "Fornication is a misdemeanor [in Massachusetts], entailing a thirty dollar fine, or three months in jail. Violation of the present statute is a felony, punishable by five years in prison. We find it hard to believe that the legislature adopted a statute carrying a five-year penalty for its possible, obviously by no means fully effective, deterrence of the commission of a ninety-day misdemeanor."...

Second. Section 21A was added to the Massachusetts General Laws [by previous amendment]. The Supreme Judicial Court in *Commonwealth v. Baird* held that the purpose of the amendment was to serve the health needs of the community by regulating the distribution of potentially harmful articles. It is plain that Massachusetts had no such purpose in mind before the enactment of 21A. As the Court of Appeals remarked, "Consistent with the fact that the statute was contained in a chapter dealing with 'Crimes Against Chastity, Morality, Decency and Good Order,' it was cast only in terms of morals. A physician was forbidden to prescribe contraceptives even when needed for the protection of health. Nor did the Court of Appeals "believe that the legislature [in enacting 21A] suddenly reversed its field and developed an interest in health. Rather, it merely made what it thought to be the precise accommodation necessary to escape the *Griswold* ruling."

Again, we must agree with the Court of Appeals. If health were the rationale of 21A, the statute would be both discriminatory and overbroad. Dissenting in *Commonwealth v. Baird*, Justices Whittemore and Cutter stated that they saw "...no public health purpose. If there is need to have a physician prescribe (and a pharmacist dispense) contraceptives, that need is as great for unmarried persons as for married persons." The Court of Appeals added: "If the prohibition [on distribution to unmarried persons]...is to be taken to mean that the same physician who can prescribe for married patients does not have sufficient skill to protect the health of patients who lack a marriage certificate, or who may be currently divorced, it is illogical to the point of irrationality."...

Third. If the Massachusetts statute cannot be upheld as a deterrent to fornication or as a health measure, may it, nevertheless, be sustained simply as a prohibition on contraception? The Court of Appeals analysis "led inevitably to the conclusion that, so far as morals are concerned, it is contraceptives per se that are considered immoral—to the extent that *Griswold* will permit such a declaration." The Court of Appeals went on to hold:

> "To say that contraceptives are immoral as such, and are to be forbidden to unmarried persons who will nevertheless persist in having intercourse, means that such persons must risk for themselves an unwanted pregnancy, for the child, illegitimacy, and for society, a possible obligation of support. Such a view of morality is not only the very mirror image of sensible legislation; we consider that it conflicts with fundamental human rights. In the absence of demonstrated harm, we hold it is beyond the competency of the state."

We need not and do not, however, decide that important question in this case because, whatever the rights of the individual to access to contraceptives may be, the rights must be the same for the unmarried and the married alike.

If under *Griswold* the distribution of contraceptives to married persons cannot be prohibited, a ban on distribution to unmarried persons would be equally impermissible. It is true that in *Griswold* the right of privacy in question inhered in the marital relationship. Yet the marital couple is not an independent entity with a mind and heart of its own, but an association of two individuals each with a separate intellectual and emotional makeup. If the right of privacy means anything, it is the right of the individual, married or single, to be free from unwarranted governmental intrusion into matters so fundamentally affecting a person as the decision whether to bear or beget a child.

On the other hand, if *Griswold* is no bar to a prohibition on the distribution of contraceptives, the State could not, consistently with the Equal Protection Clause, outlaw distribution to unmarried but not to married persons. In each case the evil, as perceived by the State, would be identical, and the underinclusion would be invidious. Justice Jackson made the point:

> "The framers of the Constitution knew, and we should not forget today, that there is no more effective practical guaranty against arbitrary and unreasonable government than to require that the principles of law which officials would impose upon a minority must be imposed generally. Conversely, nothing opens the door to arbitrary action so effectively as to allow those officials to pick and choose only a few to whom they will apply legislation and thus to escape the political retribution that might be visited upon them if larger numbers were affected. Courts can take no better measure to assure that laws will be just than to require that laws be equal in operation."

…We hold that by providing dissimilar treatment for married and unmarried persons who are similarly situated, [the Massachusetts law] violates the Equal Protection Clause.

The judgment of the Court of Appeals is affirmed.

Bowers v. Hardwick
478 U.S. 186 (1986)

Justice White delivered the opinion of the Court, in which Chief Justice Burger and Justices Powell, Rehnquist, and O'Connor joined. Chief Justice Burger and Justice Powell filed concurring opinions. Justice Blackmun filed a dissenting opinion, in which Justices Brennan, Marshall, and Stevens joined. Justice Stevens filed a dissenting opinion, in which Justices Brennan and Marshall joined.

Areas for Discussion and Ethical Reflection

1.   Justice White conceptualizes this case in terms of whether the U.S. Constitution confers upon homosexuals the right to engage in sodomy. He then concludes that there is no such right. Does Justice White understand the case correctly? It really does matter—in medical ethics, as well as constitutional law—how a problem is framed. For example, in discussions of the morality of physician-assisted suicide, the specific conceptual analysis and ethical evaluation one provides depends in large part on whether the issue is characterized as physicians helping to kill their patients or physicians fulfilling a professional obligation to alleviate suffering. Throughout this book we face this issue of the most accurate way to characterize and conceptualize problems and dilemmas in medical ethics.

2.   According to Justice White, a right will qualify for heightened judicial scrutiny if it is "a fundamental liberty implicit in the concept of ordered liberty such that neither liberty or justice would exist if [it] were sacrificed," or it is a liberty "deeply rooted in this Nation's history and tradition." What are the advantages

and disadvantages for medical ethics of these understandings of what constitutes a right?

3.   Are state laws prohibiting sodomy rational? Hardwick argued that laws are not rational when based solely on the majority's beliefs regarding what constitutes moral behavior. How does Justice White respond to this claim?

4.   In his dissent (not excerpted below), Justice Blackmun asserts, "…this case is about 'the most comprehensive of rights and the right most valued by civilized men,' namely, 'the right to be let alone.' " Justice Blackmun views Hardwick's claim within the context of a right to privacy. Do you agree? Apply and discuss your understanding of the principle of autonomy.

5.   Many in medical ethics make a distinction between the morality or immorality of actions and the morality or immorality of policies regulating or prohibiting those actions. Does such a distinction apply to homosexuality? That is, can we separate ethical arguments for and against homosexuality from ethical arguments for and against laws prohibiting homosexual sodomy?

6.   For hundreds of years many countries, including the United States, have instituted strong legal and moral prohibitions against homosexual sodomy. As a matter of fact, one could easily get the impression that sodomy is the most egregious of all sins, second only to murder. Yet, careful reflection on the reasons sodomy should be considered so morally reprehensible yields unconvincing and/or unclear answers.[8] Try to explain exactly what is wrong, morally speaking, with homosexual sodomy. Next, try to explain exactly why, morally speaking, the state should prohibit sodomy.

JUSTICE WHITE:

     …This case does not require a judgment on whether laws against sodomy between consenting adults in general, or between homosexuals in particular, are wise or desirable.

It raises no question about the right or propriety of state legislative decisions to repeal their laws that criminalize homosexual sodomy, or of state-court decisions invalidating those laws on state constitutional grounds. The issue presented is whether the Federal Constitution confers a fundamental right upon homosexuals to engage in sodomy and hence invalidates the laws of the many States that still make such conduct illegal and have done so for a very long time. The case also calls for some judgment about the limits of the Court's role in carrying out its constitutional mandate.

We first register our disagreement with the Court of Appeals and with [Hardwick] that the Court's prior cases have construed the Constitution to confer a right of privacy that extends to homosexual sodomy and for all intents and purposes have decided this case. The reach of this line of cases was sketched in *Carey v. Population Services International, Pierce v. Society of Sisters*, and *Meyer v. Nebraska*, described as dealing with child rearing and education; *Prince v. Massachusetts*, with family relationships; *Skinner v. Oklahoma*, with procreation; *Loving v. Virginia*, with marriage; *Griswold v. Connecticut*, and *Eisenstadt v. Baird*, with contraception; and *Roe v. Wade*, with abortion. The latter three cases were interpreted as construing the Due Process Clause of the Fourteenth Amendment to confer a fundamental individual right to decide whether or not to beget or bear a child....

[W]e think it evident that none of the rights announced in [prior] cases bears any resemblance to the claimed constitutional right of homosexuals to engage in acts of sodomy that is asserted in this case. No connection between family, marriage, or procreation on the one hand and homosexual activity on the other has been demonstrated, either by the Court of Appeals or by respondent. Moreover, any claim that these cases nevertheless stand for the proposition that any kind of private sexual conduct between consenting adults is constitutionally insulated from state proscription is unsupportable....

Precedent aside, however, [Hardwick] would have us announce, as the Court of Appeals did, a fundamental right to engage in homosexual sodomy. This we are quite unwilling to do. It is true that despite the language of the Due Process Clauses of the Fifth and Fourteenth Amendments, which appears to focus only on the processes by which life, liberty, or property is taken, the cases are legion in which those Clauses have been interpreted to have substantive content, subsuming rights that to a great extent are immune from federal or state regulation or proscription....

Striving to assure itself and the public that announcing rights not readily identifiable in the Constitution's text involves much more than the imposition of the justices' own choice of values on the States and the Federal Government, the Court has sought to identify the nature of the rights qualifying for heightened judicial protection. In *Palko v. Connecticut*, it was said that this category includes those fundamental liberties that are "implicit in the concept of ordered liberty," such that "neither liberty nor justice would exist if [they] were sacrificed." A different description of fundamental liberties appeared in *Moore v. East Cleveland*, where they are characterized as those liberties that are "deeply rooted in this Nation's history and tradition."

It is obvious to us that neither of these formulations would extend a fundamental right to homosexuals to engage in acts of consensual sodomy. Proscriptions against that conduct have ancient roots. Sodomy was a criminal offense at common law and was forbidden by the laws of the original 13 States when they ratified the Bill of Rights. In 1868, when the Fourteenth Amendment was ratified, all but 5 of the 37 States in the Union had criminal sodomy laws. In fact, until 1961, all 50 States outlawed sodomy, and today, 24 States and the District of Columbia continue to provide criminal penalties for sodomy performed in private and between consenting adults. Against this background, to claim that a right to engage in such conduct is "deeply rooted in

this Nation's history and tradition" or "implicit in the concept of ordered liberty" is, at best, facetious.

Nor are we inclined to take a more expansive view of
our authority to discover new fundamental rights imbed-
ded in the Due Process Clause. The Court is most vulnerable and comes nearest to illegitimacy when it deals with
judge-made constitutional law having little or no cognizable roots in the language or design of the Constitution.
That this is so was painfully demonstrated by the face-off
between the Executive and the Court in the 1930s, which
resulted in the repudiation of much of the substantive gloss
that the Court had placed on the Due Process Clauses of
the Fifth and Fourteenth Amendments. There should be,
therefore, great resistance to expand the substantive reach
of those Clauses, particularly if it requires redefining the
category of rights deemed to be fundamental. Otherwise,
the Judiciary necessarily takes to itself further authority to
govern the country without express constitutional authority. The claimed right pressed on us today falls far short of
overcoming this resistance.

[Hardwick], however, asserts that the result should
be different where the homosexual conduct occurs in the
privacy of the home. He relies on *Stanley v. Georgia* (1969),
where the Court held that the First Amendment prevents
conviction for possessing and reading obscene material in
the privacy of one's home...but the decision in *Stanley* was
firmly grounded in the First Amendment. The right pressed
upon us here has no similar support in the text of the Constitution, and it does not qualify for recognition under
the prevailing principles for construing the Fourteenth
Amendment....

Even if the conduct at issue here is not a fundamental
right, [Hardwick] asserts that there must be a rational basis
for the law and that there is none in this case other than the
presumed belief of a majority of the electorate in Georgia

that homosexual sodomy is immoral and unacceptable. This is said to be an inadequate rationale to support the law. The law, however, is constantly based on notions of morality, and if all laws representing essential moral choices are to be invalidated under the Due Process Clause, the courts will be very busy indeed. Even [Hardwick] makes no such claim, but insists that majority sentiments about the morality of homosexuality should be declared inadequate. We do not agree, and are unpersuaded that the sodomy laws of some 25 states should be invalidated on this basis.

Accordingly, the Judgment of the Court of Appeals is reversed.

Lawrence et al. v. Texas
539 U.S. ___ (2003)

Justice Kennedy delivered the opinion of the Court, in which Justices Stevens, Souter, Ginsburg, and Breyer joined. Justice O'Connor filed an opinion concurring in the judgment. Justice Scalia filed a dissenting opinion, in which Chief Justice Rehnquist and Justice Thomas joined. Justice Thomas filed a dissenting opinion.

Areas for Discussion and Ethical Reflection

1.   Justice Kennedy finds the Texas law criminalizing homosexual sodomy unconstitutional. Lay out his exact arguments for this position. Do any of these arguments entail ethical commitments on the part of Justice Kennedy? If so, what are they?

2.   In his majority opinion, Justice Kennedy employs terms such as "dignity," "autonomy," and "liberty" quite often. How does Justice Kennedy understand these terms? How do you understand these terms? If Justice Kennedy applied his understanding of autonomy to particular areas of concern in medical ethics, what would be the result? One example might be federal prohibition of marijuana use by terminally ill, suffering cancer

patients. Compare Justice Kennedy's views on autonomy and liberty in *Lawrence* to his views regarding these concepts expressed in other cases in this book.

3.   Discuss the utilitarian arguments Justice Kennedy provides in support of overturning the Texas statute. Can you think of utilitarian arguments in support of allowing Texas to continue criminalizing same-sex sodomy?

4.   From a moral perspective, would it not have been preferable for the Court to strike down Texas's law because it did not afford a specific class of individuals equal protection of the laws without good reason? Justice O'Connor was the only justice who would have invalidated the law on equal protection grounds. In her concurring opinion (not included in the excerpt below) she notes:

> Moral disapproval of a group cannot be a legitimate governmental interest under the Equal Protection Clause because legal classifications must not be "drawn for the purpose of disadvantaging the group burdened by the law." Texas' invocation of moral disapproval as a legitimate state interest proves nothing more than Texas' desire to criminalize homosexual sodomy. But the Equal Protection Clause prevents a State from creating "a classification of persons undertaken for its own sake." And because Texas so rarely enforces its sodomy law as applied to private, consensual acts, the law serves more as a statement of dislike and disapproval against homosexuals than as a tool to stop criminal behavior. The Texas sodomy law "raise[s] the inevitable inference that the disadvantage imposed is born of animosity toward the class of persons affected."

What does Justice O'Connor's position indicate about her moral commitments or value preferences with regard to homosexual sodomy?

5.   Three justices—Chief Justice Rehnquist, Justice Scalia,

and Justice Thomas—dissented from the decision, with the last two writing dissents. Justice Scalia wrote a lengthy dissent (not included in the excerpt below) in which he disagreed with practically everything the majority said. At the beginning of his dissent, Justice Scalia notes:

> Though there is discussion of "fundamental propositions," and "fundamental decisions," nowhere does the Court's opinion declare that homosexual sodomy is a "fundamental right" under the Due Process Clause....Thus, while overruling the outcome of *Bowers*, the Court leaves strangely untouched its central legal conclusion.

As you read Justice Kennedy's majority opinion, ask yourself whether Justice Scalia is correct on this point. If Justice Scalia is correct, what significance, if any, would there be for homosexual rights in particular and medical ethics in general?

6.   Justice Scalia argues against the majority by asserting that by finding a liberty interest in homosexual sodomy protected by the Due Process Clause of the Fourteenth Amendment, the Court will now have to sanction bigamy, prostitution, and homosexual marriage. Many politicians in criticizing the Court's ruling agreed with Justice Scalia. Do you think Justice Scalia is correct? How might you agree with the majority yet claim that bigamy and prostitution should remain illegal? What about homosexual marriage?

7.   Justice Thomas's dissent is very short, but two items of interest to medical ethics are worth noting. First, Justice Thomas quotes Justice Stewart from *Griswold* in calling the Texas statute an "...uncommonly silly law." Justice Thomas asserts that he would vote to repeal such a law because punishing people who engage in homosexual conduct is a waste of valuable resources. Second, Justice Thomas asserts that he is not "empowered" to help the two gay men in this case. Rather, his job is simply to interpret and apply principles of the Constitution, which does not

mention anywhere a right to privacy. What is your assessment of these assertions?

8.   What are the long-range consequences of the *Lawrence* decision for the field of medical ethics? You might return to this question after reading other cases and accompanying materials in this book. Is it possible that certain concepts or principles influential in medical ethics contributed to the outcome of the decision in *Lawrence*?

JUSTICE KENNEDY:

Liberty protects the person from unwarranted government intrusions into a dwelling or other private places. In our tradition the State is not omnipresent in the home. And there are other spheres of our lives and existence, outside the home, where the State should not be a dominant presence. Freedom extends beyond spatial bounds. Liberty presumes an autonomy of self that includes freedom of thought, belief, expression, and certain intimate conduct. The instant case involves liberty of the person both in its spatial and more transcendent dimensions.

The question before the Court is the validity of a Texas statute making it a crime for two persons of the same sex to engage in certain intimate sexual conduct....

The complaints describe their crime as "deviate sexual intercourse, namely anal sex, with a member of the same sex (man)." The applicable state law is §21.06(a). It provides: "A person commits an offense if he engages in deviate sexual intercourse with another individual of the same sex." The statute defines "[d]eviate sexual intercourse" as follows:

"(A) any contact between any part of the genitals of one person and the mouth or anus of another person; or

"(B) the penetration of the genitals or the anus of another person with an object." §21.01(1).

…We granted certiorari to consider three questions:

"1. Whether Petitioners' criminal convictions under the Texas 'Homosexual Conduct' law—which criminalizes sexual intimacy by same-sex couples, but not identical behavior by different-sex couples—violate the Fourteenth Amendment guarantee of equal protection of laws?

"2. Whether Petitioners' criminal convictions for adult consensual sexual intimacy in the home violate their vital interests in liberty and privacy protected by the Due Process Clause of the Fourteenth Amendment?

"3. Whether *Bowers v. Hardwick* (1986) should be overruled?"

…We conclude the case should be resolved by determining whether the petitioners were free as adults to engage in the private conduct in the exercise of their liberty under the Due Process Clause of the Fourteenth Amendment to the Constitution. For this inquiry we deem it necessary to reconsider the Court's holding in *Bowers*.

[Before discussing *Bowers,* Justice Kennedy discusses the scope of liberty under the Due Process Clause in past cases.]

The Court began its substantive discussion in *Bowers* as follows: "The issue presented is whether the Federal Constitution confers a fundamental right upon homosexuals to engage in sodomy and hence invalidates the laws of the many States that still make such conduct illegal and have done so for a very long time." That statement, we now conclude, discloses the Court's own failure to appreciate the extent of the liberty at stake. To say that the issue in *Bowers* was simply the right to engage in certain sexual conduct demeans the claim the individual put forward, just as it would demean a married couple were it to be said marriage is simply about the right to have sexual intercourse. The laws involved in *Bowers* and here are, to be sure, statutes that purport to do no more than prohibit a particular sexual act. Their penalties and purposes, though, have more far-reaching consequences, touching upon the most private human conduct, sexual behavior, and in the most private of places, the home. The statutes do seek to control a personal relationship that, whether or not entitled to formal recognition in the law, is within the liberty of persons to choose without being punished as criminals.

This, as a general rule, should counsel against attempts by the State, or a court, to define the meaning of the relationship or to set its boundaries absent injury to a person or abuse of an institution the law protects. It suffices for us to acknowledge that adults may choose to enter upon this relationship in the confines of their homes and their own private lives and still retain their dignity as free persons. When sexuality finds overt expression in intimate conduct with another person, the conduct can be but one element in a personal bond that is more enduring. The liberty protected by the Constitution allows homosexual persons the right to make this choice.

[At this point Justice Kennedy spends considerable time explaining then objecting to the historical premises upon which *Bowers* was based.]

It must be acknowledged, of course, that the Court in *Bowers* was making the broader point that for centuries there have been powerful voices to condemn homosexual conduct as immoral. The condemnation has been shaped by religious beliefs, conceptions of right and acceptable behavior, and respect for the traditional family. For many persons these are not trivial concerns but profound and deep convictions accepted as ethical and moral principles to which they aspire and which thus determine the course of their lives. These considerations do not answer the question before us, however. The issue is whether the majority may use the power of the State to enforce these views on the whole society through operation of the criminal law. "Our obligation is to define the liberty of all, not to mandate our own moral code."

Chief Justice Burger joined the opinion for the Court in *Bowers* and further explained his views as follows: "Decisions of individuals relating to homosexual conduct have been subject to state intervention throughout the history of Western civilization. Condemnation of those practices is firmly rooted in Judeao-Christian moral and ethical standards." As with Justice White's assumptions about history, scholarship casts some doubt on the sweeping nature of the statement by Chief Justice Burger as it pertains to private homosexual conduct between consenting adults. In all events we think that our laws and traditions in the past half century are of the most relevance here. These references show an emerging awareness that liberty gives substantial protection to adult persons in deciding how to conduct their private lives in matters pertaining to sex. "[H]istory and tradition are the starting point but not in all cases the ending point of the substantive due process inquiry."

[Justice Kennedy discusses several attempts in America and in Europe, even before *Bowers*, to decriminalize consensual sexual relations between adults.]

In our own constitutional system the deficiencies in *Bowers* became even more apparent in the years following its announcement. The 25 States with laws prohibiting the relevant conduct referenced in the *Bowers* decision are reduced now to 13, of which 4 enforce their laws only against homosexual conduct. In those States where sodomy is still proscribed, whether for same-sex or heterosexual conduct, there is a pattern of nonenforcement with respect to consenting adults acting in private. The State of Texas admitted in 1994 that as of that date it had not prosecuted anyone under those circumstances.

Two principal cases decided after *Bowers* cast its holding into even more doubt. In *Planned Parenthood of*

Southeastern Pa. v. Casey (1992), the Court reaffirmed the substantive force of the liberty protected by the Due Process Clause. The *Casey* decision again confirmed that our laws and tradition afford constitutional protection to personal decisions relating to marriage, procreation, contraception, family relationships, child rearing, and education....

The second post-*Bowers* case of principal relevance is *Romer v. Evans,* (1996). There the Court struck down class-based legislation directed at homosexuals as a violation of the Equal Protection Clause. *Romer* invalidated an amendment to Colorado's constitution, which named as a solitary class persons who were homosexuals, lesbians, or bisexual either by "orientation, conduct, practices or relationships," and deprived them of protection under state antidiscrimination laws. We concluded that the provision was "born of animosity toward the class of persons affected" and further that it had no rational relation to a legitimate governmental purpose....

Equality of treatment and the due process right to demand respect for conduct protected by the substantive guarantee of liberty are linked in important respects, and a decision on the latter point advances both interests. If protected conduct is made criminal and the law which does so remains unexamined for its substantive validity, its stigma might remain even if it were not enforceable as drawn for equal protection reasons. When homosexual conduct is made criminal by the law of the State, that declaration in and of itself is an invitation to subject homosexual persons to discrimination both in the public and in the private spheres. The central holding of *Bowers* has been brought in question by this case, and it should be addressed. Its continuance as precedent demeans the lives of homosexual persons.

The stigma this criminal statute imposes, moreover, is not trivial. The offense, to be sure, is but a class C misdemeanor, a minor offense in the Texas legal system. Still, it remains a criminal offense with all that imports for the dignity of the persons charged. The petitioners will bear on their record the history of their criminal convictions....We are advised that if Texas convicted an adult for private, consensual homosexual conduct under the statute here in question the convicted person would come within the registration laws of at least four States were he or she to be subject to their jurisdiction.

This underscores the consequential nature of the punishment and the state-sponsored condemnation attendant to the criminal prohibition. Furthermore, the Texas criminal conviction carries with it the other collateral consequences always following a conviction, such as notations on job application forms, to mention but one example....

The rationale of *Bowers* does not withstand careful analysis. In his dissenting opinion in *Bowers*, Justice Stevens came to these conclusions:

> Our prior cases make two propositions abundantly clear. First, the fact that the governing majority in a State has traditionally viewed a particular practice as immoral is not a sufficient reason for upholding a law prohibiting the practice; neither history nor tradition could save a law prohibiting miscegenation from constitutional attack. Second, individual decisions by married persons, concerning the intimacies of their physical relationship, even when not intended to produce offspring, are a form of "liberty" protected by the Due Process Clause of the Fourteenth Amendment. Moreover, this protection extends to intimate choices by unmarried as well as married persons.

Justice Stevens's analysis, in our view, should have been controlling in *Bowers* and should control here.

Bowers was not correct when it was decided, and it is not correct today. It ought not to remain binding precedent.

Bowers v. Hardwick should be and now is overruled.

The present case does not involve minors. It does not involve persons who might be injured or coerced or who are situated in relationships where consent might not easily be refused. It does not involve public conduct or prostitution. It does not involve whether the government must give formal recognition to any relationship that homosexual persons seek to enter. The case does involve two adults who, with full and mutual consent from each other, engaged in sexual practices common to a homosexual lifestyle. The petitioners are entitled to respect for their private lives. The State cannot demean their existence or control their destiny by making their private sexual conduct a crime. Their right to liberty under the Due Process Clause gives them the full right to engage in their conduct without intervention of the government. "It is a promise of the Constitution that there is a realm of personal liberty which the government may not enter." The Texas statute furthers no legitimate state interest which can justify its intrusion into the personal and private life of the individual.

Had those who drew and ratified the Due Process Clauses of the Fifth Amendment or the Fourteenth Amendment known the components of liberty in its manifold possibilities, they might have been more specific. They did not presume to have this insight. They knew times can blind us to certain truths and later generations can see that laws once thought necessary and proper in fact serve only to oppress. As the Constitution endures, persons in every generation can invoke its principles in their own search for greater freedom.

The judgment of the Court of Appeals for the Texas Fourteenth District is reversed, and the case is remanded for further proceedings not inconsistent with this opinion. It is so ordered.

Notes

1.   Tom L. Beauchamp and James F. Childress, *Principles of Biomedical Ethics*, 5th edition (New York: Oxford University Press, 2001), pp. 58–61.

2.   Ibid., pp. 293–97.

3.   Lawrence M. Hinman, ed., *Contemporary Moral Issues: Diversity and Consensus*, 2nd edition (Upper Saddle River, NJ: Prentice Hall, 2000), pp. 360–68.

4.   James Q. Wilson, "Against Homosexual Marriage," in *Contemporary Moral Issues: Diversity and Consensus*, 2nd edition, ed. Lawrence M. Hinman (Upper Saddle River, NJ: Prentice Hall, 2000), pp. 381–82.

5.   Michael H. Shapiro et al., *Bioethics and Law: Cases, Materials and Problems*, 2nd edition (St. Paul, MN: West Group, 2003), pp. 1239–40.

6.   Ibid., p. 539.

7.   John E. Nowak and Ronald D. Rotunda, *Constitutional Law*, 6th edition (St. Paul, MN: West Group, 2000), p. 857.

8.   Andrew Sullivan, "Unnatural Law," *New Republic*, March 24, 2003, 18–23.

For Further Reading

Arthur, John. "Privacy, Homosexuality, and the Constitution." In *Readings in the Philosophy of Law*, 3rd edition, John Arthur and William Shaw, eds. Upper Saddle River, NJ: Prentice Hall, 2001.

Beauchamp, Tom L., and James F. Childress. *Principles of Biomedical Ethics*, 5th edition. New York: Oxford University Press, 2001.

Halper, Thomas. "Privacy and Autonomy: From Warren and Brandeis to *Roe* and *Cruzan*." *Journal of Medicine and Philosophy* 21 (1996): 121–35.

Hinman, Lawrence M. "An Introduction to the Moral Issues: Sexual Orientation." In *Contemporary Moral Issues: Diversity and Consensus*, 2nd edition, Lawrence M. Hinman, ed. Upper Saddle River, NJ: Prentice Hall, 2000.

McKinlay, John B., ed. *Law and Ethics in Health Care*. Cambridge, MA: MIT Press, 1982.

Menikoff, Jerry. *Law and Bioethics: An Introduction*. Washington, DC: Georgetown University Press, 2001.

Rosen, Jeffrey. "Kennedy Curse: On Sodomy, the Court Overreaches." *New Republic*, July 21, 2003, 15–18.

Sullivan, Andrew. "Unnatural Law: What Sodomy Laws Really Mean." *New Republic*, March 24, 2003, 18–23.

———. "Citizens: On Sodomy, the Court Gets It Right." *New Republic*, July 21, 2003, 18–19.

Turkington, Richard C., George B. Trubow, and Anita L. Allen, eds. *Privacy: Cases and Materials*. Houston, TX: John Marshall Publishing Co., 1992.

Veatch, Robert M. *The Basics of Bioethics*. Upper Saddle River, NJ: Prentice Hall, 2000.

Warren, Samuel, and Louis Brandeis. "The Right to Privacy." *Harvard Law Review* 4 (1890): 193–220.

Wilson, James Q. "Against Homosexual Marriage." In *Contemporary Moral Issues: Diversity and Consensus*, 2nd edition, Lawrence M. Hinman, ed. Upper Saddle River, NJ: Prentice Hall, 2000.

CHAPTER TWO

THE REPRODUCTIVE FREEDOM AND MATERNAL-FETAL CONFLICT CASES

From its very creation, the Constitution was perceived as a document that sought to strike a delicate balance between, on the one hand, governmental power to accomplish the great ends of civil society and, on the other, individual liberty.

—Laurence Tribe and Michael Dorf, *On Reading the Constitution*

The Federal Constitution and the U.S. Supreme Court's interpretation of the Constitution both concern the use of power, the distribution of power, and the balancing of power. The essence of federalism entails the sharing of authority between the federal government, the individual states, and the people. The Constitution is not always clear in demarcating the proper lines of authority, thus the justices of the Supreme Court interpret the Constitution and rule upon the proper divisions of authority and power. And interpreting and deciding where government authority ends and personal freedom begins is indeed the exercise of power. That political, social, and ethical concerns exact influence on the justices is beyond dispute; interpreting the Constitution does not occur in a vacuum. The values and moral commitments of society change, and we often see this change reflected in Supreme Court decisions. Abundant examples exist, with slavery and racial segregation perhaps being the most prominent. Because many issues in medical ethics involve fundamental rights and present the opportunity for government intervention to limit those rights, examining judicial reasoning and the values behind that reasoning is especially important. This chapter examines how the justices exercise their power in addressing conflicts between individual rights and states' interests in the areas of involuntary sterilization of habitual criminals, defining and regulating relationships between parents and their children, and ascribing to and enforcing on pregnant women obligations to protect their fetuses. In and of themselves these areas are of direct and immediate concern to students of medical ethics and to health care professionals. However, we also have an opportunity, with one case in particular, to witness and evaluate ethically the exercise of power at its most basic level: deciding how to decide what should count as a fundamental right.

Constitutional Issues and Background

Our first case, *Skinner v. Oklahoma*, allows readers to revisit the Equal Protection Clause of the Fourteenth Amendment first discussed in connection with *Eisenstadt v. Baird*. At issue in *Skinner* was Oklahoma's Habitual Criminal Sterilization Act, which defined a habitual criminal as anyone convicted two or more times of a felony involving "moral turpitude." Such persons could be ordered by a trial court to undergo sterilization if the general health of the defendant would not be severely affected. The state of Oklahoma made a distinction between types of felonies such that three convictions for larceny would result in sterilization, whereas three convictions for embezzlement would not. After one conviction for stealing chickens and two convictions for robbery, Skinner was serving time in the penitentiary. In 1936, a year after the act passed, Skinner was ordered to undergo a vasectomy based on proceedings initiated by the state's attorney general. The Supreme Court of Oklahoma affirmed the trial court's finding that a vasectomy was proper by a 5-4 vote.

The justices in *Skinner*, through application of the Equal

Protection Clause, contribute to our understanding of what will count as a fundamental right and of how far the government may go in abridging that right for certain classes of individuals. A unanimous Court found the Oklahoma statute unconstitutional. Whether equal protection is the best constitutional principle to apply was a matter of some dispute, however, and at least one Justice considered the issues in the case best resolved by applying procedural due process principles.

Though very few people outside the area of constitutional law are aware of our second case, the issues under consideration and the deliberations among the justices have significant implications for not only constitutional interpretation but medical ethics as well. In the early 1980s the California Evidence Code (§621) maintained that a child born to a married woman living with her husband, who is neither impotent nor sterile, is presumed to be the child of the marriage, unless the husband or wife denies the child is of the marriage. In 1981, Carole D. gave birth to Victoria D. Carole was married to Gerald D. at the time, and he was listed as the father of Victoria on the birth certificate. But Carole had had an adulterous affair with Michael H., and blood tests showed that a very high probability existed that Michael was the father of Victoria. From 1981 until 1984, Victoria and her mother lived occasionally with Michael, occasionally with Gerald, and at times with another man. In 1982, Michael filed an action in California Superior Court asking that paternity be established and that he be given visitation rights. Victoria, through her court-appointed guardian ad litem, also filed suit asking that both Michael and Gerald be given visitation rights. Both the California Superior Court and the Court of Appeals rejected Michael and Victoria's claims.

While the Supreme Court's ultimate denial of both Michael and Victoria's claims is significant, many of the issues in this case surround definitions of parenthood and the role of genetics in determining parenthood.[1] As you will see, the debate among the justices regarding how the Court determines what will count as a fundamental right or liberty interest is quite heated. In essence, the debate between the justices is over the proper level of generality to be applied in determining what actions or liberties the Constitution should recognize as fundamental rights. The debate itself, as well as what it means for medical ethics, will be discussed in more detail below.

In our final case of this chapter, *Ferguson et al. v. Charleston et al.*, we witness the justices struggle over the meaning and application of the Fourth Amendment to issues surrounding informed consent and the gathering of evidence. In 1988 the medical staff at the Medical University of South Carolina (MUSC) became concerned about the high incidence of women giving birth to children with cocaine addiction. The staff, in conjunction with the district attorney's office and the police, developed guidelines by which pregnant women suspected of using cocaine would be identified and tested. The policy set forth procedures for obtaining urine samples of suspected women, preserving the chain of custody of the urine samples, making treatment referrals for women testing positive for drug use, arresting pregnant women, and prescribing criminal charges for drug offenses and/ or child neglect. MUSC offered to cooperate with prosecutors in convicting women suspected of using drugs. Several women, after being arrested for testing positive, filed suit asserting the policy constituted an unreasonable search. The District Court found for the women. However, on appeal, the Fourth Circuit held that MUSC's policy was valid.

Of central importance in *Ferguson* was the Fourth Amendment, which states, "The right of the people to be secure in their persons, houses, papers, and effects, against unreasonable searches and seizures shall not be violated, and no warrants shall issue, but upon probable cause, supported by oath or affirmation, and particularly describing the place to be searched, and the persons or things to be seized." Determining the conditions under which a search should be viewed as reasonable has proved quite challenging for the justices. Justice Stevens, in his majority opinion, weighed the interest of the individual in protecting privacy against what the state asserts are its legitimate needs and goals. When a search violates privacy rights, the need of the state has to be reasonable. Determinations of reasonableness are made more difficult when the search takes place in the medical context and when there is a question of valid, informed consent. While not directly at issue in *Ferguson*, the case allows us to explore the problems that occur when pregnant women refuse medical treatment deemed necessary to protect the life or health of the fetus. Imposing ethical and legal duties on pregnant women to accept medical treatment raises complex issues for both medical ethics and the law.

Ethical Issues and Background

Justice Douglas observed in his majority opinion in *Skinner v. Oklahoma*: "There is no redemption for the individual whom the law touches." He made this observation in the context of criticizing Oklahoma's mandatory sterilization law, but his comment applies with equal force to the two other cases in this chapter that address determination of paternity for child custody purposes and involuntary drug testing of pregnant women. Ethical concerns obviously surround all three issues, and consideration of the extent to which the justices confront or ignore these concerns when determining exactly what the Constitution permits or forbids is enlightening.

Involuntary sterilization raises the specter of atrocities committed in Nazi Germany and of early eugenics programs. In the United States as many as seventy thousand people were sterilized against their will during the twentieth century.[2] Two reasons—punishing criminal behavior and stopping the spread of mental retardation through heredity—generally were given for sterilization programs, although the distinction between these reasons was not always clear. In chapter 8 we will focus on eugenics in the context of involuntarily sterilizing those deemed mentally retarded, but here we examine the concept of punishment and moral reasons for punishing. Not only is the issue of punishment relevant to *Skinner*, it also applies to *Ferguson*.

Government interference with reproductive liberty requires strong moral justification. After all, if concepts of self-determination and privacy have any practical application at all, they apply to choices surrounding whether to procreate. Even those convicted of crimes should not be forced to undergo sterilization except for the strongest of reasons. Leaving aside for the moment justifications for any particular punishment, such as mandatory sterilization, several theories of punishment are commonly advanced as morally acceptable.[3] A theory of punishment based on deterrence asserts that punishment is justified by encouraging the person punished, or others likely to commit crimes, to obey the law. This theory is forward-looking in that its purpose is to stop or deter criminal behavior. Retributivism asserts that the justification for punishment lies in "paying back" the criminal for her/his acts. Punishment as retribution may stress revenge, or the seeking of justice, or even helping victims feel compensated. Another theory views punishing criminals as a means to rehabilitate them. This theory stresses the obligation of the state to devise forms of punishment that train or educate offenders to be contributing members of society.

If the state wishes to impose as criminal sanction some sort of reproductive control on individuals convicted of certain crimes, it makes sense to ask what ends the state wishes to achieve. For example, if a trial judge offers a woman convicted of child abuse the choice between a long prison sentence or a regimen of Norplant for the purpose of prohibiting reproduction for five years, we might wonder what goal the judge wishes to accomplish. Does he wish to deter other women from abusing their children? Does the choice he presents somehow represent giving her what he believes justice requires? Or, does the judge hope to rehabilitate the woman? As you read *Skinner,* try to determine to which theory of punishment Oklahoma subscribed.

Any reluctance on the part of those interested in ethical dilemmas in health care to admit that U.S. Supreme Court cases have immense implications for the study of medical ethics vanishes after considering our second case, *Michael H. v. Gerald D.* As you will discover from reading Justice Scalia's plurality opinion, the Court denied parental rights to a man who was the biological father of a child born to a woman who was married to another man. In dissent, Justice Brennan claimed that the man had a fundamental right to enjoy a relationship with his daughter. Justice Scalia, in a footnote that only one other justice joined, criticized Justice Brennan's description of the right at issue.[4] In brief, the debate between the two justices centers on the issue of how to characterize a fundamental right or liberty interest. Justice Scalia prefers to be as specific as possible when determining whether a particular activity involves a fundamental right; in addition, he wishes to ground his specificity in socially recognized traditions. Justice Brennan prefers to be as general as possible in determining whether a right is fundamental, and he is very critical of the appeal to recognized tradition as the basis for finding a liberty interest protected by the Constitution.

This debate between Justice Scalia and Justice Brennan is not at all academic, but has tremendous implications for bioethics. Over the past twenty years medical ethicists and policy makers have had to come to terms with the challenges presented by new assisted reproductive technologies. New techniques for helping women or couples bear children include in vitro fertilization, artificial insemination, freezing of embryos, gestational surrogacy, and reproductive cloning. These technologies raise new and challenging social and ethical concerns. For example, how should society determine parental obligations and responsibilities to children who may have several "mothers" and "fathers"? These new technologies challenge our traditional conceptions of family and parenthood, and it is these traditional conceptions that play an important role in the political, economic, social, and moral life of the nation. Obviously, issues surrounding the definition and rights of parenthood are important to our common understanding of the family. Often society as a whole and medical professionals in particular have to struggle over determinations of moral and legal rights and obligations for parents. Morally speaking, how might we define and determine the scope of biological parenthood as opposed to social parenthood? Does the state have an interest in supporting or favoring one type of relationship over another?

Our final case, *Ferguson v. Charleston*, permits readers to explore the ethical issues surrounding responsibilities pregnant women have toward their fetuses. A great deal of medical knowledge now exists regarding behaviors that cause harm to unborn children. Among behaviors that cause harm are drinking alcohol, smoking cigarettes, ingesting cocaine and heroin, and working under hazardous conditions. This knowledge contributes to the desire to develop policies and laws designed to ensure that pregnant women give birth to healthy children. Few people have moral qualms about developing policies designed to encourage pregnant women to adopt healthy habits; no one wishes to promote the birth of unhealthy or handicapped infants. Some, however, advocate coercive policies (imprisonment, withholding of funds) to force women to protect the health and well-being of their fetuses. The line between encouragement and coercion can be a thin one, however, and the moral justifications for any legal sanction can be quite controversial.

Though not covered explicitly in *Ferguson*, the deliberations of the justices force us to consider one of the most pressing issues in health care: developing and implementing ethically justifiable policies toward women who refuse medical treatment. On occasion a physician may determine that a delivery by caesarean section or a blood transfusion is necessary to save the life of the fetus or prevent severe birth defects. For various reasons women may refuse these medical interventions. Several morally significant issues should be kept in mind in developing and implementing policies that address such treatment refusals.[5] First, at least three parties have a stake in the outcome: the pregnant woman, with regard to self-determination and privacy interests; the state, in its promotion of the health and well-being of fetuses and children; and the fetus, with interest in its own life and well-being. Second, risks of the proposed medical procedure for both woman and fetus are morally relevant. As the risk of the procedure to the pregnant woman lessens and the benefit to the fetus increases, the stronger the obligation of the woman to consent to the procedure. Another consideration of ethical and legal significance is what one commentator calls the phenomenon of perverse incentives.[6] In determining whether the state should impose a legal duty on women to consent to treatment, one has to factor in the possibility that such a law may produce adverse consequences. That is, forcing women to consent to unwanted treatment may keep more women from seeking prenatal care in the first place. If a significant number of women are too frightened to visit their doctors, then the law may cause more harm to fetuses than otherwise would be the case.

These are only a few of the ethical and legal considerations and issues to be considered when thinking about the imposition of a moral and/or legal duty on women to prevent harm to their fetuses. In one sense or another, all three cases in this chapter are concerned with reproductive freedom and procreative liberty. The justices struggle with how to balance the rights and freedoms of individuals with the interests of the state and of other third parties. One might well wonder if the Court is consistent in its reasoning across all three cases, or even within a particular case. Clearly, the justices have set the stage for future deliberations regarding important issues in medical ethics.

Skinner v. Oklahoma
316 U.S. 535 (1942)

Justice Douglas delivered the opinion of the Court. Chief Justice Stone and Justice Jackson each issued a concurring opinion.

Areas for Discussion and Ethical Reflection

1.   How do you think Justice Douglas would define the concept of human rights? Is there really a right, human or otherwise, to reproduce? Since very few rights are absolute, what ethically justifiable limits might you place on a right to reproduce? Your answer will have implications for several social policies and laws relevant to medical ethics.

2.   Later in his opinion, Justice Douglas refers to the right to reproduce as a civil right. What might he mean by this? Is there a difference, morally speaking, between a civil right and a human right?

3.   Justice Douglas refuses to discuss whether the Oklahoma statute constitutes cruel and unusual punishment. Is he correct in ignoring this issue? How would you define cruel and unusual punishment? Readers will note that no death penalty cases are represented in this book; however, many substantive, procedural, and ethical concerns exist in relation to the right of the state to execute certain criminals for certain crimes. How, and to what extent, do you think the death penalty and constitutional concerns surrounding the death penalty are related to the concerns of medical ethics? You might return to this item after considering item #5 under *Youngberg v. Romeo* in chapter 8.

4.   Many in medical ethics place as much emphasis on the proper process for achieving a solution to a specific dilemma as they do on providing moral reasons for and against the solution itself. That is, many will claim that a rational, morally sensitive process will produce a morally defensible solution. Chief Justice Stone's main objection to the Oklahoma statute appears to be that proper procedures were not in place. Would it be morally permissible to sterilize people for certain crimes as long as fair and proper procedures were followed? Give an example of a fair and proper procedure for sterilization.

5.   Chief Justice Stone's position in *Skinner* may be what some commentators have in mind when they assert that law has nothing of value to offer to the study of medical ethics. Law, especially constitutional law, is focused on process, legal rules, and deductive reasoning. Furthermore, reliance on legal cases and legal reasoning can destroy the heart of medical ethics and render ethical justification meaningless. Keep this concern in mind as you read through this book, and be prepared to draw and defend your own conclusions.

6.   Justice Jackson states that there are limits to what a majority may do in the area of conducting biological experiments. What ethical limitations ought we to place on the majority in this context? Which moral theory might best help you in crafting reasons for concluding that the U.S. Constitution would prohibit mandatory sterilization of criminals?

7.   One commentator on the ruling in *Skinner* poses the following rather instructive thought experiment:[7] Several states pass laws requiring those convicted three times of a crime to undergo sterilization. These laws are passed in the wake of overwhelming research showing that there are certain genes that code for a predisposition to commit crimes. These states with sterilization laws sterilize only individuals who test positive for the genes and only after a hearing is held in which the defendant has ample opportunity to refute the evidence. Would such state laws be constitutional based on any of the opinions in *Skinner*? More important perhaps for our purposes, could such a law be morally justifiable? Would any ethical theory find such a law morally obligatory?

8.   From time to time trial courts will offer those convicted of such crimes as child abuse, child homicide, or sexual assault the opportunity to undergo sterilization or other reproductive interventions (castration, Depo Provera, Norplant, etc.) in exchange for a reduced prison sentence.[8] To what extent can we say that an individual confronted with such a choice freely chooses to undergo the procedure? Assuming that such court-imposed choices involve a high degree of coercion (that is, our criminal could never voluntarily choose sterilization), might we nonetheless characterize such judicially imposed choices as morally permissible?

Justice Douglas:

This case touches a sensitive and important area of human rights. Oklahoma deprives certain individuals of a right that is basic to the perpetuation of a race, the right to have offspring. Oklahoma has decreed the enforcement of its law against petitioner, overruling his claim that it violated the Fourteenth Amendment. Because that decision raised grave and substantial constitutional questions, we granted the petition for certiorari....

Several objections to the constitutionality of the Act have been pressed upon us. It is urged that the Act cannot be sustained as an exercise of the police power in view of the state of scientific authorities respecting inheritability of criminal traits. It is argued that due process is lacking because under this Act, unlike the act upheld in *Buck v. Bell*, the defendant is given no opportunity to be heard on the issue as to whether he is the probable potential parent of socially undesirable offspring. It is also suggested that the Act is penal in character and that the sterilization provided for is cruel and unusual punishment and violative of the Fourteenth Amendment. We pass those points without intimating an opinion on them, for there is a feature of the Act which clearly condemns it. That is its failure to meet the requirements of the equal protection clause of the Fourteenth Amendment.

We do not stop to point out all of the inequalities in this Act. A few examples will suffice. In Oklahoma grand larceny is a felony. Larceny is grand larceny when the property taken exceeds $20 in value. Embezzlement is punishable "in the manner prescribed for feloniously stealing property of the value of that embezzled." Hence he who embezzles property worth more than $20 is guilty of a felony. A clerk who appropriates over $20 from his employer's till and a stranger who steals the same amount are thus both guilty of felonies. If the latter repeats his act and is convicted three times, he may be sterilized. But the clerk is not subject to the pains and penalties of the Act no matter how large his embezzlements nor how frequent his convictions. A person who enters a chicken coop and steals chickens commits a felony and he may be sterilized if he is thrice convicted. If, however, he is a bailee of the property and fraudulently appropriates it, he is an embezzler. Hence no matter how habitual his proclivities for embezzlement are and no matter how often his conviction, he may not be sterilized. Thus the nature of the two crimes is intrinsically the same and they are punishable in the same manner....

It was stated in *Buck v. Bell* that the claim that state legislation violates the equal protection clause of the Fourteenth Amendment is "the usual last resort of constitutional arguments." Under our constitutional system the States in determining the reach and scope of particular legislation need not provide "abstract symmetry." They may mark and set apart the classes and types of problems according to the needs and as dictated or suggested by experience. It was in that connection that Justice Holmes, speaking for the Court stated, "We must remember that the machinery of government would not work if it were not allowed a little play in its joints." Only recently we reaffirmed the view that the equal protection clause does not prevent the legislature from recognizing "degrees of evil" that "the Constitution does not require things which are different in fact or opinion to be treated in law as though they were the same." Thus, if we had here only a question as to a State's classification of crimes, such as embezzlement or larceny, no substantial federal question would be raised. For a State is not constrained in the exercise of its police power to ignore experience which marks a class of offenders or a family of offenses for special treatment. Nor is it prevented by the equal protection clause from confining "its restrictions to those classes of cases where the need is deemed to be clearest".... But the instant legislation runs afoul of the equal protection clause, though, we give Oklahoma that large deference which the rule of the foregoing cases requires. We are dealing here with legislation which involves one of the basic civil rights of man. Marriage and procreation are fundamental to the very existence and survival of the race. The power to sterilize, if exercised, may have subtle, far-reaching and devastating effects. In evil or reckless hands it can cause races or types which are inimical to the dominant group to wither and disappear. There is no redemption for the individual whom the law touches.

Any experiment which the State conducts is to his irreparable injury. He is forever deprived of a basic liberty. We mention these matters not to reexamine the scope of the police power of the States. We advert to them merely in emphasis of our view that strict scrutiny of the classification which a State makes in a sterilization law is essential, lest unwittingly or otherwise invidious discriminations are made against groups or types of individuals in violation of the constitutional guaranty of just and equal laws. The guaranty of "equal protection of the laws is a pledge of the protection of equal laws." When the law lays an unequal hand on those who have committed intrinsically the same quality of offense and sterilizes one and not the other, it has made as an invidious a discrimination as if it had selected a particular race or nationality for oppressive treatment. Sterilization of those who have thrice committed grand larceny with immunity for those who are embezzlers is a clear, pointed, unmistakable discrimination. Oklahoma makes no attempt to say that he who commits larceny by trespass or trick or fraud has biologically inheritable traits which he who commits embezzlement lacks. Oklahoma's line between larceny by fraud and embezzlement is determined, as we have noted, "with reference to the time when the fraudulent intent to convert the property to the taker's own use" arises. We have not the slightest basis for inferring that that line has any significance in eugenics nor that the inheritability of criminal traits follows the neat legal distinctions which the law has marked between those two offenses. In terms of fines and imprisonment the crimes of larceny and embezzlement rate the same under the Oklahoma code. Only when it comes to sterilization are the pains and penalties of the law different. The equal protection clause would indeed be a formula of empty words if such conspicuously artificial lines could be drawn....

Reversed.

CHIEF JUSTICE STONE:

I concur in the result, but I am not persuaded that we are aided in reaching it by recourse to the equal protection clause....

I think the real question we have to consider is not one of equal protection, but whether the wholesale condemnation of a class to such an invasion of personal liberty, without opportunity to any individual to show that his is not the type of case which would justify resort to it, satisfies the demands of due process.

There are limits to the extent to which the presumption of constitutionality can be pressed, especially where the liberty of the person is concerned....Although [Skinner] was given a hearing to ascertain whether sterilization would be detrimental to his health, he was given none to discover whether his criminal tendencies are of an inheritable type. Undoubtedly a state may, after appropriate inquiry, constitutionally interfere with the personal liberty of the individual to prevent the transmission by inheritance of his socially injurious tendencies. But until now we have not been called upon to say that it may do so without giving him a hearing and opportunity to challenge the existence as to him of the only facts which could justify so drastic a measure....

JUSTICE JACKSON:

...There are limits to the extent to which a legislatively represented majority may conduct biological experiments at the expense of the dignity and personality and natural powers of a minority—even those who have been guilty of what the majority define as crimes....

Michael H. v. Gerald D.
491 U.S. 110 (1989)

Justice Scalia announced the opinion of the Court and delivered an opinion in which Chief Justice Rehnquist joined. Justices O'Connor and Kennedy joined in all but footnote 6. Justice O'Connor filed an opinion concurring in part, in which Justice Kennedy joined. Justice Stevens filed an opinion concurring in the judgment. Justice Brennan filed a dissenting opinion, in which Justice Marshall and Blackmun joined. Justice White filed a dissenting opinion, in which Justice Brennan joined.

Areas for Discussion and Ethical Reflection

1.   Justice Scalia, in his opinion for the Court, asserts that the facts of this case are extraordinary. But consider one commentator's observations: "Wife cheats on husband, has a child with her lover, who then wishes to be involved in raising that child. What, exactly, does Justice Scalia believe to be 'extraordinary' about the facts of this case?"[9] Does your tolerance, or lack of tolerance, for Michael's behavior, and sympathy, or lack of sympathy, for his claims, depend upon whether you agree with Justice Scalia's characterization of the facts in this case? What is your assessment, morally speaking, of Carole's behavior? Does Justice Scalia's insistence on describing the facts of this case as extraordinary serve as a defense for his appeal to both tradition and specificity in characterizing the liberty interest at stake?

2.   This case is obviously concerned with relationships and, in large measure, much of medical ethics centers on the moral significance of relationships. Try to articulate the characteristics a relationship must have in order to "deserve" constitutional

recognition and protection. From a moral perspective, what characteristics would a relationship have to have such that society would have a moral obligation to recognize and protect it? Is your answer detailed enough to provide answers to ethical questions raised by new reproductive technologies? Is Justice Scalia's approach detailed enough?

3.   Perhaps the most famous and significant part of *Michael H.* occurs in a footnote to Justice Scalia's plurality opinion. In footnote 6, Justice Scalia asserts that one must be as specific as possible when determining whether a particular activity involves a fundamental right; in addition, he wishes to ground his specificity in socially recognized traditions. This assertion was and remains extremely controversial. Justice O'Connor responded to Justice Scalia's footnote this way:

> I concur in all but footnote 6 of Justice Scalia's opinion. This footnote sketches a mode of historical analysis to be used when identifying liberty interests protected by the Due Process Clause of the Fourteenth Amendment that may be somewhat inconsistent with our past decisions in this area. On occasion the Court has characterized relevant traditions protecting asserted rights at levels of generality that might not be "the most specific level" available. I would not foreclose the unanticipated by the prior imposition of a single mode of historical analysis.

Can you think of past decisions of the Court that would make Justice Scalia's analysis inconsistent?

4.   Justice Brennan objects most vehemently to Justice Scalia's footnote 6. As you read Justice Brennan's opinion, state as clearly as possible his objections. How do you think Justice Scalia would respond?

5.   What are the ethical implications of Justice Scalia's claim that for a liberty to be protected, it must be not only fundamental but also traditionally recognized? Is Justice Scalia introducing

a notion of authority that would be unacceptable in ethical decision-making? Two commentators have noted that Justice Scalia's approach to recognizing and accepting activities as fundamental rights would result in the "near-complete abdication of the judicial responsibility to protect individual rights."[10] But is this assertion really fair? Justice Scalia might respond that indeed the obligation of justices is to protect individual rights, but such rights first have to be recognized before they can be protected. Are there moral differences between, on the one hand, recognizing a fundamental right or liberty interest and, on the other hand, taking steps to protect that same fundamental right or liberty interest? Several areas in medical ethics appear to invite application of this distinction. Can you think of an example?

6.   Justice Scalia claims that nature does not allow for dual fatherhood. What does it mean to say that "X is natural" or "X is unnatural"? How do you then translate your understanding of "natural" and "unnatural" into ethical decision-making? Even if Justice Scalia is right that dual fatherhood is unnatural, what significance, if any, would this fact have in ethics?

7.   Outline Justice Brennan's arguments for invalidating the California law. Does Justice Brennan demonstrate any prior moral commitments in his arguments? How might a rule utilitarian respond to Justice Brennan? Would someone sympathetic to a rights-based theory of ethics agree with Justice Brennan?

8.   Justice Brennan in his dissenting opinion asserts that "liberty must include the freedom not to conform." How, in the context of morality, should we interpret this statement? Are there certain ethical theories that "recommend" conformity more strongly than other theories do? For example, does rule utilitarianism necessarily assume that members of a society will conform to certain rules, be they moral, political, or social?

JUSTICE SCALIA:

...We address first the claims of Michael. At the outset, it is necessary to clarify what he sought and what he was denied. California law, like nature itself, makes no provision for dual fatherhood. Michael was seeking to be declared the father of Victoria. The immediate benefit he evidently sought to obtain from that status was visitation rights. But if Michael were successful in being declared the father, other rights would follow—most importantly, the right to be considered as the parent who should have custody, a status which "embrace[s] the sum of parental rights with respect to the rearing of a child, including the child's care; the right to the child's services and earnings; the right to direct the child's activities; the right to make decisions regarding the control, education, and health of the child; and the right, as well as the duty, to prepare the child for additional obligations, which includes the teaching of moral standards, religious beliefs, and elements of good citizenship." All parental rights, including visitation, were automatically denied by denying Michael status as the father....

Michael raises two related challenges to the constitutionality of 621 [of the California Evidence Code]. First, he asserts that requirements of procedural due process prevent the State from terminating his liberty interest in his relationship with his child without affording him an opportunity to demonstrate his paternity in an evidentiary hearing. We believe this claim derives from a fundamental misconception of the nature of the California statute. While 621 is phrased in terms of a presumption, that rule of evidence is the implementation of a substantive rule of law. California declares it to be, except in limited circumstances, irrelevant for paternity purposes whether a child conceived during, and born into, an existing marriage was begotten by someone other than the husband and had a prior relationship with him....

Michael contends as a matter of substantive due process

that, because he has established a parental relationship with Victoria, protection of Gerald's and Carole's marital union is an insufficient state interest to support termination of that relationship. This argument is, of course, predicated on the assertion that Michael has a constitutionally protected liberty interest in his relationship with Victoria....

[At this point Justice Scalia discusses issues and problems related to defining and applying the term "liberty."]

Thus, the legal issue in the present case reduces to whether the relationship between persons in the situation of Michael and Victoria has been treated as a protected family unit under the historic practices of our society, or whether on any other basis it has been accorded special protection. We think it impossible to find that it has. In fact, quite to the contrary, our traditions have protected the marital family (Gerald, Carole, and the child they acknowledge to be theirs) against the sort of claim Michael asserts.

The presumption of legitimacy was a fundamental principle of the common law. Traditionally, that presumption could be rebutted only by proof that a husband was incapable of procreation or had had no access to his wife during the relevant period. As explained by Blackstone, nonaccess could only be proved "if the husband be out of the kingdom of England (or, as the law somewhat loosely phrases it, extra quatuor maria [beyond the four seas]) for above nine months...." And, under the common law both in England and here, "neither husband nor wife [could] be a witness to prove access or nonaccess." The primary policy rationale underlying the common law's severe restrictions on rebuttal of the presumption appears to have been an aversion to declaring children illegitimate, thereby depriving them of rights of inheritance and succession, and likely making them wards of the state. A secondary policy concern was the interest in promoting the "peace and tranquillity of States and families," a goal that is obviously impaired by facilitating suits against husband and wife asserting that their children are illegitimate. Even though, as bastardy laws became less harsh, "[j]udges in both [England and the United States] gradually widened the acceptable range of evidence that could be offered by spouses, and placed restraints on the 'four seas rule'...[,] the law retained a strong bias against ruling the children of married women illegitimate."...

What Michael asserts here is a right to have himself declared the natural father and thereby to obtain parental prerogatives. What he must establish, therefore, is not that our society has traditionally allowed a natural father in his circumstances to establish paternity, but that it has traditionally accorded such a father parental rights, or at least has not traditionally denied them. Even if the law in all States had always been that the entire world could challenge the marital presumption and obtain a declaration as to who was the natural father, that would not advance Michael's claim. Thus, it is ultimately irrelevant, even for purposes of determining current social attitudes towards the alleged substantive right Michael asserts, that the present law in a number of States appears to allow the natural father—including the natural father who has not established a relationship with the child—the theoretical power to rebut the marital presumption. What counts is whether the States in fact award substantive parental rights to the natural father of a child conceived within, and born into, an extant marital union that wishes to embrace the child. We are not aware of a single case, old or new, that has done so. This is not the stuff of which fundamental rights qualifying as liberty interests are made....

We do not accept Justice Brennan's criticism that this result "squashes" the liberty that consists of "the freedom not to conform." It seems to us that reflects the erroneous view that there is only one side to this controversy—that one disposition can expand a "liberty" of sorts without contracting an equivalent "liberty" on the other side. Such a happy choice is rarely available. Here, to provide protection to an adulterous natural father is to deny protection to a marital father, and vice versa. If Michael has a "freedom not to conform" (whatever that means), Gerald must equivalently have a "freedom to conform." One of them will pay a price for asserting that "freedom"—Michael by being unable to act as father of the child he has adulterously begotten, or Gerald by being unable to preserve the integrity of the traditional family unit he and Victoria have established. Our disposition does not choose between these two "freedoms," but leaves that to the people of California. Justice Brennan's approach chooses one of them as the constitutional imperative, on no apparent basis except that the unconventional is to be preferred.

We have never had occasion to decide whether a child has a liberty interest, symmetrical with that of her parent, in maintaining her filial relationship. We need not do so here because, even assuming that such a right exists, Victoria's claim must fail. Victoria's due process challenge is, if anything, weaker than Michael's. Her basic claim is not that California has erred in preventing her from establishing that Michael, not Gerald, should stand as her legal father. Rather, she claims a due process right to maintain filial relationships with both Michael and Gerald. This assertion merits little discussion, for, whatever the merits of the guardian ad litem's belief that such an arrangement can be of great psychological benefit to a child, the claim that a State must recognize multiple fatherhood has no support in the history or traditions of this country. Moreover, even if we were to construe Victoria's argument as forwarding the lesser proposition that, whatever her status vis-a-vis Gerald, she has a liberty interest in maintaining a filial relationship with her natural father, Michael, we find that, at best, her claim is the obverse of Michael's and fails for the same reasons....

The judgment of the California Court of Appeals is affirmed.

JUSTICE BRENNAN:

In a case that has yielded so many opinions as has this one, it is fruitful to begin by emphasizing the common ground shared by a majority of this Court. Five Members of the Court refuse to foreclose "the possibility that a natural father might ever have a constitutionally protected interest in his relationship with a child whose mother was married to, and cohabiting with, another man at the time of the child's conception and birth.".̇..

Once we recognized that the "liberty" protected by the Due Process Clause of the Fourteenth Amendment encompasses more than freedom from bodily restraint, today's plurality opinion emphasizes, the concept was cut loose from one natural limitation on its meaning. This innovation paved the way, so the plurality hints, for judges to substitute their own preferences for those of elected officials. Dissatisfied with this supposedly unbridled and uncertain state of affairs, the plurality casts about for another limitation on the concept of liberty. It finds this limitation in "tradition."

It is ironic that an approach so utterly dependent on tradition is so indifferent to our precedents. Citing barely a handful of this Court's numerous decisions defining the scope of the liberty protected by the Due Process Clause to support its reliance on tradition, the plurality acts as though English legal treatises and the American Law Reports always have provided the sole source for our constitutional principles. They have not. Just as common law notions no longer define the "property" that the Constitution protects, neither do they circumscribe the "liberty" that it guarantees. On the contrary, " 'liberty' and 'property' are broad and majestic terms. They are among the 'great' [constitutional] concepts...purposely left to gather meaning from experience....[T]hey relate to the whole domain of social and economic fact, and the statesmen who founded this Nation knew too well that only a stagnant society remains unchanged" (*Board of Regents v. Roth*, 1972)....

Today's plurality, however, does not ask whether parenthood is an interest that historically has received our attention and protection; the answer to that question is too clear for dispute. Instead, the plurality asks whether the specific variety of parenthood under consideration—a natural father's relationship with a child whose mother is married to another man—has enjoyed such protection.

If we had looked to tradition with such specificity in past cases, many a decision would have reached a different result. Surely the use of contraceptives by unmarried couples, *Eisenstadt v. Baird*, or even by married couples, *Griswold v. Connecticut*, the freedom from corporal punishment in schools, *Ingraham v. Wright*, the freedom from an arbitrary transfer from a prison to a psychiatric institution, *Vitek v. Jones*, and even the right to raise one's natural but illegitimate children, *Stanley v. Illinois*, were not "interest[s] traditionally protected by our society," at the time of their consideration by this Court. If we had asked, therefore, in *Eisenstadt, Griswold, Ingraham, Vitek,* or *Stanley* itself whether the specific interest under consideration had been traditionally protected, the answer would have been a resounding "no." That we did not ask this question in those cases highlights the novelty of the interpretive method that the plurality opinion employs today.

The plurality's interpretive method is more than novel; it is misguided. It ignores the good reasons for limiting the role of "tradition" in interpreting the Constitution's deliberately capacious language. In the plurality's constitutional universe, we may not take notice of the fact that the original reasons for the conclusive presumption of paternity are out of place in a world in which blood tests can prove virtually beyond a shadow of a doubt who sired a particular child and in which the fact of illegitimacy no longer plays the burdensome and stigmatizing role it once did. Nor, in the plurality's world, may we deny "tradition" its full scope by pointing out that the rationale for the conventional rule has changed over the years, as has the rationale for [California's rule of evidence]; instead, our task is simply to identify a rule denying the asserted interest and not to ask whether the basis for that rule—which is the true reflection of the values undergirding it—has changed too often or too recently to call the rule embodying that rationale a "tradition."…

In construing the Fourteenth Amendment to offer shelter only to those interests specifically protected by historical practice, moreover, the plurality ignores the kind of society in which our Constitution exists. We are not an assimilative, homogeneous society, but a facilitative, pluralistic one, in which we must be willing to abide someone else's unfamiliar or even repellent practice because the same tolerant impulse protects our own idiosyncrasies. Even if we can agree, therefore, that "family" and "parenthood" are part of the good life, it is absurd to assume that we can agree on the content of those terms and destructive to pretend that we do. In a community such as ours, "liberty" must include the freedom not to conform. The plurality today squashes this freedom by requiring specific approval from history before protecting anything in the name of liberty.…

The atmosphere surrounding today's decision is one of make-believe. Beginning with the suggestion that the situation confronting us here does not repeat itself every day in every corner of the country, moving on to the claim that it is tradition alone that supplies the details of the liberty that the Constitution protects, and passing finally to the notion that the Court always has recognized a cramped vision of "the family," today's decision lets stand California's pronouncement that Michael—whom blood tests show to a 98 percent probability to be Victoria's father—is not Victoria's father. When and if the Court awakes to reality, it will find a world very different from the one it expects.

Ferguson et al. v. City of Charleston et al.
532 U.S. 67 (2001)

Justice Stevens delivered the opinion of the Court, in which Justices O'Connor, Souter, Ginsburg, and Breyer joined. Justice Kennedy filed an opinion concurring in the judgment. Justice Scalia filed a dissenting opinion, in which Chief Justice Rehnquist and Justice Thomas joined in part.

Areas for Discussion and Ethical Reflection

1.   What are Justice Stevens's arguments for finding the MUSC policy unconstitutional? What if any significance for medical ethics do these arguments have?

2.   What are the similarities between, on the one hand, drug testing railways employees involved in train accidents, Customs Service employees desiring promotion to sensitive positions, or high school students participating in sports programs with, on the other hand, testing pregnant women for cocaine use? Are there concepts or principles in medical ethics that could help you articulate the similarities and differences between the groups?

3.   Justice Stevens, in his majority opinion, asserts that the invasion of privacy under the policy adopted by MUSC is "far more substantial" than those under review in previous drug testing cases. How does Justice Stevens defend this assertion? Does he appeal to any ethical justification for the distinction? Is his analysis of the principle of "special need" of moral significance for medical ethics?

4.   Justice Kennedy asserts that evaluating the policy of MUSC must begin by acknowledging "…the legitimacy of the State's interest in fetal life and of the grave risk to the life and health of the fetus, and later the child, caused by cocaine ingestion." How does Justice Kennedy argue for this? Why should the beginning point not be the pregnant woman's interest in autonomy and privacy?

5.   Justice Scalia, in his dissenting opinion, notes that only 30

of 253 women who tested positive for cocaine were arrested, and that only two of those women were ever prosecuted. Does this fact have moral relevance for evaluation of the hospital's policy? For example, an act utilitarian might find the policy morally obligatory on the grounds that the benefits achieved through the policy far outweigh any negative consequences or harm resulting from the actions of the hospital and police.

6.   In his dissenting opinion Justice Scalia asserts, "…[W]e must accept the premise that the medical profession can adopt acceptable criteria for testing expectant mothers for cocaine use in order to provide prompt and effective counseling to the mother and to take proper medical steps to protect the child." Is Justice Scalia's observation relevant to the issue of whether physicians should cooperate with police in prosecuting pregnant women? What are the ethical and professional obligations of physicians in protecting third parties?

7.   Making a distinction between the intentions or goals of an action on the one hand and the means or methods for achieving those goals on the other is quite common in ethics. We often hear the claim that the end does not justify the means, which may remind you of Kantianism. Evaluate this claim in light of the following statement from Justice Scalia: "The initial goal of the doctors and nurses who conducted cocaine-testing in this case was to refer pregnant drug addicts to treatment centers, and to prepare for necessary treatment of their possibly affected children." Justice Scalia goes on to characterize the Court's decision as demonstrating that "no good deed goes unpunished." What do you think he means by this? What ethical theory would be most sympathetic to Justice Scalia's position?

8.   In his dissenting opinion Justice Scalia asserts, "…[W]e must accept the premise that the medical profession can adopt acceptable criteria for testing expectant mothers for cocaine use in order to provide prompt and effective counseling to the mother and to take proper medical steps to protect the child." What ethical arguments could you provide in support of this position?

Would Justice Scalia have any sympathy for a physician and her pregnant patient who invoke the right to self-determination and privacy as justification for the physician honoring the request of the woman not to undergo a medical procedure to save the life of the fetus?

9.   It is interesting to consider the connection between the right to procreate (see *Skinner*) and the obligations parents have toward their children (see *Ferguson* below). A Wisconsin man, David Oakley, owed twenty-five thousand dollars in child support for his nine children. He pleaded guilty and was sentenced to three years in prison and five years probation during which time he would not be allowed to have any more children unless he could take care of them and support the ones he already had. Oakley appealed on the grounds that the probation conditions violated the Constitution. In 2001 the Wisconsin Supreme Court upheld the conditions of probation.[11] What ethical arguments can you provide to support the penalty against Oakley? What might be some of the logical consequences of imposing prohibitions on reproduction on people who refuse to take care of their children? Review item 8 under *Skinner v. Oklahoma* above.

10.   As you read the excerpts of the opinions below you will note some discussion of the consequences or possible effects of a state law requiring pregnant women to be tested for cocaine use. The Court is obviously concerned with both bad and good effects of imposing on women legal duties toward their fetuses. One commentator has drawn the following conclusion: "One can assume that a legal duty will have perverse effects and oppose any legal duty for pregnant women to accept unwanted medical treatments. Alternatively, one can assume that a legal duty will have its intended effects and support a limited legal duty for pregnant women to accept unwanted medical treatments. Under a limited duty regime, treatments at the very least would have to benefit the health of the woman and her fetus. No trade-off of the woman's health for that of her fetus would be allowed. If a limited legal duty were imposed, it would be important to

monitor the effects of the duty to see whether there was evidence that pregnant women were being deterred from seeking prenatal care."[12] Is it possible to construe a hospital policy requiring testing of pregnant women suspected of cocaine use—similar to the policy under consideration in *Ferguson*—as benefiting the health of both the pregnant woman and her fetus? What moral considerations ground your position regarding a legal duty for pregnant women?

JUSTICE STEVENS:

...Because MUSC is a state hospital, the members of its staff are government actors, subject to the strictures of the Fourth Amendment. Moreover, the urine tests conducted by those staff members were indisputably searches within the meaning of the Fourth Amendment. Neither the District Court nor the Court of Appeals concluded that any of the nine criteria used to identify the women to be searched provided either probable cause to believe that they were using cocaine, or even the basis for a reasonable suspicion of such use. Rather, the District Court and the Court of Appeals viewed the case as one involving MUSC's right to conduct searches without warrants or probable cause. Furthermore, given the posture in which the case comes to us, we must assume for purposes of our decision that the tests were performed without the informed consent of the patients.

Because the hospital seeks to justify its authority to conduct drug tests and to turn the results over to law enforcement agents without the knowledge or consent of the patients, this case differs from the four previous cases in which we have considered whether comparable drug tests "fit within the closely guarded category of constitutionally permissible suspicionless searches." In three of those cases, we sustained drug tests for railway employees involved in train accidents, *Skinner v. Railway Labor Executives' Assn.*,

Treasury Employees v. Von Raab, and *Vernonia School Dist. v. Acton*. In the fourth case, we struck down such testing for candidates for designated state offices as unreasonable, *Chandler v. Miller*.

In each of those cases, we employed a balancing test that weighed the intrusion on the individual's interest in privacy against the "special needs" that supported the program. As an initial matter, we note that the invasion of privacy in this case is far more substantial than in those cases. In the previous four cases, there was no misunderstanding about the purpose of the test or the potential use of the test results, and there were protections against the dissemination of the results to third parties....The reasonable expectation of privacy enjoyed by the typical patient undergoing diagnostic tests in a hospital is that the results of those tests will not be shared with nonmedical personnel without her consent.

The critical difference between those four drug-testing cases and this one, however, lies in the nature of the "special need" asserted as justification for the warrantless searches. In each of those earlier cases, the "special need" that was advanced as a justification for the absence of a warrant or individualized suspicion was one divorced from the State's general interest in law enforcement....In this case, however, the central and indispensable feature of the policy from its inception was the use of law enforcement to coerce the patients into substance abuse treatment. This fact distinguishes this case from circumstances in which physicians or psychologists, in the course of ordinary medical procedures aimed at helping the patient herself, come across information that under rules of law or ethics is subject to reporting requirements, which no one has challenged here.

Respondents argue in essence that their ultimate purpose—namely, protecting the health of both mother and child—is a beneficent one.... In this case, a review of the M-7 policy plainly reveals that the purpose actually served by the MUSC searches "is ultimately indistinguishable from the general interest in crime control."...

While the ultimate goal of the program may well have been to get the women in question into substance abuse treatment and off of drugs, the immediate objective of the searches was to generate evidence *for law enforcement purposes* in order to reach that goal. The threat of law enforcement may ultimately have been intended as a means to an end, but the direct and primary purpose of MUSC's policy was to ensure the use of those means. In our opinion, this distinction is critical. Because law enforcement involvement always serves some broader social purpose or objective, under respondents' view, virtually any nonconsensual suspicionless search could be immunized under the special needs doctrine by defining the search solely in terms of its ultimate, rather than immediate, purpose. Such an approach is inconsistent with the Fourth Amendment. Given the primary purpose of the Charleston program, which was to use the threat of arrest and prosecution in order to force women into treatment, and given the extensive involvement of law enforcement officials at every stage of the policy, this case simply does not fit within the closely guarded category of "special needs."

The fact that positive test results were turned over to the police does not merely provide a basis for distinguishing our prior cases applying the "special needs" balancing approach to the determination of drug use. It also provides an affirmative reason for enforcing the strictures of the Fourth Amendment. While state hospital employees, like other citizens, may have a duty to provide the police with evidence of criminal conduct that they inadvertently acquire in the course of routine treatment, when they undertake to obtain such evidence from their patients *for the specific purpose of incriminating those patients*, they have a special obligation to make sure that the patients are fully informed about their constitutional rights, as standards of knowing waiver require....

Accordingly, the judgment of the Court of Appeals is reversed…It is so ordered.

JUSTICE KENNEDY:

I agree that the search procedure in issue cannot be sustained under the Fourth Amendment. My reasons for this conclusion differ somewhat from those set forth by the Court, however, leading to this separate opinion.…

The majority views its distinction between the ultimate goal and immediate purpose of the policy as critical to its analysis. The distinction the Court makes, however, lacks foundation in our special needs cases. All of our special needs cases have turned upon what the majority terms the policy's ultimate goal.… It is unsurprising that in our prior cases we have concentrated on what the majority terms a policy's ultimate goal, rather than its proximate purpose. By very definition, in almost every case the immediate purpose of a search policy will be to obtain evidence. The circumstance that a particular search, like all searches, is designed to collect evidence of some sort reveals nothing about the need it serves. Put a different way, although procuring evidence is the immediate result of a successful search, until today that procurement has not been identified as the special need which justifies the search.…

The beginning point ought to be to acknowledge the legitimacy of the State's interest in fetal life and of the grave risk to the life and health of the fetus, and later the child, caused by cocaine ingestion. Infants whose mothers abuse cocaine during pregnancy are born with a wide variety of physical and neurological abnormalities. Prenatal exposure to cocaine can also result in developmental problems which persist long after birth. There can be no doubt that a mother's ingesting this drug can cause tragic injury to a fetus and a child. There should be no doubt that South Carolina can impose punishment upon an expectant mother who has so little regard for her own unborn that she risks causing him or her lifelong damage and suffering. The State, by taking special measures to give rehabilitation and training to expectant mothers with this tragic addiction or weakness, acts well within its powers and its civic obligations....

[W]e must accept the premise that the medical profession can adopt acceptable criteria for testing expectant mothers for cocaine use in order to provide prompt and effective counseling to the mother and to take proper medical steps to protect the child. If prosecuting authorities then adopt legitimate procedures to discover this information and prosecution follows, that ought not to invalidate the testing. One of the ironies of the case, then, may be that the program now under review, which gives the cocaine user a second and third chance, might be replaced by some more rigorous system. We must, however, take the case as it comes to us; and the use of handcuffs, arrests, prosecutions, and police assistance in designing and implementing the testing and rehabilitation policy cannot be sustained under our previous cases concerning mandatory testing....

JUSTICE SCALIA:

There is always an unappealing aspect to the use of doctors and nurses, ministers of mercy, to obtain incriminating evidence against the supposed objects of their ministration—although here, it is correctly pointed out, the doctors and nurses were ministering not just to the mothers but also to the children whom their cooperation with the police was meant to protect. But whatever may be the correct social judgment concerning the desirability of what occurred here, that is not the issue in the present case. The Constitution does not resolve all difficult social questions, but leaves the vast majority of them to resolution by debate and the democratic process—which would produce a decision by the citizens of Charleston, through their elected representatives, to forbid or permit the police action at issue here. The question before us is a narrower one: whether, whatever the desirability of this police conduct, it violates the Fourth Amendment's prohibition of unreasonable searches and seizures. In my view, it plainly does not.

Until today, we have *never* held—or even suggested—that material which a person voluntarily entrusts to someone else cannot be given by that person to the police, and used for whatever evidence it may contain. Without so much as discussing the point, the Court today opens a hole in our Fourth Amendment jurisprudence, the size and shape of which is entirely indeterminate. Today's holding would be remarkable enough if the confidential relationship violated by the police conduct were at least one protected by state law. It would be surprising to learn, for example, that in a State which recognizes a spousal evidentiary privilege the police cannot use evidence obtained from a cooperating husband or wife. But today's holding goes even beyond that, since there does not exist any physician-patient privilege in South Carolina. Since the Court declines even to discuss the issue, it leaves law enforcement officials entirely in the dark as to when they can use incriminating evidence obtained from "trusted" sources. Presumably the lines will be drawn in the case-by-case development of a whole new branch of Fourth Amendment jurisprudence, taking yet another social judgment (which confidential relationships ought not be invaded by the police) out of democratic control, and confiding it to the uncontrolled judgment of this Court—uncontrolled because there is no common-law precedent to guide it. I would adhere to our established law, which says that information obtained through violation of a relationship of trust is obtained consensually, and is hence not a search.

There remains to be considered the first possible basis for invalidating this search, which is that the patients were coerced to produce their urine samples by their necessitous circumstances, to-wit, their need for medical treatment of their pregnancy. If that was coercion, it was not coercion applied by the government—and if such nongovernmental coercion sufficed, the police would never be permitted to use the ballistic evidence obtained from treatment of a patient with a bullet wound. And the Fourth Amendment would invalidate those many state laws that require physicians to report gunshot wounds, evidence of spousal abuse, and (like the South Carolina law relevant here), evidence of child abuse....

[T]he doctors here do not "ordinarily conduc[t] searches against the ordinary citizen," and they are "supposed to have in mind the welfare of the [mother and child]." That they have in mind in addition the provision of evidence to the police should make no difference. The Court suggests that if police involvement in this case was in some way incidental and after-the-fact, that would make a difference in the outcome....

Petitioners seek to distinguish [a previous case] by observing that probationers enjoy a lesser expectation of privacy than does the general public. That is irrelevant to the point I make here, which is that the presence of a law enforcement purpose does not render the special-needs doctrine inapplicable. In any event, I doubt whether [a] reasonable expectation of privacy in [a probationer's] home was any less than petitioners' reasonable expectation of privacy in their urine taken, or in the urine tests performed, in a hospital—especially in a State such as South Carolina, which recognizes no physician-patient testimonial privilege and requires the physician's duty of confidentiality to yield to public policy, and which requires medical conditions that indicate a violation of the law to be reported to authorities, *Whalen v. Roe*, (privacy interest does not forbid government to require hospitals to provide, for law enforcement purposes, names of patients receiving prescriptions of frequently abused drugs)....

The initial goal of the doctors and nurses who conducted cocaine-testing in this case was to refer pregnant drug addicts to treatment centers, and to prepare for necessary treatment of their possibly affected children. When the doctors and nurses agreed to the program providing test results to the police, they did so because (in addition to the fact that child abuse was required by law to be reported) they wanted to use the sanction of arrest as a strong incentive for their addicted patients to undertake drug-addiction treatment. And the police themselves used it for that benign purpose, as is shown by the fact that only 30 of 253 women testing positive for cocaine were ever arrested, and only two of those prosecuted. It would not be unreasonable to conclude that today's judgment, authorizing the assessment of damages against the county solicitor and individual doctors and nurses who participated in the program, proves once again that no good deed goes unpunished....

Notes

1.   Jerry Menikoff, *Law and Bioethics: An Introduction* (Washington, DC: Georgetown University Press, 2001), p. 110.

2.   Judith Areen, "Limiting Procreation," in *Medical Ethics*, 2nd ed., edited by Robert M. Veatch (Boston: Jones and Bartlett, 1997), pp.115–17.

3.   Lawrence M. Hinman, "Punishment and the Death Penalty: An Introduction to the Moral Issues," in *Contemporary Moral Issues: Diversity and Consensus*, 2nd ed., edited by Lawrence M. Hinman (Upper Saddle River, NJ: Prentice Hall, 2000), pp. 203–9.

4.   Laurence H. Tribe and Michael C. Dorf, *On Reading the Constitution* (Cambridge, MA: Harvard University Press, 1991), pp. 96–97.

5.   David Orentlicher, *Matters of Life and Death: Making Moral Theory Work in Medical Ethics and the Law* (Princeton, NJ: Princeton University Press, 2001), pp. 91–112.

6.   Ibid., pp. 113–19.

7.   Menikoff, *Law and Bioethics*, p. 47.

8.   Michael H. Shapiro et al., *Bioethics and Law: Cases, Materials and Problems*, 2nd ed. (St. Paul, MN: West Group, 2003), pp. 596–97.

9.   Menikoff, *Law and Bioethics*, p. 115.

10.   Tribe and Dorf, *On Reading the Constitution*, p. 98.

11.   Rebecca Dresser, "Procreation and Punishment," *Hastings Center Report* 31 (2001): 8–9.

12.   Orentlicher, *Matters of Life and Death*, p. 120.

For Further Reading

Areen, Judith. "Limiting Procreation." In M*edical Ethics*, 2nd edition, Robert M. Veatch, ed. Boston, MA: Jones and Bartlett, 1997.

Capron, Alexander Morgan. "Punishing Mothers." *Hastings Center Report* 28 (1998): 31–33.

Dresser, Rebecca. "Procreation and Punishment." *Hastings Center Report* 31 (2001): 8–9.

Gostin, Lawrence O. "The Rights of Pregnant Women: The Supreme Court and Drug Testing." *Hastings Center Report* 31 (2001): 8–9.

Menikoff, Jerry. *Law and Bioethics: An Introduction.* Washington, DC: Georgetown University Press, 2001.

Orentlicher, David. *Matters of Life and Death: Making Moral Theory Work in Medical Ethics and the Law.* Princeton: Princeton University Press, 2001.

Robertson, John A., and Joseph Schulman. "Pregnancy and Prenatal Harm to Offspring." In *Intervention and Reflection: Basic Issues in Medical Ethics*, 6th edition, Ronald Munson, ed. Belmont, CA: Wadsworth, 2000.

Tribe, Laurence, and Michael Dorf. *On Reading the Constitution.* Cambridge, MA: Harvard University Press, 1991.

CHAPTER THREE

THE EARLY ABORTION CASES

No comparable fact about the correct use of language can explain the supposed distinction between enumerated and unenumerated constitutional rights, however, because the Bill of Rights consists of broad and abstract principles of political morality, and correct application of these principles depends upon moral sense, not linguistic rules. The distinction between specific rights that are enumerated and those that are not is therefore simply irrelevant.

—Ronald Dworkin, *Life's Dominion: An Argument about Abortion, Euthanasia, and Individual Freedom*

No issue has raised more constitutional, ethical, political, and social concerns than whether, and under what circumstances, women may be allowed to terminate their pregnancies. In abortion we have a multitude of medical, legal, and moral problems and dilemmas, the satisfactory resolution of which can seem daunting if not impossible. Not only are concerns over autonomy, privacy, and reproductive freedom of ethical and legal importance, but such issues as the right to life, personhood, potential personhood, and what constitutes permissible state regulation of abortion are implicated as well. How these issues are resolved has implications not only for abortion, but also for such concerns as human cloning, artificial reproduction technologies, and state prosecution of fetal deaths as homicide. For more than thirty years the justices of the U.S. Supreme Court have considered, evaluated, argued about, and reconsidered the various factors and complexities involved in the legalization of abortion. Debate over the appropriateness of Supreme Court involvement rages on, but the fact remains that the Court is involved and the rulings handed down continue to impact the profession of medicine, the discipline of medical ethics, and all of society in major ways. The two cases in this chapter are the earliest that deal explicitly with the issue of abortion, and they continue to impact Court decisions to the present day. In addition, their influence on how medical ethics has approached many issues other than abortion is significant.

Constitutional Issues and Background

Roe v. Wade's landmark status in both constitutional law and medical ethics ensures that almost everyone is familiar with the issues and principles under debate by the justices. In Texas, under Articles 1191-1194 and 1196, procuring an abortion or attempting an abortion was deemed a crime, except when a physician determined that the abortion was necessary to save the life of the woman. In March 1970, Jane Roe, Dr. James Hallford, and John and Mary Doe brought suit against Texas in district court. Roe claimed that the Texas statutes violated several amendments of the U.S. Constitution in not allowing her to terminate her pregnancy under safe and clinical conditions by a licensed physician. Dr. Hallford alleged that the law interfered with the physician-patient relationship and his right to practice medicine. The Does alleged constitutional violations similar to those alleged by Roe and Hallford. The lower court refused to grant standing to the Does but did find the Texas statute unconstitutional; however, the court refused to stop enforcement of the law. The U.S. Supreme Court refused to grant Dr. Hallford and the Does standing but asserted that Roe's litigation presented a justiciable controversy.

Earlier Court decisions, most notably *Griswold*, influenced deliberations and the ultimate outcome in *Roe*. As with *Griswold*, debate over the status of unenumerated constitutional rights (privacy and abortion, for example) continued. Whether support was found in the Fourteenth Amendment or the Ninth, the Court concluded that women enjoy a right to privacy that encompasses the abortion decision. In addition, the Court ruled that fetuses are not persons under the Constitution and that the abortion decision is one that a woman with counsel from her physician should make. Introducing the trimester framework, the Court acknowledged that states have a compelling interest in fetal life such that states may prohibit abortion after viability of the fetus is reached; however, states may not prohibit abortions, even after viability, if the woman's health or life is in danger.

On the same day the Court handed down its *Roe* ruling, it also decided *Doe v. Bolton*. Mary Doe was a twenty-two-year-old married woman with three children, two of whom were in foster care because of her extreme poverty and inability to care for them. At one time she had been a mental patient at a state hospital. After being abandoned by her husband, she lived with her parents, who were raising eight other children. She became pregnant and was advised that an abortion would be better for her health. On March 25, 1970, when she was eight weeks pregnant, Mary Doe applied to an abortion committee of a local hospital. After being turned down, she and other parties filed suit against the Georgia abortion law in district court. The Georgia criminal code prohibited abortion except in cases where the woman's life was in danger, her health would be injured if she continued the pregnancy, the newborn would have severe defects, or the pregnancy was the result of rape. Georgia also had in place several procedural requirements: 1) all abortions had to be performed in hospitals accredited by the Joint Commission on Accreditation of Hospitals; 2) a hospital abortion committee had to approve all procedures; and 3) two physicians had to confirm the judgment of the physician performing the procedure. The district court ruled that many provisions of the Georgia statute were unconstitutional but refused to stop enforcement of the antiabortion law.

Near the end of his majority opinion in *Roe*, Justice Blackmun noted that it and *Doe v. Bolton* should be read together. Where *Roe* emphasizes public policy issues, *Doe* focuses on procedural concerns surrounding abortion regulations. The Supreme Court's struggle over the constitutionality of state restrictions on abortion would begin with *Doe* and continue for the next twenty years. While over time the Court changed its language and its standards of review for abortion regulations, in *Doe* a majority of the justices found Georgia's restrictions invasive of a woman's right to privacy and thus violated her right to due process.

Ethical Issues and Background

The debate over the moral and legal status of abortion is perhaps one of the most complex in medical ethics and public policy. A preliminary list of ethical issues and concerns would include moral status of the fetus, potential moral status of the fetus, autonomy rights of women, privacy rights of women, discrimination against women, the state's interest in protecting human life, the sanctity of life, the morality of killing, and considerations surrounding the appropriate method for weighing and balancing the interests of pregnant women, their fetuses, and the state. As you read the cases in this and the next chapter, you will note that the justices consider many of the items on this long list. As you examine the arguments of the justices you will want to assess their grasp of the ethical issues involved and how well their considerations help you to understand the ethical and social policy complexities of the abortion issue.

Navigating the complexities surrounding termination of pregnancy is made much easier if we keep in mind four main positions on the morality of abortion.[1] These positions—liberal, moderate, conservative, and radical conservative—are intended as a guide for considering and discussing the moral and constitutional issues involved. You should keep in mind not only that variations on each position exist, but also that two people can hold the same position but support that position in different ways. The liberal position asserts that women may terminate their pregnancies at any time during fetal development and for any reason. Aborting fetuses late in pregnancy is certainly unfortunate, but not considered immoral. The moderate view of abortion, the one perhaps with the most variation, claims that abortions up to a certain point in fetal development are morally permissible and, further, that only weighty reasons will count in support of abortion after a certain point. Many moderates choose fetal viability as that point beyond which only reasons such as maternal health, rape, incest, and fetal abnormality will count as acceptable. Conservatives usually begin with the assertion that terminating pregnancy, even in very early stages of fetal development, is morally wrong. For conservatives, morally weighty reasons for aborting a fetus may exist, but these will be few in number and may include preservation of the life of the woman, rape, and incest. Finally, radical or extreme conservatives hold that termination of pregnancy at any stage of fetal development, no matter the reason, is morally wrong. Extreme conservatives may admit that forcing women to carry fetuses to term in certain circumstances is unfortunate but nonetheless assert that choosing to terminate the pregnancy will always be morally wrong.

Much of the moral and constitutional debate over the permissibility of abortion rests on the facts of fetal development and how those facts are interpreted. Fetal development is a process beginning with one fertilized egg and ending with the birth of an infant. The stages in between—zygote, embryo, premature fetus, viable fetus—mark significant changes in function and development. (For convenience we will use the term "fetus" to mark all stages up to birth.) Determination of the moral (and legal?) weight to be assigned each stage in development is a normative issue, not a factual one. That is, at what point in fetal development, if at all, we ascribe moral status to the fetus is not an issue biology can resolve. Justice Blackmun, in his majority opinion in *Roe*, appreciates the normative nature of the debate over moral status. His discussion of whether the fetus represents human life, or potential life, from conception is shorthand for the moral debate over whether fetuses are persons or potential persons. An outline of three popular positions on the personhood of fetuses will clarify some of the issues raised in *Roe* and *Doe*.

The first position one may take is that fetuses are persons from the moment of conception. Fetuses are beings that belong to the community of moral agents and thus enjoy full moral rights. To kill a fetus is to commit murder. This view can be supported on the ground that fetuses possess the human genetic code and thus are human beings. As the product of two humans, the human fetus has a strong right to life and that right must be respected.[2] To be a human being is all that a being needs in order to have full moral status. Holders of the conservative and radical conservative positions on abortion find this view of the moral status of fetuses very attractive.

A second possibility is to view fetuses as potential moral agents. At some point in fetal development, itself a mater of dispute, a fetus attains qualities that confer upon it a right to life. One commentator uses what he calls the potentiality principle as justification for line-drawing.[3] He states the principle as follows: "If in the normal course of its development, a being will acquire a person's claim to life, then by virtue of that fact it already has some claim to life."[4] Increased probabilities for fetal survival and the adverse social consequences resulting from the killing of viable fetuses are used as the criteria for determining the potential moral status of fetuses. People subscribing to a moderate position will find this view attractive, and indeed this view seems to be that of the Court's in *Roe* and *Doe*.

Finally, there are those who claim that fetuses never acquire moral status and hence never possess a right to life. On this view, members of the moral community, persons in the moral sense if you will, possess certain characteristics that make them persons. Fetuses do not possess the requisite characteristics and hence are not moral agents. Much disagreement exists over what a list of requisite traits would include, but one commentator suggests five: consciousness, reasoning, self-motivated activity, capacity to communicate, and the presence of self-awareness.[5] Whether they use this list of characteristics or another, people subscribing to a liberal position on abortion tend to deny that fetuses are moral agents.

Because of its significance not only for the Supreme Court's decisions on abortion but also for the Court's deliberations regarding the refusal of life-sustaining treatment and physician-assisted suicide, we should explore the meaning and scope of the assertion that life is sacred. Claims that abortion is immoral and that the state is permitted to interfere with a woman's choice to terminate a pregnancy often revolve around the claim that life is sacred and should not be arbitrarily destroyed. This claim applies whether one believes fetuses are full-fledged moral agents or potential moral agents; however, it is strongest when it accompanies the claim that fetuses have the exact same rights as children and adults. But what does it mean to say that life is sacred or to assert a sanctity of life argument? In his book, *Life's Dominion: An Argument about Abortion, Euthanasia, and Individual Freedom*, Ronald Dworkin sets forth and defends a distinction with respect to the view that life is sacred.[6] Dworkin first observes that such phrases as "life begins at conception" and "human life is sacred" can be understood to have two different meanings. On the one hand, such phrases might be taken to mean that fetuses have rights and interests equivalent to those possessed by children and adults. Persons holding such a view will maintain that the government should do everything within its power to protect these rights and interests. Dworkin calls such a claim a derivative claim. On the other hand, the view that life is sacred might be taken to mean that human life is intrinsically valuable in and of itself, independent of whether a particular life has rights or interests. On this view, killing human life at any stage of development is a sort of "cosmic shame"—not because of any supposed rights or interests the life may possess, but because life, even early life, has intrinsic value. Dworkin calls this claim the detached claim.

Dworkin's contention is that a significant difference exists between the belief that life is sacred because beings, even ones at very early stages of development, have rights and interests and the belief that life is sacred just because it is human life. The former view is considered by most to be extremely difficult to defend although, as we saw above, those who consider having the human genetic code as sufficient certainly try to defend the view. The latter view holds "...that human life is sacred just in itself; and that the sacred nature of a human life begins when its biological life begins, even before the creature whose life it is has movement or sensation or interests or rights of its own."[7] This detached view of the importance of human life is a view shared by almost all of us: the atheist and the theist, the Republican and the Democrat, the conservative and the liberal. Most all of us are willing to grant that human life, at whatever stage of development, is extremely important, and we grant this whatever our particular backgrounds or worldviews. What people holding the detached view do not grant is that fetuses have the same rights as other members of the moral community.

As you read the opinions below you will have an opportunity to assess where and how the justices employ the concepts and arguments described above. Especially instructive is determining whether any particular justice discerns the distinction between detached and derivative interests. Also of interest is the discussion of personhood in the constitutional sense and the implications of that discussion for assessments of personhood in the moral sense. You will find these same concerns discussed by the justices in other cases.

Roe v. Wade
410 U.S. 113 (1973)

Justice Blackmun delivered the opinion of the Court, in which Chief Justice Burger and Justices Douglas, Brennan, Stewart, Marshall, and Powell joined. Chief Justice Burger, and Justices Douglas and Stewart each filed concurring opinions. Justice White filed a dissenting opinion, in which Justice Rehnquist joined. Justice Rehnquist filed a dissenting opinion.

Areas for Discussion and Ethical Reflection

1.   Few people realize that two years before its decision in *Roe v. Wade* the Supreme Court handed down its first decision related

to abortion in *United States v. Vuitch*, 402 U.S. 62 (1971). A Washington, DC, physician was indicted for performing abortions in violation of a Washington statute that prohibited abortion except when necessary to preserve the health or life of the woman. The United States District Court ruled that the statute was unconstitutionally vague, but the Supreme Court reversed. The case is significant because, even though the antiabortion statute was upheld, many of the justices were sympathetic toward problems faced by physicians in helping women terminate unwanted pregnancies. In addition, the majority opinion set forth a broad definition of health to include psychological as well as physical considerations.[8] Throughout this chapter and the next you will have ample opportunity to consider professional and ethical justifications surrounding physician involvement in abortion.

2.   Justice Blackmun begins his majority opinion in *Roe* by noting just how emotionally sensitive the issue of abortion is; he also notes that sincere and vigorous disagreement exists over whether abortion is moral and whether the law should allow women to terminate their pregnancies. Justice Blackmun continues by claiming that the task of the justices is to ignore emotion and preconceived notions regarding the morality of abortion as they consider the constitutionality of the Texas statute. As you read *Roe*, consider how successful the justices are in setting aside their emotions and values. Do you detect observations or arguments by the justices that indicate a utilitarian, Kantian, or natural law influence? For example, Justice Blackmun provides a list of harms that would befall the pregnant woman if the state prohibits her from having an abortion. Which ethical theory would be most receptive to ascribing moral weight to this list? Do you find the list of harms Justice Blackmun provides persuasive in striking down the Texas statute?

3.   Discuss how cases covered in chapter 1—specifically, *Griswold* and *Eisenstadt*—impact the ruling on abortion in *Roe*. What constitutional principles carry over from the two earlier cases? What ethical principles do the three cases share? What

ethical theory or framework best supports the outcomes of the three cases?

4.   Justice Blackmun grounds his rejection of the Texas antiabortion statute, at least in part, on a right to privacy, which derives from the concept of personal liberty found in the Fourteenth Amendment. He considers, but then rejects, the possibility that the right to privacy could be based on the Ninth Amendment's "reservation of rights to the people." From a moral perspective, does it matter how a constitutional right to privacy is identified and then justified? To what moral commitments might one subscribe, or what moral theory might one hold, such that one derives a right to privacy from the concept of liberty in the Fourteenth Amendment?

5.   Justice Blackmun refuses to grant women an absolute right to terminate their pregnancies. What reasons does he give? Are his reasons ethical or legal in nature? What relevance do his reasons have for medical ethics?

6.   What is the difference between a being that is a constitutional person and a being that is a moral person? Are the justices in the majority saying that fetuses have interests, but that these interests are not constitutionally relevant and only minimally relevant in a moral sense?

7.   From the Court's first analysis of a right to abortion in *Roe v. Wade* through its decision regarding a constitutional right to refuse treatment in *Cruzan v. Director, Missouri Department of Health*, two justices have consistently appealed to notions of dignity and autonomy to ground their rejection of state laws that intrude on individual rights. They are Justice Blackmun and Justice Brennan. Their arguments appealing to individual dignity are at once persuasive and reasonable, as you will discover as you read the cases in this book. Appeals to dignity, however, are ethically and conceptually problematic, no matter the context within which they are made. Christopher Miles Coope urges us to proceed with caution when applying the concept of dignity.[9] Coope

asks whether the meaning of "dignity" is subjective or objective. He asserts that we tend to define dignity subjectively; each individual is entitled to determine what it is to have or not have dignity. But a subjective meaning of dignity, Coope argues, is a meaning without substance or application. Coope is also concerned that dignity, especially as it appears in such phrases as "death with dignity," will lead to contempt and abuse of vulnerable populations. As you read passages from the justices making appeals to dignity, stop and reflect on just what the justice means. Consider also the moral and legal implications of appeals to dignity.

8.   As you no doubt are aware, the ruling and its justification have received a great deal of constitutional and moral criticism. The object of much of this criticism has been the trimester framework. Describe in detail, and as clearly as you can, the trimester framework the majority lays out in *Roe*. How would you argue that viability of the fetus has moral and/or constitutional significance? What is Justice Blackmun's argument for finding viability significant?

9.   Justice Rehnquist would reach the opposite conclusion of the majority. Justice Rehnquist asserts that the type of interaction involved between a physician and a pregnant woman seeking an abortion is not private. Can you discern whether Justice Rehnquist would ascribe a right to privacy to any type of physician-patient interaction?

10.   Some commentators have claimed that even if fetuses are not persons in the moral sense, some abortions would still be morally wrong, and that even if fetuses are full moral agents, some abortions might still be morally permissible. How might someone go about justifying such a claim? Keep your answer in mind as you review the other cases in this chapter and the next.

JUSTICE BLACKMUN:

We forthwith acknowledge our awareness of the sensitive and emotional nature of the abortion controversy, of the vigorous opposing views, even among physicians, and of the deep and seemingly absolute convictions that the subject inspires. One's philosophy, one's experiences, one's exposure to the raw edges of human existence, one's religious training, one's attitudes toward life and family and their values, and the moral standards one establishes and seeks to observe, are all likely to influence and to color one's thinking and conclusions about abortion....

The principal thrust of [Roe's] attack on the Texas statutes is that they improperly invade a right, said to be possessed by the pregnant woman, to choose to terminate her pregnancy. [Roe] would discover this right in the concept of personal "liberty" embodied in the Fourteenth Amendment's Due Process Clause; or in personal, marital, familial, and sexual privacy said to be protected by the Bill of Rights or its penumbras, or among those rights reserved to the people by the Ninth Amendment. Before addressing this claim, we feel it desirable briefly to survey, in several aspects, the history of abortion, for such insight as that history may afford us, and then to examine the state purposes and interests behind the criminal abortion laws.

It perhaps is not generally appreciated that the restrictive criminal abortion laws in effect in a majority of States today are of relatively recent vintage. Those laws, generally proscribing abortion or its attempt at any time during pregnancy except when necessary to preserve the pregnant woman's life, are not of ancient or even of common-law origin. Instead, they derive from statutory changes effected, for the most part, in the latter half of the 19th century....

Three reasons have been advanced to explain historically the enactment of criminal abortion laws in the 19th century and to justify their continued existence.

It has been argued occasionally that these laws were the product of a Victorian social concern to discourage illicit sexual conduct. Texas, however, does not advance this justification in the present case, and it appears that no court or commentator has taken the argument seriously. The appellants and amici contend, moreover, that this is not a proper state purpose at all and suggest that, if it were, the Texas statutes are overbroad in protecting it since the law fails to distinguish between married and unwed mothers.

A second reason is concerned with abortion as a medical procedure. When most criminal abortion laws were first enacted, the procedure was a hazardous one for the woman. This was particularly true prior to the development of antisepsis. Antiseptic techniques, of course, were based on discoveries by Lister, Pasteur, and others first announced in 1867, but were not generally accepted and employed until about the turn of the century. Abortion mortality was high. Even after 1900, and perhaps until as late as the development of antibiotics in the 1940s, standard modern techniques such as dilation and curettage were not nearly so safe as they are today. Thus, it has been argued that a State's real concern in enacting a criminal abortion law was to protect the pregnant woman, that is, to restrain her from submitting to a procedure that placed her life in serious jeopardy.

Modern medical techniques have altered this situation. Appellants and various amici refer to medical data indicating that abortion in early pregnancy, that is, prior to the end of the first trimester, although not without its risk, is now relatively safe. Mortality rates for women undergoing early abortions, where the procedure is legal, appear to be as low as or lower than the rates for normal childbirth. Consequently, any interest of the State in protecting the woman from an inherently hazardous procedure, except when it would be equally dangerous for her to forgo it, has largely disappeared. Of course, important state interests in the areas of health and medical standards do remain. The State has a legitimate interest in seeing to it that abortion, like any other medical procedure, is performed under circumstances that insure maximum safety for the patient. This interest obviously extends at least to the performing physician and his staff, to the facilities involved, to the availability of after-care, and to adequate provision for any complication or emergency that might arise. The prevalence of high mortality rates at illegal "abortion mills" strengthens, rather than weakens, the State's interest in regulating the conditions under which abortions are performed. Moreover, the risk to the woman increases as her pregnancy continues. Thus, the State retains a definite interest in protecting the woman's own health and safety when an abortion is proposed at a late stage of pregnancy.

The third reason is the State's interest—some phrase it in terms of duty—in protecting prenatal life. Some of the argument for this justification rests on the theory that a new human life is present from the moment of conception. The State's interest and general obligation to protect life then extends, it is argued, to prenatal life. Only when the life of the pregnant mother herself is at stake, balanced against the life she carries within her, should the interest of the embryo or fetus not prevail. Logically, of course, a legitimate state interest in this area need not stand or fall on acceptance of the belief that life begins at conception or at some other point prior to live birth. In assessing the State's interest, recognition may be given to the less rigid claim that as long as at least potential life is involved, the State may assert interests beyond the protection of the pregnant woman alone....

It is with these interests, and the weight to be attached to them, that this case is concerned.

The Constitution does not explicitly mention any right of privacy. In a line of decisions, however...the Court has recognized that a right of personal privacy, or a guarantee of certain areas or zones of privacy, does exist under the Constitution. In varying contexts, the Court or individual justices have, indeed, found at least the roots of that right in the First Amendment, in the Fourth and Fifth Amendments, in the penumbras of the Bill of Rights, in the Ninth Amendment, or in the concept of liberty guaranteed by the first section of the Fourteenth Amendment. These decisions make it clear that only personal rights that can be deemed "fundamental" or "implicit in the concept of ordered liberty" are included in this guarantee of personal privacy. They also make it clear that the right has some extension to activities relating to marriage, procreation, contraception, family relationships, and child rearing and education.

This right of privacy, whether it be founded in the Fourteenth Amendment's concept of personal liberty and restrictions upon state action, as we feel it is, or, as the District Court determined, in the Ninth Amendment's reservation of rights to the people, is broad enough to encompass a woman's decision whether or not to terminate her pregnancy. The detriment that the State would impose upon the pregnant woman by denying this choice altogether is apparent. Specific and direct harm medically diagnosable even in early pregnancy may be involved. Maternity, or additional offspring, may force upon the woman a distressful life and future. Psychological harm may be imminent. Mental and physical health may be taxed by child-care. There is also the distress, for all concerned, associated with the unwanted child, and there is the problem of bringing a child into a family already unable, psychologically and otherwise, to care for it. In other cases, as in this one, the additional difficulties and continuing stigma of unwed motherhood may be involved. All these are factors the woman and her responsible physician necessarily will consider in consultation.

On the basis of elements such as these, appellant and some amici argue that the woman's right is absolute and that she is entitled to terminate her pregnancy at whatever time, in whatever way, and for whatever reason she alone chooses. With this we do not agree. Appellant's arguments that Texas either has no valid interest at all in regulating the abortion decision, or no interest strong enough to support any limitation upon the woman's sole determination, are unpersuasive. The Court's decisions recognizing a right of privacy also acknowledge that some state regulation in areas protected by that right is appropriate. As noted above, a State may properly assert important interests in safeguarding health, in maintaining medical standards, and in protecting potential life. At some point in pregnancy, these respective interests become sufficiently compelling to sustain regulation of the factors that govern the abortion decision. The privacy right involved, therefore, cannot be said to be absolute. In fact, it is not clear to us that one has an unlimited right to do with one's body as one pleases bears a close relationship to the right of privacy previously articulated in the Court's decisions. The Court has refused to recognize an unlimited right of this kind in the past.

We, therefore, conclude that the right of personal privacy includes the abortion decision, but that this right is not unqualified and must be considered against important state interests in regulation....

Where certain "fundamental rights" are involved, the Court has held that regulation limiting these rights may be justified only by a "compelling state interest," and that legislative enactments must be narrowly drawn to express only the legitimate state interests at stake....

[Roe], as has been indicated, claims an absolute right that bars any state imposition of criminal penalties in the area. [Wade] argues that the State's determination to recognize and protect prenatal life from and after conception constitutes a compelling state interest. As noted above, we do not agree fully with either formulation.

A. [Wade] and certain amici argue that the fetus is a "person" within the language and meaning of the Fourteenth Amendment. In support of this, they outline at length and in detail the well-known facts of fetal development. If this suggestion of personhood is established, [Roe's] case, of course, collapses, for the fetus' right to life would then be guaranteed specifically by the Amendment. The appellant conceded as much on reargument. On the other hand, the appellee conceded on reargument that no case could be cited that holds that a fetus is a person within the meaning of the Fourteenth Amendment.

The Constitution does not define "person" in so many words. Section 1 of the Fourteenth Amendment contains three references to "person." The first, in defining "citizens," speaks of "persons born or naturalized in the United States." The word also appears both in the Due Process Clause and in the Equal Protection Clause. "Person" is used in other places in the Constitution...But in nearly all these instances, the use of the word is such that it has application only postnatally. None indicates, with any assurance, that it has any possible prenatal application.

All this, together with our observation that throughout the major portion of the 19th century prevailing legal abortion practices were far freer than they are today, persuades us that the word "person," as used in the Fourteenth Amendment, does not include the unborn....

This conclusion, however, does not of itself fully answer the contentions raised by Texas, and we pass on to other considerations.

B. The pregnant woman cannot be isolated in her privacy. She carries an embryo and, later, a fetus...The situation therefore is inherently different from marital intimacy, or bedroom possession of obscene material, or marriage, or procreation, or education. As we have intimated above, it is reasonable and appropriate for a State to decide that at some point in time another interest, that of health of the mother or that of potential human life, becomes significantly involved. The woman's privacy is no longer sole and any right of privacy she possesses must be measured accordingly.

Texas urges that, apart from the Fourteenth Amendment, life begins at conception and is present throughout pregnancy, and that, therefore, the State has a compelling interest in protecting that life from and after conception. We need not resolve the difficult question of when life begins. When those trained in the respective disciplines of medicine, philosophy, and theology are unable to arrive at any consensus, the judiciary, at this point in the development of man's knowledge, is not in a position to speculate as to the answer.

It should be sufficient to note briefly the wide divergence of thinking on this most sensitive and difficult question. There has always been strong support for the view that life does not begin until live birth. This was the belief of the Stoics. It appears to be the predominant, though not the unanimous, attitude of the Jewish faith. It may be taken to represent also the position of a large segment of the Protestant community, insofar as that can be ascertained; organized groups that have taken a formal position on the abortion issue have generally regarded abortion as a matter for the conscience of the individual and her family. As we have noted, the common law found greater significance in quickening. Physicians and their scientific colleagues have regarded that event with less interest and have tended to focus either upon conception, upon live birth, or upon the interim point at which the fetus becomes "viable," that is, potentially able to live outside the mother's womb, albeit with artificial aid. Viability is usually placed at about seven months (28 weeks) but may occur earlier, even at 24 weeks. The Aristotelian theory of "mediate animation," that held sway throughout the Middle Ages and the Renaissance in Europe, continued to be official Roman Catholic dogma until the 19th century, despite opposition to this "ensoulment" theory from those in the Church who would recognize the existence of life from the moment of conception. The latter is now, of course, the official belief of the Catholic Church...[T]his is a view strongly held by many non-Catholics as well, and by many physicians. Substantial problems for precise definition of this view are posed, however, by new embryological data that purport to indicate that conception is a "process" over time, rather than an event, and by new medical techniques such as menstrual extraction, the "morning-after" pill, implantation of embryos, artificial insemination, and even artificial wombs.

In areas other than criminal abortion, the law has been reluctant to endorse any theory that life, as we recognize it, begins before live birth or to accord legal rights to the unborn except in narrowly defined situations and except when the rights are contingent upon live birth. For example, the traditional rule of tort law denied recovery for prenatal injuries even though the child was born alive. That rule has been changed in almost every jurisdiction. In most States, recovery is said to be permitted only if the fetus was viable, or at least quick, when the injuries were sustained, though few courts have squarely so held. In a recent development, generally opposed by the commentators, some States permit the parents of a stillborn child to maintain an action for wrongful death because of prenatal injuries. Such an action, however, would appear to be one to vindicate the parents' interest and is thus consistent with the view that the fetus, at most, represents only the potentiality of life. Similarly, unborn children have been recognized as acquiring rights or interests by way of inheritance or other devolution of property, and have been represented by guardians ad litem. Perfection of the interests involved, again, has generally been contingent upon live birth. In short, the unborn have never been recognized in the law as persons in the whole sense.

In view of all this, we do not agree that, by adopting one theory of life, Texas may override the rights of the pregnant woman that are at stake. We repeat, however, that the State does have an important and legitimate interest in preserving and protecting the health of the pregnant woman, whether she be a resident of the State or a nonresident who seeks medical consultation and treatment there, and that it has still another important and legitimate interest in protecting the potentiality of human life. These interests are separate and distinct. Each grows in substantiality as the woman approaches term and, at a point during pregnancy, each becomes "compelling."

With respect to the State's important and legitimate interest in the health of the mother, the "compelling" point, in the light of present medical knowledge, is at approximately the end of the first trimester. This is so because of the now-established medical fact that until the end of the first trimester mortality in abortion may be less than mortality in normal childbirth. It follows that, from and after this point, a State may regulate the abortion procedure to the extent that the regulation reasonably relates to the preservation and protection of maternal health. Examples of permissible state regulation in this area are requirements as to the qualifications of the person who is to perform the abortion; as to the licensure of that person; as to the facility in which the procedure is to be performed, that is, whether it must be a hospital or may be a clinic or some other place of less-than-hospital status; as to the licensing of the facility; and the like.

This means, on the other hand, that, for the period of pregnancy prior to this "compelling" point, the attending physician, in consultation with his patient, is free to determine, without regulation by the State, that, in his medical judgment, the patient's pregnancy should be terminated. If that decision is reached, the judgment may be effectuated by an abortion free of interference by the State.

With respect to the State's important and legitimate interest in potential life, the "compelling" point is at viability. This is so because the fetus then presumably has the capability of meaningful life outside the mother's womb. State regulation protective of fetal life after viability thus has both logical and biological justifications. If the State is interested in protecting fetal life after viability, it may go so far as to proscribe abortion during that period, except when it is necessary to preserve the life or health of the mother....

The [Texas] statute makes no distinction between abortions performed early in pregnancy and those performed later, and it limits to a single reason, "saving" the mother's life, the legal justification for the procedure. The statute, therefore, cannot survive the constitutional attack made upon it here....

JUSTICE REHNQUIST:

The Court's opinion brings to the decision of this troubling question both extensive historical fact and a wealth of legal scholarship. While the opinion thus commands my respect, I find myself nonetheless in fundamental disagreement with those parts of it that invalidate the Texas statute in question, and therefore dissent....

I have difficulty in concluding, as the Court does, that the right of "privacy" is involved in this case. Texas, by the statute here challenged, bars the performance of a medical abortion by a licensed physician on a plaintiff such as Roe. A transaction resulting in an operation such as this is not "private" in the ordinary usage of that word. Nor is the "privacy" that the Court finds here even a distant relative of the freedom from searches and seizures protected by the Fourth Amendment to the Constitution....

If the Court means by the term "privacy" no more than that the claim of a person to be free from unwanted state regulation of consensual transactions may be a form of "liberty" protected by the Fourteenth Amendment, there is no doubt that similar claims have been upheld in our earlier decisions on the basis of that liberty. I agree with the statement of Justice Stewart in his concurring opinion that the "liberty," against deprivation of which without due process the Fourteenth Amendment protects, embraces more than the rights found in the Bill of Rights. But that liberty is not guaranteed absolutely against deprivation, only against deprivation without due process of law. The test traditionally applied in the area of social and economic legislation is whether or not a law such as that challenged has a rational relation to a valid state objective. The Due Process Clause of the Fourteenth Amendment undoubtedly does place a limit, albeit a broad one, on legislative power to enact laws such as this. If the Texas statute were to prohibit an abortion even where the mother's life is in jeopardy, I have little doubt that such a statute would lack a rational relation to a valid state objective…But the Court's sweeping invalidation of any restrictions on abortion during the first trimester is impossible to justify under that standard, and the conscious weighing of competing factors that the Court's opinion apparently substitutes for the established test is far more appropriate to a legislative judgment than to a judicial one.…

The fact that a majority of the States reflecting, after all, the majority sentiment in those States, have had restrictions on abortions for at least a century is a strong indication, it seems to me, that the asserted right to an abortion is not "so rooted in the traditions and conscience of our people as to be ranked as fundamental." Even today, when society's views on abortion are changing, the very existence of the debate is evidence that the "right" to an abortion is not so universally accepted as the appellant would have us believe.…

Doe v. Bolton
410 U.S. 179 (1973)

Justice Blackmun delivered the opinion of the Court, in which Chief Justice Burger, and Justices Douglas, Brennan, Stewart, Marshall, and Powell joined. Chief Justice Burger, and Justices Douglas and Stewart each filed concurring opinions. Justice White filed a dissenting opinion, in which Justice Rehnquist joined. Justice Rehnquist filed a dissenting opinion.

Areas for Discussion and Ethical Reflection

1.   Justice Blackmun asserts that *Roe* and *Doe* are companion cases and should be read together. Most medical ethics texts, however, when discussing *Roe* or providing excerpts from Justice Blackmun's opinion in that case, make no mention of *Doe v. Bolton*. As you read *Doe* consider how, if at all, the decision contributes to your appreciation and understanding of the moral and legal issues and arguments surrounding abortion.

2.   Georgia's requirement that a committee review and approve a physician's decision to perform an abortion is struck down by the Court. What exactly are Justice Blackmun's arguments for striking this requirement?

3.   The Court also finds unconstitutional Georgia's requirement that two additional physicians approve the recommendation of an abortion by the pregnant woman's own physician. As Justice Blackmun notes, this requirement brings to six the number of doctors involved in each abortion decision. What relevance, if any, do Justice Blackmun's arguments against the two-physician requirement have for ethical assessments of the physician-patient relationship?

4.   Justice Douglas, in his concurring opinion, notes that many women become pregnant under circumstances and live in situations that create "such suffering, dislocations, misery, or tragedy

as to make an early abortion the only civilized step to take." No doubt, Justice Douglas is correct in that many women find themselves pregnant in less than ideal circumstances, but how much moral weight should we give this observation? Is abortion the only "civilized" choice? Does your answer depend on your position on the moral status of the fetus?

5.   Justice Douglas's comments on the physician-patient relationship are extremely interesting and carry much significance for medical ethics. Briefly characterize his understanding of the relationship. What arguments does he provide to support his understanding? Do you find his arguments convincing enough to support the overturning of Georgia's committee and multi-physician requirements? What are the implications of Justice Douglas's conception of the doctor-patient relationship for other areas of medical ethics, such as physician-assisted suicide?

6.   Justice White, in his dissenting opinion, asserts, "The Court apparently values the convenience of the pregnant mother more than the continued existence and development of the life or potential life that she carries." Is Justice White's claim true? Is it fair? Does Justice White hold that fetuses are moral agents with the same rights as adults? Was the legislative aim of Georgia's abortion regulations to make abortion inconvenient for pregnant women? Obviously, major differences exist between Justice White and the position the majority takes in *Doe*. Do you see any way of reconciling the differences? Do the differences on the Court reflect the differences in society over the morality of abortion?

7.   Some writers have begun considering the threats new reproductive technologies pose to *Roe* and *Doe*. Writing in the *New Republic*,[10] Sacha Zimmerman describes the development of a new technology called ectogenesis, better known as the artificial womb. Cells from the lining of a woman's womb can be removed, mixed with hormones, and then grown on a model of a uterus. The model dissolves and the "new" womb continues to thrive. At this time scientists have shown that embryos will attach to the walls of the artificial womb and begin to grow. It might one day

become possible to extract embryos from women unwilling to carry them and place them in the artificial womb. Several ethical and constitutional problems and issues are raised by this new technology. Could the state force women to undergo fetal extraction in place of allowing fetal extinction? Is abortion about the right not to procreate, or is it about the right not to be pregnant? Who, from both a moral and constitutional perspective, is most appropriate for making the decision over whether fetuses should be extracted or killed? Pregnant women? The state? As you read *Roe* and *Doe* as well as the two cases in the next chapter, search for clues as to how the justices would handle new challenges posed by new reproductive technologies.

JUSTICE BLACKMUN:

...[Mary Doe and physicians] attack on several grounds those portions of the Georgia abortion statutes that remain after the District Court decision: undue restriction of a right to personal and marital privacy; vagueness; deprivation of substantive and procedural due process; improper restriction to Georgia residents; and denial of equal protection....

[Mary Doe and physicians]...argue that the District Court should have declared unconstitutional three procedural demands of the Georgia statute: (1) that the abortion be performed in a hospital accredited by the Joint Commission on Accreditation of Hospitals; (2) that the procedure be approved by the hospital staff abortion committee; and (3) that the performing physician's judgment be confirmed by the independent examinations of the patient by two other licensed physicians. [Mary Doe and physicians] attack these provisions not only on the ground that they unduly restrict the woman's right of privacy, but also on procedural due process and equal protection grounds. The physician-appellants also argue that, by subjecting a doctor's individual medical judgment to committee approval and to continuing consultations, the statute impermissibly restricts the physician's right to practice his profession and deprives him of due process.

1. JCAH accreditation. The Joint Commission on Accreditation of Hospitals is an organization without governmental sponsorship or overtones. No question whatever is raised concerning the integrity of the organization or the high purpose of the accreditation process. That process, however, has to do with hospital standards generally and has no present particularized concern with abortion as a medical or surgical procedure. In Georgia, there is no restriction on the performance of non-abortion surgery in a hospital not yet accredited by the JCAH so long as other requirements imposed by the State, such as licensing of the hospital and of the operating surgeon, are met. Furthermore, accreditation by the Commission is not granted until a hospital has been in operation at least one year. And the Uniform Abortion Act approved by the American Bar Association in February 1972 contains no JCAH-accredited hospital specification. Some courts have held that a JCAH-accreditation requirement is an overbroad infringement of fundamental rights because it does not relate to the particular medical problems and dangers of the abortion operation.

We hold that the JCAH-accreditation requirement does not withstand constitutional scrutiny in the present context. It is a requirement that simply is not "based on differences that are reasonably related to the purposes of the Act in which it is found."

This is not to say that Georgia may not or should not, from and after the end of the first trimester, adopt standards for licensing all facilities where abortions may be performed so long as those standards are legitimately related to the objective the State seeks to accomplish....

2. Committee approval. The second aspect of the appellants' procedural attack relates to the hospital abortion com-

mittee and to the pregnant woman's asserted lack of access to that committee. Relying [on previous cases], Doe first argues that she was denied due process because she could not make a presentation to the committee. It is not clear from the record, however, whether Doe's own consulting physician was or was not a member of the committee or did or did not present her case, or, indeed, whether she herself was or was not there. We see nothing in the Georgia statute that explicitly denies access to the committee by or on behalf of the woman. If the access point alone were involved, we would not be persuaded to strike down the committee provision on the unsupported assumption that access is not provided.

[Doe and physicians] attack the discretion the statute leaves to the committee. The most concrete argument they advance is their suggestion that it is still a badge of infamy "in many minds" to bear an illegitimate child, and that the Georgia system enables the committee members' personal views as to extramarital sex relations, and punishment therefore, to govern their decisions. This approach obviously is one founded on suspicion and one that discloses a lack of confidence in the integrity of physicians. To say that physicians will be guided in their hospital committee decisions by their predilections on extramarital sex unduly narrows the issue to pregnancy outside marriage. (Doe's own situation did not involve extramarital sex and its product.) The appellants' suggestion is necessarily somewhat degrading to the conscientious physician, particularly the obstetrician, whose professional activity is concerned with the physical and mental welfare, the woes, the emotions, and the concern of his female patients. He, perhaps more than anyone else, is knowledgeable in this area of patient care, and he is aware of human frailty, so-called "error," and needs. The good physician—despite the presence of rascals in the medical profession, as in all others, we trust that most physicians are "good"—will have sympathy and understanding for the pregnant patient that probably are not exceeded by those who participate in other areas of professional counseling.

[W]e see no constitutionally justifiable pertinence in the structure for the advance approval by the abortion committee. With regard to the protection of potential life, the medical judgment is already completed prior to the committee stage, and review by a committee once removed from diagnosis is basically redundant. We are not cited to any other surgical procedure made subject to committee approval as a matter of state criminal law. The woman's right to receive medical care in accordance with her licensed physician's best judgment and the physician's right to administer it are substantially limited by this statutorily imposed overview....

3. Two-doctor concurrence. The third aspect of [Doe's] attack centers on the "time and availability of adequate medical facilities and personnel." It is said that the system imposes substantial and irrational roadblocks and "is patently unsuited" to prompt determination of the abortion decision. Time, of course, is critical in abortion. Risks during the first trimester of pregnancy are admittedly lower than during later months.

[Doe and physicians] purport to show by a local study of Grady Memorial Hospital (serving indigent residents in Fulton and DeKalb Counties) that the "mechanics of the system itself forced... discontinuance of the abortion process" because the median time for the workup was 15 days. The same study shows, however, that 27% of the candidates for abortion were already 13 or more weeks pregnant at the time of application, that is, they were at the end of or beyond the first trimester when they made their applications. It is too much to say, as appellants do, that these particular persons "were victims of a system over which they [had] no control." If higher risk was incurred because of abortions in the second rather than the first trimester, much of that risk was due to delay in application, and not to the alleged cumbersomeness of the system. We note, in passing, that appellant Doe had no delay problem herself; the decision in her case was made well within the first trimester.

It should be manifest that our rejection of the accredited-hospital requirement and, more important, of the abortion committee's advance approval eliminates the major grounds of the attack based on the system's delay and the lack of facilities. There remains, however, the required confirmation by two Georgia-licensed physicians in addition to the recommendation of the pregnant woman's own consultant (making under the statute, a total of six physicians involved, including the three on the hospital's abortion committee). We conclude that this provision, too, must fall.

The statute's emphasis, as has been repetitively noted, is on the attending physician's "best clinical judgment that an abortion is necessary." That should be sufficient. The reasons for the presence of the confirmation step in the statute are perhaps apparent, but they are insufficient to withstand constitutional challenge. Again, no other voluntary medical or surgical procedure for which Georgia requires confirmation by two other physicians has been cited to us. If a physician is licensed by the State, he is recognized by the State as capable of exercising acceptable clinical judgment. If he fails in this, professional censure and deprivation of his license are available remedies. Required acquiescence by copractitioners has no rational connection with a patient's needs and unduly infringes on the physician's right to practice. The attending physician will know when a consultation is advisable—the doubtful situation, the need for assurance when the medical decision is a delicate one, and the like. Physicians have followed this routine historically and know its usefulness and benefit for all concerned. It is still true today that "[r]eliance must be placed upon the assurance given by his license, issued by an authority competent to judge in that respect, that he [the physician] possesses the requisite qualifications."

JUSTICE DOUGLAS:

While I join the opinion of the Court, I add a few words.

The questions presented in the present cases go far beyond the issues of vagueness. They involve the right of privacy, one aspect of which we considered in *Griswold v. Connecticut*, when we held that various guarantees in the Bill of Rights creates zones of privacy....

The vicissitudes of life produce pregnancies which may be unwanted, or which may impair "health," or which may imperil the life of the mother, or which in the full setting of the case may create such suffering, dislocations, misery, or tragedy as to make an early abortion the only civilized step to take. These hardships may be properly embraced in the "health" factor of the mother as appraised by a person of insight. Or they may be part of a broader medical judgment based on what is "appropriate" in a given case, though perhaps not "necessary" in a strict sense.

The "liberty" of the mother, though rooted as it is in the Constitution, may be qualified by the State for the reasons we have stated. But where fundamental personal rights and liberties are involved, the corrective legislation must be "narrowly drawn to prevent the supposed evil," and not be dealt with in an "unlimited and indiscriminate" manner. Unless regulatory measures are so confined and are addressed to the specific areas of compelling legislative concern, the police power would become the great leveler of constitutional rights and liberties.

The right of privacy has no more conspicuous place than in the physician-patient relationship, unless it be in the priest-penitent relationship. It is one thing for a patient to agree that her physician may consult with another physician about her case. It is quite a different matter for the State compulsorily to impose on that physician-patient relationship another layer or, as in this case, still a third layer of physicians. The right of privacy—the right to care for one's health and person and to seek out a physician of one's on choice protected by the Fourteenth Amendment—becomes only a matter of theory, not a reality, when a multiple-physician-approval system is mandated by the State....

The right to seek advice on one's health and the right to place reliance on the physician of one's choice are basic to Fourteenth Amendment values. We deal with fundamental rights and liberties, which, as already noted, can be contained or controlled only by discretely drawn legislation that preserves the "liberty" and regulates only those phases of the problem of compelling legislative concern. The imposition by the State of group controls over the physician-patient relationship is not made on any medical procedure apart from abortion, no matter how dangerous the medical step may be. The oversight imposed on the physician and patient in abortion cases denies them their "liberty," vix., their right of privacy, with out any compelling, discernible state interest.

Justice White:

At the heart of the controversy in these cases are those recurring pregnancies that pose no danger whatsoever to the life or health of the mother but are, nevertheless, unwanted for any one or more of a variety of reasons—convenience, family planning, economics, dislike of children, the embarrassment of illegitimacy, etc. The common claim before us is that for any one of such reasons, or for no reason at all, and without asserting or claiming any threat to life or health, any woman is entitled to an abortion at her request if she is able to find a medical advisor willing to undertake the procedure.

The Court for the most part sustains this position: During the period prior to the time the fetus becomes viable, the Constitution of the United States values the convenience, whim, or caprice of the putative mother more than the life or potential life of the fetus; the Constitution, therefore, guarantees the right to an abortion as against any state law or policy seeking to protect the fetus from an abortion not prompted by more compelling reasons of the mother.

With all due respect, I dissent. I find nothing in the language or history of the Constitution to support the Court's judgment. The Court simply fashions and announces a new constitutional right for pregnant mothers and, with scarcely any reason or authority for its action, invests that right with sufficient substance to override most existing state abortion statutes. The upshot is that the people and the legislatures of the 50 States are constitutionally disentitled to weigh the relative importance of the continued existence and development of the fetus, on the one hand, against a spectrum of possible impacts on the mother, on the other hand. As an exercise of raw judicial power, the Court perhaps has authority to do what it does today; but in my view its judgment is an improvident and extravagant exercise of the power of judicial review that the Constitution extends to this Court.

The Court apparently values the convenience of the pregnant mother more than the continued existence and development of the life or potential life that she carries. Whether or not I might agree with that marshaling of values, I can in no event join the Court's judgment because I find no constitutional warrant for imposing such an order of priorities on the people and legislatures of the States. In a sensitive area such as this, involving as it does issues over which reasonable men may easily and heatedly differ, I cannot accept the Court's exercise of its clear power of choice by interposing a constitutional barrier to state efforts to protect human life and by investing mothers and doctors with the constitutionally protected right to exterminate it. This issue, for the most part, should be left with the people and to the political processes the people have devised to govern their affairs....

Notes

1.   Rem B. Edwards and Glenn C. Graber, "Introduction to Abortion," in *Bio-Ethics*, edited by Rem B. Edwards and Glenn C. Graber (San Diego, CA: Harcourt Brace Jovanovich, 1988), pp. 533–38.

2.   John T. Noonan, Jr., "An Almost Absolute Value in History," in *Intervention and Reflection: Basic Issues in Medical Ethics*, 6th ed., edited by Ronald Munson (Belmont CA: Wadsworth, 2000), pp. 83–86.

3.   Edward Langerak, "Abortion: Listening to the Middle," in *Contemporary Moral Issues: Diversity and Consensus*, 2nd ed., edited by Lawrence M. Hinman (Upper Saddle River, NJ: Prentice Hall, 2000), pp. 53–60.

4.   Ibid., p. 55.

5.   Mary Anne Warren, "On the Moral and Legal Status of Abortion," in Noonan, *Intervention and Reflection*, pp. 101–2.

6.   Ronald Dworkin, *Life's Dominion: An Argument about Abortion, Euthanasia, and Individual Freedom* (New York: Knopf, 1993), pp. 11–24.

7.   Ibid., p. 21.

8.   Lee Epstein and Joseph F. Kobylka, *The Supreme Court and Legal Change: Abortion and the Death Penalty* (Chapel Hill: University of North Carolina Press, 1992), pp. 162–67.

9.   Christopher Miles Coope, "Death with Dignity," *Hastings Center Report* 27 (1997): 37–38.

10.   Sacha Zimmerman, "Fetal Position: The Real Threat to *Roe v. Wade*," *New Republic*, 18 & 25 August 2003, 14–17.

For Further Reading

Dworkin, Ronald. *Life's Dominion: An Argument about Abortion, Euthanasia, and Individual Freedom*. New York: Knopf, 1993.

Epstein, Lee, and Joseph Kobylka. *The Supreme Court and Legal Change: Abortion and the Death Penalty*. Chapel Hill: University of North Carolina Press, 1992.

Langerak, Edward. "Abortion: Listening to the Middle." In *Contemporary Moral Issues: Diversity and Consensus*, 2nd edition, Lawrence M. Hinman, ed. Upper Saddle River, NJ: Prentice Hall, 2000.

Munson, Ronald. "Introduction to Abortion." In *Intervention and Reflec-

tion: Basic Issues in Medical Ethics, 6th edition, Ronald Munson, ed. New York: McGraw-Hill, 2000.

Noonan, Jr., John T. "An Almost Absolute Value in History." In Munson, *Intervention and Reflection*.

Warren, Mary Ann. "On the Moral and Legal Status of Abortion." In Munson, *Intervention and Reflection*.

Zimmerman, Sacha. "Fetal Position: The Real Threat to *Roe v. Wade*." *New Republic*, 18 and 25 August 2003, 14–17.

CHAPTER FOUR

THE LATER ABORTION CASES

Most of the cases that reach the Supreme Court cannot be decided on the basis of mere logical inference from the language of preexisting legal rules applied to the facts of the cases. They take judgment, choices among different reasonable ways to understand what has been meant. There is disagreement among lawyers and judges about whether that entails going outside the law and applying something that is not law to help make legal decisions, or whether law as it is and has been practiced in the Anglo-American system includes and requires that judges and justices understand the "rules" in light of fundamental American principles of ethics, morality, and humanity. In most of the cases that the Supreme Court considers, the justices have no choice but to allow themselves to be influenced by their understanding of those fundamental principles.

—Stephen Gottlieb, *Morality Imposed: The Rehnquist Court and Liberty in America*

The division between early and later Supreme Court decisions is useful in reminding us that in *Roe v. Wade* the Court was preoccupied with basic issues surrounding the personhood and the potential personhood of embryos and fetuses, as well as privacy and autonomy rights of women. In later cases, the justices were confronted with state regulations designed to make engaging in abortion activities more difficult for women and their doctors. Although the distinction between "early" and "later" is useful, we should keep in mind as we consider two of the most famous "later" cases that fundamental issues of moral status and autonomy are inextricably linked to laws regulating abortion. Even in *Doe v. Bolton*, *Roe*'s immediate successor, we see the justices applying their understanding of the abortion right to procedural concerns surrounding the Georgia statutes. In the twenty years following *Roe* and *Doe*, the Court was presented with ample opportunities to clarify, modify, and even change its approach to the constitutional (and moral?) underpinnings of the basic abortion right. Several states seemed determined to find a way around *Roe*'s justifications for permitting women to terminate their pregnancies. Many of these regulations were designed specifically to apply to the relationship between a woman and her doctor, and these included twenty-four-hour waiting periods, informed consent requirements, provision of information on fetal development and available resources for women who elected not to undergo abortion, and new definitions of viability. The two cases covered in this chapter examine the constitutionality of these regulations, with the majorities in each case reaching different conclusions. These two cases have had a dramatic impact on the ethics of the physician-patient relationship.

Constitutional Issues and Background

Thornburgh v. American College of Obstetricians and Gynecologists is the last case in which a majority of the justices explicitly subscribed to the reasoning of *Roe v. Wade*. Justice Powell, who consistently upheld principles espoused in *Roe*, retired from the Court in 1987. At issue in this case was the Pennsylvania Abortion Control Act of 1982, which was the latest in several attempts by Pennsylvania to restrict a woman's access to abortion and to control the manner in which physicians performed abortions. Among the provisions of the act under challenge were requirements for informed consent; women to be given printed, detailed information regarding physical and psychological risks of the procedure; the availability of financial assistance for prenatal care; determination of viability; and second-physician consultation. The U.S. Court of Appeals for the Third Circuit ruled that many of the provisions were unconstitutional.

Thornburgh is an important case for many reasons. The case provides readers with an excellent summary of how many of the justices view the role and scope of judicial review with respect to abortion regulations. In addition, the majority opinion expresses a conception of the physician-patient relationship that many in medical ethics find intriguing. Finally, since much of the majority's holding was overturned six years later in *Casey*, reading *Thornburgh* and *Casey* together provides an excellent exercise in comparing arguments and the different uses by the justices of important concepts. The majority based its finding in *Thornburgh* on the principle that the state could only enact laws designed to protect the health of the pregnant woman or to protect a viable fetus.

Our second case, *Planned Parenthood of Southeastern Pennsylvania v. Casey*, is the most famous and most important abortion decision since *Roe v. Wade*. The specifics of *Casey* were almost identical to those in *Thornburgh*. At issue were several provisions of the Pennsylvania Abortion Control Act, including a twenty-four-hour waiting period, informed consent, reporting requirements, notification of the husband of a married woman, and the consent of one parent of a minor who wished to obtain an abortion albeit with a judicial bypass exception. Five abortion clinics and one doctor brought suit in District Court seeking to stop enforcement of the statutes. The District Court found all the provisions unconstitutional and stopped their enforcement. On appeal, the Court of Appeals found only the husband notification provision unconstitutional.

Casey can be a somewhat confusing case on first reading. As the list of the distribution of opinions demonstrates, the ruling was divided; the ruling was in part a majority opinion and in part a plurality opinion (an opinion receiving more votes than any other opinion but lacking sufficient votes to constitute a majority). A majority of the justices asserted that the concept

of liberty in the Due Process Clause of the Fourteenth Amendment protected a woman's right to choose to abort a nonviable
fetus. A plurality ruled that the appropriate principle for determining the constitutionality of a particular abortion regulation
was whether the regulation constituted an undue burden for the
woman. A particular abortion regulation would constitute an
"undue burden" if it had the purpose or effect of placing substantial obstacles in the way of the woman exercising her constitutionally protected right to have an abortion. The establishment
of the "undue burden" test and the fact that *Roe*'s central holding
remained intact are two of the reasons this case is significant. As
we shall see, much disagreement existed among the justices as to
the meaning and legitimacy of the "undue burden" test.

Ethical Issues and Background

In the last chapter we focused on the moral status of the fetus
and the obligations the state has in prohibiting the killing of a
biological human being, even in the earliest stages of development. This focus was appropriate given that the justices in *Roe*
struggled over the meaning and scope of moral agency; for the
justices this struggle was couched in terms of whether the fetus
is "human life" or "potential human life." We also examined the
meaning and scope of the assertion that "life is sacred." In preparation for reading the two cases in this chapter we focus briefly
on ethical concerns surrounding autonomy and privacy interests
of pregnant women. We examine, as the justices do, the weight of
these interests and the issue of whether these interests are strong
enough to outweigh a fetus's interest in continued existence. In
so doing we have an opportunity to explore one of the most
important concepts in medical ethics and law, the concept of a
Good Samaritan.

Both *Thornburgh* and *Casey* allow us to ask some very
important questions. How ought we to characterize a woman's
right to control her own body and her own destiny? What are
the ethical justifications for these rights and what should be the

limits on the exercise of these rights? Might we say that even if a fetus is a moral agent with a right to life, a woman may legitimately continue to exercise control over her body such that she could, if she wishes, abort the fetus? May the state take steps to ensure that women give serious and sustained thought to the abortion decision?

Judith Jarvis Thomson answers some of these questions as she argues that even if we consider fetuses persons with a right to life, that right does not outweigh the right of a pregnant woman to terminate her pregnancy. Thomson supports her position by examining the phrase "right to life."[1] What does it mean to have a right to life? After considering and discarding several possibilities—the right to life means the right to be given anything one needs to stay in existence, or the right to life means the right not to be killed—Thomson settles on defining the right to life as the right not to be killed unjustly. A woman's interests in bodily self-determination and privacy outweigh a fetus's right to life, hence killing it is not unjust. Thomson admits that as the moment of birth grows nearer and the reasons a woman gives for aborting become frivolous, the abortion becomes problematic. Thomson's account, whatever its shortcomings, forces us to consider exactly what we mean when we assert that a fetus, or any person for that matter, has a right to life. Try to determine how the justices are using the phrase "right to life" as you read the cases in this chapter.

Related to questions surrounding the meaning and scope of a right to life is the concept of the Good Samaritan. This concept has a great deal of ethical and legal significance especially in discussions of the morality of state regulations severely restricting abortion. A Good Samaritan is one who makes sacrifices, perhaps even significant sacrifices, in coming to the aid of another. Of course, disagreement exists over what constitutes a significant sacrifice, but most people generally think activities that affect your health or that endanger your life constitute significant sacrifice. Neither the law nor moral theory requires people to make major sacrifices in order that others may be helped. However, morality may require that you make some sacrifice to help others. Examples would include dialing 911 upon witnessing someone being robbed or murdered and saving a drowning child from a river when you know how to swim. Thomson calls these kinds of actions the actions of a Minimally Decent Samaritan.[2] But the law does not even require people to be either Good Samaritans or Minimally Decent Samaritans except for one category of persons, pregnant women. Thomson asserts that laws requiring women to carry fetuses to term are compelling women to be Good Samaritans. Thomson admits, however, that perhaps society should require everyone to be at least Minimally Decent Samaritans, but until it does, it is unjust to require women to be Good Samaritans.

As you think about the meaning and scope of the phrase "right to life" and consider the implications of the Good Samaritan concept, try to determine exactly how they would apply to the undue burden principle espoused by Justices O'Connor, Kennedy, and Souter in *Casey*. The three justices explain that the principle of undue burden is a method for characterizing the conclusion that a state has passed into law a regulation that has "the purpose or effect of placing a substantial obstacle in the path of a woman seeking an abortion of a nonviable fetus." As you read the opinion of the three justices you will note that they continue by explaining the distinction between "purpose" and "effect" as those terms are used in the undue burden principle. As you come to understand this distinction and the undue burden principle as a whole, consider its relevance within the context of the idea of the Good Samaritan. Specifically, do you agree that, when applying the undue burden principle to a state law requiring a twenty-four-hour waiting period before abortion, the law should be upheld? What would the Good Samaritan principle conclude about the law?

As you already know, much of our discussion on abortion, and that of the Court's as well, relates to the social equality of women. Any concerns for the autonomy and privacy interests of women have consequences for their social and political equality. While many tend to believe that full reproductive freedom is necessary for women's equality, there are writers who take the position that state restrictions on abortion, even those that are quite severe, do not endanger women's goals of equal treatment. This position, sometimes referred to as pro-life feminism,[3] holds that one can find abortion immoral and advocate for strict laws regulating abortion without sacrificing the autonomy and privacy interests of women and without endangering their search for equality. Defenses of pro-life feminism usually begin with assertions that fetuses have intrinsic value, thus making abortion immoral. From the assertion of intrinsic value, pro-life feminists then move to asserting that women must take responsibility for their lives and for the children that will be born. Moreover, social and sexual equality for women will be realized when society in general and men in particular see that women are willing to take responsibility.

As you read these two cases representing the Court's position on abortion you will certainly have an opportunity to think about the ethical and conceptual complexity of abortion. In addition, you can determine just how much of this ethical and conceptual complexity the justices take into account in their deliberations. You might also take note of any differences in ethical analysis that occur from one case to the other.

Thornburgh v. American College of Obstetricians and Gynecologists 476 U.S. 747 (1986)

Justice Blackmun delivered the opinion of the Court, in which Justices Brennan, Marshall, Powell, and Stevens joined. Justice Stevens filed a concurring opinion. Chief Justice Burger filed a dissenting opinion. Justices White and O'Connor each filed dissenting opinions, both of which were joined by Justice Rehnquist.

Areas for Discussion and Ethical Reflection

1.   What are Justice Blackmun's arguments for finding many of the informed consent and informational requirements un-

constitutional? Do any of those arguments strike you as ethical arguments?

2.   From a moral perspective, who is better situated to determine what types of information a woman should receive before consenting to an abortion, the state or a physician? How does Justice Blackmun support his position that the physician is better situated to determine the type of information to be offered? Are there problems with Justice Blackmun's position? For example, with regard to medical procedures other than abortion, do you think Justice Blackmun would be comfortable with sole discretion resting with the physician? Would you be comfortable?

3.   In his dissenting opinion, Justice White observes that, "... the fact that many men and women of goodwill and high commitment to constitutional government place themselves on both sides of the abortion controversy strengthens my own conviction that the values animating the Constitution do not compel recognition of the abortion liberty as fundamental." For Justice White, what specific values animate the Constitution? Would specific moral theories recommend specific values?

4.   Justice White makes the following observation:

> However one answers the metaphysical or theological question whether the fetus is a "human being" or the legal question whether it is a "person" as that term is used in the Constitution, one must at least recognize, first, that the fetus is an entity that bears in its cells all the genetic information that characterizes a member of the species homo sapiens and distinguishes an individual member of that species from all others....

This observation should recall our discussion of personhood in the previous chapter. What problems do you find with Justice White's observation? Is Justice White subscribing to natural law theory in supporting his understanding of the status of a fetus?

From a natural law ethics perspective, what might you say to help Justice White make a more convincing argument?

5.   Justice White is very skeptical of the majority's position that the state should not "structure" the patient-physician relationship. His support of professional freedom within the medical profession is certainly not as strong as that of the majority's. Explain Justice White's position and his arguments for the position. Do you think Justice White's position should prevail?

6.   Even people who find abortion morally permissible and legally acceptable admit that there would be some instances when terminating a pregnancy would be immoral. Under what circumstances would you find abortion immoral? Would you be willing to accept legal prohibition of abortion in those circumstances?

JUSTICE BLACKMUN:

> ...This case, as it comes to us, concerns the constitutionality of six provisions of the Pennsylvania Act that the Court of Appeals struck down as facially invalid: 3205 ("informed consent"); 3208 ("printed information"); 3214(a) and (h) (reporting requirements); 3211(a) (determination of viability); 3210(b) (degree of care required in postviability abortions); and 3210(c) (second-physician requirement)....

> In the years since this Court's decision in *Roe*, States and municipalities have adopted a number of measures seemingly designed to prevent a woman, with the advice of her physician, from exercising her freedom of choice...But the constitutional principles that led this Court to its decisions in 1973 still provide the compelling reason for recognizing the constitutional dimensions of a woman's right to decide whether to end her pregnancy. "[I]t should go without saying that the vitality of these constitutional principles cannot be allowed to yield simply because of disagreement with them." The States are not free, under the guise of protect-

ing maternal health or potential life, to intimidate women into continuing pregnancies. [Pennsylvania] claims that the statutory provisions before us today further legitimate compelling interests of the Commonwealth. Close analysis of those provisions, however, shows that they wholly subordinate constitutional privacy interests and concerns with maternal health in an effort to deter a woman from making a decision that, with her physician, is hers to make.

We turn to the challenged statutes:

[Only the Court's observations and arguments regarding informed consent, printed information, reporting requirements, determination of viability, and degree of care for postviability abortions are excerpted below.]

1. Section 3205 ("informed consent") and 3208 ("printed information"). Section 3205(a) requires that the woman give her "voluntary and informed consent" to an abortion. Failure to observe the provisions of 3205 subjects the physician to suspension or revocation of his license, and subjects any other person obligated to provide information relating to informed consent to criminal penalties. A requirement that the woman give what is truly a voluntary and informed consent, as a general proposition, is, of course, proper and is surely not unconstitutional. But the State may not require the delivery of information designed "to influence the woman's informed choice between abortion or childbirth."

[The Court describes what it calls the *Akron* test by which a state may not subject women to "a litany of information" or "a parade of horribles" designed to influence the woman's choice.]

We conclude that...3205 and 3208 fail the *Akron* measurement. The two sections prescribe in detail the method for securing "informed consent." Seven explicit kinds of information must be delivered to the woman at least 24 hours before her consent is given, and five of these must be presented by the woman's physician. The five are: (a) the name of the physician who will perform the abortion, (b) the "fact that there may be detrimental physical and psychological effects which are not accurately foreseeable," (c) the "particular medical risks associated with the particular abortion procedure to be employed," (d) the probable gestational age, and (e) the "medical risks associated with carrying her child to term." The remaining two categories are (f) the "fact that medical assistance benefits may be available for prenatal care, childbirth and neonatal care," and (g) the "fact that the father is liable to assist" in the child's support, "even in instances where the father has offered to pay for the abortion." The woman also must be informed that materials printed and supplied by the Commonwealth that describe the fetus and that list agencies offering alternatives to abortion are available for her review. If she chooses to review the materials but is unable to read, the materials "shall be read to her," and any answer she seeks must be "provided her in her own language." She must certify in writing, prior to the abortion, that all this has been done. The printed materials "shall include the following statement":

> There are many public and private agencies willing and able to help you to carry your child to term, and to assist you and your child after your child is born, whether you choose to keep your child or place her or him for adoption. The Commonwealth of Pennsylvania strongly urges you to contact them before making a final decision about abortion. The law requires that your physician or his agent give you the opportunity to call agencies like these before you undergo an abortion.

The materials must describe the "probable anatomical and physiological characteristics of the unborn child at two-week gestational increments from fertilization to full term, including any relevant information on the possibility of the unborn child's survival."

In *Akron*, this Court noted: "The validity of an informed consent requirement thus rests on the State's interest in protecting the health of the pregnant woman."... The informational requirements in the *Akron* ordinance were invalid for two "equally decisive" reasons. The first was that "much of the information required is designed not to inform the woman's consent but rather to persuade her to withhold it altogether." The second was that a rigid requirement that a specific body of information be given in all cases, irrespective of the particular needs of the patient, intrudes upon the discretion of the pregnant woman's physician and thereby imposes the "undesired and uncomfortable straitjacket" with which the Court in *Danforth* was concerned.

These two reasons apply with equal and controlling force to the specific and intrusive informational prescriptions of the Pennsylvania statutes. The printed materials...seem to us to be nothing less than an outright attempt to wedge the Commonwealth's message discouraging abortion into the privacy of the informed-consent dialogue between the woman and her physician. The mandated description of fetal characteristics at 2-week intervals, no matter how objective, is plainly overinclusive. This is not medical information that is always relevant to the woman's decision, and it may serve only to confuse and punish her and to heighten her anxiety, contrary to accepted medical practice. Even the listing of agencies in the printed Pennsylvania form presents serious problems; it contains names of agencies that well may be out of step with the needs of the particular woman and thus places the physician in an awkward position and infringes upon his or her professional responsibilities. Forcing the physician or counselor to present the materials and the list to the woman makes him or her in effect an agent of the State in treating the woman and places his or her imprimatur upon both the materials and the list. All this is, or comes close to being, state medicine imposed upon the woman, not the professional medical guidance she seeks, and it officially structures—as it obviously was intended to do—the dialogue between the woman and her physician.

[The Court dismisses for the same reasons the requirement that women be informed of the possibility of financial assistance.]

The requirements that the woman be informed by the physician of "detrimental physical and psychological effects" and of all "particular medical risks" compound the problem of medical attendance, increase the patient's anxiety, and intrude upon the physician's exercise of proper professional judgment. This type of compelled information is the antithesis of informed consent....

2. Sections 3214(a) and (h) (reporting) and 3211(a) (determination of viability). Section 3214(a)(8), part of the general reporting section, incorporates 3211(a). Section 3211(a) requires the physician to report the basis for his determination "that a child is not viable." It applies only after the first trimester. The report required is detailed and must include, among other things, identification of the performing and referring physicians and of the facility or agency; information as to the woman's political subdivision and State of residence, age, race, marital status, and number of prior pregnancies; the date of her last menstrual period and the probable gestational age; the basis for any judgment that a medical emergency existed; the basis for any determination of nonviability; and the method of payment for the abortion. The report is to be signed by the attending physician.

Despite the fact that [the state claims reports will not become public knowledge] each report "shall be made available for public inspection and copying within 15 days of receipt in a form which will not lead to the disclosure of the identity of any person filing a report." Similarly, the report of complications "shall be open to public inspection and copying." A willful failure to file a report required under 3214 is "unprofessional conduct" and the noncomplying physician's license "shall be subject to suspension or revocation."

The scope of the information required and its availability to the public belie any assertions by the Commonwealth that it is advancing any legitimate interest....Pennsylvania would require information as to method of payment, as to the woman's personal history, and as to the bases for medical judgments.

[The Court notes that reporting requirements will be upheld if they meet health-related concerns of the state.]

The required Pennsylvania reports, on the other hand, while claimed not to be "public," are available nonetheless to the public for copying. Moreover, there is no limitation on the use to which the Commonwealth or the public copiers may put them...The decision to terminate a pregnancy is an intensely private one that must be protected in a way that assures anonymity....

A woman and her physician will necessarily be more reluctant to choose an abortion if there exists a possibility that her decision and her identity will become known publicly... We note as we reach this conclusion, that the Court consistently has refused to allow government to chill the exercise of constitutional rights by requiring disclosure of protected, but sometime unpopular, activities....Pennsylvania's reporting requirements raise the specter of public exposure and harassment of women who choose to exercise their personal, intensely private, right, with their physician, to end a pregnancy. Thus, they pose an unacceptable danger of deterring the exercise of that right, and must be invalidated....

3. Section 3210(b) sets forth two independent requirements for a postviability abortion. First, it demands the exercise of that degree of care "which such person would be required to exercise in order to preserve the life and health of any unborn child intended to be born and not aborted." Second, "the abortion technique employed shall be that which would provide the best opportunity for the

unborn child to be aborted alive unless," in the physician's good-faith judgment, that technique "would present a significantly greater medical risk to the life or health of the pregnant woman."...

The Court of Appeals ruled that the [degree of care for postviability abortion] was unconstitutional because it required a "trade off" between the woman's health and fetal survival, and failed to require that maternal health be the physician's paramount consideration. In [a previous case] we the Court recognized the undesirability of any "trade off" between the woman's health and additional percentage points of fetal survival....We agree with the Court of Appeals and therefore find the statute to be facially invalid....

Constitutional rights do not always have easily ascertainable boundaries, and controversy over the meaning of our Nation's most majestic guarantees frequently has been turbulent. As judges, however, we are sworn to uphold the law even when its content gives rise to bitter dispute. We recognized at the very beginning of our opinion in *Roe*, that abortion raises moral and spiritual questions over which honorable persons can disagree sincerely and profoundly. But those disagreements did not then and do not now relieve us of our duty to apply the Constitution faithfully.

Our cases long have recognized that the Constitution embodies a promise that a certain private sphere of individual liberty will be kept largely beyond the reach of government. That promise extends to women as well as to men. Few decisions are more personal and intimate, more properly private, or more basic to individual dignity and autonomy, than a woman's decision—with the guidance of her physician and within the limits specified in *Roe*—whether to end her pregnancy. A woman's right to make that choice freely is fundamental. Any other result, in our view, would protect inadequately a central part of the sphere of liberty that our law guarantees equally to all.

The Court of Appeals correctly invalidated the specified provisions of Pennsylvania's 1982 Abortion Control Act. Its judgment is affirmed. It is so ordered.

JUSTICE WHITE:

Today the Court carries forward the "difficult and continuing venture in substantive due process" that began with the decision in *Roe v. Wade*, and has led the Court further and further afield in the 13 years since that decision was handed down. I was in dissent in *Roe v. Wade* and am in dissent today....

The Court has justified the recognition of a woman's fundamental right to terminate her pregnancy by invoking decisions upholding claims of personal autonomy in connection with the conduct of family life, the rearing of children, marital privacy, the use of contraceptives, and the preservation of the individual's capacity to procreate. Even if each of these cases were correctly decided and could be properly grounded in rights that are "implicit in the concept of ordered liberty" or "deeply rooted in this Nation's history and tradition," the issues [just listed] differ from those at stake where abortion is concerned. As the Court appropriately recognized in *Roe v. Wade*, "[t]he pregnant woman cannot be isolated in her privacy;" the termination of a pregnancy typically involves the destruction of another entity: the fetus. However one answers the metaphysical or theological question whether the fetus is a "human being" or the legal question whether it is a "person" as that term is used in the Constitution, one must at least recognize, first, that the fetus is an entity that bears in its cells all the genetic information that characterizes a member of the species homo sapiens and distinguishes an individual member of that species from all others, and second, that there is no nonarbitrary line separating a fetus from a child or, indeed, an adult human being. Given that the continued existence and development—that is to say, the life—of such an entity are so directly at stake in the woman's decision whether or not to terminate her pregnancy, that decision must be recognized as sui generis, different in kind from the others that the Court has protected under the rubric of person or family privacy and autonomy....

The majority's opinion evinces no deference toward the State's legitimate policy. Rather, the majority makes it clear from the outset that it simply disapproves of any attempt by Pennsylvania to legislate in this area. The history of the state legislature's decade-long effort to pass a constitutional abortion statute is recounted as if it were evidence of some sinister conspiracy. In fact, of course, the legislature's past failure to predict the evolution of the right first recognized in *Roe v. Wade* is understandable and is in itself no ground for condemnation. Moreover, the legislature's willingness to pursue permissible policies through means that go to the limits allowed by existing precedents is no sign of mens rea. The majority, however, seems to find it necessary to respond by changing the rules to invalidate what before would have seemed permissible. The result is a decision that finds no justification in the Court's previous holdings, departs from sound principles of constitutional and statutory interpretation, and unduly limits the State's power to implement the legitimate (and in some circumstances compelling) policy of encouraging normal childbirth in preference to abortion.

The Court begins by striking down statutory provisions designed to ensure that the woman's choice of an abortion is fully informed—that is, that she is aware not only of the reasons for having an abortion, but also of the risks associated with an abortion and the availability of assistance that might make the alternative of normal childbirth more attractive than it might otherwise appear....Indeed, maximization of the patient's freedom of choice—not restriction of his or her liberty—is generally perceived to be the principal value justifying the imposition of disclosure requirements upon physicians....

One searches the majority's opinion in vain for a convincing reason why the apparently laudable policy of promoting informed consent becomes unconstitutional when the subject is abortion. The majority purports to find support in *Akron v. Akron Center for Reproductive Health, Inc.* But *Akron* is not controlling. The informed-consent provisions struck down in that case, as characterized by the majority, required the physician to advance tendentious statements concerning the unanswerable question of when human life begins, to offer merely speculative descriptions of the anatomical features of the fetus carried by the woman seeking the abortion, and to recite a "parade of horribles" suggesting that abortion is "a particularly dangerous procedure." I have no quarrel with the general proposition...that a campaign of state-promulgated disinformation cannot be justified in the name of "informed consent" or "freedom of choice." But the Pennsylvania statute before us cannot be accused of sharing the flaws of the ordinance at issue in *Akron*. As the majority concedes, the statute does not, on its face, require that the patient be given any information that is false or unverifiable. Moreover, it is unquestionable that all of the information required would be relevant in many cases to a woman's decision whether or not to obtain an abortion.

Why, then, is the statute unconstitutional? The majority's argument, while primarily rhetorical, appears to offer three answers. First, the information that must be provided will in some cases be irrelevant to the woman's decision. This is true. Its pertinence to the question of the statute's constitutionality, however, is beyond me. Legislators are ordinarily entitled to proceed on the basis of rational generalizations about the subject matter of legislation, and the existence of particular cases in which a feature of a statute performs no function (or is even counterproductive) ordinarily does not render the statute unconstitutional or even constitutionally suspect. Only where the statute is subject to heightened scrutiny by virtue of its impingement on some fundamental right or its employment of a suspect classification does the imprecision of the "fit" between the statute's ends and means become potentially damning. Here, there is nothing to trigger such scrutiny, for the statute does not directly infringe the allegedly fundamental right at issue—the woman's right to choose an abortion. Indeed, I fail to see how providing a woman with accurate information—whether relevant or irrelevant—could ever be deemed to impair any constitutionally protected interest....

Second, the majority appears to reason that the informed-consent provisions are invalid because the information they require may increase the woman's "anxiety" about the procedure and even "influence" her in her choice. Again, both observations are undoubtedly true; but they by no means cast the constitutionality of the provisions into question. It is in the very nature of informed-consent provisions that they may produce some anxiety in the patient and influence her in her choice. This is in fact their reason for existence, and—provided that the information required is accurate and nonmisleading—it is an entirely salutary reason. If information may reasonably affect the patient's choice, the patient should have that information....

Third, the majority concludes that the informed-consent provisions are invalid because they "intrud[e] upon the discretion of the pregnant woman's physician," violate "the privacy of the informed-consent dialogue between the woman and her physician," and "officially structur[e]" that dialogue. The provisions thus constitute "state medicine" that "infringes upon [the physician's] professional responsibilities." This is nonsensical. I can concede that the Constitution extends its protection to certain zones of personal autonomy and privacy, and I can understand, if not share, the notion that that protection may extend to a woman's decision regarding abortion. But I cannot concede the possibility that the Constitution provides more than minimal protection for the manner in which a physician practices his or her profession or for the "dialogues" in which he or she chooses to participate in the course of treating patients. I had thought it clear that regulation of the practice of medicine, like regulation of other professions and of economic affairs generally, was a matter peculiarly within the competence of legislatures, and that such regulation was subject to review only for rationality.

Were the Court serious about the need for strict scrutiny of regulations that infringe on the "judgment" of medical professionals, "structure" their relations with their patients, and amount to "state medicine," there is no telling how many state and federal statutes (not to mention principles of state tort law) governing the practice of medicine might be condemned. And of course, there would be no reason why a concern for professional freedom could be confined to the medical profession: nothing in the Constitution indicates a preference for the liberty of doctors over that of lawyers, accountants, bakers, or brickmakers. Accordingly, if the State may not "structure" the dialogue between doctor and patient, it should also follow that the State may not, for example, require attorneys to disclose to their clients information concerning the risks of representing the client in a particular proceeding.

The rationale for state efforts to regulate the practice of a profession or vocation is simple: the government is entitled not to trust members of a profession to police themselves, and accordingly the legislature may for the most part impose such restrictions on the practice of a profession or business as it may find necessary to the protection of the public. This is precisely the rationale for infringing the professional freedom of doctors by imposing disclosure requirements upon them: "Respect for the patient's right of self-determination on particular therapy demands a standard set by law for physicians rather than one which physicians may or may not impose upon themselves."...

The majority's decision to strike down the reporting requirements of the statute is equally extraordinary. The requirements obviously serve legitimate purposes. The information contained in the reports is highly relevant to the State's efforts to enforce the statute, which forbids abortion of viable fetuses except when necessary to the mother's health. The information concerning complications plainly serves the legitimate goal of advancing the state of medical knowledge concerning maternal and fetal health. Given that the subject of abortion is a matter of considerable public interest and debate (constrained to some extent, of course, by the pre-emptive effect of this Court's ill-conceived constitutional decisions), the collection and dissemination of demographic information concerning abortions is clearly a legitimate goal of public policy....

[Justice White then spends some time criticizing on procedural grounds the majority's decision to strike down the reporting requirements.]

Finally, in addition to being procedurally flawed, the majority's holding is substantively suspect. The information contained in the reports identifies the patient on the basis of age, race, marital status, and "political subdivision" of residence; the remainder of the information included in the reports concerns the medical aspects of the abortion. It is implausible that a particular patient could be identified on the basis of the combination of the general identifying information and the specific medical information in these reports by anyone who did not already know (at a minimum) that the woman had been pregnant and obtained an abortion. Accordingly, the provisions pose little or no threat to the woman's privacy....

Planned Parenthood of Southeastern Pennsylvania v. Casey
505 U.S. 833 (1992)

Justices O'Connor, Kennedy, and Souter announced the judgment of the Court and delivered the opinion of the Court with respect to select parts, in which Justices Blackmun and Stevens joined. Justice Stevens filed an opinion concurring in part and dissenting in part. Justice Blackmun filed an opinion concurring in part, concurring in the judgment in part, and dissenting in part. Chief Justice Rehnquist filed an opinion concurring in the judgment in part and dissenting in part, in which Justices White, Scalia, and Thomas joined. Justice Scalia filed an opinion concurring in the judgment in part and dissenting in part, in which Chief Justice Rehnquist and Justices White and Thomas joined.

Areas for Discussion and Ethical Reflection

1.   In an early section of their plurality opinion (not included in the excerpt below), Justices O'Connor, Kennedy, and Souter noted that an attorney representing the parties trying to overturn the Pennsylvania statutes asserted at oral arguments that upholding even one of the restrictions would necessarily entail the overturning of *Roe*. What justification might you give for this position? Obviously, the plurality disagreed. Do you think they were correct?

2.   The first sentence of Justices O'Connor, Kennedy, and Souter's opinion is only nine words in length. What does that sentence mean to you? What ethical significance, if any, does the sentence have? Does the sentence make more sense if viewed from a utilitarian framework? Justice Scalia certainly finds the sentence troubling and, at the end of his critique of the sentence, shows his disdain with a reworded version: "Reason finds no refuge in this jurisprudence of confusion." After reading the excerpts below, you might consider with whom you are more sympathetic.

3.   Another sentence written by the plurality also has garnered a great deal of attention. Justices O'Connor, Kennedy, and Souter

assert, "At the heart of liberty is the right to define one's own concept of existence, of meaning, of the universe, and of the mystery of human life." What does this sentence mean to you? Try to discuss the ethical implications of the plurality's assertion for other areas of medical ethics.

4.   What exactly is the undue burden test? Try providing an ethical justification for the test. Does a particular ethical framework—utilitarianism, Kantianism, natural law theory, rights based theory—seem much more supportive of such a test than the others do?

5.   The Court abandons the trimester standard and puts in its place a viability standard for examining state restrictions on abortion. What is the viability standard? Is it a clearer, more morally defensible standard than the trimester framework from *Roe*?

6.   At the very beginning of his opinion (concurring in part and dissenting in part), Justice Stevens asserts that, "…as a matter of federal constitutional law, a developing organism that is not yet a 'person' does not have what is sometimes described as a right to life." By way of support, Justice Stevens in footnote 2 of his opinion quotes at length Ronald Dworkin:

> The suggestion that states are free to declare a fetus a person…assumes that a state can curtail some persons' constitutional rights by adding new persons to the constitutional population. The constitutional rights of one citizen are, of course, very much affected by who or what else also has constitutional rights, because the rights of others may compete or conflict with his. So any power to increase the constitutional population by unilateral decision would be, in effect, a power to decrease rights the national Constitution grants to others…. If a state could declare trees to be persons with a constitutional right to life, it could prohibit publishing newspapers or books in spite of the First Amendment's guarantee of free speech, which could not be understood as

a license to kill....Once we understand that the suggestion
we are considering has that implication, we must reject it.
If a fetus is not part of the constitutional population under
the national constitutional arrangement, then states have no
power to overrule that national arrangement by themselves
declaring that fetuses have rights competitive with the constitutional rights of pregnant women.

What exactly does Dworkin mean by these observations? Why
do you think Justice Stevens cites Dworkin? If our task is to con-
nect judicial decision-making with ethical reflection, what conclusions might we draw regarding how Justice Stevens views the
morality of abortion?

7.   Justice Blackmun, in an opinion concurring in part and dissenting in part (not excerpted below), asserts, "Make no mistake,
the joint opinion of Justices O'Connor, Kennedy, and Souter is
an act of personal courage and constitutional principle." Is the
plurality opinion really an act of courage, personal or otherwise?
The concept of courage occupies a special place in ethics, especially virtue ethics. What does it mean to be courageous, or to
have the virtue of courage? Is it possible to judge that a person
acts courageously, yet immorally? Do you think the justices who
would like to see *Roe* overruled thought the plurality opinion
was a courageous one?

8.   Justice Scalia is quite critical of the plurality opinion in
Casey. He thinks that on the issue of the permissibility of abortion and the permissibility of states restricting a woman's access
to abortion, people in a democracy should strive to convince each
other of their views and then vote. No doubt, Justice Scalia continues, the ability of a woman to abort a fetus is a liberty, but it is
not a liberty protected by the Constitution. Does Justice Scalia's
position emanate from his views on the proper methodology for
interpreting the Constitution? Or, does his position represent his
values and moral commitments regarding abortion? Is it both?
The reader should note that these questions can be asked of al-

most all the justices in almost all the cases we cover in this book.

9.   Suppose the Supreme Court decided to adopt Justice Scalia's view by which the legal permissibility of abortion and the constitutionality of state restrictions on abortion should be left to the voters of the individual states. What impact do you think this would have on the discipline of medical ethics? For example, would articles exploring the dimensions of autonomy, privacy, and bodily integrity (at least as those concepts apply to women) disappear from bioethics textbooks? Does Justice Scalia's position advocating for state control of abortion say anything about his moral commitments?

10.   Up to this point we have not discussed moral issues related to whether minors may terminate their pregnancies or the constitutional concerns raised by state laws prohibiting or severely restricting abortion for minors. The U.S. Supreme Court has ruled on the constitutional questions raised by state laws several times. Relevant Court decisions include: *Planned Parenthood of Central Missouri v. Danforth* 428 U.S. 52 (1976), *Bellotti v. Baird* (*Bellotti* II) 443 U.S. 622 (1979), *H. L. v. Matheson* 450 U.S. 398 (1981), *City of Akron v. Akron Center for Reproductive Health* 462 U.S. 416 (1983), *Hodgson v. Minnesota* 497 U.S. 417 (1990), and, of course, *Casey*. The Court considered such state restrictions of a minor's access to abortion as two-parent notification, one-parent notification, various parental consent statutes, physician involvement in obtaining parental consent, and a judicial bypass provision for minors who, because of emergency or the prospect of harm from parents, could not obtain parental consent. In general, the Supreme Court recognizes that the state has an interest in severely restricting a minor's access to abortion. The Court will normally uphold restrictions on minors as long as a judicial bypass procedure is in place. However, the burden of proof rests with the minor in showing that an abortion is in her best interest. What ethical justifications would you employ in implementing restrictions on minors? Are some restrictions more morally problematic than others? List examples.

11.   As you think about the restrictions on abortion set in place by Pennsylvania's Abortion Control Act, and the motives state legislators had for implementing the statutes, consider the very real possibility that some abortions are truly immoral, or done for trivial reasons. Even the strongest advocate for a woman's right to terminate a pregnancy will admit that such instances of immoral abortion occur. Consider the following example.[4] A woman learns she is pregnant and tells her husband, who is extremely happy. Although the woman is happily married and knows that she and her husband would make excellent parents, she decides to have an abortion. Her reason is that she will be pregnant during the summer and thus unable to wear a bikini. She has never really thought much about fetal development, or personhood, or the sanctity of life (for some reason she never attended a biology, or philosophy, or medical ethics class) and besides, she really loves wearing bikinis. She remains determined even in the face of her husband's promises that he will take care of the baby. Almost everyone would consider abortion under these circumstances immoral, or at least sadly unnecessary. Might a state, Pennsylvania for instance, enact statutes designed to encourage women like our bikini lover to take the abortion decision more seriously? How do you think Justice Stevens would respond to this question?

12.   Neither law nor ethics requires people to be Good Samaritans. That is, we normally are not required to make major sacrifices in order to come to the aid of others. Locate sections in the plurality opinion where the justices seem sensitive to the Good Samaritan concept. Can you provide examples of state restrictions on abortion—past, present, or future—that you would interpret as forcing women to be Good Samaritans?

Justices O'Connor, Kennedy, and Souter:

Liberty finds no refuge in a jurisprudence of doubt. Yet, 19 years after our holding that the Constitution protects a woman's right to terminate her pregnancy in its early stages, that definition of liberty is still questioned. Joining the respondents as amicus curiae, the United States, as it has done in five other cases in the last decade, again asks us to overrule *Roe*.

At issue in these cases are five provisions of the Pennsylvania Abortion Control Act of 1982, as amended in 1988 and 1989. The Act requires that a woman seeking an abortion give her informed consent prior to the abortion procedure, and specifies that she be provided with certain information at least 24 hours before the abortion is performed. For a minor to obtain an abortion, the Act requires the informed consent of one of her parents, but provides for a judicial bypass option if the minor does not wish to or cannot obtain a parent's consent. Another provision of the Act requires that, unless certain exceptions apply, a married woman seeking an abortion must sign a statement indicating that she has notified her husband of her intended abortion. The Act exempts compliance with these three requirements in the event of a "medical emergency," which is defined in §3203 of the Act. In addition to the above provisions regulating the performance of abortions, the Act imposes certain reporting requirements on facilities that provide abortion services....

After considering the fundamental constitutional questions resolved by *Roe,* principles of institutional integrity, and the rule of stare decisis, we are led to conclude this: the essential holding of *Roe v. Wade* should be retained and once again reaffirmed.

It must be stated at the outset and with clarity that *Roe*'s essential holding, the holding we reaffirm, has three parts. First is a recognition of the right of the woman to choose to have an abortion before viability and to obtain it without undue interference from the State. Before viability, the State's interests are not strong enough to support a prohibition of abortion or the imposition of a substantial obstacle to the woman's effective right to elect the procedure. Second is a confirmation of the State's power to restrict abortions after fetal viability if the law contains exceptions for pregnancies which endanger the woman's life or health. And third is the principle that the State has legitimate interests from the outset of the pregnancy in protecting the health of the woman and the life of the fetus that may become a child. These principles do not contradict one another; and we adhere to each....

Men and women of good conscience can disagree, and we suppose some always shall disagree, about the profound moral and spiritual implications of terminating a pregnancy, even in its earliest stage. Some of us as individuals find abortion offensive to our most basic principles of morality, but that cannot control our decision. Our obligation is to define the liberty of all, not to mandate our own moral code. The underlying constitutional issue is whether the State can resolve these philosophic questions in such a definitive way that a woman lacks all choice in the matter, except perhaps in those rare circumstances in which the pregnancy is itself a danger to her own life or health, or is the result of rape or incest....At the heart of liberty is the right to define one's own concept of existence, of meaning, of the universe, and of the mystery of human life. Beliefs about these matters could not define the attributes of personhood were they formed under compulsion of the State.

These considerations begin our analysis of the woman's interest in terminating her pregnancy, but cannot end it, for this reason: though the abortion decision may originate within the zone of conscience and belief, it is more than a philosophic exercise. Abortion is a unique act. It is an act fraught with consequences for others: for the woman who must live with the implications of her decision; for the persons who perform and assist in the procedure; for the spouse, family, and society which must confront the knowledge that these procedures exist, procedures some deem nothing short of an act of violence against innocent human life; and, depending on one's beliefs, for the life or potential life that is aborted. Though abortion is conduct, it does not follow that the State is entitled to proscribe it in all instances. That is because the liberty of the woman is at stake in a sense unique to the human condition, and so, unique to the law. The mother who carries a child to full term is subject to anxieties, to physical constraints, to pain that only she must bear.

That these sacrifices have from the beginning of the human race been endured by woman with a pride that ennobles her in the eyes of others and gives to the infant a bond of love cannot alone be grounds for the State to insist she make the sacrifice. Her suffering is too intimate and personal for the State to insist, without more, upon its own vision of the woman's role, however dominant that vision has been in the course of our history and our culture. The destiny of the woman must be shaped to a large extent on her own conception of her spiritual imperatives and her place in society....

From what we have said so far, it follows that it is a constitutional liberty of the woman to have some freedom to terminate her pregnancy. We conclude that the basic decision in *Roe* was based on a constitutional analysis which we cannot now repudiate. The woman's liberty is not so unlimited, however, that, from the outset, the State cannot show its concern for the life of the unborn and, at a later point in fetal development, the State's interest in life has sufficient force so that the right of the woman to terminate the pregnancy can be restricted....

We conclude the line should be drawn at viability, so that, before that time, the woman has a right to choose to terminate her pregnancy. We adhere to this principle for two reasons. First, as we have said, is the doctrine of stare decisis. Any judicial act of line-drawing may seem some-what arbitrary, but *Roe* was a reasoned statement, elaborated with great care. We have twice reaffirmed it in the face of great opposition. Although we must overrule those parts of *Thornburgh* and *Akron I* which, in our view, are inconsistent with *Roe*'s statement that the State has a legitimate interest in promoting the life or potential life of the unborn, the central premise of those cases represents an unbroken commitment by this Court to the essential holding of *Roe*. It is that premise which we reaffirm today.

The second reason is that the concept of viability, as we noted in *Roe*, is the time at which there is a realistic possibility of maintaining and nourishing a life outside the womb, so that the independent existence of the second life can, in reason and all fairness, be the object of state protection that now overrides the rights of the woman. Consistent with other constitutional norms, legislatures may draw lines which appear arbitrary without the necessity of offering a justification. But courts may not. We must justify the lines we draw. And there is no line other than viability which is more workable....

The woman's right to terminate her pregnancy before viability is the most central principle of *Roe v. Wade*. It is a rule of law and a component of liberty we cannot renounce.

Yet it must be remembered that *Roe v. Wade* speaks with clarity in establishing not only the woman's liberty but also the State's "important and legitimate interest in potential life." That portion of the decision in *Roe* has been given too little acknowledgment and implementation by the Court in its subsequent cases. Those cases decided that any regulation touching upon the abortion decision must survive strict scrutiny, to be sustained only if drawn in narrow terms to further a compelling state interest. Not all of the cases decided under that formulation can be reconciled with the holding in *Roe* itself that the State has legitimate interests in the health of the woman and in protecting the potential life within her. In resolving this tension, we choose to rely upon *Roe,* as against the later cases.

[The Court briefly discusses the trimester framework and its impact on state regulation of abortion.]

Though the woman has a right to choose to terminate or continue her pregnancy before viability, it does not at all follow that the State is prohibited from taking steps to ensure that this choice is thoughtful and informed. Even in the earliest stages of pregnancy, the State may enact rules and regulations designed to encourage her to know that there are philosophic and social arguments of great weight that can be brought to bear in favor of continuing the pregnancy to full term, and that there are procedures and institutions to allow adoption of unwanted children as well as a certain degree of state assistance if the mother chooses to raise the child herself. "[T]he Constitution does not forbid a State or city, pursuant to democratic processes, from expressing a preference for normal childbirth." It follows that States are free to enact laws to provide a reasonable framework for a woman to make a decision that has such profound and lasting meaning. This, too, we find consistent with *Roe*'s central premises, and indeed the inevitable consequence of our holding that the State has an interest in protecting the life of the unborn.

We reject the trimester framework, which we do not consider to be part of the essential holding of *Roe*. Measures aimed at ensuring that a woman's choice contemplates the consequences for the fetus do not necessarily interfere with the right recognized in *Roe*, although those measures have been found to be inconsistent with the rigid trimester framework announced in that case. A logical reading of the central holding in *Roe* itself, and a necessary reconciliation of the liberty of the woman and the interest of the State in promoting prenatal life, require, in our view, that we abandon the trimester framework as a rigid prohibition on all pre-viability regulation aimed at the protection of fetal life. The trimester framework suffers from these basic flaws: in its formulation, it misconceives the nature of the pregnant woman's interest; and in practice, it undervalues the State's interest in potential life, as recognized in *Roe....*

Numerous forms of state regulation might have the incidental effect of increasing the cost or decreasing the availability of medical care, whether for abortion or any other medical procedure. The fact that a law which serves a valid purpose, one not designed to strike at the right itself, has the incidental effect of making it more difficult or more expensive to procure an abortion cannot be enough to invalidate it. Only where state regulation imposes an undue burden on a woman's ability to make this decision does the power of the State reach into the heart of the liberty protected by the Due Process Clause....

These considerations of the nature of the abortion right illustrate that it is an overstatement to describe it as a right to decide whether to have an abortion "without interference from the State." All abortion regulations interfere to some degree with a woman's ability to decide whether to terminate her pregnancy. It is, as a consequence, not surprising that, despite the protestations contained in the original *Roe* opinion to the effect that the Court was not recognizing an absolute right, the Court's experience applying the trimester framework has led to the striking down of some abortion regulations which in no real sense deprived women of the ultimate decision. Those decisions went too far, because the right recognized by *Roe* is a right to be free from unwarranted governmental intrusion into matters so fundamentally affecting a person as the decision whether to bear or beget a child. Not all governmental intrusion is, of necessity, unwarranted, and that brings us to the other basic flaw in the trimester framework: even in *Roe*'s terms, in practice, it undervalues the State's interest in the potential life within the woman....

The very notion that the State has a substantial interest in potential life leads to the conclusion that not all regulations must be deemed unwarranted. Not all burdens on the right to decide whether to terminate a pregnancy will be undue. In our view, the undue burden standard is the appropriate means of reconciling the State's interest with the woman's constitutionally protected liberty....

A finding of an undue burden is a shorthand for the conclusion that a state regulation has the purpose or effect of placing a substantial obstacle in the path of a woman seeking an abortion of a nonviable fetus. A statute with this purpose is invalid because the means chosen by the State to further the interest in potential life must be calculated to inform the woman's free choice, not hinder it. And a statute which, while furthering the interest in potential life or some other valid state interest, has the effect of placing a substantial obstacle in the path of a woman's choice cannot be considered a permissible means of serving its legitimate ends...In our considered judgment, an undue burden is an unconstitutional burden. Understood another way, we answer the question, left open in previous opinions discussing the undue burden formulation, whether a law designed to further the State's interest in fetal life which imposes an undue burden on the woman's decision before fetal viability could be constitutional. The answer is no.

Some guiding principles should emerge. What is at stake is the woman's right to make the ultimate decision, not a right to be insulated from all others in doing so. Regulations which do no more than create a structural mechanism by which the State, or the parent or guardian of a minor, may express profound respect for the life of the unborn are permitted, if they are not a substantial obstacle to the woman's exercise of the right to choose. Unless it has that effect on her right of choice, a state measure designed to persuade her to choose childbirth over abortion will be upheld if reasonably related to that goal. Regulations designed to foster the health of a woman seeking an abortion are valid if they do not constitute an undue burden....

JUSTICE STEVENS:

My disagreement with the joint opinion begins with its understanding of the trimester framework established in *Roe*. Contrary to the suggestion of the joint opinion, it is not a "contradiction" to recognize that the State may have a legitimate interest in potential human life and, at the same time, to conclude that that interest does not justify the regulation of abortion before viability (although other interests, such as maternal health, may). The fact that the State's interest is legitimate does not tell us when, if ever, that interest outweighs the pregnant woman's interest in personal liberty. It is appropriate, therefore, to consider more carefully the nature of the interests at stake.

First, it is clear that, in order to be legitimate, the State's interest must be secular; consistent with the First Amendment, the State may not promote a theological or sectarian interest. Moreover, the state interest in potential human life is not an interest in loco parentis, for the fetus is not a person.

Identifying the State's interests—which the States rarely articulate with any precision—makes clear that the interest in protecting potential life is not grounded in the Constitution. It is, instead, an indirect interest supported by both humanitarian and pragmatic concerns. Many of our citizens believe that any abortion reflects an unacceptable disrespect for potential human life, and that the performance of more than a million abortions each year is intolerable; many find third-trimester abortions performed when the fetus is approaching personhood particularly offensive. The

State has a legitimate interest in minimizing such offense. The State may also have a broader interest in expanding the population, believing society would benefit from the services of additional productive citizens—or that the potential human lives might include the occasional Mozart or Curie. These are the kinds of concerns that comprise the State's interest in potential human life.

In counterpoise is the woman's constitutional interest in liberty. One aspect of this liberty is a right to bodily integrity, a right to control one's person. This right is neutral on the question of abortion: the Constitution would be equally offended by an absolute requirement that all women undergo abortions as by an absolute prohibition on abortions. "Our whole constitutional heritage rebels at the thought of giving government the power to control men's minds." The same holds true for the power to control women's bodies.

The woman's constitutional liberty interest also involves her freedom to decide matters of the highest privacy and the most personal nature....

Weighing the State's interest in potential life and the woman's liberty interest, I agree with the joint opinion that the State may "expres[s] a preference for normal childbirth," that the State may take steps to ensure that a woman's choice "is thoughtful and informed," and that States are free to enact laws to provide a reasonable framework for a woman to make a decision that has such profound and lasting meaning. Serious questions arise, however, when a State attempts to "persuade the woman to choose childbirth over abortion." Decisional autonomy must limit the State's power to inject into a woman's most personal deliberations its own views of what is best. The State may promote its preferences by funding childbirth, by creating and maintaining alternatives to abortion, and by espousing the virtues of family; but it must respect the individual's freedom to make such judgments.

[Justice Stevens then notes that he would distinguish between those Pennsylvania statutes that require women to receive information intended to dissuade abortion from those statutes intended to truly inform women about the procedure. Justice Stevens would find only the latter constitutional.]

The 24-hour waiting period required by the Pennsylvania statute raises even more serious concerns. Such a requirement arguably furthers the Commonwealth's interests in two ways, neither of which is constitutionally permissible.

First, it may be argued that the 24-hour delay is justified by the mere fact that it is likely to reduce the number of abortions, thus furthering the Commonwealth's interest in potential life. But such an argument would justify any form of coercion that placed an obstacle in the woman's path. The Commonwealth cannot further its interests by simply wearing down the ability of the pregnant woman to exercise her constitutional right.

Second, it can more reasonably be argued that the 24-hour delay furthers the Commonwealth's interest in ensuring that the woman's decision is informed and thoughtful. But there is no evidence that the mandated delay benefits women, or that it is necessary to enable the physician to convey any relevant information to the patient. The mandatory delay thus appears to rest on outmoded and unacceptable assumptions about the decision-making capacity of women....Just as we have left behind the belief that a woman must consult her husband before undertaking serious matters, so we must reject the notion that a woman is less capable of deciding matters of gravity.

In the alternative, the delay requirement may be premised on the belief that the decision to terminate a pregnancy is presumptively wrong. This premise is illegitimate. Those who disagree vehemently about the legality and morality of abortion agree about one thing: the decision to terminate a pregnancy is profound and difficult. No person undertakes such a decision lightly—and States may not presume that a woman has failed to reflect adequately merely because her conclusion differs from the State's preference. A woman who has, in the privacy of her thoughts and conscience, weighed the options and made her decision cannot be forced to reconsider all, simply because the State believes she has come to the wrong conclusion.

Part of the constitutional liberty to choose is the equal dignity to which each of us is entitled. A woman who decides to terminate her pregnancy is entitled to the same respect as a woman who decides to carry the fetus to term. The mandatory waiting period denies women that equal respect.

In my opinion, a correct application of the "undue burden" standard leads to the same conclusion concerning the constitutionality of these requirements. A state-imposed burden on the exercise of a constitutional right is measured both by its effects and by its character: a burden may be "undue" either because the burden is too severe or because it lacks a legitimate, rational justification.

The 24-hour delay requirement fails both parts of this test. The findings of the District Court establish the severity of the burden that the 24-hour delay imposes on many pregnant women. Yet even in those cases in which the delay is not especially onerous, it is, in my opinion, "undue," because there is no evidence that such a delay serves a useful and legitimate purpose. As indicated above, there is no legitimate reason to require a woman who has agonized over her decision to leave the clinic or hospital and return again another day. While a general requirement that a physician notify her patients about the risks of a proposed medical procedure is appropriate, a rigid requirement that all patients wait 24 hours or (what is true in practice) much longer to evaluate the significance of information that is either common knowledge or irrelevant is an irrational, and therefore "undue," burden.

The counseling provisions are similarly infirm. Whenever government commands private citizens to speak or to listen, careful review of the justification for that command is particularly appropriate. In this case, the Pennsylvania statute directs that counselors provide women seeking abortions with information concerning alternatives to abortion, the availability of medical assistance benefits, and the possibility of child support payments. The statute requires that this information be given to all women seeking abortions, including those for whom such information is clearly useless, such as those who are married, those who have undergone the procedure in the past and are fully aware of the options, and those who are fully convinced that abortion is their only reasonable option. Moreover, the statute requires physicians to inform all of their patients of "[t]he probable gestational age of the unborn child." This information is of little decisional value in most cases, because 90% of all abortions are performed during the first trimester, when fetal age has less relevance than when the fetus nears viability. Nor can the information required by the statute be justified as relevant to any "philosophic" or "social" argument, either favoring or disfavoring the abortion decision in a particular case. In light of all of these facts, I conclude that the information requirements in [the provisions] do not serve a useful purpose, and thus constitute an unnecessary—and therefore undue—burden on the woman's constitutional liberty to decide to terminate her pregnancy....

Justice Scalia:

...The States may, if they wish, permit abortion on demand, but the Constitution does not require them to do so. The permissibility of abortion, and the limitations upon it, are to be resolved like most important questions in our democracy: by citizens trying to persuade one another and then voting. As the Court acknowledges, "where reasonable people disagree, the government can adopt one position or the other." The Court is correct in adding the qualification that this "assumes a state of affairs in which the choice does not intrude upon a protected liberty"—but the crucial part of that qualification is the penultimate word. A State's choice between two positions on which reasonable people can disagree is constitutional even when (as is often the case) it intrudes upon a "liberty" in the absolute sense. Laws against bigamy, for example—with which entire societies of reasonable people disagree—intrude upon men and women's liberty to marry and live with one another. But bigamy happens not to be a liberty specially "protected" by the Constitution.

That is, quite simply, the issue in this case: not whether the power of a woman to abort her unborn child is a "liberty" in the absolute sense; or even whether it is a liberty of great importance to many women. Of course it is both. The issue is whether it is a liberty protected by the Constitution of the United States. I am sure it is not. I reach that conclusion not because of anything so exalted as my views concerning the "concept of existence, of meaning, of the universe, and of the mystery of human life." Rather, I reach it for the same reason I reach the conclusion that bigamy is not constitutionally protected—because of two simple facts: (1) the Constitution says absolutely nothing about it, and (2) the longstanding traditions of American society have permitted it to be legally proscribed....

Notes

1.   Judith Jarvis Thomson, "A Defense of Abortion," in *Ethical Issues in Modern Medicine*, 6th ed., edited by Bonnie Steinbock et al. (Boston: McGraw Hill, 2003), pp. 483–92.

2.   Ibid., pp. 489–90.

3.   For a detailed explanation and support of this view see Sidney Callahan, "A Case for Pro-Life Feminism," in *Intervention and Reflection: Basic Issues in Medical Ethics*, 6th ed., edited by Ronald Munson (Belmont, CA: Wadsworth, 2000), pp. 116–22.

4.   Bonnie Steinbock, "Why Most Abortions Are Not Wrong," in *Ethical Issues in Modern Medicine*, p. 480.

For Further Reading

Annas, George J. "*Roe v. Wade* Reaffirmed Again." *Hastings Center Report* 16 (1986): 26–27.

Callahan, Sidney. "A Case for Pro-Life Feminism." In *Intervention and Reflection: Basic Issues in Medical Ethics*, 6th edition, Ronald Munson, ed. Belmont, CA: Wadsworth, 2000.

Dworkin, Ronald. *Life's Dominion: An Argument about Abortion, Euthanasia, and Individual Freedom*. New York: Knopf, 1993.

Epstein, Lee, and Joseph Kobylka. *The Supreme Court & Legal Change: Abortion and the Death Penalty*. Chapel Hill: University of North Carolina Press, 1992.

Steinbock, Bonnie. "Why Most Abortions Are Not Wrong." In *Ethical Issues in Modern Medicine*, 6th edition, Bonnie Steinbock et al., eds. New York: McGraw-Hill, 2003.

Thomson, Judith Jarvis. "A Defense of Abortion." In *Ethical Issues in Modern Medicine*.

CHAPTER FIVE

THE RELIGIOUS OBJECTIONS TO MEDICAL TREATMENT AND PUBLIC HEALTH CASES

It is at most a small exaggeration to say that legal rules and litigation have become Americans' civil religion and that if we share one sacred text, it is our Constitution. Whether the issue is abortion, race discrimination, sexual harassment, the environment, criminal justice, religious liberty, freedom of speech, or almost any other aspect of how we live and even how we die, Americans have come almost routinely to expect the courts, especially the Supreme Court, to take sides on every issue of national urgency and help resolve our most vexing social problems.

—Edward Lazarus, *Closed Chambers: The Rise, Fall, and Future of the Modern Supreme Court*

Although the two cases covered in this chapter are not recent—the first is one hundred years old and the second is sixty—they are two of the most often cited cases in the context of religious objections to medical interventions and in the area of public health. Medical interventions, whether designed to benefit one person or an entire community, often can be intrusive, costly, painful, or even deeply offensive to one's (or a community's) sincerely held religious beliefs. On occasion rational adults do refuse medical treatment, thus running the risk of death. Also, there are instances when parents will refuse, usually for religious reasons, to grant permission for their children to receive medical treatment, knowing that such refusal may well result in the child's death. Respect for the preservation of autonomy, bodily integrity, and parental rights come into direct conflict with obligations on the part of the state to protect and promote the welfare of children and that of the community. The ethical and constitutional issues raised by the refusal of medical interventions—especially when such refusal adversely affects the community or young children—are dramatic and demand careful attention by policy makers and health care professionals. The two influential Supreme Court cases excerpted in this chapter provide an excellent opportunity to grapple with ethical issues surrounding the concept of paternalism, the harm principle, (these two are covered in chapter 7) the protection of the welfare of children, and the protection of the health and safety of the community. Medical ethics, at both the clinical and public policy levels, has certainly been impacted by the deliberations of the justices in these early cases.

Constitutional Issues and Background

Our first case, *Jacobson v. Commonwealth of Massachusetts*, has significantly impacted medical ethics, especially in the areas of refusal by adults of medical treatment and state legislation to promote public health. In 1902, Cambridge, Massachusetts, enacted a regulation whereby all residents over the age of twenty-one would be vaccinated against smallpox. The board of health of Cambridge empowered a physician to enforce the regulation. On July 17th, 1902, Henning Jacobson refused to be vaccinated and subsequently was arraigned. After pleading not guilty, Jacobson asked the trial judge to give the jury several reasons in support of his acquittal. Jacobson argued that he did not have to comply with the mandatory vaccination regulation, because such a regulation violated the privileges and immunities clause, the Due Process Clause, and the Equal Protection of the Laws provision of the Fourteenth Amendment. Jacobson was claiming, among other things, that his religious beliefs did not allow him to receive vaccinations and, in any case, that every person has a right to control his own body even against the dictates of the state. The judge refused to give the jury Jacobson's instructions and he was subsequently found guilty. On appeal, the Supreme Judicial Court of Massachusetts affirmed.

At issue in *Jacobson* was the First Amendment to the Federal Constitution, which begins, "Congress shall make no law respecting an establishment of religion, or prohibiting the free exercise thereof...." Both the first part of this provision—called the establishment clause—and the second part—called the free exercise clause—are applicable to the states as well as the federal government. On first appearance a certain degree of tension or conflict exists between the two clauses: The first prohibits the establishment of a religion while the second prohibits state interference with the practice of religion. In the areas of constitutional law and interpretation the Supreme Court addresses this tension by asserting that state and federal governments should enact only laws and regulations that meet secular goals and that such goals should be achieved in a way that is as religiously neutral as possible.[1] The free exercise clause was at issue in *Jacobson* in that the Court had to balance the right to practice freely one's religious beliefs with the obligations of the state to protect public welfare. A majority of the justices found that the state's interest outweighed Jacobson's freedom to refuse vaccination on religious grounds and that the state could use its police power to enforce the vaccination law.

As with *Jacobson*, overemphasizing the significance of our second case for medical ethics is almost impossible. *Prince v. Commonwealth of Massachusetts* has special relevance for examining and applying ethical concepts and principles surrounding refusal of life-saving interventions by children or by parents on behalf of their children. In 1941, Sarah Prince was a Jehovah's Witness living in Brockton, Massachusetts. She had two sons, and she was the aunt and guardian of nine-year-old Betty Simons. Ms. Prince was in the habit of distributing Jehovah's Witness publications on the streets of Brockton and sometimes allowed the children to accompany her. On the night of December 18, 1941, she and Betty went to a street corner where they began preaching and handing out religious publications. When a school officer approached Ms. Prince to ask Betty's name and age, she refused to tell him. Ms. Prince insisted that she and Betty were doing God's work and had a right to be on the street. The school officer reminded Ms. Prince that she had been warned several times to stop allowing the children to distribute religious literature on the streets, and he reminded her that she was prohibited from allowing the children to engage in such activities. Ms. Prince was charged and found guilty of violating Massachusetts' child labor laws.

Again the High Court had to consider the free exercise clause of the First Amendment; in addition, the Court considered Ms. Prince's claim that Massachusetts was interfering with her parental rights, which in turn were guaranteed by the Due Process Clause of the Fourteenth Amendment. Rights associated with parental discretion were in direct conflict with state obligations to protect children from harm. A majority of the justices concluded that neither the free exercise clause nor the Due Process Clause outweighed the state's obligations to protect the welfare of children. As with *Jacobson*, the Supreme Court struggled over legitimate use of the state's police power.

Ethical Issues and Background

Jacobson and *Prince* afford us an opportunity to evaluate arguments of the justices that continue to have a dramatic impact on dilemmas in medical ethics. Refusal by adults of life-saving medical interventions, parental refusal of medical treatment for children, and government interventions, directed at both individuals and groups, designed to protect or promote the public's health, raise many troubling ethical and constitutional issues. We begin to understand and appreciate the significance of our two cases for the relationship between medical ethics and constitutional law by briefly discussing the concept of competency, issues surrounding parental responsibility, and ethical and public policy standards surrounding the permissibility of coercive public health measures. These three areas—competency, parental responsibility, and standards for protecting public health—play a major role in the justices' deliberations. Assessing how well the justices understand and employ these concepts is, of course, quite enlightening. In addition, much of the material outlined below will be relevant to your study of issues surrounding physician-assisted suicide in chapter 9.

Earlier considerations of autonomy in this book, both by the justices and in the background material, lead naturally to the conclusion that competent adults may decline medical interventions, even if death is the result. And indeed, medical ethics, the common law, and constitutional law are in agreement that autonomy, privacy, and informed consent (refusal) are controlling principles here. However, the situation is not as clear-cut as it may first appear. When ethical and legal problems surrounding refusal of medical interventions by adults arise, they do so usually in the context of questions and concerns over whether the individual's refusal constitutes a genuinely rational, competent, autonomous decision. Concerns over competency and rationality usually occur on those occasions when an individual's expressed choice or preference is radically different from what we believe we would choose under identical circumstances. As we have noted previously, it is one thing to acknowledge that we ought to honor the autonomous, rational choices of others; it is quite another to actually honor those choices.

Consider one of the most famous cases of treatment refusal by an adult in medical ethics.[2] On a July afternoon in 1973, in east Texas, Donald (Dax) Cowart and his father were looking at a piece of land Dax was considering buying. Dax was twenty-five years old, had served in the air force, and was working for his father in real estate while waiting for an opening to be a commercial airline pilot. As Dax tried to start the car, gas from a leak in a propane gas transmission line ignited. The blast and resulting fire were tremendous. Dax's father died on the way to the hospital and Dax received serious injuries. He suffered third-degree burns over 65 percent of his body, both ears were destroyed, one eye had to be surgically removed, the other became useless, his fingers were burned off, and he suffered horrible pain for more than a year. Even as an ambulance was taking him and his father to the hospital, Dax begged to be killed. His requests to be allowed to die continued during months of painful treatment for his burns. Two psychiatric consults concluded that Dax was rational. Yet throughout Dax's ordeal, various physicians refused to grant his request to terminate treatment and let him die.

The Dax Cowart story raises many ethical questions. Were Dax's persistent and continued requests to be allowed to die rational? What criteria should physicians and judges use in determining rationality? How strongly should physicians and judges value autonomy? Is respect for autonomy so important that physicians ought to let patients make "wrong" decisions? If we somehow could be sure that in the future a patient would be grateful to be alive, does that justify violating the patient's autonomy in the present? Who is the best judge of what is in the patient's best interest? The import of these questions can be expressed in the following observation: "Not to respect a patient's freedom is undoubtedly wrong. But to respect what may be an expression of freedom only in appearance would be a violation of another basic principle of ethical medicine: promotion of the patient's well-being."[3]

Judgments regarding competence to refuse treatment as well as judgments regarding what is in the patient's best interests or will promote her/his well-being are notoriously difficult to make and defend. Competency determinations usually address such factors as accurate understanding of the present situation, accurate appreciation of the consequences of various actions or inactions, absence of clinically diagnosed depression or mental illness, and absence of unwarranted fears. Determinations of best interest are just as controversial. Some will argue that simply being alive is in the patient's best interest. Others strongly disagree and argue for a focus on expected quality of life, with the judgment being made by the patient or family members. But, of course, quality of life assessments carry their own conceptual problems.

Very little of what the justices have to say in either *Jacobson* or *Prince* directly addresses the issue of whether to honor refusal of life-saving treatment by adults. However, both cases do address issues surrounding the autonomy and competency of adults and hence are indirectly relevant to more modern concerns. You will note that in *Jacobson*, Justice Harlan argues that society is not necessarily obligated to honor an adult's refusal of a medical intervention, even a refusal that is clearly autonomous and rational. More will be said on this below when we examine standards for justifying coercive public health measures. We turn now to a concern in clinical ethics that has been directly impacted by the decision in *Prince*: what justifications, if any, would permit a state to intervene in a parental refusal of medical treatment for their children.

In both ethics and law, two views of parental responsibility toward children are dominant. First, springing from the values of protecting and promoting family privacy and autonomy, parents enjoy wide latitude in raising their children in the manner they deem most appropriate. Such freedom not only protects important values of privacy and independence; it also results in beneficial consequences for society. Second, parents have obligations to prevent unnecessary harm from occurring to their children. Children are generally recognized by both law and ethics to be incompetent and thus vulnerable to various physical, emotional, and mental harms. Generally, these two views of parental rights and responsibilities work very well together. Conflict occurs, however, when parents, usually out of genuinely held religious reasons, refuse medical treatment for their children. When this happens, our two views come into conflict. This conflict raises dramatic and immediate concerns for both constitutional law and medical ethics. On what grounds may the state impose its authority over parental discretion? On what grounds may health care professionals impose medical interventions on children against the wishes of parents?

When Justice Rutledge, in *Prince v. Commonwealth of Massachusetts*, declared that parents are not free to make martyrs of their children, he and the U.S. Supreme Court provided both constitutional and moral justification for limits on parental authority. This justification is in place today and serves as the foundation for invalidating parental discretion when the lives of their children are in jeopardy. The justices concluded that the state has an obligation to identify and protect the best interests of children. Clearly, receiving medical treatment that will prevent premature death or serious debilitation is in the child's best interest. Children, once they have matured, are certainly free to disagree with judgments of the state and the medical profession, but that is exactly the point. Until they are able to exercise autonomous discretion, neither children nor their parents should be allowed to make choices that will preclude future choices.

Most health care professionals are in agreement that on occasion parental authority should be overridden. Some professional organizations have attempted to provide concrete guidance to health care workers when they are confronted with a case of parental refusal. In its document, "Religious Objections to Medical Care," the American Academy of Pediatrics Committee on Bioethics recommends that health care professionals report to child protective service agencies or the courts instances of parental refusal involving "medical interventions of clear efficacy that can prevent, ameliorate, or cure serious disease, incapacity, or loss of life and interventions that will clearly result in prevention of future handicaps or disability for the child."[4] As you read *Prince*, search for other arguments that might be relevant to medical ethics.

Children are not the only ones government may have an obligation to protect. The task of detailing under what circumstances, if any, government may interfere with the liberty of action of individuals in order to promote public welfare has come before the Court many times. *Jacobson v. Commonwealth of Massachusetts* is probably the best example of how the Supreme Court has blended constitutional and ethical concerns in the public health context. Lawrence O. Gostin notes that the *Jacobson* Court articulated four standards for determining when public health authorities may override the choices of individuals.[5] First, states may act only from necessity; that is, the measures taken must be necessary to prevent an avoidable harm. Second, states may exercise only reasonable means. Even if government has a valid goal, the methods for achieving that goal must be reasonable in that they must not constitute a blatant violation of individual rights. Third, states must exercise proportionality. The burdens imposed by government on individuals must be proportional to the expected benefit. The fourth standard used by the majority in *Jacobson* in judging the constitutionality of public health regulations is harm avoidance. A measure used by public health officials must not pose an undue risk on the individual to whom the measure is directed. As you read Justice Harlan's opinion, try to identify each of these four standards and the arguments he uses in their defense. You may wish to return to *Jacobson* and *Prince* after reviewing discussions of paternalism and the harm principle included in chapter 7.

Jacobson v. Commonwealth of Massachusetts
197 U.S. 11 (1905)

Justice Harlan delivered the opinion of the Court.

Areas for Discussion and Ethical Reflection

1.   Justice Harlan begins his opinion by noting that, under the police power, a state has the authority to "enact quarantine laws and health laws of every description." What constitutional justification does Justice Harlan offer? What ethical justification does he offer? Are there similarities between the two?

2.   After reading Justice Harlan's decision, are you able to judge whether Henning Jacobson's refusal of the vaccination was rational? Physicians are well aware of the public health benefits of many medical treatments and they are also aware that many of

their patients could care less about public health. Brock and Wartman employ the concept of the "prevention paradox"[6] to describe occurrences in which physicians offer patients a treatment that benefits both the patient and the community, but the patient finds the treatment not worth the trouble. Brock and Wartman assert that a patient's choice to decline such a treatment does not constitute grounds upon which to judge the patient irrational. However, they are quick to point out that there is no absolute obligation to honor even the rational choices of individuals. You should find Justice Harlan's observations enlightening on this point.

3.   On first appearance at least Justice Harlan's reasoning in support of the Massachusetts statute conforms to rule utilitarianism. Formulate as clearly as possible the rule utilitarian justification for compulsory vaccination of adults. Can you give a Kantian rationale for a program of mandatory vaccination? If both theories would find such programs morally permissible, where exactly do they differ?

4.   Justice Harlan acknowledges that there could be instances in which government, in an effort to protect the health and safety of its citizens, enacts legislation that is arbitrary and unreasonable, either in general or with respect to certain groups of people. How should we decide what regulations count as arbitrary or unreasonable? Justice Harlan does provide an answer to this question. What ethical problems does his answer raise?

5.   Do you detect in Justice Harlan's opinion a justification (constitutional or moral) for allowing competent adults to refuse medical treatment even when doing so would not jeopardize the public's health in any way? Can you determine whether Justice Harlan would make a moral distinction between, on the one hand, refusal of treatment where the benefits to the patient are great and the risks are low and, on the other, refusal of treatment where the benefits to the patient are minimal and the risks are great? Of course, keep in mind that Justice Harlan was writing long before society and medical ethicists became interested in issues surrounding refusal of treatment by adults.

6.   Imagine an emergency room physician working in a hospital in a large urban area. In the event of a large-scale biological weapons attack, this hospital and this physician are responsible for treating thousands of victims. Because smallpox is likely to be the weapon of choice for terrorists launching such an attack, all physicians on the "front lines" are asked to inoculate themselves against smallpox so that they can aid as many people as possible. Such inoculations are not without risk: a very small number of people will get sick and an even smaller number will die. Now imagine this physician refusing to be vaccinated for smallpox. What guidance does Justice Harlan's opinion provide here? Would the physician's motives for refusal matter to Justice Harlan? Would it matter to you?

7.   At the end of 2002, the Bush administration implemented a vaccination plan for smallpox covering military personnel, health care workers, and members of police and fire departments. Inoculation is voluntary for health care workers and first-responders but mandatory for the military. The administration had hoped that 450,000 health care workers would be vaccinated by the end of January 2003. Figures indicate, however, that by the end of February, only 1 percent of that number had been vaccinated. In an effort to persuade people to undergo the vaccination, Congress in April 2003 passed a compensation package for any health care professional who becomes ill or dies after receiving the vaccination.[7] What are the ethical arguments for and against a nationwide plan for vaccinating health care professionals? Should Congress have passed a compensation package for health care professionals? What is it about the nature of medicine and the ethical obligations of the medical profession that might lead you to believe that health care workers have an obligation to participate in the vaccination plan whether or not a compensation package exists? You might wish to return to this item after reviewing the goals of medicine outlined in chapter 7.

JUSTICE HARLAN:

...The authority of the state to enact this statute is to be referred to what is commonly called the police power—a power which the state did not surrender when becoming a member of the Union under the Constitution. Although this court has refrained from any attempt to define the limits of that power, yet it has distinctly recognized the authority of a state to enact quarantine laws and health laws of every description; indeed, all laws that relate to matters completely within its territory and which do not by their necessary operation affect the people of other states. According to settled principles, the police power of a state must be held to embrace, at least, such reasonable regulations established directly by legislative enactment as will protect the public health and the public safety.

It is equally true that the state may invest local bodies called into existence for purposes of local administration with authority in some appropriate way to safeguard the public health and the public safety. The mode or manner in which those results are to be accomplished is within the discretion of the state, subject, of course, so far as federal power is concerned, only to the condition that no rule prescribed by a state, nor any regulation adopted by a local governmental agency acting under the sanction of state legislation, shall contravene the Constitution of the United States, nor infringe any right granted or secured by that instrument. A local enactment or regulation, even if based on the acknowledged police powers of a state, must always yield in case of conflict with the exercise by the general government of any power it possesses under the Constitution, or with any right which that instrument gives or secures....

The defendant insists that his liberty is invaded when the state subjects him to fine or imprisonment for neglecting or refusing to submit to vaccination; that a compulsory vaccination law is unreasonable, arbitrary, and oppressive, and, therefore, hostile to the inherent right of every freeman to care for his own body and health in such way as to him seems best; and that the execution of such a law against one who objects to vaccination, no matter for what reason, is nothing short of an assault upon his person. But the liberty secured by the Constitution of the United States to every person within its jurisdiction does not import an absolute right in each person to be, at all times and in all circumstances, wholly freed from restraint. There are manifold restraints to which every person is necessarily subject for the common good. On any other basis organized society could not exist with safety to its members. Society based on the rule that each one is a law unto himself would soon be confronted with disorder and anarchy. Real liberty for all could not exist under the operation of a principle which recognizes the right of each individual person to use his own, whether in respect of his person or his property, regardless of the injury that may be done to others....Even liberty itself, the greatest of all rights, is not unrestricted license to act according to one's own will. It is only freedom from restraint under conditions essential to the equal enjoyment of the same right by others. It is, then, liberty regulated by law. In the Constitution of Massachusetts adopted in 1780, it was laid down as a fundamental principle of the social compact that the whole people covenants with each citizen, and each citizen with the whole people, that all shall be governed by certain laws for "the common good," and that government is instituted "for the common good, for the protection, safety, prosperity, and happiness of the people, and not for the profit, honor, or private interests of any one man, family, or class of men." The good and welfare of the commonwealth, of which the legislature is primarily the judge, is the basis on which the police power rests in Massachusetts.

Applying these principles to the present case, it is to be observed that the legislature of Massachusetts required the inhabitants of a city or town to be vaccinated only when, in the opinion of the board of health, that was necessary for the public health or the public safety. The authority to determine for all what ought to be done in such an emergency must have been lodged somewhere or in some body; and surely it was appropriate for the legislature to refer that question, in the first instance, to a board of health composed of persons residing in the locale affected, and appointed, presumably, because of their fitness to determine such questions. To invest such a body with authority over such matters was not an unusual, nor an unreasonable or arbitrary, requirement. Upon the principle of self-defense, of paramount necessity, a community has a right to protect itself against an epidemic of disease which threatens the safety of its members. It is to be observed that when the regulation in question was adopted smallpox...was prevalent to some extent in the city of Cambridge, and the disease was increasing....

If the mode adopted by Massachusetts for the protection of its local communities against smallpox proved to be distressing, inconvenient, or objectionable to some—if nothing more could be reasonably affirmed of the statute in question—the answer is that it was the duty of the constituted authorities primarily to keep in view the welfare, comfort, and safety of the many, and not permit the interests of the many to be subordinated to the wishes or convenience of the few. There is, of course, a sphere within which the individual may assert the supremacy of his own will, and rightfully dispute the authority of any human government—especially of any free government existing under a written constitution—to interfere with the exercise of that will. But it is equally true that in every well-ordered society charged with the duty of conserving the safety of its members the rights of the individual in respect to his liberty may at times, under the pressures of great dangers, be subjected to such restraint, to be enforced by reasonable regulations, as the safety of the general public may demand....

The liberty secured by the Fourteenth Amendment consists, in part, in the right of a person to live and work where he will. [Y]et he may be compelled, by force if need be, against his will and without regard to his personal wishes or his pecuniary interests, or even his religious or political convictions, to take his place in the ranks of the army of his country, and risk the chance of being shot down in its defense....

The state legislature proceeded upon the theory which recognized vaccination as at least an effective, if not the best-known, way in which to meet and suppress the evils of a smallpox epidemic that imperiled an entire population. Upon what sound principles as to the relations existing between the different departments of government can the review this action of the legislature? If there is any such power in the judiciary to review legislative action in respect of a matter affecting the general welfare, it can only be when that which the legislature has done comes within the rule that, if a statute purporting to have been enacted to protect the public health, the public morals, or the public safety, has no real or substantial relation to those objects, or is, beyond all question, a plain, palpable invasion of rights secured by the fundamental law, it is the duty of the courts to so adjudge, and thereby give effect to the Constitution.

Whatever may be thought of the expediency of this statute, it cannot be affirmed to be, beyond question, in palpable conflict with the Constitution. Nor, in view of the methods employed to stamp out the disease of smallpox, can anyone confidently assert that the means prescribed by the state to that end has no real or substantial relation to the protection of the public health and the public safety. Such an assertion would not be consistent with the experience of this and other countries whose authorities have dealt with the disease of smallpox. And the principle of vaccination as a means to prevent the spread of smallpox had been enforced in many states by statutes making the vaccination of children a condition of their right to enter or remain in public schools....

Nearly every state in the Union has statutes to encourage, or directly or indirectly to require, vaccination; and this is true of most nations of Europe. A common belief, like common knowledge, does not require evidence to establish its existence, but may be acted upon without proof by the legislature and the courts. The fact that the belief is not universal is not controlling, for there is scarcely any belief that is accepted by everyone. The possibility that the belief may be wrong, and that science may yet show it to be wrong, is not conclusive; for the legislature has the right to pass laws which, according to the common belief of the people, are adapted to prevent the spread of contagious diseases. In a free country, where the government is by the people, through their chosen representatives, practical legislation admits of no other standard of action, for what the people believe is for the common welfare, whether it does in fact or not. Any other basis would conflict with the spirit of the Constitution, and would sanction measures opposed to a Republican form of government. While we do not decide, and cannot decide, that vaccination is a preventative of smallpox, we take judicial notice of the fact that this is the common belief of the people of the state, and, with this fact as a foundation, we hold that the statute in question is a health law, enacted in a reasonable and proper exercise of the police power....

We are not prepared to hold that a minority...may defy the will of [the community's] constituted authorities....If such be the privilege of a minority, then a like privilege would belong to each individual of the community, and the spectacle would be presented of the welfare and safety of an entire population being subordinated to the notions of a single individual who chooses to remain a part of that population. We are unwilling to hold it to be an element in the liberty secured by the Constitution that one person, or a minority of persons, should have to power to dominate the majority when supported in their action by the authority of the state. While this Court should guard with firmness every right appertaining to life, liberty, or property as secured to the individual by the supreme law of the land, it is of the last importance that it should not invade the domain of local authority except when it is plainly necessary in order to enforce that law. The safety and the health of the people of Massachusetts are, in the first instance, for that commonwealth to guard and protect. They are matters that do not ordinarily concern the national government. So far as they can be reached by any government, they depend, primarily, upon such action as the state, in its wisdom, may take; and we do not perceive that this legislation has invaded any right secured by the Federal Constitution....

The judgment of the court below must be affirmed. It is so ordered.

Prince v. Commonwealth of Massachusetts
321 U.S. 158 (1944)

Justice Rutledge delivered the opinion of the Court. Justice Jackson filed a dissenting opinion.

Areas for Discussion and Ethical Reflection

1.   Almost all would agree that parents have obligations toward their children. Specify exactly what these obligations are. Avoid phrases such as "take care of" in your description of parental obligations; such a phrase has numerous meanings and applications. For example, a Jehovah's Witness sincerely believes that by refusing a needed blood transfusion for his daughter, he is taking care of her. Use two different ethical theories to justify your set of obligations. Do specific obligations differ from one ethical theory to another?

2.   Perhaps the most famous passage from *Prince* is this assertion by Justice Rutledge: "Parents may be free to become martyrs

themselves. But it does not follow they are free, in identical circumstances, to make martyrs of their children...." State as clearly as you can Justice Rutledge's meaning. What moral theory and ethical arguments are employed to support his assertion? Can you think of an ethical argument or moral theory that would support parents making martyrs of their children? Perhaps Justice Jackson in his dissent offers one justification. Recall that the free exercise clause of the First Amendment prohibits both the federal government and the states from interfering with how individuals practice their religious. Why should it not be the case that parents, sincerely and deeply concerned about the eternal life of their children's souls, be allowed to deny medical care for their children for religious reasons?

3.   What significance, if any, should one's religious beliefs have in determinations of competency? If one's religious beliefs and practices are "outside the norm," how should you go about determining whether that person is acting in a genuinely autonomous manner? Should you rely simply on the chronological age of the individual?

4.   From a social policy perspective does it make sense to prosecute under homicide statutes parents whose child has died because the parents denied medical care to the child for religious reasons? Many states have religious exemption statutes that do not allow charges of child abuse or neglect to be brought against parents who seek spiritual healing for their children in place of medical care. However, upon the death of a child, many of these same states seek to prosecute the parents under homicide or manslaughter statutes. Does it logically follow that a state can make exceptions to its child welfare laws for religious reasons and, at the same time, prosecute parents whose children have died as a result of the parents' refusal to seek treatment?[8]

5.   Justice Jackson in his dissenting opinion asserts that religious training and activity are protected from interference by the state except to the extent that such training and activity "violate reasonable regulations adopted for the protection of the public

health, morals and welfare." A few paragraphs later Justice Jackson seems to define reasonableness to mean that the state must prove the existence of a "grave and immediate danger to the state or to the health, morals or welfare of the child." What do you suppose Justice Jackson means by reasonable? What moral presuppositions underlie his claims regarding the impermissibility of interfering with how parents raise their children?

6.   What guidance for the treatment of children does *Prince* provide health care professionals working in the real world of clinical medicine? Physicians often encounter parents from religious backgrounds or cultural traditions different from their own who refuse medical intervention for their children. What should a physician do when the treatment she wishes to offer is both clinically sound and ethically appropriate?

7.   Another kind of situation arises in clinical medicine that raises both ethical and legal dilemmas, and it involves disputes between parents and health care professionals over the treatment of severely deformed newborns. Often, parents will decline medical treatment for a severely deformed infant on grounds that the child will have a poor quality of life. Physicians may observe that quality of life determinations are uncertain and try to talk the parents into consenting to medical treatment. Does the *Prince* decision offer any guidance for such tragic situations?

JUSTICE RUTLEDGE:

…[Sarah Prince] does not stand on freedom of the press. Regarding it as secular, she concedes it may be restricted as Massachusetts has done. Hence, she rests squarely on freedom of religion under the First Amendment, applied by the Fourteenth by the states. She buttresses this foundation, however, with a claim of parental right as secured by due process clause of the latter Amendment. These guarantees, she thinks, guard alike herself and the child in what they have done. Thus, two claimed liberties are at stake. One is the parent's, to bring up the child in the way he should go, which for appellant means to teach him the tenets and the practices of their faith. The other freedom is the child's, to observe these; and among them is "to preach the gospel…by public distribution" of "Watchtower" and "Consolation," in conformity with the scripture: "A little lamp shall lead them."…

To make accommodation between these freedoms and an exercise of state authority always is delicate. It hardly could be more so than in such a clash as this case presents. On one side is the obviously earnest claim for freedom of conscience and religious practice. With it is allied the parent's claim to authority in her own household and in the rearing of her children. The parent's conflict with the state over control of the child and his training is serious enough when only secular matters are concerned. It becomes the more so when an element of religious conviction enters. Against these sacred private interests, basic in a democracy, stands the interests of society to protect the welfare of children, and the state's assertion of authority to that end, made here in a matter conceded valid if only secular things were involved. The last is no mere corporate concern of official authority. It is the interest of youth itself, and of the whole community, that children be both safeguarded from abuses and given opportunities for growth into free and independent well-developed men and citizens. Between contrary pulls of such weight, the safest and most objective recourse is to the lines already marked out, not precisely but for guides, in narrowing the no man's land where this battle has gone on.

The rights of children to exercise their religion, and of parents to give them religious training and to encourage them in the practice of religious belief, as against preponderant sentiment and assertion of state power voicing it, have had recognition here… It is cardinal with us that the custody, care and nurture of the child reside first in the parents, whose primary function and freedom include preparation for obligations the state can neither supply nor hinder. And it is in recognition of this that [our previous] decisions have respected the private realm of family life which the state cannot enter.

But the family itself is not beyond regulation in the public interest, as against a claim of religious liberty. And neither rights of religion nor rights of parenthood are beyond limitation. Acting to guard the general interest in youth's well-being the state as parens patriae may restrict the parent's control by requiring school attendance, regulating or prohibiting the child's labor, and in many other ways. Its authority is not nullified merely because the parent grounds his claim to control the child's course of conduct on religion or conscience. Thus, he cannot claim freedom from compulsory vaccination for the child more than for himself on religious grounds. The right to practice religion freely does not include liberty to expose the community or the child to communicable disease or the latter to ill health or death. The catalogue need not be lengthened. It is sufficient to show what indeed appellant hardly disputes, that the state has a wide range of power for limiting parental freedom and authority in things affecting the child's welfare; and that this includes, to some extent, matters of conscience and religious conviction.

But it is said the state cannot do so here. [F]irst, because when state action impinges upon a claimed religious freedom, it must fall unless shown to be necessary for or conducive to the child's protection against some clear and present danger, and there was no showing here. The child's presence on the street, with her guardian, distributing, or offering to distribute the magazines, was in no way harmful to her, nor in any event no more so than the presence of many other children at the same time and place, engaged in shopping and other activities not prohibited. And, finally, it is said, the statute is, as to children, an absolute prohibition, not merely a reasonable regulation, of the denounced activity....

The state's authority over children's activities is broader than over like actions of adults. This is peculiarly true of public activities and in matters of employment. A democratic society rests, for its continuance, upon the healthy, well-rounded growth of young people into full maturity as citizens, with all that implies. It may secure this against impending restraints and dangers, within a broad range of selection. Among evils most appropriate for such action are the crippling effects of child employment, more especially in public places, and the possible harms arising from other activities subject to all the diverse influences of the street. It is too late now to doubt that legislation appropriately designed to reach such evils is within the state's police power, whether against the parent's claim to control of the child or one that religious scruples dictate contrary action....

The case reduces itself therefore to the question whether the presence of the child's guardian puts a limit to the state's power. That fact may lessen the likelihood that some evils the legislation seeks to avert will occur. But it cannot forestall all of them. The zealous though lawful exercise of the right to engage in propagandizing the community, whether in religious, political or other matters, may and at times does create situations difficult enough for adults to cope with and wholly inappropriate for children, especially of tender years, to face. Other harmful possibilities could be stated, of emotional excitement and psychological or physical injury. Parents may be free to become martyrs themselves. But it does not follow they are free, in identical circumstances, to make martyrs of their children before they have reached the age of full and legal discretion when they can make that choice for themselves....

The judgment is affirmed.

JUSTICE JACKSON:

...Religious training and activity, whether performed by adult or child, are protected by the Fourteenth Amendment against interference by state action, except insofar as they violate reasonable regulations adopted for the protection of the public health, morals and welfare. Our problem here is whether a state, under the guise of enforcing its child labor laws, can lawfully prohibit girls under the age of eighteen and boys under the age of twelve from practicing their religious faith insofar as it involves the distribution or sale of religious tracts on the public streets....Criminal sanctions are imposed on the parents and guardians who compel or permit minors in their control to engage in the prohibited transactions. The state court has construed these statutes to cover the activities here involved, thereby imposing an indirect restraint through the parents and guardians on the free exercise by minors of their religious beliefs. This indirect restraint is no less effective than a direct one. A square conflict between the constitutional guarantee of religious freedom and the state's legitimate interest in protecting the welfare of its children is thus presented....

In dealing with the validity of statutes which directly or indirectly infringe religious freedom and the right of parents to encourage their children in the practice of a religious belief, we are not aided by any strong presumption of the constitutionality of such legislation. On the contrary, the human freedoms enumerated in the First Amendment and carried over into the Fourteenth Amendment are to be presumed to be invulnerable and any attempt to sweep away those freedoms is prima facie invalid. It follows that any restriction or prohibition must be justified by those who deny that the freedoms have been unlawfully invaded. The burden was therefore on the state of Massachusetts to prove the reasonableness and necessity of prohibiting children from engaging in religious activity of the type involved in this case....The state, in my opinion, has completely failed to sustain its burden of proving the existence of any grave or immediate danger to any interest which it may lawfully protect....

No chapter in human history has been so largely written in terms of persecution and intolerance as the one dealing with religious freedom. From ancient times to the present day, the ingenuity of man has known no limits in its ability to forge weapons of oppression for use against rights of those who dare to express or practice unorthodox religious beliefs. And the Jehovah's Witnesses are living proof of the fact that even in this nation, conceived as it was in the ideals of freedom, the right to practice religion in unconventional ways is still far from secure. Theirs is a militant and unpopular faith, pursued with a fanatical zeal. They have suffered brutal beatings; their property has been destroyed; they have been harassed at every turn by the resurrection and enforcement of little used ordinances and statutes. To them, along with other present-day religious minorities, befalls the burden of testing our devotion to the ideals and constitutional guarantees of religious freedom. We should therefore hesitate before approving the application of a statute that might be used as another instrument of oppression. Religious freedom is too sacred a right to be restricted or prohibited in any degree without convincing proof that a legitimate interest of the state is in grave danger.

Notes

1.   John E. Nowak and Ronald D. Rotunda, *Constitutional Law*, 6th ed. (St. Paul, MN: West Group, 2000), p. 1307.

2.   Ronald Munson, "Donald (Dax) Cowart Rejects Treatment—and Is Ignored," in *Intervention and Reflection: Basic Issues in Medical Ethics*, 6th ed., edited by Ronald Munson (Belmont, CA: Wadsworth, 2000), pp. 378–81. This account by Munson is very powerful and well worth reading in its entirety.

3.   James F. Drane, "Competency to Give an Informed Consent: A Model for Making Clinical Assessments," in *Intervention and Reflection: Basic Issues*

in Medical Ethics, p. 415.

4.   Albert R. Jonsen, Mark Siegler, and William J. Winslade, *Clinical Ethics: A Practical Approach To Ethical Decisions in Clinical Medicine*, 4th ed., (New York: McGraw-Hill, 1998), p. 93.

5.   Lawrence O. Gostin, ed., *Public Health Law and Ethics* (Berkeley: University of California Press, 2002), pp. 215–16.

6.   Dan Brock and Steven Wartman, "When Competent Patients Make Irrational Choices," in *Contemporary Issues in Bioethics*, 4th ed., edited by Tom Beauchamp and LeRoy Walters (Belmont, CA: Wadsworth, 1994), pp. 109–14.

7.   Jennifer Gray, "Public Health: Bush's Smallpox Vaccination Plan," *Journal of Law, Medicine & Ethics* 31 (2003): 312–14.

8.   Carl E. Schneider, "Justification by Faith," *Hastings Center Report* 29 (1999): 24–25.

For Further Reading

Beauchamp, Tom L., and James F. Childress. *Principles of Biomedical Ethics*, 5th edition. New York: Oxford University Press, 2001.

Brock, Dan, and Steven Wartman. "When Competent Patients Make Irrational Choices." In *Contemporary Issues in Bioethics*, 4th edition, Tom L. Beauchamp and LeRoy Walters, eds. Belmont, CA: Wadsworth, 1994.

Cowart, Dax, and Robert Burt. "Confronting Death: Who Chooses, Who Controls? A Dialogue." In *Intervention and Reflection: Basic Issues in Medical Ethics*, 6th edition, Ronald Munson, ed. Belmont, CA: Wadsworth, 2000.

Drane, James F. "Competency to Give an Informed Consent: A Model for Making Clinical Assessments." In *Intervention and Reflection: Basic Issues in Medical Ethics*.

Gostin, Lawrence O., ed. *Public Health Law and Ethics*. Berkeley: University of California Press, 2002.

Gray, Jennifer. "Public Health: Bush's Smallpox Vaccination Plan." *Journal of Law, Medicine & Ethics* 31 (2003): 312–14.

Jonsen, Albert R., Mark Siegler, and William Winslade. *Clinical Ethics: A Practical Approach to Ethical Decisions in Clinical Medicine*, 4th edition. New York: McGraw-Hill, 1998.

Munson, Ronald. "Case Presentation: The Death of Robyn Twitchell and Christian Science." In *Intervention and Reflection: Basic Issues in Medical Ethics.*

———. "Case Presentation: Donald (Dax) Cowart Rejects Treatment—And Is Ignored." In *Intervention and Reflection: Basic Issues in Medical Ethics.*

Schneider, Carl E. "Justification by Faith." *Hastings Center Report* 29 (1999): 24–25.

CHAPTER SIX

THE CONFIDENTIALITY AND PROFESSIONALISM CASES

Any medical ethics includes a set of ethical standards, principles, rules, or codes for physicians or other health care professionals. In many cases these are articulated by professional groups themselves for their members. When groups do this, we have...a professional ethic. For an ethic to be a professional ethic...the group must make the claim that the professional group generates the norms, principles, or correct professional conduct or at least that it is the only body having knowledge of what is ethically required for members of the profession.

—Robert M. Veatch, *A Theory of Medical Ethics*

No profession has faced more challenges to its values, norms, practices, and authority than medicine. The demands placed on physicians, nurses, therapists, and others directly involved in patient care are significant and pervasive. Different constituencies have different expectations. Licensing boards and accrediting agencies demand that high standards of competency are met; third party payers demand cost-effective and efficient care; government demands that medical professionals follow the law; communities, usually through legal sanction, demand prevention of communicable diseases and promotion of health; and patients and their loved ones demand quality, compassionate, respectful, and affordable health care. Even within the same group, different and conflicting demands can be placed on health care professionals. For example, society desires and demands that physicians keep information learned during the clinical encounter confidential, yet society also demands that professionals breach confidentiality when the health or well-being of one or more individuals in the community is in danger. Health care professionals are forced to practice under significant pressure to maintain a sense of identity, authority, and autonomy. Several principles and concepts prominent in constitutional law and medical ethics address issues surrounding the degree to which health professionals, especially physicians, may practice absent undue state interference. The three cases below highlight the justices' views on such concepts as professional autonomy, trust, and confidentiality within the health care professional–patient relationship.

Constitutional Issues and Background

As we are well aware, the right to privacy and the limitations on that right occupy an important role in constitutional law and medical ethics. Our first case, *Whalen v. Roe*, continues our discussion of when and under what circumstances the state may infringe on that right within the physician-patient relationship. In 1972, the state of New York passed legislation requiring physicians to report all prescriptions for Schedule II drugs and to file that report with the state health department. The statute required that the report include the patient's name, address, dispensing pharmacy, name of drug, and dosage. Reports were to be destroyed after five years, and public disclosure of patient information was prohibited. The legislation was enacted in an attempt by the state to curtail the illegal use of Schedule II drugs. Suit was brought in district court by patients using Schedule II drugs, prescribing physicians, and two associations of physicians challenging the constitutionality of the patient-identification portions of the law. Asserting that the doctor-patient relationship is a "zone of privacy" deserving constitutional protection and that the statute violated that zone, the District Court halted New York's enforcement of the statute.

The Supreme Court concluded that although patients and physicians enjoy privacy interests deserving of constitutional protection, protection is not absolute. That is, the state has legitimate interests in preventing the illegal distribution and use of narcotics and in collecting data on medication prescriptions, especially when the state makes good faith efforts to keep private all information gathered. In writing for a unanimous Court, Justice Stevens found New York's law "...the product of an orderly and rational legislative decision." The justices discussed but then dismissed the possibility that the Fourth Amendment might prohibit the collection and storage of patient information.

In *Rust v. Sullivan* considerable disagreement existed among the justices regarding the history and interpretation of a specific regulation and regarding the interpretation of both the First and Fifth Amendments. In 1988, the Secretary of Health and Human Services (HHS) issued guidelines prohibiting federal funds in support of Title X family planning services from being used in activity that could be construed to advocate abortion. At the time of the new regulations there were about four thousand family planning clinics receiving Title X money serving about 4 million poor women a year. Physicians, nurses, and others were prohibited from discussing, referring, or counseling women regarding abortion—a prohibition referred to as a "gag rule." Physicians supervising the use of Title X funds filed suit alleging that the new regulations ran counter to congressional intent and violated First Amendment rights of physicians and nurses who deem it necessary to talk to select women about abortion. The First and Tenth Circuit courts had ruled the regulations unconstitutional, but the Second Circuit had ruled in favor of the secretary of HHS.

The Court ruled, in a 5-4 decision, that the federal government may prohibit doctors from discussing abortion with their Title X patients. Of major importance in *Rust* is the constitutional status of the physician-patient relationship and how much control of physicians the federal government can impose in programs it funds. Chief Justice Rehnquist was unwilling to accord the relationship First and Fifth Amendment protection. No doubt, this case has implications for the constitutional status of a woman's right to abortion, but the free speech rights of physicians and the rights of poor people to receive information take center stage in this case. These concerns are echoed quite forcibly in the dissents.

The last case in this chapter, *Jaffee v. Redmond*, examines Rule 501 of the Federal Rules of Evidence and considers whether constitutional protection should be extended to the psychotherapist-client relationship. In June 1991, Mary Lu Redmond was a police officer employed by the village of Hoffman Estates, Illinois. In responding to a "fight in progress" call at an apartment complex, Redmond shot and killed Ricky Allen, who, she later testified, was threatening to kill another man with a butcher knife. The administrator of Allen's estate filed suit, charging that Redmond had violated Allen's constitutional rights by using excessive force. Before trial, Allen's estate learned that Redmond had participated in about fifty counseling sessions with Karen Beyer, a clinical social worker licensed by Illinois and employed by the Village of Hoffman Estates. When the trial court ordered records of the sessions turned over, Beyer and Redmond asserted a privilege between psychotherapist and client. The trial court judge instructed the jury that refusal to turn over the records was not legally justified, and a verdict was returned for the estate of Allen. The Seventh Circuit reversed, arguing that Section 501 of the Federal Rules of Evidence would recognize such a privilege.

The Supreme Court began its analysis by noting that federal courts are authorized under Rule 501 to define new privileges by interpreting "the principles of the common law…in the light of reason and experience." Several professions, most notably law and medicine, have enjoyed a long-standing, legally recognized communication privilege. Only under extreme circumstances may attorneys or physicians be compelled to testify regarding the content of conversations they conduct with their clients. The justices in *Jaffee* debated the issue of what constitutes an extreme circumstance. The justices also discussed whether social work is a profession deserving the same status as psychiatry and psychology. Justice Stevens's majority opinion appears heavily influenced by principles of medical ethics.

Ethical Issues and Background

The three cases covered in this chapter have not received very much attention from medical ethicists, which is unfortunate for two reasons. First, and perhaps most important, all three cases provide us with an opportunity to assess how members of the Court view the physician-patient relationship. Although the abortion cases have certainly provided us with clues of how the justices view interactions between physicians and patients, the justices are much more explicit about their views regarding the limits of state intervention in that relationship in the cases covered in this chapter. Second, two of these cases provide us with insight into regulatory and public policy concerns surrounding one of the most important rules in medical ethics, the rule to preserve confidentiality. A substantial literature exists detailing justifications for an obligation of health care professionals to preserve confidential information as well as the limits on such an obligation. Try to determine if you detect in the justices' reasoning any influence by this literature.

We begin by examining the physician-patient relationship, which serves as an effective method for studying many of the ethical problems arising in medicine. Two of those problems—confidentiality and physician as financial gatekeeper—are discussed explicitly in this book. Because of its central importance and relevance to many issues in medical ethics, many commentators have analyzed and evaluated the physician-patient relationship.[1] In articulating and justifying an ethically defensible conception of the relationship, medical ethicists strive to address two different considerations: "general ethical theory that is pertinent to other human relationships, and the factual reality of medical practice."[2] Below we briefly describe four models of the relationship.

Robert M. Veatch begins his critical discussion of models of the relationship with the following observation:

> ...[W]ith the biological revolution, health care really is essential to "life, liberty, and the pursuit of happiness." And health care is a right for everyone because of the social revolution which is really a revolution in our conception of justice. If the obscure phrase "all men are created equal" means anything in the medical context where biologically it is clear that they are not equal, it means that they are equal in the legitimacy of their moral claim. They must be treated equally in what is essential to their humanity: dignity, freedom, individuality.[3]

Veatch's observation, with its references to constitutional concepts and justice, is well worth revisiting as you read other chapters. For now, we note his insistence that the physician-patient relationship is deserving of careful study.

The oldest model of the physician-patient relationship is the priestly model. Since the beginning of medicine, both physicians and patients have subscribed to this understanding of the relationship. In the priestly model, the physician is the high priest, the one person who knows what is best for the patient, and the patient listens and obeys. Physicians promise to always benefit and to do no harm toward their patients. The physician "knows best" not only with regard to medical procedures or treatments, but also with regard to values and morality. Patients question or ignore the advice of their physicians at great peril not only to their physical health but to their mental and emotional health as well. Obviously, this model makes little room for respect for freedom and dignity of the patient.

Significant advances in both medical technology and the capability of medical interventions to prolong life have led to the view that physicians should be considered as engineers or scientists. On this engineering model, health care professionals know and understand the facts of medical science, and their sole obligation is to present those facts to their patients. Unlike the priestly model, the physician-as-engineer stays completely value-neutral; all that matters are the biological and medical data at hand. Such a stance, of course, recalls memories of Nazi physicians conducting experiments and research on vulnerable groups. Too, medicine and medical practice are not value-neutral. Options always exist, and patients will ascribe different values to these options.

Concerns over the lack of moral integrity exemplified in the engineering model and violations of freedom and dignity evident in the priestly model have led theorists to posit the collegial model of physician-patient interactions. On this model, the physician is the patient's "pal." Both doctor and patient are joined in the common endeavor of fighting disease and promoting patient well-being. In a relationship where both parties are committed to the same goals, confidence and trust are the dominant themes and respect for equality is paramount. Although such a model appears very pleasant, even morally praiseworthy, the realities of modern medicine, costly services, and social relationships make the model unrealistic. Doctors and patients do not in fact share the same goals, thus making the collegial model unrealistic.

Concerns over current medical and social realities have led several medical ethicists to set forth and defend what they call the contractual or covenant model of the physician-patient relationship. In a contractual relationship, individuals or groups recognize and appreciate the obligations and duties of each other. Each party respects the other as "free moral agents with their own goals and interests."[4] Physicians take responsibility for technical decisions appropriate to their education and training, and patients take responsibility for decisions regarding their lifestyle and personal moral values. Critics of this account of the relationship note the implicit nature of many of the expectations between physicians and patients and that the relationship is too formal or legalistic.

Other conceptualizations of the relationship have been put forth and defended by ethicists, but these four are probably the most popular. As you read the excerpts from *Whalen, Rust,* and *Jaffee* you have the opportunity to evaluate how individual justices view the relationship between health care professionals and their patients. Do the justices subscribe to a model of the relationship that properly accounts for the values and obligations that each party should have toward the other? Do the justices understand the consequences—personal, professional, and social—of specific models? As you will see, specific models have specific consequences for issues in medical ethics. One such issue, one playing a central role in the cases in this chapter, is obligations to confidentiality. We briefly discuss that issue before turning to the actual Court decisions.

The value of confidentiality and obligations of health care professionals to maintain commitments to preserve confidential information are commonly recognized as significant. In medicine, commitment to confidentiality has been recognized for thousands of years. Medicine's earliest code, the Hippocratic Oath, asserts: "What I may see or hear in the course of the treatment or even outside of the treatment in regard to the life of men, which on no account one must spread abroad, I will keep to myself holding such things shameful to be spoken about." Today, codes of ethics for most health care professions recognize obligations to preserve information gathered during interactions with patients or clients. However, problems emerge for practitioners and patients regarding how to justify not only a commitment to confidentiality but also exceptions to the commitment. We first examine various justifications for a commitment to confidentiality.

Rem Edwards takes up the challenge of listing and explaining the reasons that both health care professionals and their patients should value professional commitments to confidentiality.[5] He provides these reasons or justifications with no particular rank ordering in mind. First, confidentiality in the physician-patient relationship is valuable because it "affirms and protects the more fundamental value of privacy." Second, the social status of clients and patients is protected by commitments to confidentiality. Third, respecting confidentiality is economically advantageous to clients and patients since social stigma may attach to some mental and physical disorders. Fourth, openness between practitioner and client is promoted by respecting confidential communications. Fifth, serious commitment to confidentiality encourages individuals to seek help from appropriate professionals. Sixth, confidentiality is valuable because it promotes trust within the relationship. And finally, confidentiality is valuable because it promotes autonomous control over information the client wishes to keep from others. As you read *Whalen* and *Jaffee*, search for mention of these justifications in the justices' opinions.

Finally, we must reinforce the fact that no one believes that obligations to preserve confidentiality are absolute. Health care professionals are permitted, sometimes even obligated, to divulge to third parties information gained from patient contact under certain circumstances and for certain reasons. Obviously, much disagreement exists over what should count as a justifiable circumstance or reason and whether a health care professional is merely permitted or is obligated to notify third parties. Consider the following candidates for justifiable reasons to breach confidentiality: 1) to protect a client from harm, 2) to protect identifiable third parties from harm; 3) to further a particular state public health measure; 4) to inform insurance companies paying for care, and 5) to meet the requirement of a criminal or civil proceeding. As you read *Whalen* and *Jaffee*, consider the weight specific justices attach to some of these justifications.

Whalen v. Roe
429 U.S. 589 (1977)

Justice Stevens delivered the opinion for a unanimous Court. Justices Brennan and Stewart each filed concurring opinions.

Areas for Discussion and Ethical Reflection

1.   As we all know, and as the Court acknowledges, many drugs have legitimate and illegitimate uses. Society clearly has an

interest in promoting the former and curtailing the latter. What moral arguments can you employ in support of state practices to collect the names and addresses of all people using Schedule II medications prescribed by a physician? What moral considerations can be raised against the practice? Justice Stevens's opinion for the Court seems influenced by concerns voiced by medical ethicists. What are these concerns?

2.   Discuss in some detail your understanding of the "zone of privacy" as it applies to the physician-patient relationship. In his opinion for the Court, Justice Stevens notes that two interests are served by a commitment to protect privacy. The first is an "individual interest in avoiding disclosure of personal matters." The second interest centers on "independence in making certain kinds of important decisions." Provide both a utilitarian and a Kantian justification for acknowledging and respecting these interests.

3.   Justice Stevens characterizes the disclosure of prescription information to the New York Department of Health as an "unpleasant invasion of privacy." Would you characterize the disclosure of the information as "unpleasant"? Undoubtedly, the physicians and patients who filed suit against the New York law would not characterize the disclosure as "unpleasant." What ethically significant reasons might they give?

4.   One commentator in medical ethics asserts: "Medical confidentiality, as it has traditionally been understood by patients and doctors, no longer exists…it is a decrepit concept."[6] That is, confidentiality, along with laws and professional codes of ethics designed to promote it, is no longer of much use since modern health care has become so complex. In addition to serving the legitimate interests of third parties, the patient's interest in receiving quality care is also served by divulging information to others. Justice Stevens echoes this sentiment in his decision for the Court. Do you believe patients' expectations that the information they share with physicians will remain private and confidential are now outdated? Is such a belief relevant to the facts as presented in *Whalen*?

5.   In footnote 16 of his opinion, Justice Stevens details some of the adverse effects of New York's central filing law. These include: 1) parents so concerned that their children would be stigmatized by the law that they took their children off medications, 2) three patients so fearful of disclosure that they ended their medication; 3) four physicians reporting reactions of fear and shock from their patients informed of the law, and 4) one physician no longer prescribing Schedule II medications. After noting these unfortunate results of the law, Justice Stevens continues by observing that over 100,00 prescriptions are written each month, hence any adverse effects of the reporting requirement are limited. Which ethical theory is Justice Stevens using? Do you find Justice Stevens's reasoning in footnote 16 persuasive?

6. What is the most morally defensible conception of the doctor-patient relationship? What would it mean to say that a doctor has a right to practice medicine? Once we have determined what such a right would mean, what would constitute morally acceptable constraints on the right?

7.   In commenting on the privacy of personal medical records and the problem of unauthorized persons receiving and using that information, one commentator provides several recent examples:

>...[A] database created by the state of Maryland in 1993 to keep the medical records of all its residents for cost-containment purposes was used by state employees to sell confidential information on Medicaid recipients to health maintenance organizations, and was accessed by a banker who employed the information to call in the loans of customers who he discovered had cancer. A medical student in Colorado sold the medical records of patients to malpractice lawyers. In Newton, Massachusetts, a convicted child rapist working at a local hospital used a former employee's computer password to access nearly 1,000 patient files to make obscene phone calls to young girls. In Florida, a state health department worker used state computers to compile

a list of 4,000 people who tested positive for HIV and forwarded it to two newspapers....[7]

These examples are, of course, rather frightening. Do they help support the concerns of the patients and physicians in *Whalen*? How would the justices who supported the New York law respond to such horror stories?

8.   On April 14, 2003, the first standards developed by the federal government to protect the privacy of patient medical records went into effect. These new standards are part of the Health Insurance Portability and Accountability Act (HIPAA) passed by Congress in 1996. The new privacy regulations apply to hospitals, health plans, pharmacies, and nursing homes. The standards allow patients access to their medical information, require facilities to inform patients of their privacy rights, prohibit use of patient information for marketing, and set limits on how health plans and hospitals may use individual patient information. HIPAA and the privacy regulations were developed by Health and Human Services partially in response to widespread concern over misuse of confidential information. Many have complained that the new standards are burdensome to follow and that patients actually may be harmed because it is now more difficult for health care professionals to share information.

9. Justice Brennan, in his concurring opinion, makes the observation that: "...I am not prepared to say that future developments will not demonstrate the necessity of some curb on such technology." In the almost 30 years since Justice Brennan made this comment a great deal of progress has been made in technology designed to gather and store personal information. Can you think of particular methods and uses of gathering information on citizens that Justice Brennan might now find troubling?

10.   Several weeks after the terrorist attacks on the United States in September 2001, Congress at the urging of the Bush administration and the Department of Justice passed the United States Patriot Act (USPA). The act gives the government expanded power

to collect personal information on citizens and noncitizens with very little or no judicial oversight. What constitutional and moral insight does *Whalen* provide in assessing the USPA?

JUSTICE STEVENS:

> The constitutional question presented is whether the State of New York may record, in a centralized computer file, the names and addresses of all persons who have obtained, pursuant to a doctor's prescription, certain drugs for which there is both a lawful and an unlawful market....
>
> [Patients taking Schedule II drugs and prescribing doctors] contend that the statute invades a constitutionally protected zone of privacy. The cases sometimes characterized as protecting privacy have in fact involved at least two different kinds of interests. One is the individual interest in avoiding disclosure of personal matters, and another is the interest in independence in making certain kinds of important decisions. [Patients and doctors] argue that both of these interests are impaired by this statute. The mere existence in readily available form of the information about patients' use of Schedule II drugs creates a genuine concern that the information will become publicly known and that it will adversely affect their reputations. This concern makes some patients reluctant to use, and some doctors reluctant to prescribe, such drugs even when their use is medically indicated. It follows, they argue, that the making of decisions about matters vital to the care of their health is inevitably affected by the statute. Thus, the statute threatens to impair both their interest in nondisclosure of private information and also their interest in making important decisions independently.
>
> We are persuaded, however, that the New York program does not, on its face, pose a sufficiently grievous threat to either interest to establish a constitutional violation.
>
> [The Court notes three ways patient information can

be revealed: 1) health department employees might reveal information deliberately or negligently; 2) the stored data may be used in a judicial proceeding; and 3) the doctor, pharmacist, or patient may voluntarily reveal information.]

...[There are] a host of other unpleasant invasions of privacy that are associated with many facets of health care. Unquestionably, some individuals' concern for their own privacy may lead them to avoid or to postpone needed medical attention. Nevertheless, disclosures of private medical information to doctors, to hospital personnel, to insurance companies, and to public health agencies are often an essential part of modern medical practice even when the disclosure may reflect unfavorably on the character of the patient.

[Patients and doctors] also argue, however, that even if unwarranted disclosures do not actually occur, the knowledge that the information is readily available in a computerized file creates a genuine concern that causes some persons to decline needed medication. The record supports the conclusion that some use of Schedule II drugs has been discouraged by that concern; it also is clear, however, that about 100,000 prescriptions for such drugs were being filled each month prior to the District Court's injunction. Clearly, therefore, the statute did not deprive the public of access to the drugs....

We hold that neither the immediate nor the threatened impact of the patient-identification requirements [of the act] is sufficient to constitute an invasion of any right or liberty protected by the Fourteenth Amendment.

...The doctors argue separately that the statute impairs their right to practice medicine free of unwarranted state interference. If the doctors' claim has any reference to the impact of the 1972 statute on their own procedures, it is clearly frivolous. For even the prior statute required the doctor to prepare a written prescription identifying the name and address of the patient and the dosage of the prescribed drug. To the extent that their claim has reference to the possibility that the patients' concern about disclosure may induce them to refuse needed medication, the doctors' claim is derivative from, and therefore no stronger than, the patients'. Our rejection of their claim therefore disposes of the doctors' as well....

Reversed.

JUSTICE BRENNAN:

I write only to express my understanding of the opinion of the Court, which I join.

The New York statute under attack requires doctors to disclose to the State information about prescriptions for certain drugs with a high potential for abuse, and provides for the storage of that information in a central computer file. The Court recognizes that an individual's "interest in avoiding disclosure of personal matters" is an aspect of the right to privacy, but holds that in this case, any such interest has not been seriously enough invaded by the State to require a showing that its program was indispensable to the State's effort to control drug abuse.

The information disclosed by the physician under this program is made available only to a small number of public health officials with a legitimate interest in the information....Broad dissemination by state officials of such information, however, would clearly implicate constitutionally protected privacy rights, and would presumably be justified only by compelling state interests.

What is more troubling about this scheme, however, is the central computer storage of the data thus collected. Obviously, as the State argues, collection and storage of data by the State that is in itself legitimate is not rendered unconstitutional simply because new technology makes the State's operations more efficient. However, as the example of the Fourth Amendment shows, the Constitution puts limits not only on the type of information the State may gather, but also on the means it may use to gather it. The central storage and easy accessibility of computerized data vastly increase the potential for abuse of that information, and I am not prepared to say that future developments will not demonstrate the necessity of some curb on such technology.

In this case, as the Court's opinion makes clear, the State's carefully designed program includes numerous safeguards intended to forestall the danger of indiscriminate disclosure. Given this serious and, so far as the record shows, successful effort to prevent abuse and limit access to the personal information at issue, I cannot say that the statute's provisions for computer storage, on their face, amount to a deprivation of constitutionally protected privacy interests, any more than the more traditional reporting provisions.

Rust v. Sullivan
500 U.S. 173 (1991)

Chief Justice Rehnquist delivered the opinion of the Court, in which Justices White, Kennedy, Scalia, and Souter joined. Justice Blackmun filed a dissenting opinion, in which Justices Marshall, O'Connor, and Stevens joined in part. Justices Stevens and O'Connor each filed dissenting opinions.

Areas for Discussion and Ethical Reflection

1.   What exactly are Chief Justice Rehnquist's arguments for upholding the constitutionality of the gag rules? Which of these arguments are most relevant to medical ethics and to understanding the physician-patient relationship?

2.   We discussed very briefly above four different models of

the physician-patient relationship. Can you discern, after reading his opinion, Chief Justice Rehnquist's conception of the physician-patient relationship? Can you discern Justice Blackmun's conception in his dissenting opinion? What model is held by the patients and physicians who filed suit to overturn the regulations? Do you think the patients and physicians who wished to overturn the federal regulations prohibiting counseling women about abortion subscribe to a model of the relationship that is ethically defensible? Is it realistic?

3.   Chief Justice Rehnquist asserts that it is constitutional for the government to encourage (through funding) certain protected activities and to discourage (through withholding of funds) other activities, even those that are constitutionally protected. Can you make the argument that although Chief Justice Rehnquist is correct, his assertion misses the point of the case?

4.   In footnote 3 to his dissenting opinion, Justice Blackmun quotes Justice Marshall: "It is perfectly proper for judges to disagree about what the Constitution requires. But it is disgraceful for an interpretation of the Constitution to be premised upon unfounded assumptions about how people live." Justice Blackmun uses this quote to criticize as "uninformed fantasy" the majority's conception of the physician-patient relationship. Justice Blackmun maintains that everyone, including poor pregnant women, expects physicians to provide accurate and complete information; such expectations cannot be met when physicians are not allowed to provide information regarding abortion. How persuasive do you find Justice Marshall's quote? Is it really "disgraceful" to apply the Constitution based upon "unfounded assumptions about how people live"? In what other cases in this book might you be tempted to quote Justice Marshall?

5.   Consider Justice Marshall's quote for another moment or two. Given your understanding of the scope and meaning of medical ethics, evaluate the significance of this quote for judicial decision-making. Would you be more likely or less likely to recommend Justice Marshall's approach to justices of the Supreme Court?

6.   Is the relationship between poor women and their physicians one such that it is deserving of special protection? Justice Blackmun asserts that such a relationship is not "an all-encompassing" one. What does he mean by this? What is the ethical import of his argument?

7.   At least one commentator in bioethics has asserted that *Rust* has more to say about poverty and the medical profession than it does about abortion.[8] In federally funded programs that provide health care, such as Medicare and Medicaid, how much control over the physician-patient dialogue should the government have?

8.   After reading *Rust*, what do you think are the most important issues in the case? Justice Rehnquist asserts that the case concerns whether women may receive information about abortion from clinics receiving federal money. Justice Blackmun views the case as concerning poverty and the physician-patient relationship. With whom do you most agree? Why?

CHIEF JUSTICE REHNQUIST:

...We begin by pointing out the posture of the cases before us. [Doctors and their patients] are challenging the facial validity of the regulations. Thus, we are concerned only with the question whether, on their face, the regulations are both authorized by the Act, and can be construed in such a manner that they can be applied to a set of individuals without infringing upon constitutionally protected rights....

We turn first to [the claim by doctors and their patients] that the regulations exceed the Secretary's authority under Title X, and are arbitrary and capricious. We begin with an examination of the regulations concerning abortion counseling, referral, and advocacy, which every Court of Appeals has found to be authorized by the statute, and then turn to the "program integrity requirement," with respect to which the courts below have adopted conflicting positions. We then address [the claim by doctors and their patients] that the regulations must be struck down because they raise a substantial constitutional question.

We need not dwell on the plain language of the statute, because we agree with every court to have addressed the issue that the language is ambiguous…[but] the Secretary's construction of Title X may not be disturbed as an abuse of discretion if it reflects a plausible construction of the plain language of the statute and does not otherwise conflict with Congress's expressed intent. In determining whether a construction is permissible, "[t]he court need not conclude that the agency construction was the only one it could permissibly have adopted…or even the reading the court would have reached if the question initially had arisen in a judicial proceeding." Rather, substantial deference is accorded to the interpretation of the authorizing statute by the agency authorized with administering it….

We turn next to the "program integrity" requirements embodied in the regulations, mandating separate facilities, personnel, and records. These requirements are not inconsistent with the plain language of Title X. [Doctors and their patients] contend, however, that they are based on an impermissible construction of the statute because they frustrate the clearly expressed intent of Congress that Title X programs be an integral part of a broader, comprehensive, health care system. They argue that this integration is impermissibly burdened because the efficient use of non–Title X funds by Title X grantees will be adversely affected by the regulations.

The Secretary defends the separation requirements of [the statute] on the grounds that they are necessary to assure that Title X grantees apply federal funds only to federally authorized purposes and that grantees avoid creating the appearance that the government is supporting abor-

tion-related activities....The Secretary further argues that
the separation requirements do not represent a deviation
from past policy because the agency has consistently taken
the position that 1008 requires some degree of physical and
financial separation between Title X projects and abortion-
related activities.

We agree that the program integrity requirements are
based on a permissible construction of the statute, and are
not inconsistent with Congressional intent....

[Doctors and their patients] contend that the regulations violate the First Amendment by impermissibly
discriminating based on viewpoint because they prohibit
"all discussion about abortion as a lawful option—including counseling, referral, and the provision of neutral and
accurate information about ending a pregnancy—while
compelling the clinic or counselor to provide information
that promotes continuing a pregnancy to term." They assert that the regulations violate the "free speech rights of
private health care organizations that receive Title X funds,
of their staff, and of their patients" by impermissibly imposing "viewpoint-discriminatory conditions on government subsidies," and thus penaliz[e] speech funded with
non-Title X monies. Because "Title X continues to fund
speech ancillary to pregnancy testing in a manner that is
not evenhanded with respect to views and information
about abortion, it invidiously discriminates on the basis
of viewpoint."...[Doctors and their patients] also assert
that, while the Government may place certain conditions
on the receipt of federal subsidies, it may not "discriminate
invidiously in its subsidies in such a way as to 'ai[m] at the
suppression of dangerous ideas.' "

There is no question but that the statutory prohibition
contained in 1008 is constitutional....The Government
can, without violating the Constitution, selectively fund
a program to encourage certain activities it believes to be

in the public interest, without at the same time funding an alternate program which seeks to deal with the problem in another way. In so doing, the Government has not discriminated on the basis of viewpoint; it has merely chosen to fund one activity to the exclusion of the other. "[A] legislature's decision not to subsidize the exercise of a fundamental right does not infringe the right." "A refusal to fund protected activity, without more, cannot be equated with the imposition of a 'penalty' on that activity." "There is a basic difference between direct state interference with a protected activity and state encouragement of an alternative activity consonant with legislative policy."...

The Title X program is designed not for prenatal care, but to encourage family planning. A doctor who wished to offer prenatal care to a project patient who became pregnant could properly be prohibited from doing so because such service is outside the scope of the federally funded program. The regulations prohibiting abortion counseling and referral are of the same ilk; "no funds appropriated for the project may be used in programs where abortion is a method of family planning," and a doctor employed by the project may be prohibited in the course of his project duties from counseling abortion or referring for abortion. This is not a case of the Government "suppressing a dangerous idea," but of a prohibition on a project grantee or its employees from engaging in activities outside of its scope.

To hold that the Government unconstitutionally discriminates on the basis of viewpoint when it chooses to fund a program dedicated to advance certain permissible goals because the program, in advancing those goals, necessarily discourages alternate goals would render numerous government programs constitutionally suspect.... Petitioners' assertions ultimately boil down to the position that, if the government chooses to subsidize one protected right, it must subsidize analogous counterpart rights. But the Court has soundly rejected that proposition. Within far broader limits than [doctors and their patients] are willing to concede, when the Government appropriates public funds to establish a program, it is entitled to define the limits of that program....

[Chief Justice Rehnquist next discusses prior cases of the Court and how they relate to the issues at hand.]

The same principles apply to [the claim of doctors and their patients] that the regulations abridge the free speech rights of the grantee's staff. Individuals who are voluntarily employed for a Title X project must perform their duties in accordance with the regulation's restrictions on abortion counseling and referral. The employees remain free, however, to pursue abortion-related activities when they are not acting under the auspices of the Title X project. The regulations, which govern solely the scope of the Title X project's activities, do not in any way restrict the activities of those persons acting as private individuals. The employees' freedom of expression is limited during the time that they actually work for the project; but this limitation is a consequence of their decision to accept employment in a project, the scope of which is permissibly restricted by the funding authority....

It could be argued by analogy that traditional relationships such as that between doctor and patient should enjoy protection under the First Amendment from government regulation, even when subsidized by the Government. We need not resolve that question here, however, because the Title X program regulations do not significantly impinge upon the doctor-patient relationship. Nothing in them requires a doctor to represent as his own any opinion that he does not in fact hold. Nor is the doctor-patient relationship established by the Title X program sufficiently all-encompassing so as to justify an expectation on the part of the patient of comprehensive medical advice. The program does not provide post-conception medical care, and therefore a doctor's silence with regard to abortion cannot reasonably be thought to mislead a client into thinking that the doctor does not consider abortion an appropriate option for her. The doctor is always free to make clear that advice regarding abortion is simply beyond the scope of the program. In these circumstances, the general rule that the Government may choose not to subsidize speech applies with full force....

We turn now to [the argument made by doctors and their patients] that the regulations violate a woman's Fifth Amendment right to choose whether to terminate her pregnancy. We recently reaffirmed the long-recognized principle that " 'the Due Process Clauses generally confer no affirmative right to governmental aid, even where such aid may be necessary to secure life, liberty, or property interests of which the government itself may not deprive the individual.' " The Government has no constitutional duty to subsidize an activity merely because the activity is constitutionally protected, and may validly choose to fund childbirth over abortion and " 'implement that judgment by the allocation of public funds' " for medical services relating to childbirth, but not to those relating to abortion. The Government has no affirmative duty to "commit any resources to facilitating abortions," and its decision to fund childbirth but not abortion "places no governmental obstacle in the path of a woman who chooses to terminate her pregnancy, but rather, by means of unequal subsidization of abortion and other medical services, encourages alternative activity deemed in the public interest....

[Doctors and their patients] also argue that by impermissibly infringing on the doctor/patient relationship and depriving a Title X client of information concerning abortion as a method of family planning, the regulations violate a woman's Fifth Amendment right to medical self-determination and to make informed medical decisions free of government-imposed harm. They argue that, under our decisions in *Akron v. Akron Center for Reproductive Health*

Inc. and *Thornburg v. American College of Obstetricians and Gynecologists* the government cannot interfere with a woman's right to make an informed and voluntary choice by placing restrictions on the patient/doctor dialogue.

[Doctors and their patients] contend…that most Title X clients are effectively precluded by indigency and poverty from seeing a health-care provider who will provide abortion-related services. But once again, even these Title X clients are in no worse position than if Congress had never enacted Title X. "The financial constraints that restrict an indigent woman's ability to enjoy the full range of constitutionally protected freedom of choice are the product not of governmental restrictions on access to abortion, but rather of her indigency."

The Secretary's regulations are a permissible construction of Title X, and do not violate either the First or Fifth Amendments to the Constitution. Accordingly, the judgment of the Court of Appeals is Affirmed.

JUSTICE BLACKMUN:

…[T]he majority upholds direct regulation of dialogue between a pregnant woman and her physician when that regulation has both the purpose and the effect of manipulating her decision as to the continuance of her pregnancy. I conclude that the Secretary's regulation of referral, advocacy, and counseling activities exceeds his statutory authority, and also that the Regulations violate the First and Fifth Amendments of our Constitution….

[Justice Blackmun discusses in detail his belief that the Court has misapplied its prior cases.]

Remarkably, the majority concludes that "the Government has not discriminated on the basis of viewpoint; it has merely chosen to fund one activity to the exclusion of another." But the majority's claim that the Regulations merely limit a Title X project's speech to preventive or preconceptional services, ibid., rings hollow in light of the broad range of non-preventive services that the Regulations authorize Title X projects to provide. By refusing to fund those family planning projects that advocate abortion because they advocate abortion, the Government plainly has targeted a particular viewpoint. The majority's reliance on the fact that the Regulations pertain solely to funding decisions simply begs the question. Clearly, there are some bases upon which government may not rest its decision to fund or not to fund. For example, the Members of the majority surely would agree that government may not base its decision to support an activity upon considerations of race. As demonstrated above, our cases make clear that ideological viewpoint is a similarly repugnant ground upon which to base funding decisions....

[I]n addition to their impermissible focus upon the viewpoint of regulated speech, the provisions intrude upon a wide range of communicative conduct, including the very words spoken to a woman by her physician. By manipulating the content of the doctor/patient dialogue, the Regulations upheld today force each of the petitioners "to be an instrument for fostering public adherence to an ideological point of view [he or she] finds unacceptable." This type of intrusive, ideologically based regulation of speech goes far beyond the narrow lobbying limitations...and cannot be justified simply because it is a condition upon the receipt of a governmental benefit.

The Court concludes that the challenged Regulations do not violate the First Amendment rights of Title X staff members, because any limitation of the employees' freedom of expression is simply a consequence of their decision to accept employment at a federally funded project. But it has never been sufficient to justify an otherwise unconstitutional condition upon public employment that the employee may escape the condition by relinquishing his or her job. It is beyond question "that a government may not require an individual to relinquish rights guaranteed him by the First Amendment as a condition of public employment."...

The majority attempts to circumvent this principle by emphasizing that Title X physicians and counselors "remain free...to pursue abortion-related activities when they are not acting under the auspices of the Title X project." "The regulations," the majority explains, "do not in any way restrict the activities of those persons acting as private individuals." Under the majority's reasoning, the First Amendment could be read to tolerate any governmental restriction upon an employee's speech so long as that restriction is limited to the funded workplace. This is a dangerous proposition, and one the Court has rightly rejected in the past. [In previous decisions the Court has ruled that lower courts are required] to balance the speaker's interest in the message against those of government in preventing its dissemination....

[T]he speaker's interest in the communication is both clear and vital. In addressing the family planning needs of their clients, the physicians and counselors who staff Title X projects seek to provide them with the full range of information and options regarding their health and reproductive freedom. Indeed, the legitimate expectations of the patient and the ethical responsibilities of the medical profession demand no less. "The patient's right of self-decision can be effectively exercised only if the patient possesses enough information to enable an intelligent choice.... The physician has an ethical obligation to help the patient make choices from among the therapeutic alternatives consistent with good medical practice." When a client becomes pregnant, the full range of therapeutic alternatives includes the abortion option, and Title X counselors' interest in providing this information is compelling.

The Government's articulated interest in distorting the doctor/patient dialogue—ensuring that federal funds are not spent for a purpose outside the scope of the program—falls far short of that necessary to justify the suppression of truthful information and professional medical opinion regarding constitutionally protected conduct. Moreover, the offending Regulation is not narrowly tailored to serve this interest. For example, the governmental interest at stake could be served by imposing rigorous bookkeeping standards to ensure financial separation or adopting content-neutral rules for the balanced dissemination of family planning and health information. By failing to balance or even to consider the free speech interests claimed by Title X physicians against the Government's asserted interest in suppressing the speech, the Court falters in its duty to implement the protection that the First Amendment clearly provides for this important message.

By far the most disturbing aspect of today's ruling is the effect it will have on the Fifth Amendment rights of the women who, supposedly, are beneficiaries of Title X programs. The majority rejects petitioners' Fifth Amendment claims summarily.

Until today, the Court has allowed to stand only those restrictions upon reproductive freedom that, while limiting the availability of abortion, have left intact a woman's ability to decide without coercion whether she will continue her pregnancy to term. Today's decision abandons that principle, and with disastrous results.

Contrary to the majority's characterization, this is not a case in which individuals seek government aid in exercising their fundamental rights. The Fifth Amendment right asserted by petitioners is the right of a pregnant woman to be free from affirmative governmental interference in her decision. *Roe v. Wade* and its progeny are not so much about a medical procedure as they are about a woman's fundamental right to self-determination. Those cases serve to vindicate the idea that "liberty," if it means anything, must entail freedom from governmental domination in making the most intimate and personal of decisions. By suppressing medically pertinent information and injecting a restrictive ideological message unrelated to considerations of maternal health, the Government places formidable obstacles in the path of Title X clients' freedom of choice and thereby violates their Fifth Amendment rights.

It is crystal clear that the aim of the challenged provisions—an aim the majority cannot escape noticing—is not simply to ensure that federal funds are not used to perform abortions, but to "reduce the incidence of abortion."...[T]he regulations require Title X physicians and counselors to provide information pertaining only to childbirth, to refer a pregnant woman for prenatal care irrespective of her medical situation, and, upon direct inquiry, to respond that abortion is not an "appropriate method" of family planning.

The undeniable message conveyed by this forced speech, and the one that the Title X client will draw from it, is that abortion nearly always is an improper medical option. Although her physician's words, in fact, are strictly controlled by the Government, and wholly unrelated to her particular medical situation, the Title X client will reasonably construe them as professional advice to forgo her right to obtain an abortion. As would most rational patients, many of these women will follow that perceived advice and carry their pregnancy to term, despite their needs to the contrary and despite the safety of the abortion procedure for the vast majority of them. Others, delayed by the Regulations' mandatory prenatal referral, will be prevented from acquiring abortions during the period in which the process is medically sound and constitutionally protected....

The substantial obstacles to bodily self-determination that the Regulations impose are doubly offensive because they are effected by manipulating the very words spoken by physicians and counselors to their patients. In our society, the doctor/patient dialogue embodies a unique relationship of trust. The specialized nature of medical science and the emotional distress often attendant to health-related decisions requires that patients place their complete confidence, and often their very lives, in the hands of medical professionals. One seeks a physician's aid not only for medication or diagnosis, but also for guidance, professional judgment, and vital emotional support. Accordingly, each of us attaches profound importance and authority to the words of advice spoken by the physician....

The manipulation of the doctor/patient dialogue achieved through the Secretary's Regulations is clearly an effort "to deter a woman from making a decision that, with her physician, is hers to make." As such, it violates the Fifth Amendment.

Jaffee v. Redmond
518 U.S. 1 (1996)

Justice Stevens delivered the opinion of the Court, in which Justices O'Connor, Kennedy, Souter, Thomas, Ginsburg, and Breyer joined. Justice Scalia filed a dissenting opinion, in which Chief Justice Rehnquist joined in part.

Areas for Discussion and Ethical Reflection

1.   At the beginning of his majority opinion Justice Stevens makes a distinction between disclosure of information in general medicine and disclosure in psychotherapy. What do you think of that distinction? Is the distinction even important?

2.   Both John Stuart Mill and Immanuel Kant would find elements of Justice Stevens's opinion satisfactory. Which arguments of Justice Stevens are consequentialist in nature? Which are nonconsequentialist? Justice Stevens distinguishes between serving private interests and serving public ends in upholding a

privilege for social workers. Does this distinction dovetail with the distinction between Kant's ethics and Mill's utilitarianism? If not, why not?

3.   In constitutional law as well as in medical ethics, the notion of balancing plays a vital role. Most people recognize that there are competing legitimate interests and arguments involved in constitutional and ethical disputes. Reviewing the previous chapters of this book should aptly demonstrate the central role balancing has occupied in medical ethics and law. But in his majority opinion, Justice Stevens rejects the exercise of balancing the client's interest in privacy with the government's need to obtain evidence in cases where a social worker–client privilege is asserted. What is his argument for this rejection? Does such a rejection bestow too much autonomy on the social work profession?

4.   Acquaint yourself with some of the responsibilities and duties of social work. You might even locate and read the current National Association of Social Workers Code of Ethics. Obviously, *Jaffee* is extremely important for the profession of social work. Why do you think this case has such significance for that profession?

5.   The current NASW Code of Ethics became effective six months after the decision in *Jaffee*. The preamble to the current code reads in part, "The primary mission of the social work profession is to enhance human well-being and help meet the basic human needs of all people, with particular attention to the needs and empowerment of people who are vulnerable, oppressed, and living in poverty."[9] Do you think Justice Scalia might have softened his unflattering stance toward the profession, or perhaps even ruled differently, if he had read the NASW Code of Ethics? Does the Code provide explicit or implicit recognition and resolution of the problems faced by the social worker in *Jaffee*? Might the NASW Code recommend that Karen Beyer provide the information the lower court was seeking?

6.   Justice Scalia, at the end of his dissenting opinion, asserts that the need for a social worker–client privilege has not been

made clear. Do you agree that the need for legal recognition of the duty to preserve confidentiality has not been made clear? What other evidence, or what additional arguments, do you think Justice Scalia would need to change his mind?

JUSTICE STEVENS:

> ...The common-law principles underlying the recognition of testimonial privileges can be stated simply. " 'For more than three centuries it has now been recognized as a fundamental maxim that the public...has a right to every man's evidence.' " When we come to examine the various claims of exemption, we start with the primary assumption that there is a general duty to give what testimony one is capable of giving, and that any exemptions which may exist are distinctly exceptional.... Exceptions from the general rule disfavoring testimonial privileges may be justified, however, by a " 'public good transcending the normally predominant principle of utilizing all rational means for ascertaining the truth.' "

> Guided by these principles, the question we address today is whether a privilege protecting confidential communications between a psychotherapist and her patient "promotes sufficiently important interests to outweigh the need for probative evidence...." Both "reason and experience" persuade us that it does.

> Like the spousal and attorney-client privileges, the psychotherapist-patient privilege is "rooted in the imperative need for confidence and trust." Treatment by a physician for physical ailments can often proceed successfully on the basis of a physical examination, objective information supplied by the patient, and the results of diagnostic tests. Effective psychotherapy, by contrast, depends upon an atmosphere of confidence and trust in which the patient is willing to make a frank and complete disclosure of facts, emotions, memories, and fears. Because of the sensitive nature of the

problems for which individuals consult psychotherapists, disclosure of confidential communications made during counseling sessions may cause embarrassment or disgrace. For this reason, the mere possibility of disclosure may impede development of the confidential relationship necessary for successful treatment....

By protecting confidential communications between a psychotherapist and her patient from involuntary disclosure, the proposed privilege serves important private interests.

Our cases make clear that an asserted privilege must also "serv[e] public ends."...The psychotherapist privilege serves the public interest by facilitating the provision of appropriate treatment for individuals suffering the effects of a mental or emotional problem. The mental health of our citizenry, no less than its physical health, is a public good of transcendent importance.

In contrast to the significant public and private interests supporting recognition of the privilege, the likely evidentiary benefit that would result from the denial of the privilege is modest. If the privilege were rejected, confidential conversations between psychotherapists and their patients would surely be chilled, particularly when it is obvious that the circumstances that give rise to the need for treatment will probably result in litigation. Without a privilege, much of the desirable evidence to which litigants such as petitioner seek access—for example, admissions against interest by a party—is unlikely to come into being. This unspoken "evidence" will therefore serve no greater truth-seeking function than if it had been spoken and privileged.

That it is appropriate for the federal courts to recognize a psychotherapist privilege under Rule 501 is confirmed by the fact that all 50 States and the District of Columbia have enacted into law some form of psychotherapist privilege. We have previously observed that the policy decisions of the

States bear on the question whether federal courts should recognize a new privilege or amend the coverage of an existing one. Because state legislatures are fully aware of the need to protect the integrity of the factfinding functions of their courts, the existence of a consensus among the States indicates that "reason and experience" support recognition of the privilege. In addition, given the importance of the patient's understanding that her communications with her therapist will not be publicly disclosed, any State's promise of confidentiality would have little value if the patient were aware that the privilege would not be honored in a federal court. Denial of the federal privilege therefore would frustrate the purposes of the state legislation that was enacted to foster these confidential communications....

All agree that a psychotherapist privilege covers confidential communications made to licensed psychiatrists and psychologists. We have no hesitation in concluding in this case that the federal privilege should also extend to confidential communications made to licensed social workers in the course of psychotherapy. The reasons for recognizing a privilege for treatment by psychiatrists and psychologists apply with equal force to treatment by a clinical social worker such as Karen Beyer. Today, social workers provide a significant amount of mental health treatment. Their clients often include the poor and those of modest means who could not afford the assistance of a psychiatrist or psychologist, but whose counseling sessions serve the same public goals. Perhaps in recognition of these circumstances, the vast majority of States explicitly extend a testimonial privilege to licensed social workers. We therefore agree with the Court of Appeals that "[d]rawing a distinction between the counseling provided by costly psychotherapists and the counseling provided by more readily accessible social workers serves no discernible public purpose."

We part company with the Court of Appeals on a separate point. We reject the balancing component of the privilege implemented by that court and a small number of States. Making the promise of confidentiality contingent upon a trial judge's later evaluation of the relative importance of the patient's interest in privacy and the evidentiary need for disclosure would eviscerate the effectiveness of the privilege. As we explained in [a previous case], if the purpose of the privilege is to be served, the participants in the confidential conversation "must be able to predict with some degree of certainty whether particular discussions will be protected. An uncertain privilege, or one which purports to be certain but results in widely varying applications by the courts, is little better than no privilege at all."…

The conversations between Officer Redmond and Karen Beyer and the notes taken during their counseling sessions are protected from compelled disclosure under Rule 501 of the Federal Rules of Evidence. The judgment of the Court of Appeals is affirmed.

It is so ordered.

JUSTICE SCALIA:

The Court has discussed at some length the benefit that will be purchased by creation of the evidentiary privilege in this case: the encouragement of psychoanalytic counseling. It has not mentioned the purchase price: occasional injustice. That is the cost of every rule which excludes reliable and probative evidence—or at least every one categorical enough to achieve its announced policy objective. In the case of some of these rules, such as the one excluding confessions that have not been properly "Mirandized," the victim of the injustice is always the impersonal State or the faceless "public at large." For the rule proposed here, the victim is more likely to be some individual who is prevented from proving a valid claim—or (worse still) prevented from establishing a valid defense. The latter is particularly unpalatable for those who love justice, because it causes the courts of law not merely to let stand a wrong, but to become themselves the instruments of wrong…The Court today…ends up creating a privilege that is new, vast, and ill-defined. I respectfully dissent….

To say that the Court devotes the bulk of its opinion to the much easier question of psychotherapist-patient privilege is not to say that its answer to that question is convincing. At bottom, the Court's decision to recognize such a privilege is based on its view that "successful [psycho-therapeutic] treatment" serves "important private interests" (namely those of patients undergoing psychotherapy) as well as the "public good" of "[t]he mental health of our citizenry." I have no quarrel with these premises. Effective psychotherapy undoubtedly is beneficial to individuals with mental problems, and surely serves some larger social interest in maintaining a mentally stable society. But merely mentioning these values does not answer the critical question: are they of such importance, and is the contribution of psychotherapy to them so distinctive, and is the application of normal evidentiary rules so destructive to psycho-therapy, as to justify making our federal courts occasional instruments of injustice? On that central question I find the Court's analysis insufficiently convincing to satisfy the high standard we have set for rules that "are in derogation of the search for truth."

When is it, one must wonder, that the psychotherapist came to play such an indispensable role in the maintenance of the citizenry's mental health? For most of history, men and women have worked out their difficulties by talking to, inter alios, parents, siblings, best friends and bartenders—none of whom was awarded a privilege against testifying in court. Ask the average citizen: Would your mental health be more significantly impaired by preventing you from seeing a psy-chotherapist, or by preventing you from getting advice from your mom? I have little doubt what the answer would be.

Yet there is no mother-child privilege.

How likely is it that a person will be deterred from seeking psychological counseling, or from being completely truthful in the course of such counseling, because of fear of later disclosure in litigation? And even more pertinent to today's decision, to what extent will the evidentiary privilege reduce that deterrent? The Court does not try to answer the first of these questions; and it cannot possibly have any notion of what the answer is to the second, since that depends entirely upon the scope of the privilege, which the Court amazingly finds it "neither necessary nor feasible to delineate."...

Even where it is certain that absence of the psychotherapist privilege will inhibit disclosure of the information, it is not clear to me that that is an unacceptable state of affairs. Let us assume the very worst in the circumstances of the present case: that to be truthful about what was troubling her, the police officer who sought counseling would have to confess that she shot without reason, and wounded an innocent man. If (again to assume the worst) such an act constituted the crime of negligent wounding under Illinois law, the officer would of course have the absolute right not to admit that she shot without reason in criminal court. But I see no reason why she should be enabled both not to admit it in criminal court (as a good citizen should), and to get the benefits of psychotherapy by admitting it to a therapist who cannot tell anyone else. And even less reason why she should be enabled to deny her guilt in the criminal trial—or in a civil trial for negligence—while yet obtaining the benefits of psychotherapy by confessing guilt to a social worker who cannot testify. It seems to me entirely fair to say that if she wishes the benefits of telling the truth she must also accept the adverse consequences. To be sure, in most cases the statements to the psychotherapist will be only marginally relevant, and one of the purposes of the privilege (though not one relied upon by the Court) may be simply to spare patients needless intrusion upon their privacy, and to spare psychotherapists needless expenditure of their time in deposition and trial. But surely this can be achieved by means short of excluding even evidence that is of the most direct and conclusive effect....

The Court's conclusion that a social-worker psycho-therapeutic privilege deserves recognition is even less persuasive....[The Court's] brief analysis—like the earlier, more extensive, discussion of the general psychotherapist privilege—contains no explanation of why the psycho-therapy provided by social workers is a public good of such transcendent importance as to be purchased at the price of occasional injustice. Moreover, it considers only the respects in which social workers providing therapeutic ser-vices are similar to licensed psychiatrists and psychologists; not a word about the respects in which they are different. A licensed psychiatrist or psychologist is an expert in psycho-therapy—and that may suffice (though I think it not so clear that this Court should make the judgment) to justify the use of extraordinary means to encourage counseling with him, as opposed to counseling with one's rabbi, minister, family or friends. One must presume that a social worker does not bring this greatly heightened degree of skill to bear, which is alone a reason for not encouraging that consultation as generously. Does a social worker bring to bear at least a sig-nificantly heightened degree of skill—more than a minister or rabbi, for example? I have no idea, and neither does the Court. The social worker in the present case, Karen Beyer, was a "licensed clinical social worker" in Illinois, a job title whose training requirements consist of "master's degree in social work from an approved program," and "3,000 hours of satisfactory, supervised clinical professional experience." It is not clear that the degree in social work requires any training in psychotherapy....

[Justice Scalia discusses training requirements for social workers in Illinois. He concludes such requirements are not as rigorous as those for lawyers and physicians.]

Another critical distinction between psychiatrists and psychologists, on the one hand, and social workers, on the other, is that the former professionals, in their consultations with patients, do nothing but psychotherapy. Social workers, on the other hand, interview people for a multitude of reasons....

Thus, in applying the "social worker" variant of the "psychotherapist" privilege, it will be necessary to determine whether the information provided to the social worker was provided to him in his capacity as psychotherapist, or in his capacity as an administrator of social welfare, a community organizer, etc. Worse still, if the privilege is to have its desired effect (and is not to mislead the client), it will presumably be necessary for the social caseworker to advise, as the conversation with his welfare client proceeds, which portions are privileged and which are not....

The question before us today is not whether there should be an evidentiary privilege for social workers providing therapeutic services. Perhaps there should. But the question before us is whether (1) the need for that privilege is so clear, and (2) the desirable contours of that privilege are so evident, that it is appropriate for this Court to craft it in common-law fashion, under Rule 501. Even if we were writing on a clean slate, I think the answer to that question would be clear. But given our extensive precedent to the effect that new privileges "in derogation of the search for truth" "are not lightly created," the answer the Court gives today is inexplicable....

Notes

1.   The following discussion is influenced by three excellent articles on the physician-patient relationship. See Robert M. Veatch, "Models for Ethical Medicine in a Revolutionary Age," in *Bio-Ethics*, edited by Rem B. Edwards and Glenn C. Graber (San Diego, CA: Harcourt Brace Jovanovich, 1988), pp. 51–55; Howard Brody, "The Physician-Patient Relationship," in *Medical Eth-*

ics, 2nd ed., edited by Robert M. Veatch (Boston: Jones and Bartlett, 1997), pp. 75–101; Ezekiel Emanuel and Linda Emanuel, "Four Models of the Physician-Patient Relationship," in *Ethical Issues in Modern Medicine*, 6th ed., edited by Bonnie Steinbock et al. (Boston: McGraw-Hill, 2003), pp. 67–76.

2.   Brody, "The Physician-Patient Relationship," in *Medical Ethics*, p. 76.

3.   Veatch, "Models for Ethical Medicine in a Revolutionary Age," in *Bio-Ethics*, p. 52.

4.   Brody, "The Physician-Patient Relationship," in *Medical Ethics*, p. 78.

5.   Rem B. Edwards, "Confidentiality and the Professions," in *Bio-Ethics*, pp. 74–78. The following discussion of confidentiality is indebted to this article.

6.   Mark Siegler, "Confidentiality in Medicine—A Decrepit Concept," in *Intervention and Reflection: Basic Issues in Medical Ethics*, 6th ed., edited by Ronald Munson (Belmont, CA: Wadsworth, 2000), p. 443.

7.   Amitai Etzioni, "Medical Records: Enhancing Privacy, Preserving the Common Good," *Hastings Center Report* 29 (1999): p.14.

8.   George J. Annas, *Standard of Care: The Law of American Bioethics* (New York: Oxford University Press, 1993), pp. 19–21. George Annas provides what is possibly the best summary and analysis of *Rust v. Sullivan*.

9.   The National Association of Social Workers, *NASW Code of Ethics*, 1997.

For Further Reading

Annas, George J. *Standard of Care: The Law of American Bioethics*. New York: Oxford University Press, 1993.

Brody, Howard. "The Physician-Patient Relationship." In *Medical Ethics*, 2nd edition, Robert M. Veatch, ed. Boston: Jones and Bartlett, 1997.

Edwards, Rem B. "Confidentiality and the Professions." In *Bio-Ethics*, Rem B. Edwards and Glenn C. Graber, eds. San Diego, CA: Harcourt Brace Jovanovich, 1988.

Etzioni, Amitai. "Medical Records: Enhancing Privacy, Preserving the Common Good." *Hastings Center Report* 29 (1999): 14–23.

Roberts, Dorothy E. "Reconstructing the Patient: Starting with Women of Color." In *Feminism and Bioethics: Beyond Reproduction*, Susan M. Wolf, ed. New York: Oxford University Press, 1996.

Siegler, Mark. "Confidentiality in Medicine—A Decrepit Concept." In *Intervention and Reflection: Basic Issues in Medical Ethics*, 6th edition, Ronald Munson, ed. Belmont, CA: Wadsworth, 2000.

Veatch, Robert M. "Models for Ethical Medicine in a Revolutionary Age." In *Bio-Ethics*.

CHAPTER SEVEN

THE SCOPE AND REGULATION OF MEDICAL TREATMENT CASES

It should be emphasized at the outset that any medical treatment done primarily to protect the physician from potential lawsuits (rather than to benefit the patient), although sometimes legal, is by definition unethical. And to the extent that exaggerated legal concerns, rather than patient-centered and sound professional practice concerns, determine treatment decisions, medicine both abuses patients and abdicates its responsibility to set the standard of care.

—George Annas, *Standard of Care: The Law of American Bioethics*

One need not engage in the study of medical ethics in depth or for a long period of time before realizing that the practice of medicine—no matter how ethically laudable it may be, no matter how much it exemplifies the highest standards of the profession—often comes into conflict with values and norms of other institutions in society. The health care professions in general, and medicine in particular, enjoy a degree of autonomy and independence enjoyed by few other professions. The reasons for this autonomy and independence are historical, political, legal, and moral in nature. The ability to actually save lives through medical intervention and technology bestowed upon medicine power and prestige. Professional associations, such as the American Medical Association, have used this prestige to acquire political influence and to affect social and political agendas. Both common law and constitutional law have recognized and honored medicine's special place in society. And, finally, with power, influence, and recognition have come moral and ethical obligations on the part of medicine to act responsibly and professionally. Yet medicine's power and independence are not absolute. Often, professional values and moral obligations conflict with legal commitments and responsibilities of the state. A physician's choice to exercise her/his duty to promote patient welfare by prescribing marijuana to alleviate suffering, for example, may conflict with the state's responsibility to prohibit distribution of substances it considers dangerous. Thus, on many occasions the Supreme Court has had to consider how to resolve conflicts between professional judgment and state regulation. This conflict is, of course, a central concern of medical ethics.

Constitutional Issues and Background

Our first case, *United States v. Rutherford*, does not involve debate over interpretation and application of one or more constitutional principles, but instead centers around statutory interpretation and the power of a federal agency to interpret certain terms. The case concerned the drug Laetrile and Section 505 of the Federal Food, Drug, and Cosmetic Act, which prohibited interstate distribution of any "new drug" unless the safety and effectiveness of the drug could be demonstrated to the secretary of health, education, and welfare. Suit was brought in Federal District Court in 1975 by terminally ill cancer patients and their spouses to stop the government from interfering with their ability to obtain and use Laetrile. After being ordered to consider the status of Laetrile, the commissioner of the Food and Drug Administration ruled that Laetrile was a "new drug," hence prohibiting its use by cancer patients was proper. The district court found the drug safe and effective in proper doses and concluded that the commissioner's decision violated privacy interests of patients who wished to use the drug under a doctor's supervision. The

Court of Appeals for the Tenth Circuit, though not addressing the privacy issues, agreed with the District Court that patients should have access to the drug on the grounds that safety and effectiveness had no relevance for terminally ill cancer patients.

The Supreme Court examined both the legislative history of the act and the meanings of "safe and effective." In a unanimous opinion written by Justice Marshall, the Court concluded that the federal government could prohibit the distribution of Laetrile. Justice Marshall was not sympathetic with the Tenth Circuit's assertion that the statute's definitions of "safe" and "effective" had no relevance to terminally ill cancer patients. Of particular note is the fact that the Court was unwilling to consider the privacy interests of the terminally ill patients, although the Court did observe that terminally ill patients are vulnerable and must be protected from practices and substances that could do them harm. Eighteen years later the Supreme Court's comments on the vulnerability of terminally ill patients would take on new meaning. Justice Rehnquist, in his opinion in *Washington v. Glucksberg*, quoted from *Rutherford* in supporting the state of Washington's position that all human life is valuable and worthy of state protection.

Our second case concerns partial-birth abortion and the lengths to which a state may go in prohibiting a medical procedure. Not since *Casey* had the Supreme Court dealt with issues surrounding abortion and the regulation of medicine as controversial as the issues raised in *Stenberg v. Carhart*. At issue in *Stenberg* was whether Nebraska's law prohibiting the D&X procedure (partial-birth abortion) violated a woman's constitutional right to privacy as that right is interpreted and understood in *Roe* and *Casey*. In the late 1990s, Dr. LeRoy Carhart was a practicing physician in Nebraska who performed abortions. In an effort to stop physicians from performing what it termed partial-birth abortions, Nebraska passed legislation prohibiting the procedure unless necessary to save the life of the woman. Violating the law could result in a twenty-five-thousand-dollar fine, a prison term of up to twenty years, and revocation of the physician's license to practice medicine. Carhart brought suit in district court claiming that the legislation violated the U.S. Constitution. The district court agreed, and the Eighth Circuit Court of Appeals affirmed.

The Supreme Court gave two basic reasons for finding the Nebraska statute unconstitutional. First, the law made no exception for preserving the woman's health, and second, the law constituted an "undue burden" on the woman's right to choose an abortion. The reasons the Court provided in support of these conclusions rested in its previous decisions in *Casey* and *Roe*. Much of the majority's concern regarding the Nebraska statute centered on the role of physicians and the state's desire to interfere with medical judgment. The dissents in this case are particularly vigorous since several justices desired that *Roe* be overruled.

Our third case returns us to the problem of responsibly meeting the needs of suffering cancer patients. But where the patients in *Rutherford* were seeking a cure for their disease, the patients in *United States v. Oakland Cannabis Buyers Cooperative et al.* were seeking relief from physical pain and suffering. In 1996, California voters approved a measure allowing for medical uses of marijuana. The Compassionate Use Act made exceptions to existing laws prohibiting cultivation and possession of marijuana; for example, patients and caregivers could possess and patients could use marijuana if there was a medical purpose for the use and a physician prescribed the drug. The Oakland Cannabis Buyers Cooperative, a not-for-profit organization, distributed marijuana to patients who provided a written order for marijuana therapy from a physician and who came for an interview. In January 1998 the United States sued the cooperative and its medical director seeking to stop the organization from manufacturing and distributing marijuana. The district court found that medical necessity was not a legitimate reason for violating the Controlled Substances Act (CSA) and issued an injunction against the cooperative, but the cooperative openly violated the order. On appeal, the Ninth Circuit overruled the district court and asserted that medical necessity was a legitimate defense.

The issue before the Supreme Court was how to interpret relevant provisions of the Controlled Substances Act. Specifically, the Court examined whether a medical necessity exception in the act permits the use of marijuana by patients who are suffering and who have consulted with a physician. In writing for a unanimous Court, Justice Thomas rejected the claim that medical necessity could be used as a defense against violations of the act. Justice Thomas also rejected any appeal to public interest as a reason for overriding congressional intent to ban marijuana except for use in research projects. The Court concluded that the symptoms and needs of patients cannot override the interests of the government in regulating marijuana. The Court's interpretation of the CSA, as well as its ruling that federal regulations override state initiatives, has implications for a host of issues in medical ethics, most notably physician-assisted suicide. More on this is provided below.

Ethical Issues and Background

The opinions excerpted from the three cases covered in this chapter allow us to explore further the relationship between physicians and their patients and the debate over what constitutes justifiable interference by the state in that relationship. Various models of the physician-patient relationship were covered in the previous chapter, and you may wish to keep these models in mind as you read and evaluate the decisions in this chapter. Two of the three cases provide additional insight into how the justices view the plight of terminally ill and suffering patients, and what if any obligations the federal government has toward such patients. Interesting parallels exist between the limits that the Constitution permits the government to impose on medical interventions for terminally ill patients and how the Court deals with physician-assisted suicide. Our consideration of the justices' moral commitments will be aided by briefly discussing the concepts of the goals of medicine, paternalism, and John Stuart Mill's harm principle.

All three cases in this chapter directly involve state or federal regulation of medical treatment. Consequently, all three cases require an understanding of the proper meaning and scope of medicine. In considering, from an ethical perspective, what constitutes legitimate versus illegitimate regulation of medical practice, identifying the proper goals of medicine is helpful. In other words, we as individuals and as a society must articulate and justify exactly what it is we expect medicine to do. Jonsen, Siegler, and Winslade address this challenge directly by articulating seven goals of medicine.[1] These goals are: 1) promotion of health and prevention of disease; 2) relief of symptoms, pain, and suffering; 3) cure of disease; 4) prevention of untimely death; 5) improvement of functional status or maintenance of compromised status; 6) education and counseling of patients regarding their condition and its prognosis; and 7) avoiding harm to the patient in the course of care. If we consider as the major responsibility of medicine the benefit of patients, then these goals are part of that responsibility. In many cases all of these goals can be achieved simultaneously; however, in clinical settings two or more of these goals may come into conflict or the goals may be simply unclear. Prevention of untimely death may conflict with the goal of pain relief, for example.

In making explicit the relationship between constitutional adjudication and medical ethics and in discerning the influence of medical ethics on the High Court, you should try determining whether one or more of the justices is sympathetic to any or all of the above goals. Would the outcomes in *Rutherford* and *Oakland Cannabis Buyers Cooperative* have been different if Justice Marshall or Justice Thomas had adopted a different perspective on the responsibilities of medicine? This question assumes that interpretation of administrative regulations, acts of Congress, and even constitutional provisions could or should be influenced by one's position regarding the responsibilities of medicine. Defending this assumption is left to the reader.

Another conceptual issue of great ethical significance for all three cases is paternalism. We begin with a straightforward and somewhat simplistic definition of paternalism. Paternalism consists of "acting in a way that is believed to protect or advance the interest of a person, although acting in this way goes against the person's own immediate desires or limits the person's freedom of choice."[2] When we grant or acquiesce in a person's wishes or desires we are respecting the moral principle of autonomy; however, when we act paternalistically we override a person's wishes or desires, in accord with either respect for the moral principle of beneficence or respect for the moral principle of nonmaleficence.[3] Paternalism, and the ethical and legal problems associated with it, is made much clearer if we make two sets of distinctions: weak and strong paternalism, and personal and state paternalism.

When we interfere with a person's desires, either because we wish to promote her/his good or to prevent harm, and the person is acting with diminished autonomy, we are engaging in weak paternalism. That is, we intervene on grounds that the person is about to act in a "substantially nonvoluntary or nonautonomous" way.[4] If a five-year-old child wishes to play in heavy traffic, to stop the child would be to intervene in an action that clearly is substantially nonvoluntary or nonautonomous. On the other hand, when we interfere with a person's desires, either because we wish to promote her/his good or prevent harm, and the person's desires result from rational, autonomous deliberations, we are engaging in strong paternalism. That is, the need to protect individuals from harm appears to justify overriding or not acquiescing in a person's desires. When a wife forbids her husband from taking skydiving lessons on the grounds that she is convinced he will hurt himself, and we have every reason to believe the husband's desire is sustained and rational, the wife is engaging in strong paternalism.

This brief discussion of weak and strong paternalism leads naturally into a discussion of another relevant distinction, personal versus state paternalism.[5] Personal (sometimes called private) paternalism results when individuals intervene in the actions of others from a motive of preventing harm to or promoting the good of individuals. The two above examples—stopping the child from playing in heavy traffic and forbidding the husband from taking skydiving lessons—are instances of personal paternalism, with the former weak and the latter strong. State (sometimes called public) paternalism occurs when government entities—the legislative, executive, and judicial branches—enact laws, approve regulations, or interpret constitutional provisions in such a way as to interfere with the practices or wishes of groups or individuals, for the purpose of preventing harm to the group or individual. Simple examples of state paternalism include state regulations requiring seventy-two-hour commitment for individuals attempting suicide and laws prohibiting individuals from riding motorcycles unless they wear helmets. As with personal paternalism, state paternalism can be either weak or strong. Mandatory seventy-two-hour commitment for those who attempt suicide is usually considered weak paternalism, and motorcycle helmet laws are usually considered strong. We should note, however, that how to characterize a specific law can be controversial. For example, some would argue that choosing to ride a motorcycle without a helmet is clearly irrational, thus making laws requiring their use an example of weak paternalism.

Indeed, disputes over characterizations do have ethical and constitutional significance. Very few problems arise when individuals or the state, acting from the motive of preventing harm or promoting good, interfere with the nonautonomous, irrational choices of others. Significant problems and concerns do arise, however, when the state, acting to promote the interests of individuals, interferes with the choices of those individuals that are the result of rational, autonomous reflection. That is, strong ethical argumentation is needed to justify the state infringing on the liberty of individuals (or groups) in order to protect their interests when all evidence suggests that these individuals (or groups) know full well what their interests are and are acting rationally. One's understanding and commitment to such principles as autonomy and beneficence will dictate one's position on the moral permissibility of strong paternalistic actions undertaken by the state. From the perspective of constitutional law, justifications of strong paternalism may depend in part on how one views the functions of government and then reconciling that view with specific provisions in the Constitution. The three cases in this chapter are prime examples of how the Supreme Court considers the constitutionality of state and federal regulations that interfere with liberty of action. As you read the cases, keep in mind that few people argue against state interference with individual choice to protect others from harm (see *Jacobson* in chapter 5).

Perhaps the strongest opponent of state interference with the autonomous choices of others was John Stuart Mill. Mill's position was that the only justifiable reason for the state coercing autonomous individuals was to protect others from harm. Mill states his position succinctly in what has come to be known as the harm principle. Mill asserts:

> ...[T]he sole end for which mankind are warranted, in-
> dividually or collectively, in interfering with the liberty of
> action of any of their number, is self-protection. That the
> only purpose for which power can be rightfully exercised
> over any member of a civilized community, against his will,
> is to prevent harm to others. His own good, either physical
> or moral, is not a sufficient warrant.[6]

Mill's principle seems to have at least two meanings.[7] First, individuals and governments are entitled to interfere with the liberty of others if such interference is necessary to prevent harm to third parties. For example, the state may certainly criminalize murder and rape. Very few would object to this understanding of the harm principle. Second, interfering with the liberty of another for the purpose of promoting either that individual's good or the good of society is never permissible. No doubt, Mill would find laws requiring the wearing of motorcycle helmets an unjustifiable violation of autonomous action and liberty. But, as you will see from reading the Court's decisions below, this second meaning is much more controversial.

We all value freedom to make choices, especially when those choices are the result of sustained, reflective, and careful thought. But even if we are sympathetic with Mill's insistence on placing absolute value on autonomy and self-determination, we cannot help but think that there are times, perhaps not often, when government is entitled to implement compulsory measures designed to promote individual and community welfare. Gerald Dworkin notes that health care is a good of such importance that it may justify government coercion to realize important health benefits for individuals and the community.[8] In addition, he notes that many people are careless and do not think through the consequences of their actions, and that if people were sufficiently far-sighted they would realize government coercion is justified. As you read the cases in this chapter and others in this book, you have an opportunity to think further about the problems associated with the harm principle.

United States v. Rutherford
442 U.S. 544 (1979)

Justice Marshall delivered the opinion for a unanimous Court.

Areas for Discussion and Ethical Reflection

1.   Justice Marshall provides several arguments in support of the Court's position that the Food, Drug, and Cosmetic Act should not be interpreted to allow terminally ill cancer patients access to Laetrile. What are those arguments? Which, if any, are morally significant? What, if any, arguments used by Justice Marshall are relevant to justifications of state paternalism? Indeed, the actions of both the FDA and the Supreme Court seem to be instances of strong paternalism. How do you make and defend the distinction between justifiable and unjustifiable instances of strong paternalism undertaken by the state?

2.   Is it morally significant that, as Justice Marshall points out,

the FDA has never made exceptions to its policy for terminally ill patients? As a simple matter of legitimate ethical argumentation, are we entitled to make appeals to tradition?

3.   What weight does the issue of whether Laetrile is "safe and effective" carry in Justice Marshall's arguments? Might we define "safe and effective" differently in different contexts? Take note of the definition of "effective" provided by Justice Marshall. Does anything about this definition strike you as strange? That is, does it seem ironic to worry over the safety and effectiveness of medications that will be used by terminally ill cancer patients? How might Justice Marshall respond? This issue carries implications for the morally permissible limits that a state may place on the regulation of medicine. Also take note of what it means for a drug to be "safe." Do you find the notion of safety as used by the act convincing? Would evaluating the distinction between weak and strong paternalism help you here?

4.   Justice Marshall concludes his decision by pointing out the disastrous consequences of waiving the safety and effectiveness standards of the act for terminally ill patients. What are these disastrous consequences? Do you think Justice Marshall's concerns are justified?

5.   Everyone would agree that the right to receive as well as the obligation to provide any medical treatment one wishes is not absolute. However, tremendous disagreement exists over the morally acceptable limits to the right or obligation. May a patient require physicians to provide any treatment the patient wishes as long as no direct harm results? What exactly should be the ethical limits on patients' requests? Of course, this question assumes we have a well-considered position on the obligations of physicians.

6.   Interesting parallels exist between this case and *Oakland Cannabis Buyers Cooperative*. What are the similarities between the two cases? After you have had a chance to consider physician-assisted suicide and have read the decisions in *Washington v. Glucksberg* and *Vacco v. Quill* in chapter 9, you may wish to

return to *Rutherford* and *Oakland Cannabis*. For now, pay attention to how the Court views suffering and the extent to which the government may interfere in efforts by physicians to ameliorate the pain and suffering experienced by patients. What are the moral arguments in favor of allowing states to make quality of life determinations? What moral arguments might a state use to justify its refusal to make such determinations?

Justice Marshall:

The question presented in this case is whether the Federal Food, Drug, and Cosmetic Act precludes terminally ill cancer patients from obtaining Laetrile, a drug not recognized as "safe and effective" within the meaning of 201 (p) (1) of the Act.

Section 505 of the Federal Food, Drug, and Cosmetic Act prohibits interstate distribution of any "new drug" unless the Secretary of Health, Education, and Welfare approves an application supported by substantial evidence of the drug's safety and effectiveness. As defined in 201 (p) (1) of the Act, the term "new drug" includes

"[a]ny drug...not generally recognized, among experts qualified by scientific training and experience to evaluate the safety and effectiveness of drugs, as safe and effective for use under the conditions prescribed, recommended, or suggested in the labeling...."

Exemptions from premarketing approval procedures are available for drugs intended solely for investigative use and drugs qualifying under either of the Act's two grandfather provisions.

[The Court goes on to note that terminally ill cancer patients and their spouses went to District Court to stop the government from interfering with the interstate shipment and sale of Laetrile, a drug that many patients and their doctors considered safe and perhaps effective in treating various types of cancer. Both the District Court and the Court of Appeals ruled that an implied exemption to the act for terminally ill cancer patients was justified.]

We granted certiorari and now reverse....

When construing a statute so explicit in scope, a court must act within certain well-defined constraints. If a legislative purpose is expressed in "plain and unambiguous language,...the...duty of the courts is to give it effect according to its terms." Exceptions to clearly delineated statutes will be implied only where essential to prevent "absurd results" or consequences obviously at variance with the policy of the enactment as a whole. In the instant case, we are persuaded by the legislative history and consistent administrative interpretation of the Act that no implicit exemption for drugs used by the terminally ill is necessary to attain congressional objectives or to avert an unreasonable reading of the terms "safe" and "effective" in 201 (p) (1).

> Nothing in the history of the 1938 Food, Drug, and Cosmetic Act, which first established procedures for review of drug safety, or of the 1962 Amendments, which added the current safety and effectiveness standards in 201 (p) (1), suggests that Congress intended protection only for persons suffering from curable diseases. To the contrary, in deliberations preceding the 1938 Act, Congress expressed concern that individuals with fatal illnesses, such as cancer, should be shielded from fraudulent cures....

In implementing the statutory scheme, the FDA has never made exception for drugs used by the terminally ill. As this Court has often recognized, the construction of a statute by those charged with its administration is entitled to substantial deference....Unless and until Congress does so, we are reluctant to disturb a longstanding administrative policy that comports with the plain language, history, and prophylactic purpose of the Act.

In the Court of Appeals' view, an implied exemption from the Act was justified because the safety and effectiveness standards set forth in 201 (p) (1) could have "no reasonable application" to terminally ill patients. We disagree. Under our constitutional framework, federal courts do not sit as councils of revision, empowered to rewrite legislation in accord with their own conceptions of prudent public policy. Only when a literal construction of a statute yields results so manifestly unreasonable that they could not fairly be attributed to congressional design will an exception to statutory language be judicially implied. Here, however, we have no license to depart from the plain language of the Act, for Congress could reasonably have intended to shield terminal patients from ineffectual or unsafe drugs.

A drug is effective within the meaning of 201 (p) (1) if there is general recognition among experts, founded on substantial evidence, that the drug in fact produces the results claimed for it under prescribed conditions. Contrary to the Court of Appeals' apparent assumption, effectiveness does not necessarily denote capacity to cure. In the treatment of any illness, terminal or otherwise, a drug is effective if it fulfills, by objective indices, its sponsor's claims of prolonged life, improved physical condition, or reduced pain.

So too, the concept of safety under 201 (p) (1) is not without meaning for terminal patients. Few if any drugs are completely safe in the sense that they may be taken by all persons in all circumstances without risk. Thus, the Commissioner generally considers a drug safe when the expected therapeutic gain justifies the risk entailed by its use. For the terminally ill, as for anyone else, a drug is unsafe if its potential for inflicting death or physical injury is not offset by the possibility of therapeutic benefit. Indeed, the Court of Appeals implicitly acknowledged that safety considerations have relevance for terminal cancer patients by restricting authorized use of Laetrile to intravenous injections for persons under a doctor's supervision.

Moreover, there is a special sense in which the relationship between drug effectiveness and safety has meaning in the context of incurable illnesses. An otherwise harmless drug can be dangerous to any patient if it does not produce its purported therapeutic effect. But if an individual suffering from a potentially fatal disease rejects conventional therapy in favor of a drug with no demonstrable curative properties, the consequences can be irreversible. For this reason, even before the 1962 Amendments incorporated an efficacy standard into new drug application procedures, the FDA considered effectiveness when reviewing the safety of drugs used to treat terminal illness. The FDA's practice also reflects the recognition, amply supported by expert medical testimony in this case, that with diseases such as cancer it is often impossible to identify a patient as terminally ill except in retrospect. Cancers vary considerably in behavior and in responsiveness to different forms of therapy. Even critically ill individuals may have unexpected remissions and may respond to conventional treatment. Thus, as the Commissioner concluded, to exempt from the Act drugs with no proved effectiveness in the treatment of cancer "would lead to needless deaths and suffering among…patients characterized as 'terminal' who could actually be helped by legitimate therapy."

It bears emphasis that although the Court of Appeals' ruling was limited to Laetrile, its reasoning cannot be so readily confined. To accept the proposition that the safety and efficacy standards of the Act have no relevance for terminal patients is to deny the Commissioner's authority over all drugs, however toxic or ineffectual, for such individuals. If history is any guide, this new market would not be long overlooked. Since the turn of the century, resourceful entrepreneurs have advertised a wide variety of purportedly simple and painless cures for cancer, including liniments of turpentine, mustard, oil, eggs, and ammonia; peat moss; arrangements of colored floodlamps; pastes made from glycerin and limburger cheese; mineral tablets; and "Fountain of Youth" mixtures of spices, oil, and suet. In citing these examples, we do not, of course, intend to deprecate the sincerity of Laetrile's current proponents, or to imply any opinion on whether that drug may ultimately prove safe and effective for cancer treatment. But this historical experience does suggest why Congress could reasonably have determined to protect the terminally ill, no less than other patients, from the vast range of self-styled panaceas that inventive minds can devise....

The judgment of the Court of Appeals is reversed, and the case is remanded for further proceedings consistent with this opinion. So ordered.

Stenberg v. Carhart
530 U.S. 914 (2000)

Justice Breyer delivered the opinion of the Court, in which Justices Stevens, O'Connor, Souter, and Ginsburg joined. Justice Stevens filed a concurring opinion, in which Justice Ginsburg joined. Justice O'Connor filed a concurring opinion. Justice Ginsburg filed a concurring opinion, in which Justice Stevens joined. Chief Justice Rehnquist and Justice Scalia each filed dissenting opinions. Justice Kennedy filed a dissenting opinion, in which Chief Justice Rehnquist joined. Justice Thomas filed a dissenting opinion, in which Chief Justice Rehnquist and Justice Scalia joined.

Areas for Discussion and Ethical Reflection

1. *Stenberg v. Carhart* is placed in this chapter on the scope and regulation of medical treatment because of the ethical concerns it raises regarding legitimate state intervention into one area of

the doctor-patient relationship. However, many commentators discuss this case in the context of abortion. Indeed, Justice Breyer begins his opinion by stating, "We again consider the right to an abortion." What do you think the case is about? Do the justices in the majority and those dissenting agree over the central issues involved in the case? If, after reading the case, you determine that the author of your book was wrong in placing *Stenberg* in this chapter, formulate an argument in support of your position. Feel free to allow the dissenters in *Stenberg* to help you.

2.   How might you claim that the actions of the Nebraska legislature, in prohibiting the use of the D&X procedure, constitute an example of strong state paternalism? If you determine that Nebraska's law does constitute paternalism, consider whether the law is morally justifiable.

3.   Justice Breyer gives two basic reasons for claiming that Nebraska's partial-birth abortion law violates the Constitution as interpreted in *Roe* and *Casey*. First, the law makes no exception for the preservation of the health of the woman. Second, the law places an undue burden on a woman's ability to choose a D&E abortion. How does Justice Breyer support these two basic reasons? To what explicit or implicit values are the justices in the majority subscribing?

4.   From a constitutional jurisprudence perspective, do you agree that the holdings in *Roe* and *Casey*, and the reasoning in support of those holdings, support the decision in *Stenberg*? Do you agree from a purely moral perspective?

5.   From a moral perspective, do you agree with Nebraska that a health exception in its law is not needed? Nebraska claims that the ban on the D&X procedure poses no risk to women because there are alternative procedures. What do the facts of the matter suggest to you? Justice Breyer points out that "…it would have been a simple matter" for the ban to include language that would allow for the D&E procedure. Why did Nebraska not include such language? Would the motives of the Nebraska legislators

who passed the ban matter to you? Do their motives matter with regard to whether we should characterize the law as an example of strong state paternalism?

6.   Justice Kennedy, in his dissenting opinion, asserts: "A State may take measures to ensure the medical profession and its members are viewed as healers…." Evaluate this assertion within the context of our discussion of the proper goals of medicine. Is it possible that Justice Kennedy is wrong in his assertion, that in actuality the state should not take steps to ensure that the medical profession and its members are viewed as healers? Discuss this possibility in detail.

7.   Justice Stevens, in his very short concurrence, notes his failure to understand how a state could prevent a physician from performing a procedure that the physician reasonably believes will protect the health of the woman. What is Justice Stevens's argument?

8.   In his very brief dissenting opinion (not excerpted below), Justice Scalia uses phrases such as "killing a human child," "shudder of revulsion," "give live-birth abortion free reign," and "eliminating our half-born posterity." Are such emotively charged phrases appropriate for a justice of the Supreme Court? Would it be appropriate for students in a medical ethics course debating the morality of partial-birth abortion to use such phrases?

9.   How would you go about arguing that early abortions are morally permissible but late-term or partial-birth abortions are not? Your answer should not rely on the facts of the matter; that is, the gruesomeness of the D&X procedure should not be the controlling factor in your decision-making. If you also think early abortions should remain legal but partial-birth abortions should not, how do you explain the distinction?

10.   On June 4, 2003, the U.S. House voted 282-139 to make a federal crime the performance by doctors of second or third trimester abortions. Members who voted for the law insisted that saving the life of the mother would count as the only exception to the ban. In addition, the House refused, by a vote of

256-165, to grant a health waiver to the legislation. From a moral perspective, evaluate the House's actions. How do you think the majority in *Stenberg* would respond to the House action? If the House measure were actually to become law, what constitutional problems would it pose? What moral problems?

Justice Breyer:

We again consider the right to an abortion. We understand the controversial nature of the problem. Millions of Americans believe that life begins at conception and consequently that an abortion is akin to causing the death of an innocent child; they recoil at the thought of a law that would permit it. Other millions fear that a law that forbids abortion would condemn many American women to lives that lack dignity, depriving them of equal liberty and leading those with least resources to undergo illegal abortions with the attendant risks of death and suffering. Taking account of these virtually irreconcilable points of view, aware that constitutional law must govern a society whose different members sincerely hold directly opposing views, and considering the matter in light of the Constitution's guarantees of fundamental individual liberty, this Court, in the course of a generation, has determined and then redetermined that the Constitution offers basic protection to the woman's right to choose. We shall not revisit those legal principles. Rather, we apply them to the circumstances of this case.

Three established principles determine the issue before us. We shall set them forth in the language of the joint opinion in *Casey*. First, before "viability…the woman has a right to choose to terminate her pregnancy."

Second, "a law designed to further the State's interest in fetal life which imposes an undue burden on the woman's decision before fetal viability" is unconstitutional. An "undue burden is…shorthand for the conclusion that a state regulation has the purpose or effect of placing a substantial obstacle in the path of a woman seeking an abortion of a nonviable fetus."

Third, " 'subsequent to viability, the State in promoting its interest in the potentiality of human life may, if it chooses, regulate, and even proscribe, abortion except where it is necessary, in appropriate medical judgment, for the preservation of the life or health of the mother.' "

We apply these principles to a Nebraska law banning "partial birth abortion." The statute reads as follows:

> "No partial birth abortion shall be performed in this state, unless such procedure is necessary to save the life of the mother whose life is endangered by a physical disorder, physical illness, or physical injury, including a life-endangering physical condition caused by or arising from the pregnancy itself."

The statute defines "partial birth abortion" as:

> "an abortion procedure in which the person performing the abortion partially delivers vaginally a living unborn child before killing the unborn child and completing the delivery."

It further defines "partially delivers vaginally a living unborn child before killing the unborn child" to mean

> "deliberately and intentionally delivering into the vagina a living unborn child, or a substantial portion thereof, for the purpose of performing a procedure that the person performing such procedure knows will kill the unborn child and does kill the unborn child."

The law classifies violation of the statute as a "Class III felony" carrying a prison term of up to 20 years, and a fine of up to $25,000. It also provides for the automatic revocation of a doctor's license to practice medicine in Nebraska.

We hold that this statute violates the Constitution....

Because Nebraska law seeks to ban one method of aborting a pregnancy, we must describe and then discuss several different abortion procedures. Considering the fact that those procedures seek to terminate a potential human life, our discussion may seem clinically cold or callous to some, perhaps horrifying to others. There is no alternative way, however, to acquaint the reader with the technical distinctions among different abortion methods and related factual matters, upon which the outcome of this case depends. For that reason, drawing upon the findings of the trial court, underlying testimony, and related medical texts, we shall describe the relevant methods of performing abortions in technical detail.

1. About 90% of all abortions performed in the United States take place during the first trimester of pregnancy, before 12 weeks of gestational age. During the first trimester, the predominant abortion method is "vacuum aspiration," which involves insertion of a vacuum tube (cannula) into the uterus to evacuate the contents. Such an abortion is typically performed on an outpatient basis under local anesthesia. Vacuum aspiration is considered particularly safe. The procedure's mortality rates for first trimester abortion are, for example, 5 to 10 times lower than those associated with carrying the fetus to term. Complication rates are also low. As the fetus grows in size, however, the vacuum aspiration method becomes increasingly difficult to use.

2. Approximately 10% of all abortions are performed during the second trimester of pregnancy (12 to 24 weeks)....[T]he medical profession has switched from medical induction of labor to surgical procedures for most second trimester abortions. The most commonly used procedure is called "dilation and evacuation" (D&E).

That procedure (together with a modified form of vacuum aspiration used in the early second trimester) accounts for about 95% of all abortions performed from 12 to 20 weeks of gestational age.

3. D&E "refers generically to transcervical procedures performed at 13 weeks gestation or later."…There are variations in D&E operative strategy. However, the common points are that D&E involves (1) dilation of the cervix; (2) removal of at least some fetal tissue using nonvacuum instruments; and (3) (after the 15th week) the potential need for instrumental disarticulation or dismemberment of the fetus or the collapse of fetal parts to facilitate evacuation from the uterus.

4. When instrumental disarticulation incident to D&E is necessary, it typically occurs as the doctor pulls a portion of the fetus through the cervix into the birth canal.…

5. The D&E procedure carries certain risks. The use of instruments within the uterus creates a danger of accidental perforation and damage to neighboring organs. Sharp fetal bone fragments create similar dangers. And fetal tissue accidentally left behind can cause infection and various other complications. Nonetheless studies show that the risks of mortality and complication that accompany the D&E procedure between the 12th and 20th weeks of gestation are significantly lower than those accompanying induced labor procedures (the next safest midsecond trimester procedures).

6. At trial, Dr. Carhart and Dr. Stubblefield described a variation of the D&E procedure, which they referred to as an "intact D&E." Like other versions of the D&E technique, it begins with induced dilation of the cervix. The procedure then involves removing the fetus from the uterus through the cervix "intact," *i.e.*, in one pass, rather than in several passes. It is used after 16 weeks at the earliest, as vacuum aspiration becomes ineffective and the fetal skull becomes

too large to pass through the cervix....

7. The intact D&E procedure can also be found described in certain obstetric and abortion clinical textbooks, where two variations are recognized....

8. The American College of Obstetricians and Gynecologists describes the D&X procedure in a manner corresponding to a breech-conversion intact D&E, including the following steps:

1. deliberate dilatation of the cervix, usually over a sequence of days;

2. instrumental conversion of the fetus to a footling breech;

3. breech extraction of the body excepting the head; and

4. partial evacuation of the intracranial contents of a living fetus to effect vaginal delivery of a dead but otherwise intact fetus.

Despite the technical differences we have just described, intact D&E and D&X are sufficiently similar for us to use the terms interchangeably.

9. Dr. Carhart testified he attempts to use the intact D&E procedure during weeks 16 to 20 because (1) it reduces the dangers from sharp bone fragments passing through the cervix, (2) minimizes the number of instrument passes needed for extraction and lessens the likelihood of uterine perforations caused by those instruments, (3) reduces the likelihood of leaving infection-causing fetal and placental tissue in the uterus, and (4) could help to prevent potentially fatal absorption of fetal tissue into the maternal circulation. The District Court made no findings about the D&X procedure's overall safety. The District Court concluded, however, that "the evidence is both clear and convincing that Carhart's D&X procedure is superior to, and safer than, the...other abortion procedures used during the relevant

gestational period in the 10 to 20 cases a year that present to Dr. Carhart."

10. The materials presented at trial referred to the potential benefits of the D&X procedure in circumstances involving nonviable fetuses, such as fetuses with abnormal fluid accumulation in the brain (hydrocephaly)....Others have emphasized its potential for women with prior uterine scars, or for women for whom induction of labor would be particularly dangerous.

11. There are no reliable data on the number of D&X abortions performed annually. Estimates have ranged between 640 and 5,000 per year.

The question before us is whether Nebraska's statute, making criminal the performance of a "partial birth abortion," violates the Federal Constitution, as interpreted in *Planned Parenthood of Southeastern Pa. v. Casey,* and *Roe v. Wade.* We conclude that it does for at least two independent reasons. First, the law lacks any exception " 'for the preservation of the...health of the mother.' " Second, it "imposes an undue burden on a woman's ability" to choose a D&E abortion, thereby unduly burdening the right to choose abortion itself. We shall discuss each of these reasons in turn.

The *Casey* joint opinion reiterated what the Court held in *Roe;* that " 'subsequent to viability, the State in promoting its interest in the potentiality of human life may, if it chooses, regulate, and even proscribe, abortion *except where it is necessary, in appropriate medical judgment, for the preservation of the life or health of the mother.' "*

The fact that Nebraska's law applies both pre- and postviability aggravates the constitutional problem presented. The State's interest in regulating abortion previability is considerably weaker than postviability. Since the law requires a health exception in order to validate even a postviability abortion regulation, it at a minimum requires the same in respect to previability regulation.

The quoted standard also depends on the state regulations "promoting [the State's] interest in the potentiality of human life." The Nebraska law, of course, does not directly further an interest "in the potentiality of human life" by saving the fetus in question from destruction, as it regulates only a *method* of performing abortion. Nebraska describes its interests differently. It says the law " 'show[s] concern for the life of the unborn,' " "prevent[s] cruelty to partially born children," and "preserve[s] the integrity of the medical profession." But we cannot see how the interest-related differences could make any difference to the question at hand, namely, the application of the "health" requirement.

Consequently, the governing standard requires an exception "where it is necessary, in appropriate medical judgment for the preservation of the life or health of the mother," *Casey* for this Court has made clear that a State may promote but not endanger a woman's health when it regulates the methods of abortion....

Nebraska responds that the law does not require a health exception unless there is a need for such an exception. And here there is no such need, it says. It argues that "safe alternatives remain available" and "a ban on partial-birth abortion/D&X would create no risk to the health of women." The problem for Nebraska is that the parties strongly contested this factual question in the trial court below; and the findings and evidence support Dr. Carhart. The State fails to demonstrate that banning D&X without a health exception may not create significant health risks for women, because the record shows that significant medical authority supports the proposition that in some circumstances, D&X would be the safest procedure....

The Eighth Circuit found the Nebraska statute unconstitutional because, in *Casey*'s words, it has the "effect of placing a substantial obstacle in the path of a woman seeking an abortion of a nonviable fetus." It thereby places an "undue burden" upon a woman's right to terminate her pregnancy before viability. Nebraska does not deny that the statute imposes an "undue burden" *if* it applies to the more commonly used D&E procedure as well as to D&X and we agree with the Eighth Circuit that it does so apply....

[Justice Breyer repeats his discussion of the similarities between D&E and D&X.]

Even if the statute's basic aim is to ban D&X, its language makes clear that it also covers a much broader category of procedures. The language does not track the medical differences between D&E and D&X—though it would have been a simple matter, for example, to provide an exception for the performance of D&E and other abortion procedures. Nor does the statute anywhere suggest that its application turns on whether a portion of the fetus' body is drawn into the vagina as part of a process to extract an intact fetus after collapsing the head as opposed to a process that would dismember the fetus. Thus, the dissenters' argument that the law was generally intended to bar D&X can be both correct and irrelevant. The relevant question is *not* whether the legislature wanted to ban D&X, it is whether the law was intended to apply *only* to D&X. The plain language covers both procedures....Both procedures can involve the introduction of a "substantial portion" of a still living fetus, through the cervix, into the vagina—the very feature of an abortion that leads Justice Thomas to characterize such a procedure as involving "partial birth."...

In sum, using this law some present prosecutors and future Attorneys General may choose to pursue physicians who use D&E procedures, the most commonly used method for performing previability second trimester abortions. All those who perform abortion procedures using that method must fear prosecution, conviction, and imprisonment. The result is an undue burden upon a woman's right to make an abortion decision. We must consequently find the statute unconstitutional.

The judgment of the Court of Appeals is *affirmed.*

JUSTICE STEVENS:

...The rhetoric is almost, but not quite, loud enough to obscure the quiet fact that during the past 27 years, the central holding of *Roe v. Wade* has been endorsed by all but 4 of the 17 Justices who have addressed the issue. That holding—that the word "liberty" in the Fourteenth Amendment includes a woman's right to make this difficult and extremely personal decision—makes it impossible for me to understand how a State has any legitimate interest in requiring a doctor to follow any procedure other than the one that he or she reasonably believes will best protect the woman in her exercise of this constitutional liberty. But one need not even approach this view today to conclude that Nebraska's law must fall. For the notion that either of these two equally gruesome procedures performed at this late stage of gestation is more akin to infanticide than the other, or that the State furthers any legitimate interest by banning one but not the other, is simply irrational.

JUSTICE KENNEDY:

...States may take sides in the abortion debate and come down on the side of life, even life in the unborn....

States also have an interest in forbidding medical procedures which, in the State's reasonable determination, might cause the medical profession or society as a whole to become insensitive, even disdainful, to life, including life in the human fetus. Abortion, *Casey* held, has consequences beyond the woman and her fetus. The States' interests in regulating are of concomitant extension. *Casey* recognized that abortion is, "fraught with consequences for...the persons who perform and assist in the procedure [and for] society which must confront the knowledge that these procedures exist, procedures some deem nothing short of an act of violence against innocent human life."

A State may take measures to ensure the medical profession and its members are viewed as healers, sustained by a compassionate and rigorous ethic and cognizant of the dignity and value of human life, even life which cannot survive without the assistance of others.

Casey demonstrates that the interests asserted by the State are legitimate and recognized by law. It is argued, however, that a ban on the D&X does not further these interests. This is because, the reasoning continues, the D&E method, which Nebraska claims to be beyond its intent to regulate, can still be used to abort a fetus and is no less dehumanizing than the D&X method. While not adopting the argument in express terms, the Court indicates tacit approval of it by refusing to reject it in a forthright manner...The issue is not whether members of the judiciary can see a difference between the two procedures. It is whether Nebraska can. The Court's refusal to recognize Nebraska's right to declare a moral difference between the procedure is a dispiriting disclosure of the illogic and illegitimacy of the Court's approach to the entire case.

Nebraska was entitled to find the existence of a consequential moral difference between the procedures. We are referred to substantial medical authority that D&X perverts the natural birth process to a greater degree than D&E, commandeering the live birth process until the skull is pierced. American Medical Association (AMA) publications describe the D&X abortion method as "ethically wrong." The D&X differs from the D&E because in the D&X the fetus is "killed *outside* of the womb" where the fetus has "an autonomy which separates it from the right of the woman to choose treatments for her own body." ("Intact D&X is aberrant and troubling because the technique confuses the disparate role of a physician in childbirth and abortion in such a way as to blur the medical, legal, and ethical line between infanticide and abortion.") Witnesses to the procedure relate that the fingers and feet of the fetus are moving prior to the piercing of the skull; when the scissors are inserted in the back of the head, the fetus' body, wholly outside the woman's body and alive, reacts as though startled and goes limp. D&X's stronger resemblance to infanticide means Nebraska could conclude the procedure presents a greater risk of disrespect for life and a consequent greater risk to the profession and society, which depend for their sustenance upon reciprocal recognition of dignity and respect. The Court is without authority to second-guess this conclusion.

Those who oppose abortion would agree, indeed would insist, that both procedures are subject to the most severe moral condemnation, condemnation reserved for the most repulsive human conduct. This is not inconsistent, however, with the further proposition that as an ethical and moral matter D&X is distinct from D&E; and is a more serious concern for medical ethics and the morality of the larger society the medical profession must serve. Nebraska must obey the legal regime which has declared the right of the woman to have an abortion before viability. Yet it retains its power to adopt regulations which do not impose an undue burden on the woman's right. By its regulation, Nebraska instructs all participants in the abortion process, including the mother, of its moral judgment that all life, including the life of the unborn, is to be respected. The participants, Nebraska has determined, cannot be indifferent to the procedure used and must refrain from using the natural delivery process to kill the fetus. The differentiation between the procedures is itself a moral statement, serving to promote respect for human life; and if the woman and her physician in contemplating the moral consequences of the prohibited procedure conclude that grave moral consequences pertain to the permitted abortion process as well, the choice to elect or not to elect abortion is more informed; and the policy of promoting respect for life is advanced.

It ill-serves the Court, its institutional position, and the constitutional sources it seeks to invoke to refuse to issue a forthright affirmation of Nebraska's right to declare that critical moral differences exist between the two procedures. The natural birth process has been appropriated; yet the Court refuses to hear the State's voice in defining its interests in its law. The Court's holding contradicts *Casey*'s assurance that the State's constitutional position in the realm of promoting respect for life is more than marginal....

United States v. Oakland Cannabis Buyers Cooperative
532 U.S. 483 (2001)

Justice Thomas delivered the opinion of the Court, in which Chief Justice Rehnquist and Justices O'Connor, Scalia, and Kennedy joined. Justice Stevens filed an opinion concurring in the judgment, in which Justices Souter and Ginsburg joined. Justice Breyer did not participate in either the consideration or decision of the case.

Areas for Discussion and Ethical Reflection

1.   What are Justice Thomas's arguments for denying Oakland Cannabis Buyers Cooperative the right to distribute marijuana to seriously ill cancer patients who, upon the advice and consent of a physician, use marijuana to ease their suffering? Do any of Justice Thomas's arguments demonstrate prior moral commitments? As you did in *U.S. v. Rutherford*, discuss the role of state paternalism and its justification in the present case. Would you

consider the federal government's prohibition on the distribution of marijuana to suffering patients a case of strong state paternalism? Perhaps the prohibition is simply an example of weak state paternalism. Discuss in detail.

2. If you asked Justice Thomas for his position regarding the central responsibilities of physicians, what do you think would be his response? For Justice Thomas, what are the goals of medicine?

3. Justice Stevens agrees with the judgment of the Court, but he very much disapproves of its reasoning. At one point in his opinion, Justice Stevens focuses on medical necessity and wonders whether the defense of necessity might be available under the Controlled Substances Act for seriously ill patients who are suffering. What reasons does he provide for maintaining that seriously ill patients should have marijuana available to them for use? Do any of his arguments have relevance for medical ethics?

4. In a footnote to his opinion, Justice Stevens cites a story from the *Dallas Morning News* titled, "Bush Backs States Rights on Marijuana: He Opposes Medical Use but Favors Local Control." The reporter notes that as governor of Texas, George W. Bush supported state control over medical marijuana use, but as President has opposed state self-determination. Is this fact relevant to the ethical analysis of the issues in this case? Is it appropriate for Justice Stevens to note this fact?

5. How similar are the issues presented in this case to those in *Rutherford*? Suppose Laetrile is much more dangerous than marijuana. Would that fact matter in your evaluation of the Court's ruling in *Oakland Cannabis Buyers Cooperative*?

6. What exactly are the moral and professional obligations of physicians in California who wish to prescribe marijuana to their patients? On what ethical theory do you ground those obligations? What principles of medical ethics are relevant here?

7. As you know by now, Supreme Court decisions can have far-reaching, even unforeseen consequences. A few months after

the Supreme Court's decision in *Oakland Cannabis Buyers Co-operative*, U.S. Attorney General John Ashcroft sent a memo to Asa Hutchinson, head of the Drug Enforcement Administration (DEA). In the memo John Ashcroft asserted his judgment that assisting in a suicide was not a legitimate medical purpose for which physicians could prescribe medications. Ashcroft directed the DEA to monitor medication-dispensing records of physicians in Oregon for instances where physicians were prescribing pain medications sufficient for use in assisting terminally ill patients in suicide. Physicians who prescribed pain medication for the purpose of assisting in a suicide were to have their licenses revoked. Ashcroft intended to override the Oregon Death with Dignity Act, which makes assistance in suicide by physicians legal in Oregon. A federal district court issued a permanent injunction against Ashcroft, the Department of Justice, and the DEA. After you have read *Oakland Cannabis Buyers Cooperative*, consider whether the ruling supports John Ashcroft's contention that the Controlled Substances Act supercedes state law. Also consider who should decide what is and what is not a legitimate medical purpose.[9]

8.   Do the three decisions in this chapter provide you with any guidance in determining, morally speaking, under what circumstances the state may interfere with medical judgment? Recall the concept of a "zone of privacy" introduced in previous chapters. What role, if any, does that concept play in these three cases?

JUSTICE THOMAS:

> The Controlled Substances Act, 84 Stat. 1242, 21 U. S. C. §801, prohibits the manufacture and distribution of various drugs, including marijuana. In this case, we must decide whether there is a medical necessity exception to these prohibitions. We hold that there is not....
>
> The Controlled Substances Act provides that, "[e]xcept as authorized by this subchapter, it shall be unlawful for any

person knowingly or intentionally…to manufacture, distribute, or dispense, or possess with intent to manufacture, distribute, or dispense, a controlled substance." The subchapter, in turn, establishes exceptions. For marijuana (and other drugs that have been classified as "schedule I" controlled substances), there is but one express exception, and it is available only for Government-approved research projects. Not conducting such a project, the Cooperative cannot, and indeed does not, claim this statutory exemption.

The Cooperative contends, however, that notwithstanding the apparently absolute language of [the Act], the statute is subject to additional, implied exceptions, one of which is medical necessity. According to the Cooperative, because necessity was a defense at common law, medical necessity should be read into the Controlled Substances Act. We disagree.…

[Justice Thomas discusses the controversial nature of the necessity defense at common law, and then asserts that the defense is at odds with the terms of the act.]

Under any conception of legal necessity, one principle is clear: The defense cannot succeed when the legislature itself has made a "determination of values." In the case of the Controlled Substances Act, the statute reflects a determination that marijuana has no medical benefits worthy of an exception (outside the confines of a Government-approved research project). Whereas some other drugs can be dispensed and prescribed for medical use, the same is not true for marijuana. Indeed, for purposes of the Controlled Substances Act, marijuana has "no currently accepted medical use" at all.…

The Cooperative…argues that use of Schedule I drugs generally—whether placed in Schedule I by Congress or the Attorney General—can be medically necessary, notwithstanding that they have "no currently accepted medical use." According to the Cooperative, a drug may not yet have achieved general acceptance as a medical treatment but may nonetheless have medical benefits to a particular patient or class of patients. We decline to parse the statute in this manner. It is clear from the text of the Act that Congress has made a determination that marijuana has no medical benefits worthy of an exception. The statute expressly contemplates that many drugs "have a useful and legitimate medical purpose and are necessary to maintain the health and general welfare of the American people," but it includes no exception at all for any medical use of marijuana. Unwilling to view this omission as an accident, and unable in any event to override a legislative determination manifest in a statute, we reject the Cooperative's argument.

Finally, the Cooperative contends that we should construe the Controlled Substances Act to include a medical necessity defense in order to avoid what it considers to be difficult constitutional questions. In particular, the Cooperative asserts that, shorn of a medical necessity defense, the statute exceeds Congress' Commerce Clause powers, violates the substantive due process rights of patients, and offends the fundamental liberties of the people under the Fifth, Ninth, and Tenth Amendments. As the Cooperative acknowledges, however, the canon of constitutional avoidance has no application in the absence of statutory ambiguity. Because we have no doubt that the Controlled Substances Act cannot bear a medical necessity defense to distributions of marijuana, we do not find guidance in this avoidance principle. Nor do we consider the underlying constitutional issues today. Because the Court of Appeals did not address these claims, we decline to do so in the first instance....

In this case, the Court of Appeals erred by considering relevant the evidence that some people have "serious medical conditions for whom the use of cannabis is necessary in order to treat or alleviate those conditions or their symptoms," that these people "will suffer serious harm if they are denied cannabis," and that "there is no legal alternative to cannabis for the effective treatment of their medical conditions." As explained above, in the Controlled Substances Act, the balance already has been struck against a medical necessity exception. Because the statutory prohibitions cover even those who have what could be termed a medical necessity, the Act precludes consideration of this evidence. It was thus error for the Court of Appeals to instruct the District Court on remand to consider "the criteria for a medical necessity exemption, and, should it modify the injunction, to set forth those criteria in the modification order."

The judgment of the Court of Appeals is reversed, and the case is remanded for further proceedings consistent with this opinion.

It is so ordered.

JUSTICE STEVENS:

Lest the Court's narrow holding be lost in its broad dicta, let me restate it here: "[W]e hold that medical necessity is not a defense to *manufacturing* and *distributing* marijuana." This confined holding is consistent with our grant of certiorari, which was limited to the question "[w]hether the Controlled Substances Act forecloses a medical necessity defense to the Act's prohibition against *manufacturing* and *distributing* marijuana, a Schedule I controlled substance." And, at least with respect to distribution, this holding is consistent with how the issue was raised and litigated....

Apart from its limited holding, the Court takes two unwarranted and unfortunate excursions that prevent me from joining its opinion. First, the Court reaches beyond its holding, and beyond the facts of the case, by suggesting that the defense of necessity is unavailable for anyone under the Controlled Substances Act. Because necessity was raised in this case as a defense to distribution, the Court need not venture an opinion on whether the defense is available to anyone other than distributors. Most notably, whether the defense might be available to a seriously ill patient for whom there is no alternative means of avoiding starvation or extraordinary suffering is a difficult issue that is not presented here.

Second, the Court gratuitously casts doubt on "whether necessity can ever be a defense" to *any* federal statute that does not explicitly provide for it, calling such a defense into question by a misleading reference to its existence as an "open question." By contrast, our precedent has expressed no doubt about the viability of the common-law defense, even in the context of federal criminal statutes that do not provide for it in so many words.... Indeed, the Court's comment on the general availability of the necessity defense is completely unnecessary because the Government has made no such suggestion. The Court's opinion on this point is pure dictum....

The overbroad language of the Court's opinion is especially unfortunate given the importance of showing respect for the sovereign States that comprise our Federal Union. That respect imposes a duty on federal courts, whenever possible, to avoid or minimize conflict between federal and state law, particularly in situations in which the citizens of a State have chosen to serve as a laboratory in the trial of novel social and economic experiments without risk to the rest of the country. In my view, this is such a case. By passing Proposition 215, California voters have decided that seriously ill patients and their primary caregivers should be exempt from prosecution under state laws for cultivating and possessing marijuana if the patient's physician recommends using the drug for treatment. This case does not call upon the Court to deprive *all* such patients of the benefit of the necessity defense to federal prosecution, when the case itself does not involve *any* such patients.

Notes

1.   Albert R. Jonsen, Mark Siegler, and William J. Winslade, *Clinical Ethics: A Practical Approach To Ethical Decisions in Clinical Medicine*, 4th ed. (New York: McGraw-Hill, 1998), p. 16.

2.   Ronald Munson, "Introduction to Physicians, Patients, and Others: Autonomy, Truth Telling, and Confidentiality," in *Intervention and Reflection: Basic Issues in Medical Ethics*, 6th ed., edited by Ronald Munson (Belmont, CA: Wadsworth, 2000), p. 390.

3.   Tom L. Beauchamp and James F. Childress, *Principles of Biomedical Ethics*, 5th ed. (New York: Oxford University Press, 2001), p. 179.

4.   Ibid., p. 181.

5.   Munson, "Introduction to Physicians, Patients and Others," pp. 391–93.

6.   John Stuart Mill, *On Liberty*, in *The English Philosophers from Bacon to Mill*, edited by Edwin A. Burtt (New York: The Modern Library, 1967), p. 956.

7.   Gerald Dworkin, "Paternalism," in *Intervention and Reflection*, pp. 402–11.

8.   Ibid., p. 409.

9.   Ben A. Rich, "*Oregon v. Ashcroft*: The Battle over the Soul of Medicine," *Cambridge Quarterly of Health Care Ethics* 12 (2003): 310–21. This article provides a detailed analysis of Attorney General John Ashcroft's attack on the Oregon Death with Dignity Act and the subsequent court decision.

For Further Reading

Carpenter, Joan. " 'Partial-Birth' Abortion: Let's Be Reasonable." In *Intervention and Reflection: Basic Issues in Medical Ethics*, 6th edition, Ronald Munson, ed. Belmont, CA: Wadsworth, 2000.

Dworkin, Gerald. "Paternalism." In *Intervention and Reflection: Basic Issues in Medical Ethics*.

Halpern, Aviva. "Pain: No Medical Necessity Defense for Marijuana to Controlled Substances Act." *Journal of Law, Medicine & Ethics* 29 (2001): 410–11.

Jonsen, Albert R., Mark Siegler, and William J. Winslade. *Clinical Ethics: A Practical Approach to Ethical Decisions in Clinical Medicine*, 4th edition. New York: McGraw-Hill, 1998.

Mill, John Stuart. *On Liberty*. In *The English Philosophers from Bacon to Mill*, Edwin A. Burtt, ed. New York: Random House, 1967.

Munson, Ronald. "Physicians, Patients, and Others: Autonomy, Truth Telling, and Confidentiality." In *Intervention and Reflection: Basic Issues in Medical Ethics*.

Wiley, Lindsay F. "Assisted Suicide: Court Strikes Down Ashcroft Directive." *Journal of Law, Medicine & Ethics* 30 (2002): 459–60.

CHAPTER EIGHT

THE TREATMENT AND CONFINEMENT OF PEOPLE WITH MENTAL ILLNESS AND MENTAL RETARDATION CASES

The makers of our Constitution undertook to secure conditions favorable to the pursuit of happiness. They recognized the significance of man's spiritual nature, of his feelings and of his intellect. They knew that only a part of the pain, pleasure and satisfactions of life are to be found in material things. They sought to protect Americans in their beliefs, their thoughts, their emotions and their sensations. They conferred, as against the Government, the right to be let alone—the most comprehensive of rights and the right most valued by civilized men.

—Justice Louis Brandeis, dissenting in *Olmstead v. United States*

History demonstrates that society has not been kind to people suffering from mental illness and mental retardation. Practices such as forced sterilization, imprisonment, warehousing, denial of educational and employment opportunities, and forced medication all have formed part of society's response to people deemed "abnormal" or "different." One of the most intractable problems in medical ethics concerns developing ethically appro-

priate principles and procedures for the treatment and confinement of individuals with diminished competence and autonomy. Principles of beneficence and nonmaleficence require that
treatment and confinement of mentally ill and mentally retarded
individuals take place within a context of utmost respect for individual dignity, safety, and best interest. Concurrently, however,
concerns over scarce health care resources and over protecting
clients and third parties from harm demand attention. Ethical
and legal requirements for obtaining voluntary, informed consent (or refusal) before treating such individuals are difficult if
not impossible to meet. Measures taken to promote client dignity
often conflict with the need to keep the client or other third parties safe. Although the challenges and tragedies of physical illness
and incapacitation are great, meeting the needs of this population in an ethically appropriate manner is especially challenging.
Pressure to act in the most morally defensible manner comes
from all sides—political, social, legal, and medical—yet these
same parties may exert pressure to engage in activities that seem
unethical to many. People suffering from mental illness or mental retardation are vulnerable, and this vulnerability gives rise to
ethical problems. The three Supreme Court cases excerpted in
this chapter highlight this vulnerability and the ethical problems
associated with state and federal practices to treat and confine
the mentally ill and mentally retarded.

Constitutional Issues and Background

All students of medical ethics and health law should be familiar
with our first case, *Buck v. Bell*. Justice Holmes's remark, "Three
generations of imbeciles are enough," is only one reason this case
is one of the most famous, or infamous, in U.S. Supreme Court
history. In 1924, Virginia passed a law allowing the sterilization
of people the state deemed "socially inadequate" as long as it
benefited society and the procedure did not negatively impact
the individual's health. Virginia, along with several other states,
had passed laws allowing for mandatory sterilization of indi-

viduals (vasectomy for men and salpingectomy, the cutting and tying of the fallopian tubes, for women). These laws were the result of a popular eugenics movement in the United States that began in the 1890s and was founded on the premise that genetics determined whether a person would be mentally ill or a criminal. After giving birth to a daughter, Vivian, Carrie Buck was placed in the State Colony for Epileptics and Feeble Minded. Her mother, Emma, was also housed at the same institution. Carrie's daughter was taken away from her and Carrie was ordered to undergo sterilization. Vivian died at the age of eight, and Carrie Buck died in early January 1983. In 2002 the state of Virginia formally issued an apology for forcibly sterilizing Carrie Buck. Today universal agreement exists that neither Carrie nor her daughter was a "mental defective."

Very few people are aware that the state of Virginia filed the original sterilization petition. The superintendent of the facility where Carrie and her mother were housed, Dr. A. S. Priddy, desired judicial recognition and sanction of involuntary sterilization and played a significant role in helping the case make its way through the lower courts.[1] The issue came to the U.S. Supreme Court as an equal protection case. As Justice Holmes noted in his opinion, the claim could be made that Virginia's sterilization law was discriminatory because it applied only to those individuals in state custody and ignored the large number of "mental defectives" not in state custody. Justice Holmes summarily dismissed this argument. The analysis used by the Court in applying the Equal Protection Clause has evolved since the decision in *Buck*, at which time the three-tiered analysis (see the introduction) had not been developed. While the Court has never concluded that involuntary sterilization in and of itself is unconstitutional, few doubt the Court would reach the same result today that it did in 1927.[2]

Fifty-five years after its decision in *Buck*, the High Court considered for the first time whether involuntarily committed mentally retarded persons have substantive due process rights. Nicholas Romeo was thirty-three years old yet considered to have the mental capacity of an eighteen-month-old with an IQ of between 8 and 10. When Romeo was twenty-six, his mother had him institutionalized in a Pennsylvania state facility because she could no longer take care of him. After his commitment to the institution, Romeo's mother became concerned about injuries he was suffering. She filed for damages in federal district court asserting that Romeo had constitutional rights, under the Eighth and Fourteenth Amendments, to safe conditions, freedom from bodily restraints, and training. The federal district court found for the state and refused to consider Fourteenth Amendment issues. On appeal, the Third Circuit reversed, arguing that the Fourteenth Amendment was indeed the proper guide.

Justice Powell, in his opinion for the High Court, weighed the postcommitment interests of mentally retarded persons against the legitimate interests of the state. The Court had no problem concluding that mentally retarded individuals have a liberty interest in safe living conditions and in freedom from bodily restraint; however, the claim that such individuals have a liberty interest in training proved much more "troubling" for the Court. In deciding this issue, Justice Powell found it proper to use a professional judgment standard. That is, psychiatrists and psychologists must be free to make determinations regarding proper levels of training for residents without fear of suits for damages.

The professional judgment standard played a prominent role in a Court decision that remains influential, *Washington v. Harper*. By the time his case reached the Supreme Court in late 1989, Walter Harper had been in the Washington state prison system since 1976. After being convicted and serving four years for robbery, he assaulted two nurses while on parole. Throughout his incarceration Harper received psychiatric treatment, including administration of antipsychotic medications (Haldol, Mellaril, and Prolixin injections), on the basis of an initial diagnosis of manic-depressive disorder and a later diagnosis of schizoaffective disorder. Periodically he engaged in violent conduct when his condition deteriorated. On two occasions he was transferred to the Special Offender Center (a state facility for convicted felons with mental illness), and antipsychotic drugs were administered against his will. Harper asserted that involuntary medication without a judicial proceeding constituted a violation of both procedural and substantive due process. The trial court ruled against Harper, but the Washington State Supreme Court reversed, finding that the Due Process Clause required a judicial hearing before administering antipsychotic medications against a patient's will.

The task before the Supreme Court was to determine what the Due Process Clause of the Fourteenth Amendment would require in implementing procedures for involuntarily medicating a mentally ill person. The Court found that Washington's policy adequately addressed any substantive or procedural constitutional concerns on the part of Harper. The policy requires that inmates be subjected to involuntary medication only if the inmate "suffers from a 'mental disorder' and is 'gravely disabled' or possesses a 'likelihood of serious harm' to himself, others, or their property." The policy also requires that inmates be given twenty-four-hour notice and that a committee in the institution where the inmate is housed periodically review medication decisions. Much of the Court's rationale for supporting the policy rests on the professional judgment standard.

Ethical Issues and Background

On August 14, 2003, in an interview on C-SPAN, Dr. Thomas Insel, director of the National Institute of Mental Health, observed that the largest number of mentally ill people residing in one place in the United States was confined in the Los Angeles County jail. In the year 2002, Dr. Insel continued, LA County spent $10 million on psychotropic medications for its inmates. Such facts are undoubtedly disturbing from both a moral and a public policy perspective. The three Supreme Court decisions in this chapter allow us to examine some of the ethical, medical, and social concerns surrounding the treatment and confinement of people with mental illness and mental retardation. Obviously, we want to assess how well the justices understand and employ some of the concepts and arguments medical ethicists have used in addressing issues surrounding government involvement with people who are mentally ill or mentally retarded. We begin by briefly examining ethical issues surrounding eugenics. We then consider the professional judgment standard and the proposition that psychiatrists' and psychologists' judgments regarding specific medical interventions are value laden. As problematic as conflicts of interest are in medicine, they are especially troubling in decisions regarding the treatment of individuals with diminished decision-making capacity. Because this chapter involves issues related to treatment and confinement of individuals for their own best interests, you may wish to review and keep in mind our discussion of strong and weak paternalism in the previous chapter.

Those who have studied the events surrounding *Buck v. Bell* have concluded that Emma, Carrie, and Vivian were not "imbeciles." In the 1920s, "imbecile" was a technical term denoting individuals with a mental age between six and nine years of age; this fact in part explains Justice Holmes's use of the word in his famous comment.[3] Recognition that the Bucks were not mentally retarded has led one commentator to observe: "I don't know that such correction of cruel but forgotten errors of history counts for much, but I find it both symbolic and satisfying to learn that forced eugenic sterilization, a procedure of such dubious morality, earned its official justification (and won its most quoted line of rhetoric) on a patent falsehood."[4] Most people would agree that forced sterilization is of "dubious morality." But why? And what moral arguments did Justice Holmes marshal in support of finding Virginia's forced sterilization law constitutional? We briefly address the second question first.

Justice Holmes seemed to believe, as did many Americans in the early years of the twentieth century, that heredity played a major role in the spread of "undesirable" traits such as blindness, deafness, criminal behavior, mental illness, and moral deficiency. Moreover, they believed that if heredity played a causal role in behavior society found objectionable, then perhaps society could control, even eliminate, this behavior. Many in society became interested in eugenics, the study of how to improve humanity through genetic means. Eugenics programs spread to many states throughout the country in the 1890s and continued into the 1930s and 40s. As a result of alarm over the increasing number of "feeble minded" people in institutions, worry over the rising number of immigrants settling in America, and enthusiasm by scientists that "antisocial behavior" could be eliminated through genetic interventions, states began adopting laws mandating the sterilization of people who would pass along "undesirable traits." Physicians working in state institutions and many of the nation's wealthiest people were enthusiastic about these laws.[5] In the beginning, many of these laws were struck down as unconstitutional. By the 1920s, however, state legislatures became much more sophisticated in drafting legislation: New laws required that consent from parents or guardians be obtained and that jury trials be provided to determine if the patient was "the potential parent of socially undesirable offspring."[6]

As you read Justice Holmes's decision, keep the social, legal, and political context described above in mind. The justices in *Buck* were deliberating the constitutionality of a mandatory eugenics program, a program with widespread moral, scientific, and political support. Sterilizing Carrie Buck, Justice Holmes believed, would relieve society of the burden of taking care of mentally deficient people. Justice Holmes also noted that the state had put into place measures designed to ensure that no physical harm would come to Carrie. He argued further that many citizens are called upon to make sacrifices for their country; surely Carrie Buck and others similarly situated could make sacrifices as well. But are these arguments persuasive? What do they reveal about the moral commitments of the justices?

Any attempt to control or prohibit reproduction based on eugenics raises concerns regarding privacy, autonomy, self-determination, and reproductive freedom (all issues and concepts discussed in the first two chapters). The ability to choose whether or not to reproduce is a vital part of self-determination and goes to the heart of a sense of self. Justice Holmes seems to ignore both the ethical and constitutional significance of privacy and autonomy and their implications for the right to reproduce. Of course, at that point in the Court's history recognition of autonomy and privacy as constitutional values was limited. But even if we overlook the Court's failure to consider privacy rights, Justice Holmes's argument is less than convincing. No doubt exists that Justice Holmes was placing a higher value on social benefit than on individual well-being, but he never made clear how the concept of "social benefit" should be understood and applied. Even today, a great deal of debate exists in ethics and public policy over the meaning of "social benefit." In any event, with the hindsight that history affords, we now are very skeptical that eugenics programs, especially mandatory ones, can be ethically or constitutionally justified. One need only recall the atrocities of Nazi Germany to realize the disastrous effects of such programs. Although the Court had the opportunity to reassess its position fifteen years later in *Skinner*, it still has not been able to resolve definitively the problems of weighing and balancing values of social benefit, individual welfare, and scientific expertise.

Some of the Court's most difficult cases in the realm of bioethics law involve issues surrounding treatment and confinement of people with mental illness and mental retardation. The Court recognizes that individuals have rights to liberty and autonomy, but identifying and determining the scope of these rights has proved difficult. Does a constitutionally recognized liberty interest in autonomy require the state to provide training to mentally retarded individuals in its custody *(Romeo)*? Is a state's practice of medicating mentally ill inmates against their will *(Harper)* violative of the same liberty interest? The Supreme Court's answer to these questions as well as its justification provides insight into some of the ethical issues concerning state responsibilities and obligations toward vulnerable populations.

The Supreme Court's answer to the above two questions is relatively clear and straightforward: States are required only to employ professional medical judgment in determining the kind and extent of training to which mentally retarded patients are entitled, and in determining whether forced administration of antipsychotic drugs to mentally ill patients is appropriate. In the areas of habilitation and forced medication, any rights mentally retarded and mentally ill patients enjoy are substantially limited. States are entitled to limit rights in these areas if, in the judgment of psychologists or psychiatrists, states are providing the type of training or the program of forced medication that professionals deem necessary. In essence the Court is saying that professional judgments regarding treatment will satisfy any constitutional requirements to respect the liberty of confined individuals.

This medical judgment standard is especially interesting, from both a constitutional and ethical perspective, in cases of forced medication. The Court acknowledges that mentally ill patients, even those patients involuntarily committed, have a right to be free from "arbitrary administration of antipsychotic medication." However, if a psychiatrist determines that the patient is 1) mentally ill, 2) gravely disabled or dangerous, and 3) medication is in the best medical interests of the patient, then the Due Process Clause is not violated. The state is allowed to weigh the medical interests of patients with the interests of the institution; no outside review of an institution's decision to involuntarily medicate patients is necessary.

As purely a matter of ethics, several problems arise from the Court's deference to the professional judgment standard. First, such reliance on the judgment of professionals ignores the problem of conflict of interest or divided loyalty. The psychiatrists and psychologists making judgments regarding training and forced medication are employed by the state. The decisions of these professionals are subject to review by administrative boards, but the board members are also in the employ of the state, often working at the same institutions where the patients are housed. Even if everyone could agree that medical professionals may weigh the interests of both the patient and the institution—a claim that carries its own moral problems—how can we determine that clinicians are not swayed unduly by the interests of the institution? Is it unreasonable to believe that a psychiatrist's determination of dangerousness and medical best interest might be based, at least in part, on value judgments? If indeed the professional's medical judgment is influenced by loyalty to the state, then patients may be subject to coercion and manipulation.

The second problem relates to the first and concerns the assertion that medical diagnoses, treatment regimens, and predictions of future behavior are value neutral. But are the judgments of professionals value neutral? In concluding that professional judgment is the appropriate standard for determining a patient's interest in autonomy, freedom, and well-being, the Court seems to assume that scientific or medical judgment is somehow separate from value judgments. But consider the observations of one commentator:

> The purpose of gathering data and building scientific theories is to describe, explain, predict, or control events. Such claims serve in medicine as the empirical basis for the activities of diagnosis, prognosis, prevention, or treatment of illness. Scientific judgments are necessary, but not sufficient for the practice of psychiatry, because psychiatry also includes values, duties, goods, goals, and virtues as an internal part of this tradition.[7]

Does the Supreme Court overlook the possibility that medical judgments are at least in part value judgments? That is, do "pure," empirically based decisions exist regarding the diagnosis and treatment of patients? Surely judgments regarding treatment will be impacted by such factors as loyalty to the institution, time and effort required to treat the patient if forced medication is not used, and even the extent to which the professional "likes" or "dislikes" the patient. You will note that some justices raise this concern as well as the issue of divided loyalty in their opinions. As you read the excerpts, you can weigh the ethical significance of these concerns for yourself.

Buck v. Bell
274 U.S. 200 (1927)

Justice Holmes delivered the opinion of the Court. Justice Butler dissented.

Areas for Discussion and Ethical Reflection

1.   Identify and outline Justice Holmes's arguments in support of the sterilization of Carrie Buck. Which of these arguments do you find especially relevant to medical ethics? Which argument do you find the strongest? Which do you find the weakest?

2.   In arguing that Virginia may sterilize Carrie Buck, Justice Holmes employs two analogies. First, he notes that it is entirely proper for government to require its best citizens to sacrifice their lives in time of war. Second, in order that communities may protect themselves from disease, mandatory vaccination of individuals against their will is considered a legitimate aim of government. Do you find these analogies convincing? Do the analogies demonstrate logical confusion on the part of Justice Holmes? Do they demonstrate moral confusion?

3.   What moral arguments would you make in favoring a program of involuntary sterilization for "mentally deficient" individuals? Would you feel more comfortable supporting such a program if the state could ensure fair procedures were in place? What would constitute a fair procedure for determining whether an individual should be sterilized?

4.   In many instances sterilization procedures can be reversed. In addition, many types of long- and short-acting contraceptives are available. If a state limited the ability of persons to procreate only through means that were temporary, would the same ethical concerns that accompany forced, permanent sterilization still apply?[8] Would it be morally permissible for states, in an effort to curb the number of births of severely retarded or otherwise mentally deficient children, to force some individuals to under-

go sterilization?[9] Would such state action be constitutional? Of course, other options are available to states that wish to promote a social goal of fewer children born with heritable diseases. For example, a state could impose a mandatory genetic screening process and then order abortion for any fetus likely to be born with abnormalities.[10] Would such actions be moral? Would such actions be constitutional?

5.   A state could adopt noncoercive or less coercive forms of eugenic control than those listed above. For example, a state could develop and implement tax and funding policies in order to persuade people believed likely to reproduce defective children not to procreate.[11] What ethical arguments might you provide in support of such a policy? What ethical concerns would be raised by such a policy?

6.   After reading *Buck*, return to chapter 2 and review *Skinner* and *Ferguson*. Obviously, *Buck* and *Skinner* have much in common: They both consider the permissibility of forced sterilization. Do you think Justice Holmes would have reached a different result if he had read the arguments in *Skinner*? Does anything in the opinion by Justice Holmes strike you as ethically relevant to the issues in *Ferguson*? Note that this might be a much more interesting question than it first appears.

JUSTICE HOLMES:

> ...Carrie Buck is a feeble-minded white woman who was committed to the State Colony [for Epileptics and Feeble Minded] in due form. She is the daughter of a feeble-minded mother in the same institution, and the mother of an illegitimate feeble-minded child. She was eighteen years old at the time of the trial of her case in the Circuit Court in the latter part of 1924. An Act of Virginia approved March 20, 1924 recites that the health of the patient and the welfare of society may be promoted in certain cases by the sterilization of mental defectives, under careful safeguard,

etc.; that the sterilization may be effected in males by vasectomy and in females by salpingectomy, without serious pain or substantial danger to life; that the Commonwealth is supporting in various institutions many defective persons who if now discharged would become a menace but if incapable of procreating might be discharged with safety and become self-supporting with benefit to themselves and to society; and that experience has shown that heredity plays an important part in the transmission of insanity, imbecility, etc. The statute then enacts that whenever the superintendent of certain institutions including the above named State Colony shall be of opinion that it is for the best interest of the patients and of society that an inmate under his care should be sexually sterilized, he may have the operation performed upon any patient afflicted with hereditary forms of insanity, imbecility, etc., on complying with the very careful provisions by which the act protects the patients from possible abuse....

There can be no doubt that so far as procedure is concerned the rights of the patient are most carefully considered, and as every step in this case was taken in scrupulous compliance with the statute and after months of observation, there is no doubt that in that respect the plaintiff in error has had due process at law.

The attack is not upon the procedure but upon the substantive law. It seems to be contended that in no circumstances could such an order be justified. It certainly is contended that the order cannot be justified upon the existing grounds. The judgment finds the facts that have been recited and that Carrie Buck "is the probable potential parent of socially inadequate offspring, likewise afflicted, that she may be sexually sterilized without detriment to her general health and that her welfare and that of society will be promoted by her sterilization," and thereupon makes the order. In view of the general declarations of the Legislature and the specific findings of the Court obviously we cannot say as matter of law that the grounds do not exist, and if they exist they justify the result. We have seen more than once that the public welfare may call upon the best citizens for their lives. It would be strange if it could not call upon those who already sap the strength of the State for these lesser sacrifices, often not felt to be such by those concerned, in order to prevent our being swamped with incompetence. It is better for all the world, if instead of waiting to execute degenerate offspring for crime, or to let them starve for their imbecility, society can prevent those who are manifestly unfit from continuing their kind. The principle that sustains compulsory vaccination is broad enough to cover cutting the Fallopian tubes. Three generations of imbeciles are enough. But, it is said, however it might be if this reasoning were applied generally, it fails when it is confined to the small number who are in the institutions named and is not applied to the multitudes outside. It is the usual last resort of constitutional arguments to point out shortcomings of this sort.

But the answer is that the law does all that is needed when it does all that it can, indicates a policy, applies it to all within the lines, and seeks to bring within the lines all similarly situated so far and so fast as its means allow. Of course so far as the operations enable those who otherwise must be kept confined to be returned to the world, and thus open the asylum to others, the equality aimed at will be more nearly reached.

Judgment affirmed.

Youngberg v. Romeo
457 U.S. 307 (1982)

Justice Powell delivered the opinion of the Court, in which Justices Brennan, White, Marshall, Blackmun, Rehnquist, Stevens, and O'Connor joined. Justice Blackmun filed a concurring opinion, in which Justices Brennan and O'Connor joined. Chief Justice Burger filed an opinion concurring in the judgment.

Areas for Discussion and Ethical Reflection

1.   From the perspective of medical ethics, both *Youngberg* and *Harper* are similar. After reading both decisions, list the similarities. To avoid repetition, some of the items for discussion and ethical reflection listed below are also appropriate for discussion in *Harper*, and vice versa.

2.   At the beginning of his majority opinion Justice Powell asserts that Romeo has a constitutional right to safe conditions and to freedom from bodily restraint. Other than noting that both rights involve liberty interests, Justice Powell defends these rights claims by citing prior cases of the Court. What ethical arguments might you give for claiming that involuntarily committed persons have a right to safety and a right to freedom from bodily restraint?

3.   Justice Blackmun notes that the Court in *Youngberg* leaves two issues unresolved. What are these issues? What is their significance for medical ethics in general and the ethics of mental health care in particular?

4.   In the last paragraph of his opinion in *Youngberg* excerpted below, Justice Blackmun asserts that mentally retarded persons can suffer a loss of liberty if they enter a state institution with one level of self-care skills and then fall below that level as they remain in state custody. Do you agree? Which principle of medical ethics (autonomy, nonmaleficence, or beneficence) might we employ to justify an obligation on the part of physicians employed by the state to "maintain" mentally retarded residents? Note also that Justice Blackmun seems to think that mentally retarded individuals are aware of when they have lost their liberty. Do you agree? Does it matter?

5.   Chief Justice Burger asserts: "I agree with much of the Court's opinion. However, I would hold flatly that [Romeo] has no constitutional right to training, or 'habilitation,' per se." What exactly is his argument for this position? What moral arguments might you provide to assist the chief justice? Discuss some of the consequences of Chief Justice Burger's position for federal and

state policies toward vulnerable populations. Are any of these consequences ethically problematic?

6.   What are the ethical arguments for and against the moral permissibility of executing mentally retarded persons convicted of murder? In June 2002, the Supreme Court ruled in *Atkins v. Virginia*, 536 U.S. 304 (2002) that the execution of mentally retarded criminals violated the Eighth Amendment's prohibition against excessive punishment. Daryl Renard Atkins was convicted of abduction, armed robbery, and capital murder, then sentenced to death. At trial, school records were presented showing that Atkins had an IQ of 59, but experts for the state testified that he was of normal intelligence. The Virginia Supreme Court affirmed the conviction, but two judges dissented. They wrote in part:

> ...[I]t is indefensible to conclude that individuals who are mentally retarded are not to some degree less culpable for their criminal acts. By definition, such individuals have substantial limitations not shared by the general population. A moral and civilized society diminishes itself if its system of justice does not afford recognition and consideration of those limitations in a meaningful way.

In reversing the Virginia Supreme Court, Justice Stevens, writing for a 6-3 majority, seemed quite impressed with the above statement and cited it as one of the reasons for finding the imposition of the death penalty on mentally retarded defendants unconstitutional. With *Atkins* and *Youngberg* in mind, what specific obligations are owed by a "moral and civilized society" toward the mentally retarded?

JUSTICE POWELL:

The question presented is whether [Romeo], involuntarily committed to a state institution for the mentally retarded, has substantive rights under the Due Process Clause of the Fourteenth Amendment to (i) safe conditions of confinement; (ii) freedom from bodily restraints; and (iii) training or "habilitation." [Romeo] sued under 42 U.S.C. 1983 three administrators of the institution, claiming damages for the alleged breach of his constitutional rights....

We consider here for the first time the substantive rights of involuntarily committed mentally retarded persons under the Fourteenth Amendment to the Constitution. In this case, [Romeo] has been committed under the laws of Pennsylvania, and he does not challenge the commitment. Rather, he argues that he has a constitutionally protected liberty interest in safety, freedom of movement, and training within the institution; and that petitioners infringed these rights by failing to provide constitutionally required conditions of confinement.

The mere fact that Romeo has been committed under proper procedures does not deprive him of all substantive liberty interests under the Fourteenth Amendment. Indeed, the State concedes that [Romeo] has a right to adequate food, shelter, clothing, and medical care. We must decide whether liberty interests also exist in safety, freedom of movement, and training. If such interests do exist, we must further decide whether they have been infringed in this case.

[Romeo's] first two claims involve liberty interests recognized by prior decisions of this Court, interests that involuntary commitment proceedings do not extinguish. The first is a claim to safe conditions. In the past, this Court has noted that the right to personal security constitutes a "historic liberty interest" protected substantively by the Due Process Clause. And that right is not extinguished by lawful confinement, even for penal purposes. If it is cruel and unusual punishment to hold convicted criminals in unsafe conditions, it must be unconstitutional to confine the involuntarily committed—who may not be punished at all—in unsafe conditions.

Next, [Romeo] claims a right to freedom from bodily restraint. In other contexts, the existence of such an interest is clear in the prior decisions of this Court. Indeed, "[l]iberty from bodily restraint always has been recognized as the core of the liberty protected by the Due Process Clause from arbitrary governmental action." This interest survives criminal conviction and incarceration. Similarly, it must also survive involuntary commitment.

[Romeo's] remaining claim is more troubling. In his words, he asserts a "constitutional right to minimally adequate habilitation." This is a substantive due process claim that is said to be grounded in the liberty component of the Due Process Clause of the Fourteenth Amendment. The term "habilitation," used in psychiatry, is not defined precisely or consistently in the opinions below or in the briefs of the parties or the amici. As noted previously the term refers to "training and development of needed skills." Respondent emphasizes that the right he asserts is for "minimal" training, and he would leave the type and extent of training to be determined on a case-by-case basis "in light of present medical or other scientific knowledge."

In addressing the asserted right to training, we start from established principles. As a general matter, a State is under no constitutional duty to provide substantive services for those within its border. When a person is institutionalized—and wholly dependent on the State—it is conceded by petitioners that a duty to provide certain services and care does exist, although even then a State necessarily has considerable discretion in determining the nature and scope of its responsibilities. Nor must a State "choose between attacking every aspect of a problem or not attacking the problem at all."

[Romeo], in light of the severe character of his retardation, concedes that no amount of training will make possible his release. And he does not argue that if he were still at home, the State would have an obligation to provide training at its expense. The record reveals that [Romeo's] primary needs are bodily safety and a minimum of physical restraint, and respondent clearly claims training related to these needs. As we have recognized that there is a constitutionally protected liberty interest in safety and freedom from restraint, training may be necessary to avoid unconstitutional infringement of those rights. On the basis of the record before us, it is quite uncertain whether respondent seeks any "habilitation" or training unrelated to safety and freedom from bodily restraints. Romeo indicates that even the self-care programs he seeks are needed to reduce his aggressive behavior… If, as seems the case, [Romeo] seeks only training related to safety and freedom from restraints, this case does not present the difficult question whether a mentally retarded person, involuntarily committed to a state institution, has some general constitutional right to training per se, even when no type or amount of training would lead to freedom.

[Justice Powell concludes that the state has an obligation to provide "minimally adequate or reasonable training to ensure safety and freedom from undue restraint."]

Yet these interests are not absolute; indeed to some extent they are in conflict. In operating an institution such as Pennhurst, there are occasions in which it is necessary for the State to restrain the movement of residents—for example, to protect them as well as others from violence. Similar restraints may also be appropriate in a training program. And an institution cannot protect its residents from all danger of violence if it is to permit them to have any freedom of movement. The question then is not simply whether a liberty interest has been infringed but whether the extent or nature of the restraint or lack of absolute safety is such as to violate due process….

Accordingly, whether [Romeo's] constitutional rights have been violated must be determined by balancing his liberty interests against the relevant state interests. If there is to be any uniformity in protecting these interests, this balancing cannot be left to the unguided discretion of a judge or jury. We therefore turn to consider the proper standard for determining whether a State adequately has protected the rights of the involuntarily committed mentally retarded.

We think the standard articulated by Chief Judge Seitz [Third Circuit] affords the necessary guidance and reflects the proper balance between the legitimate interests of the State and the rights of the involuntarily committed to reasonable conditions of safety and freedom from unreasonable restraints. He would have held that "the Constitution only requires that the courts make certain that professional judgment in fact was exercised. It is not appropriate for the courts to specify which of several professionally acceptable choices should have been made." Persons who have been involuntarily committed are entitled to more considerate treatment and conditions of confinement than criminals whose conditions of confinement are designed to punish. At the same time, this standard is lower than the "compelling" or "substantial" necessity tests the Court of Appeals would require a State to meet to justify use of restraints or conditions of less than absolute safety. We think this requirement would place an undue burden on the administration of institutions such as Pennhurst and also would restrict unnecessarily the exercise of professional judgment as to the needs of residents.

Moreover, we agree that [Romeo] is entitled to minimally adequate training. In this case, the minimally adequate training required by the Constitution is such training as may be reasonable in light of respondent's liberty interests in safety and freedom from unreasonable restraints. In determining what is "reasonable"—in this and in any case presenting a claim for training by a State—we emphasize that courts must show deference to the judgment exercised by a qualified professional. By so limiting judicial review of challenges to conditions in state institutions, interference by the federal judiciary with the internal operations of these institutions should be minimized. Moreover, there certainly is no reason to think judges or juries are better qualified than appropriate professionals in making such decisions. (Courts should not " 'second-guess the expert administrators on matters on which they are better informed.' ") For these reasons, the decision, if made by a professional, is presumptively valid; liability may be imposed only when the decision by the professional is such a substantial departure from accepted professional judgment, practice, or standards as to demonstrate that the person responsible actually did not base the decision on such a judgment. In an action for damages against a professional in his individual capacity, however, the professional will not be liable if he was unable to satisfy his normal professional standards because of budgetary constraints; in such a situation, good-faith immunity would bar liability....

[Romeo] thus enjoys constitutionally protected interests in conditions of reasonable care and safety, reasonably nonrestrictive confinement conditions, and such training as may be required by these interests. Such conditions of confinement would comport fully with the purpose of [Romeo's] commitment. In determining whether the State has met its obligations in these respects, decisions made by the appropriate professional are entitled to a presumption of correctness. Such a presumption is necessary to enable institutions of this type—often, unfortunately, overcrowded and understaffed—to continue to function. A single professional may have to make decisions with respect to a number of residents with widely varying needs and problems in the course of a normal day. The administrators, and particularly professional personnel, should not be required to make each decision in the shadow of an action for damages....

We vacate the decision of the Court of Appeals...So Ordered.

Justice Blackmun:

I join the Court's opinion. I write separately, however, to make clear why I believe that opinion properly leaves unresolved two difficult and important issues.

The first is whether the Commonwealth of Pennsylvania could accept [Romeo] for "care and treatment," as it did under the Pennsylvania Mental Health and Mental Retardation Act of 1966, and then constitutionally refuse to provide him any "treatment," as that term is defined by state law. Were that question properly before us, in my view there would be a serious issue whether, as a matter of due process, the State could so refuse....

The second difficult question left open today is whether [Romeo] has an independent constitutional claim, grounded in the Due Process Clause of the Fourteenth Amendment, to that "habilitation" or training necessary to preserve those basic self-care skills he possessed when he first entered Pennhurst—for example, the ability to dress himself and care for his personal hygiene. In my view, it would be consistent with the Court's reasoning today to include within the "minimally adequate training required by the Constitution," such training as is reasonably necessary to prevent a person's pre-existing self-care skills from deteriorating because of his commitment.

The Court makes clear, that even after a person is committed to a state institution, he is entitled to such training as is necessary to prevent unreasonable losses of additional liberty as a result of his confinement—for example, unreasonable bodily restraints or unsafe institutional conditions. If a person could demonstrate that he entered a state institution with minimal self-care skills, but lost those skills after commitment because of the State's unreasonable refusal to provide him training, then, it seems to me, he has alleged a loss of liberty quite distinct from—and as serious as—the loss of safety and freedom from unreasonable restraints. For many mentally retarded people, the difference between the capacity to do things for themselves within an institution and total dependence on the institution for all of their needs is as much liberty as they ever will know....

CHIEF JUSTICE BURGER:

I agree with much of the Court's opinion. However, I would hold flatly that [Romeo] has no constitutional right to training, or "habilitation," per se. The parties, and the Court, acknowledge that [Romeo] cannot function outside the state institution, even with the assistance of relatives. Indeed, even now neither [Romeo] nor his family seeks his discharge from state care. Under these circumstances, the State's provision of food, shelter, medical care, and living conditions as safe as the inherent nature of the institutional environment reasonably allows, serves to justify the State's custody of respondent. The State did not seek custody of [Romeo]; his family understandably sought the State's aid to meet a serious need....

Washington v. Harper
494 U.S. 210 (1990)

Justice Kennedy delivered the opinion for a unanimous Court with respect to one part of the opinion as well as the opinion of the Court with respect to the remaining parts, in which Chief Justice Rehnquist and Justices White, Blackmun, O'Connor, and Scalia joined. Justice Blackmun filed a concurring opinion. Justice Stevens filed an opinion concurring in part and dissenting in part, in which Justices Brennan and Marshall joined.

Areas for Discussion and Ethical Reflection

1.   The Court concludes that a judicial hearing is not necessary in order for the state to administer antipsychotic medication to a mentally ill patient against her/his will. Outline Justice Kennedy's arguments in support of the Court's position. Would you be willing to argue, from a purely moral perspective, that it would be permissible, but not obligatory, for states to put in place judicial proceedings before such actions are taken? If we assume that Justice Kennedy would agree that such procedures are permissible, why would he not conclude that they are necessary? In other words, discuss morally relevant factors that bear on the distinction between an action being morally permissible and morally obligatory.

2.   Justice Kennedy is claiming that the professional judgment standard is sufficient to protect Harper's liberty interest. Do you agree? Does such a claim rest on a particular model of the physician-patient relationship? Review the models outlined in chapter 6. As you will see when you read *Harper*, the Court describes the liberty interest at stake as one "in avoiding the unwanted administration of antipsychotic drugs." But, as one commentator notes, the liberty interest involved might best be described as one in "bodily integrity" or "mentational integrity."[12] Discuss ethical arguments and considerations that might recommend one description over another. You might wish to return to our discussion of *Michael H. v. Gerald D.* in chapter 2 for help.

3.   In a footnote to his decision, Justice Kennedy details why the majority disagrees with Justice Stevens's contention that Harper is being treated with antipsychotic medications without first determining the medical appropriateness of the medications. Justice Kennedy points out: "That an inmate is mentally ill and dangerous is a necessary condition to medication, but not a sufficient condition...." In addition, Justice Kennedy contends, the inmate's treating physician must also find that the medication is appropriate. What does it mean to make a distinction between necessary and sufficient conditions? Do you find Justice Kennedy's assertion reassuring?

4.   Justice Kennedy quotes the American Psychological Association as claiming, "Psychotropic medication is widely accepted within the psychiatric community as an extraordinarily effective treatment for both acute and chronic psychoses, particularly schizophrenia." Even if this assertion is true, what ethical concerns might you raise against forcing patients to take psychotropic medications against their will? How would you define "extraordinarily effective treatment"?

5.   Look again at the very brief passage that opens this chapter; Justice Brandeis wrote this in 1928 in his dissenting opinion in *Olmstead v. United States*. Justice Stevens quotes this passage in the part of his opinion in *Washington v. Harper* that is a dissent. Since the majority agrees with Justice Stevens that individuals have a liberty interest against unwanted bodily invasion, why does Justice Stevens cite this passage from *Olmstead*? Discuss two ethical principles that support the passage.

6.   Justice Stevens asserts: "A competent individual's right to refuse psychotropic medication is an aspect of liberty requiring the highest order of protection under the Fourteenth Amendment." That is, judicial review of orders to involuntarily medicate inmates is required. Justice Stevens appeals to respect for dignity in support of his position. What other ethical arguments can you provide in support of Justice Stevens's position?

7.   Are there, or should there be, different ethical concerns between common medical practice in the field of mental health and common medical practice in the field of mental health in prisons?[13] Obviously, the mission of a prison is different from that of an inpatient mental health facility. What is the ethical significance of the differing missions for the treatment of mentally ill patients/inmates? One might well imagine, using another example, that informed consent requirements and procedures would be quite different in one area than in the other. What would be these differences? Is one set of differences more morally suspect than the other?

8.   The influence of *Harper* on both the Court and on medical ethics continues. In June 2003, in a 6-3 ruling, the Court handed down its decision in *Sell v. United States*, 539 U.S. ___ (2003). At issue in the case was whether the Constitution permitted the government to administer antipsychotic medication against an individual's will in order to allow him to become competent enough to stand trial. Charles Sell, a dentist with a long history of mental illness, had been charged with fraud and other crimes. After a lower court ordered Sell to take medication, he appealed. On appeal, the Eighth Circuit concluded that, while Sell was not a danger to himself or others, he could be forced to take antipsychotic medications in order to help him attain competence for standing trial against the charges. The Eighth Circuit reasoned that the government had an "essential interest" in bringing Sell to trial and that the medication was "medically appropriate." Justice Breyer, writing for the majority, overturned the Eighth Circuit. Citing *Harper*, Justice Breyer noted that individuals have a substantial liberty interest in avoiding unwanted administration of antipsychotic medications. The Court ruled that government can force individuals to take antipsychotic medication against their will for the purpose of helping defendants achieve competence to stand trial, but several conditions have to be met. These conditions are: 1) important governmental interests must be at stake, 2) forced medication will significantly advance those government interests, 3) the forced medication is necessary to advance the interests of the state, and 4) the administration of drugs must be medically appropriate. Justice Breyer concluded that in this case these conditions were not met. From a moral perspective, what do you conclude regarding the adequacy of these four conditions? Does the type of crime a defendant is accused of committing make a moral difference in your assessment of the moral permissibility of the defendant being forced to take antipsychotic medication?

Justice Kennedy:

The central question before us is whether a judicial hearing is required before the State may treat a mentally ill prisoner with antipsychotic drugs against his will. Resolution of the case requires us to discuss the protections afforded the prisoner under the Due Process Clause of the Fourteenth Amendment....

In February 1985, [Walter Harper] filed suit in state court under 42 U.S.C. 1983 against various individual defendants and the State, claiming that the failure to provide a judicial hearing before the involuntary administration of antipsychotic medication violated the Due Process, Equal Protection, and Free Speech Clauses of both the Federal and State Constitutions, as well as state tort law. [The trial court ruled against Harper, but the Washington State Supreme Court held that] under the Due Process Clause, the State could administer antipsychotic medication to a competent, nonconsenting inmate only if, in a judicial hearing at which the inmate had the full panoply of adversarial procedural protections, the State proved by "clear, cogent, and convincing" evidence that the administration of antipsychotic medication was both necessary and effective for furthering a compelling state interest.

We granted certiorari, and we reverse....

The Washington Supreme Court...required that a different set of determinations than those set forth in the policy be made as a precondition to medication without the inmate's consent. Instead of having to prove, pursuant to the Policy, only that the mentally ill inmate is "gravely disabled" or that he presents a "serious likelihood of harm" to himself for others, the court required the State to prove that it has a compelling interest in administering the medication and that the administration of the drugs is necessary and effective to further that interest. The decision-maker was required further to consider and make written findings regarding either the inmate's desires or a "substituted judgment" for the inmate analogous to the medical treatment decision for an incompetent person. The Washington Supreme Court's decision, as a result, has both substantive and procedural aspects....

As a matter of state law, the Policy itself undoubtedly confers upon respondent a right to be free from the arbitrary administration of antipsychotic medication...Policy 600.30 is...mandatory in character. By permitting a psychiatrist to treat an inmate with antipsychotic drugs against his wishes only if he is found to be (1) mentally ill and (2) gravely disabled or dangerous, the Policy creates a justifiable expectation on the part of the inmate that the drugs will not be administered unless those conditions exist....

[Harper] contends that the State, under the mandate of the Due Process Clause, may not override his choice to refuse antipsychotic drugs unless he has been found to be incompetent, and then only if the fact finder makes a substituted judgment that he, if competent, would consent to drug treatment. We disagree. The extent of a prisoner's right under the Clause to avoid the unwanted administration of antipsychotic drugs must be defined in the context of the inmate's confinement. The Policy under review requires the State to establish, by a medical finding, that a mental disorder exists which is likely to cause harm if not treated. Moreover, the fact that the medication must first be prescribed by a psychiatrist, and then approved by a reviewing psychiatrist, ensures that the treatment in question will be ordered only if it is in the prisoner's medical interests, given the legitimate needs of his institutional confinement. These standards, which recognize both the prisoner's medical interests and the State's interests, meet the demands of the Due Process Clause.

[Justice Kennedy then cites and discusses previous cases establishing that the state has an interest in prison safety and security.]

We hold that, given the requirements of the prison environment, the Due Process Clause permits the State to treat a prison inmate who has a serious mental illness with antipsychotic drugs against his will, if the inmate is dangerous to himself or others and the treatment is in the inmate's medical interest....

[W]e address next what procedural protections are necessary to ensure that the decision to medicate an inmate against his will is neither arbitrary nor erroneous under the standards we have discussed above....

The primary point of disagreement between the parties is whether due process requires a judicial decisionmaker. As written, the Policy requires that the decision whether to medicate an inmate against his will be made by a hearing committee composed of a psychiatrist, a psychologist, and the Center's Associate Superintendent...

[Harper] contends that only a court should make the decision to medicate an inmate against his will...

[Harper's] interest in avoiding the unwarranted administration of antipsychotic drugs is not insubstantial. The forcible injection of medication into a nonconsenting person's body represents a substantial interference with that person's liberty. The purpose of the drugs is to alter the chemical balance in a patient's brain, leading to changes, intended to be beneficial, in his or her cognitive processes. While the therapeutic benefits of antipsychotic drugs are well documented, it is also true that the drugs can have serious, even fatal, side effects. One such side effect identified by the trial court is acute dystonia, a severe involuntary spasm of the upper body, tongue, throat, or eyes. The trial court found that it may be treated and reversed within a few minutes through use of the medication Cogentin. Other side effects include akathesia (motor restlessness, often characterized by an inability to sit still); neuroleptic malignant syndrome (a relatively rare condition which can lead to death from cardiac dysfunction); and tardive dyskinesia, perhaps the most discussed side effect of antipsychotic drugs. Tardive dyskinesia is a neurological disorder, irreversible in some cases, that is characterized by involuntary, uncontrollable movements of various muscles, especially around the face. The State, respondent, and amici sharply disagree about the frequency with which tardive dyskinesia occurs, its severity, and the medical profession's ability to treat, arrest, or reverse the condition. A fair reading of the evidence, however, suggests that the proportion of patients treated with antipsychotic drugs who exhibit the symptoms of tardive dyskinesia ranges from 10% to 25%. According to the American Psychiatric Association, studies of the condition indicate that 60% of tardive dyskinesia is mild or minimal in effect, and about 10% may be characterized as severe.

Notwithstanding the risks that are involved, we conclude that an inmate's interests are adequately protected, and perhaps better served, by allowing the decision to medicate to be made by medical professionals rather than a judge. The Due Process Clause "has never been thought to require that the neutral and detached trier of fact be law trained or a judicial or administrative officer." Though it cannot be doubted that the decision to medicate has societal and legal implications, the Constitution does not prohibit the State from permitting medical personnel to make the decision under fair procedural mechanisms....We cannot make the facile assumption that the patient's intentions, or a substituted judgment approximating those intentions, can be determined in a single judicial hearing apart from the realities of frequent and ongoing clinical observation by medical professionals.... Nor can we ignore the fact that requiring judicial hearings will divert scarce prison resources, both money and the staff's time, from the care and treatment of mentally ill inmates.

Under Policy 600.30, the decision-maker is asked to review a medical treatment decision made by a medical professional. That review requires two medical inquiries: first, whether the inmate suffers from a "mental disorder"; and second, whether, as a result of that disorder, he is dangerous to himself, others, or their property. Under the Policy, the hearing committee reviews on a regular basis the staff's choice of both the type and dosage of drug to be administered, and can order appropriate changes. The risks associated with antipsychotic drugs are for the most part medical ones, best assessed by medical professionals. A State may conclude with good reason that a judicial hearing will not be as effective, as continuous, or as probing as administrative review using medical decisionmakers. We hold that due process requires no more.

In sum, we hold that the regulation before us is permissible under the Constitution. It is an accommodation between an inmate's liberty interest in avoiding the forced administration of antipsychotic drugs and the State's interests in providing appropriate medical treatment to reduce the danger that an inmate suffering from a serious mental disorder represents to himself or others. The Due Process Clause does require certain essential procedural protections, all of which are provided by the regulation before us. The judgment of the Washington Supreme Court is reversed....

It is so ordered.

JUSTICE STEVENS:

...The Court has undervalued [Harper's] liberty interest; has misread the Washington involuntary medication Policy...and has concluded that a mock trial before an institutionally biased tribunal constitutes "due process of law." Each of these errors merits separate discussion.

The Court acknowledges that under the Fourteenth Amendment "[Harper] possesses a significant liberty interest in avoiding the unwanted administration of antipsychotic drugs," but then virtually ignores the several dimensions of that liberty. They are both physical and intellectual. Every violation of a person's bodily integrity is an invasion of his or her liberty. The invasion is particularly intrusive if it creates a substantial risk of permanent injury and premature death. Moreover, any such action is degrading if it overrides a competent person's choice to reject a specific form of medical treatment. And when the purpose or effect of forced drugging is to alter the will and the mind of the subject, it constitutes a deprivation of liberty in the most literal and fundamental sense…The liberty of citizens to resist the administration of mind-altering drugs arises from our Nation's most basic values.

[Justice Stevens, after reading from a record of one of Harper's medication hearings, in which Harper said he would rather die than take medication, Stevens concludes: "There is no doubt… that a competent individual's right to refuse such medication is a fundamental liberty interest deserving the highest order of protection."]

Arguably, any of three quite different state interests might be advanced to justify a deprivation of this liberty interest. The State might seek to compel Harper to submit to a mind-altering drug treatment program as punishment for the crime he committed in 1976, as a "cure" for his mental illness, or as a mechanism to maintain order in the prison. The Court today recognizes Harper's liberty interest only as against the first justification.

Forced administration of antipsychotic medication may not be used as a form of punishment. This conclusion follows inexorably from our holding in *Vitek v. Jones* that the Constitution provides a convicted felon the protection of due process against an involuntary transfer from the prison population to a mental hospital for psychiatric treatment...

...[A]lthough the Court does not find, as Harper urges, an absolute liberty interest of a competent person to refuse psychotropic drugs, it does recognize that the substantive protections of the Due Process Clause limit the forced administration of psychotropic drugs to all but those inmates whose medical interests would be advanced by such treatment....

Policy 600.30 permits forced administration of psychotrophic drugs on a mentally ill inmate based purely on the impact that his disorder has on the security of the prison environment. The provisions of the Policy make no reference to any expected benefit to the inmate's medical condition.

Although any application of Policy 600.30 requires a medical judgment as to a prisoner's mental condition and the cause of his behavior, the Policy does not require a determination that forced medication would advance his medical interest. Use of psychotropic drugs, the State readily admits, serves to ease the institutional and administrative burdens of maintaining prison security and provides a means of managing an unruly prison population and preventing property damage. By focusing on the risk that the inmate's mental condition poses to other people and property, the Policy allows the State to exercise either parens patriae authority or police authority to override a prisoner's liberty interest in refusing psychotropic drugs. Thus, most unfortunately, there is simply no basis for the Court's assertion that medication under the Policy must be to advance the prisoner's medical interest.

[Justice Stevens next discusses at length how the Court has misapplied rulings from previous decisions regarding issues surrounding security concerns.]

The State, and arguably the Court, allows the SOC to

blend the state interests in responding to emergencies and in convenient prison administration with the individual's interest in receiving beneficial medical treatment. The result is a muddled rationale that allows the "exaggerated response" of forced psychotropic medication on the basis of purely institutional concerns. So serving institutional convenience eviscerates the inmate's substantive liberty interest in the integrity of his body and mind.

The procedures of Policy 600.30 are also constitutionally deficient. Whether or not the State ever may order involuntary administration of psychotropic drugs to a mentally ill person who has been committed to its custody but has not been declared incompetent, it is at least clear that any decision approving such drugs must be made by an impartial professional concerned not with institutional interests, but only with the individual's best interests. The critical defect in Policy 600.30 is the failure to have the treatment decision made or reviewed by an impartial person or tribunal.

The psychiatrists who diagnose and provide routine care to SOC inmates may prescribe psychotropic drugs and recommend involuntary medication under Policy 600.30.

These decision makers have two disqualifying conflicts of interest. First, the panel members must review the work of treating physicians who are their colleagues and who, in turn, regularly review their decisions. Such an in-house system pits the interests of an inmate who objects to forced medication against the judgment not only of his doctor, but often his doctor's colleagues. Furthermore, the Court's conclusion that "[n]one of the hearing committee members may be involved in the inmate's current treatment or diagnosis," overlooks the fact that Policy 600.30 allows a treating psychiatrist to participate in all but the initial 7-day medication approval. This revolving door operated in Harper's case....

Second, the panel members, as regular staff of the

Center, must be concerned not only with the inmate's best medical interests, but also with the most convenient means of controlling the mentally disturbed inmate. The mere fact that a decision is made by a doctor does not make it "certain that professional judgment in fact was exercised." [See *Youngberg.*] The structure of the SOC committee virtually ensures that it will not be....

[Justice Stevens continues by discussing the presence of institutional bias.]

In sum, it is difficult to imagine how a committee convened under Policy 600.30 could conceivably discover, much less be persuaded to overrule, an erroneous or arbitrary decision to medicate or to maintain a specific dosage or type of drug. Institutional control infects the decision makers and the entire procedure....I continue to believe that "even the inmate retains an unalienable interest in liberty—at the very minimum the right to be treated with dignity—which the Constitution may never ignore." A competent individual's right to refuse psychotropic medication is an aspect of liberty requiring the highest order of protection under the Fourteenth Amendment....

Notes

1.   Phillip R. Reilly, "Eugenic Sterilization in the United States," in *Contemporary Issues in Bioethics*, 4th ed., edited by Tom L. Beauchamp and LeRoy Walters (Belmont, CA: Wadsworth, 1994), p. 602.

2.   Jerry Menikoff, *Law and Bioethics: An Introduction* (Washington, DC: Georgetown University Press, 2001), pp. 40–42.

3.   Stephen Jay Gould, "Carrie Buck's Daughter," in *Contemporary Issues in Bioethics*, p. 611.

4.   Ibid., p. 613.

5.   Reilly, "Eugenic Sterilization in the United States," p. 600.

6.   Ibid., p. 602.

7.   Loretta M. Kopelman, "Moral Problems in Psychiatry: The Role of

Value Judgments in Psychiatric Practice," in *Medical Ethics*, 2nd ed., edited by Robert M. Veatch (Boston: Jones and Bartlett, 1997), pp. 279–80.

8.   Michael H. Shapiro et al., *Bioethics and Law: Cases, Materials and Problems*, 2nd ed. (St. Paul, MN: West Group, 2003), p. 815.

9.   Ibid.

10.   Ibid.

11.   Ibid., p. 808.

12.   Ibid., p. 338.

13.   Ibid., p. 339.

For Further Reading

Beauchamp, Tom L., and LeRoy Walters. "Introduction to Eugenics and Human Genetics." In *Contemporary Issues in Bioethics*, 4th edition, Tom L. Beauchamp and LeRoy Walters, eds. Belmont, CA: Wadsworth, 1994.

Gould, Stephen Jay. "Carrie Buck's Daughter." In *Contemporary Issues in Bioethics*.

Kopelman, Loretta M. "Moral Problems in Psychiatry: The Role of Value Judgments in Psychiatric Practice." In *Medical Ethics*, 2nd edition, Robert M. Veatch, ed. Boston: Jones and Bartlett, 1997.

Lombardo, Paul A. "Facing Carrie Buck." *Hastings Center Report* 33 (2003): 14–17.

Reilly, Phillip R. "Eugenic Sterilization in the United States." In *Contemporary Issues in Bioethics*.

Shapiro, Michael H., et al. *Bioethics and Law: Cases, Materials and Problems*, 2nd edition. St. Paul, MN: West Publishing Company, 2003.

CHAPTER NINE

THE RIGHT TO REFUSE TREATMENT AND ASSISTED SUICIDE CASES

Because issues of bioethics have started to come before the courts only over the past few decades, the courts have looked elsewhere to find principles upon which to base their judgments. Courts have regularly looked both to the traditions of the common law and the traditions of ethics and medicine. Analogously, judicial decisions have often formed the basis of new ethical and medical approaches....The law is not merely looking to ethics for potential methods of analysis, it is usurping ethics in debate on these issues.

—Barry Furrow et al., *Bioethics: Health Care Law and Ethics*

Nowhere do we see the influence of constitutional law on medical ethics and that of medical ethics on constitutional law more clearly than in the area of death and dying. Ethical and legal concerns surrounding when and how we die are dramatic and give rise to intense emotions. Intelligent people of goodwill often disagree vehemently with one another over what constitutes morally and legally permissible actions and policies. Determining whether family members of once-competent patients who are now terminally or chronically ill may request the removal of medical interventions raises all manner of ethical, social, and legal concerns. Many of these same problems, and different ones as well, revolve around allowing physicians to assist their terminally ill, competent patients to die. Respect for autonomy, privacy, and dignity on the one hand, and avoiding harm to third parties, prohibiting suicide, and respect for biological life on the other, inform the debate over how, if at all, medicine may sanction and participate in the hastening of death. In this chapter we examine three of the most famous cases in bioethics law. Such has been the impact of these three cases in the constitutional and ethical debate over death and dying that even those students and professionals with no interest in judicial decision-making or public policy are familiar with these decisions. The moral arguments and value judgments underlying the justices' reasoning in these cases are very often quite obvious. But for all their familiarity and influence, these cases are often misunderstood.

Constitutional Issues and Background

At issue in our first case, *Cruzan v. Director, Missouri Department of Health*, was whether the U.S. Constitution grants incompetent, chronically ill individuals the right to refuse medical interventions necessary to sustain life. On the night of January 11, 1983, Nancy Beth Cruzan lost control of her car and was thrown into a ditch, where she lay for as long as twelve to fourteen minutes without oxygen. When paramedics arrived, they discovered no evidence of breathing or heartbeat but initiated treatment to revive her. Later Cruzan was diagnosed with permanent brain damage and determined to be in a permanent vegetative state. Cruzan was not placed on a respirator, but artificial nutrition and hydration were begun, the removal of which would result in Cruzan's death. Cruzan was being kept in a state facility, and Missouri was paying for her care. When it became clear that Nancy would never regain normal mental capacity, her parents asked that nutrition and hydration be removed. The hospital refused, but a state trial court granted the parents' request. Upon appeal, the Missouri State Supreme Court refused to grant the parents' request. The court asserted that the right to refuse treatment did not apply in this case and that Nancy Cruzan did not enjoy a right to privacy in these circumstances. The Missouri Supreme Court insisted on applying a clear and convincing evidence standard whereby a surrogate decision-maker (in this case, Nancy's parents) would have to show that Nancy would, beyond a reasonable doubt, wish treatment withdrawn under the present circumstances.

In a 5-4 decision, the Court ruled that nothing in the Due Process Clause of the Fourteenth Amendment prohibited Missouri from requiring clear and convincing evidence of a formerly competent patient's wishes before honoring a request to remove life-sustaining treatment. Chief Justice Rehnquist, in his majority opinion, did acknowledge that competent patients have a right to refuse life-sustaining treatment. The Court also took the position that artificial nutrition and hydration are medical procedures, an acknowledgment that held great ethical and legal significance in that competent patients could now refuse artificial nutrition and hydration as medical treatment. The various opinions of the justices demonstrate the degree to which they differed over the rights of formerly competent patients and over the lengths to which a state could go in keeping patients alive.

Seven years later the Court once again considered issues surrounding death and dying, this time in the context of physician-assisted suicide (PAS). In two cases, the Court considered whether the Constitution permitted states to prohibit physicians from assisting their terminally ill, competent patients to die. In the first case, *Washington v. Glucksberg*, the justices considered a Washington statute making it a felony for anyone to assist another in committing suicide. Four physicians who treated terminally ill, suffering patients, a nonprofit organization that counseled the terminally ill, and three patients brought suit against the state. They filed suit in federal district court asserting that Washington's law constituted a violation of the Due Process Clause of the Fourteenth Amendment. Relying on the Court's previous decisions in *Casey* and *Cruzan*, the lower court ruled that, indeed, terminally ill, competent patients have a right to assistance from physicians in ending their lives. The Ninth Circuit

Court of Appeals, in a widely discussed decision authored by Judge Reinhardt, affirmed the decision.

In overruling the Ninth Circuit, Chief Justice Rehnquist asserted that the right to assistance in committing suicide is not a liberty interest protected by the Due Process Clause. Rehnquist also asserted that Washington's ban on suicide is rationally related to a legitimate state interest. All nine justices concurred in the judgment, but disagreement existed among the justices regarding the reasons the Washington statute could be upheld. This disagreement among the justices was related, at least in part, to the distinction between constitutional challenges that are facial in nature and challenges that are as-applied. That is, several justices seemed to think they were finding the Washington law only facially constitutional, which would mean that these justices might be willing to reconsider the constitutionality of the prohibition if it were applied to a particularized group. Of course, the doctors and terminally ill, suffering patients who were challenging the law thought they were challenging the law as it applied to them.

Our third decision is the companion case to *Washington v. Glucksberg*; both cases concern physician-assisted suicide, both were argued together, and both decisions were handed down on the same day in 1997. The state of New York had made it a crime for anyone to assist in a suicide, although competent, terminally ill patients were allowed to refuse life-saving treatment. A group of New York physicians and three terminally ill patients brought suit claiming the law violated the Equal Protection Clause of the Fourteenth Amendment. The law, so physicians and patients argued, allows some patients to choose the manner and timing of their deaths but denies that privilege to other similarly situated patients. The federal district court ruled in favor of New York, but the Second Circuit reversed, finding that, indeed, New York state was treating similar groups differently and that this different treatment had no rational basis.

Chief Justice Rehnquist, as he did with the ruling from the Ninth Circuit in *Glucksberg*, overruled the Second Circuit. He concluded that New York's ban on assisted suicide was a rational method to meet a legitimate goal of the state legislature. That is, New York could make a distinction between patients who wished to refuse life-saving medical treatment and patients who wished to request assistance from a physician in hastening death. In addition, the Court determined that New York's recognition of treatment refusals and prohibition of requests for assistance from a physician in committing suicide is constitutional. As with *Glucksberg*, all the justices agreed with the judgment of the Court, but widespread disagreement existed over the reasons for the judgment.

Ethical Issues and Background

We begin our discussion of ethical issues and background by clarifying what is *not* the focus of debate in this chapter. First, generally speaking, it is a settled matter in constitutional law and medical ethics that competent patients, whether terminally ill or not, may refuse to begin or may request the cessation of medical treatment. Respect for principles of autonomy, privacy, and informed consent usually dictates that medical professionals may not start or continue treatment that the rational person does not want. Second, and again generally speaking, a "standard wisdom about the decision-making process"[1] exists regarding the withholding or withdrawing of life-saving therapy for once-competent, terminally ill patients. Both law and ethics usually recognize the use of advance directives, proxy directives, or surrogate decision-makers in determining what treatments should be initiated, stopped, or never even considered for once-competent, terminally ill patients. This is not to say that ethical problems and tensions do not arise with respect to treatment decisions regarding these two groups of patients. Concerns and controversies over the meaning and scope of autonomy, competency, and best interests do arise in such treatment decisions, as the Supreme Court recognizes in the cases below. However, law and medical ethics typically address these tensions effectively.

Our focus, and that of the Court as well, centers around two other groups of patients. In *Cruzan* the justices examine the moral and legal complexities surrounding the permissibility of withholding or withdrawing life-sustaining treatment from formerly competent patients who are not terminally ill and who have no written advance health care directives. In *Glucksberg* and *Vacco,* ethical and legal issues accompanying the request by competent, suffering, terminally ill patients to have death hastened with the assistance of a physician are the focus of attention. As one can imagine, determining proper societal responses to the needs of these two groups of patients raises very troubling and complex ethical questions. What exactly are the professional obligations of physicians toward these patients? Might the norms and values of the medical profession require a physician to end a patient's suffering even if the measures taken result in the patient's death? Is it a case of unjustified killing to honor the request of a family member who wishes to have life-sustaining treatment withdrawn from a loved one who is not dying but will remain in a coma for many years? How can the state morally justify keeping patients alive who, their families are convinced, would rather die? What moral justifications can the state employ for prohibiting physicians from honoring the request of their competent, terminally ill patients who wish to end their suffering? The justices in the three cases below address these questions and others. As background we examine select arguments for and against honoring requests of patients' families and for and against physician-assisted suicide.

In determining whether Nancy Cruzan's parents have a right to discontinue artificial hydration and nutrition, we have to ask whether Nancy herself has rights or interests. If Nancy Cruzan has an interest in, for example, not being kept alive in a condition where she has no experiences, then Missouri appears to violate that interest by requiring clear and convincing evidence of her wishes before allowing her to die. John Robertson maintains that people in permanent vegetative state (PVS) have no interests and hence no rights to violate.[2] He claims patients in this condition do not feel pain and are not aware of their situation, thus they have no interests that can be harmed. The most powerful response to Robertson's position comes from Ronald Dworkin who, by making a distinction between experiential and critical interests, argues that Nancy Cruzan does have interests that must be legally and morally respected. By experiential interests Dworkin means the pursuit of experiences we find pleasurable and the avoidance of experiences we find painful. Patients in PVS have no experiential interests that can be respected or violated. Critical interests, on the other hand, refer to the interests an individual has in ensuring that her/his life goes well; critical interests are a person's convictions about what makes her/his own life worth living.[3] Thus keeping patients in PVS alive when they would rather die is a violation of their critical interests.

The rights and interests of the family are also relevant in ethical and constitutional assessments of state interference in treatment decisions for PVS patients. Similar to the above claims regarding Nancy's interests, John Robertson asserts that forcing Nancy to stay alive does not violate any rights or interests of Nancy's family.[4] Robertson acknowledges that the Supreme Court has long recognized the rights of families to raise and educate their children in ways they see fit; such activities emanate from a right to privacy. But, Robertson contends, the Supreme Court is correct not to extend this privacy right to decision-making regarding medical treatment for patients in PVS, since the treatment is neither harming nor helping the family member. Of course, many disagree with Robertson. Anyone believing, as Ronald Dworkin does, that Nancy has critical interests, would claim that the state is harming Nancy by refusing her family's request. Other commentators note that families bear most of the burden when a state refuses to grant the request for cessation of treatment. Larry Gostin observes: "Whether the burden of continued life is measured by emotional suffering, by economic cost, or by any other standard, it is not society, the medical profession, or the state that has to pay the cost. The family must live with the consequences."[5] The severity and nature of these burdens lead many to conclude that if a right to family privacy means anything, it means the right to have medical treatment stopped for loved ones in PVS.

Leaving behind the interests of Nancy and her family, we turn to a broader concern, the sanctity of life. An argument in support of Missouri's imposition of a clear and convincing evidence standard is that human life is sacred and the state is permitted, even obligated, to take measures to protect human life. Not only does the state have an interest in human life itself, it also has an interest in preventing abuses that would occur if human life were devalued. Not to require a very high standard for granting a family's request for termination of treatment could possibly lead to denying treatment to patients who would have wanted to live and to the pressuring of families and medical professionals to discontinue treatment in inappropriate circumstances. Some medical ethicists as well as some of the justices writing in the *Cruzan* case have strenuously objected to the notion that the state has an unqualified interest in human life. You may recall Ronald Dworkin's distinction between derivative and detached meanings of the phrase "life is sacred" discussed in chapter 3. Dworkin argues that states have only a detached interest in the sanctity of life (that is, life has intrinsic value, but no rights stem from this recognition), thus the state can legitimately act only to protect that kind of interest. Larry Gostin asserts that Missouri's interest in keeping Nancy Cruzan alive is at best an abstraction. He also maintains that any authority the state has in preserving human life surely diminishes in circumstances where patients do not have and will never have conscious experiences.[6] Justice Brennan voices other objections in his dissenting opinion in *Cruzan*.

The above debate over the extent to which the state may assert and protect an interest in human life is our segue into a brief discussion of some of the ethical concerns underlying the Supreme Court's two physician-assisted suicide (PAS) cases. In both *Glucksberg* and *Vacco* the Supreme Court found appropriate a state's wish to assert an unqualified interest in the preservation of human life. In part, it is this interest in the protection of life that allows the state to refuse to make quality of life judgments. If a state can refuse to make quality of life judgments, then it follows that states are free, if they wish, to designate suicide and assistance in suicide crimes. The above considerations regarding sanctity of life and state interest will help you assess just how comprehensive and convincing some of the justices' arguments are. Keep in mind that although all the justices concurred in the judgments in both *Glucksberg* and *Vacco*, major disagreements existed over the proper reasoning to be used. Much of this disagreement, as you will see, has ethical implications.

Of course, the justices consider many other arguments of ethical importance in ruling on the constitutionality of state prohibitions of PAS. As a matter of fact, both cases are a rich source of conceptual analysis and moral argumentation related to dilemmas in clinical medicine and public policy on PAS. Arguments in support of PAS that rely on the principle of autonomy are contrasted with the state's interest in protecting human life. You also will discover arguments in these cases relying on the right of competent, terminally ill patients to die with dignity. These arguments are contrasted with fears that a constitutional right (and a moral right) to PAS will lead to the unjustified killing of handicapped patients. Related to the concern over the potential abuse of patients is the fear of the slippery slope. Several of the justices employ the slippery slope argument as support for continued prohibition of PAS. That is, once the state allows physicians to assist in suicide of terminally ill patients, assisting in the suicides of chronically ill patients will be next. Soon physicians will no longer take measure to learn how to control pain and suffering. Finally, society will be witness to medical killing on a mass scale. Slippery slope arguments of this type are extremely problematic. For example, they assume that adequate procedures cannot be put in place to prevent abuses from happening; however, one need only turn to Oregon's Death with Dignity Act, which legalized PAS in 1994, to realize that so far abuses have not occurred.

Much has been written on how well or how poorly the justices recognize and appreciate the conceptual and ethical complexity of the arguments for and against PAS. As you read the excerpts, you have an opportunity to become familiar with this analysis and argumentation. Because of its relevance to other arguments and concepts discussed in the cases, we examine briefly the principle of double effect.

The principle of double effect is a venerable concept in ethics and medical ethics. Its origins are in Roman Catholicism and natural law ethics, but many have found the principle useful no matter their ethical persuasion. The principle is also the subject of sustained attack on both theoretical and practical grounds. We can provide a formal statement of the principle as follows: It is morally permissible to perform an action that has both a good effect and a bad effect if a) the act considered in itself is good, or at least morally neutral; b) the bad effect cannot be avoided if the good effect is to be achieved; c) the bad effect is an unintended side effect to achieving the good effect; and d) the bad effect and the good effect are both equally important.[7] The principle of double effect can be difficult to understand and even more difficult to apply. These difficulties serve as the foundation for many objections to the principle. For our purposes, however, it is the third criterion—the bad effect must be unintended to achieve the good effect—that is most relevant and perhaps the most problematic.

In *Vacco v. Quill,* Justice Rehnquist employs the principle of double effect to demonstrate that PAS is legally and morally suspect. Physicians commonly withdraw, or they honor the request to never begin, life-sustaining treatment. In addition, physicians engage in a practice called terminal sedation or barbiturate coma. This practice involves the administration of drugs designed to reduce the patient's pain and suffering, but have the effect of keeping the patient unconscious until death results. Justice Rehnquist employs the criterion of intentionality to distinguish these two practices from the practice of a physician prescribing a lethal dose of drugs to a terminally ill patient. In PAS the physician intends the death of the patient, but in the case of treatment refusal or terminal sedation the physician intends to honor the request of a competent patient or to ease the suffering of the patient. The physician certainly foresees that death will result in these cases, but she/he need not intend death. Justice Rehnquist concludes that, since the distinction between intending and foreseeing death is ethically and legally recognized, patients have no right to receive assistance from a physician in hastening their deaths.

Justice Rehnquist is correct in asserting that the role of intention is significant in ethics. The American Medical Association relies on the distinction as a means of justifying withdrawal of life-sustaining treatment but not permitting euthanasia. Whether the distinction between intending death and merely foreseeing death is as successful in justifying prohibitions on PAS (or euthanasia for that matter) as Justice Rehnquist, the AMA, and others believe is open to debate. As a practical matter, it is difficult to believe that physicians never intend the deaths of their patients when they withdraw treatment or honor treatment refusals. Another practical difficulty revolves around access to a physician's mental state; we cannot know with certainty what a physician is thinking. In addition, employing the distinction in order to justify the practice of terminal sedation seems strained.[8] For many, the practice of terminal sedation is hard to distinguish from PAS. One final observation, especially appropriate for evaluating the Court's handling of PAS, concerns the connection between physician integrity and the principle of double effect. Applying the principle of double effect seems to assume that physicians should never intend death. But asserting that physicians should never intend death involves presuppositions regarding the proper goals of medicine that may not be warranted given the circumstances in which terminally ill, suffering patients often find themselves. Many patients now fear that they will die under conditions that do not constitute dignity or comport with their wishes. An evaluation of medicine's responsibilities and sense of integrity with respect to end of life issues might well require a reassessment of when physicians are permitted or obligated to hasten death.

As you read the three cases in this chapter you will have an opportunity to carefully consider some of the most important ethical issues and concerns surrounding the circumstances of how Americans die. Patients and their families have an immense interest in how the medical profession, state and federal governments, and the courts address practices at the end of life. The manner in which the Supreme Court considers and the extent to which it appreciates the myriad ethical concerns and moral concepts surrounding the treatment of terminally and chronically ill patients provide new insight into these very issues.

Cruzan v. Director, Missouri Department of Health
497 U.S. 261 (1990)

Chief Justice Rehnquist delivered the opinion of the Court, in which Justices White, O'Connor, Scalia, and Kennedy joined. Justices O'Connor and Scalia each filed a concurring opinion. Justice Brennan filed a dissenting opinion, in which Justices Marshall and Blackmun joined. Justice Stevens filed a dissenting opinion.

Areas for Discussion and Ethical Reflection

1.   After the U.S. Supreme Court's ruling in June 1990, the state of Missouri withdrew from the case. Nancy Cruzan's parents and the state-appointed guardian asked the trial court that originally granted the Cruzan's request for removal of treatment to reconsider the case. Additional testimony from Nancy's friends supporting the withdrawal of nutrition and hydration was presented. The trial court ruled that the clear and convincing evidence standard had been met and, on December 14, granted the parents' request for removal of the feeding tube. Twelve days later and more than seven years after she was diagnosed with permanent vegetative state, Nancy died.[9] What feelings does the Cruzan family ordeal raise in you? Why do you suppose Missouri, after "winning" at the Supreme Court level, withdrew

from the case? Why do you suppose Nancy's parents refused to give up? As you think about these questions, and as you read the opinions in *Cruzan*, try to answer two additional questions posed by Ronald Dworkin. "Why do we care so much, one way or the other, about dying when there is nothing to live for but also no pain or suffering that death will stop? Why aren't more of us simply indifferent about what happens to us, or to those we love, in that circumstance?"[10]

2.   The written opinions in this case are extremely interesting and rather detailed. After you have read each excerpt, try outlining each argument you find. Where do the justices address each other's concerns? Where do they ignore one another? Which of the arguments seem relevant to ethical justifications for and against terminating life-sustaining treatment for incompetent adults?

3.   Is *Cruzan* about the right to refuse treatment, the right to die, or the right to commit suicide? Explain why this question matters to any ethical analysis of the permissibility of allowing formerly competent patients to refuse treatment.

4.   Does Chief Justice Rehnquist sincerely believe that competent adult patients have a constitutionally protected right to refuse artificial hydration and nutrition? Identify those portions of his opinion that might call into question his sincerity. What ethical principles would you use to support a right to refuse life-saving medical treatment for competent adults?

5.   Chief Justice Rehnquist notes that "...[W]e do not think a state is required to remain neutral in the face of an informed and voluntary decision by a physically able adult to starve to death." This statement seems to have absolutely no relevance to the Cruzan case. Why does Chief Justice Rehnquist say it?[11] He may, of course, be providing a subtle hint of his own value judgments regarding the morally permissible course of action for Nancy Cruzan. What might be those value judgments?

6.   Chief Justice Rehnquist asserts that the state has an unqualified interest in the preservation of human life. How does he

argue for this? What ethical theories would support this absolut-ist position? What problems might you raise against Rehnquist?

7.   Near the end of his majority opinion, Chief Justice Rehnquist asserts that keeping patients alive who really would have preferred death is better than granting the wishes of sur-rogates because the risk of error is not as great. What argu-ments does Rehnquist give for this claim? Do you agree with Rehnquist's claim?

8.   Justice O'Connor is much more emphatic than Rehnquist in characterizing a competent adult's refusal of medical treat-ment, including artificial food and fluids, as a liberty interest protected by the Due Process Clause of the Fourteenth Amend-ment. What are her arguments for considering the right to treat-ment refusal a liberty interest? When O'Connor uses the term "dignity" do you think she means death with dignity?

9.   Justice O'Connor claims that states may well have a duty to recognize and honor the decisions of surrogate decision-makers. Such a duty on the part of the state, she claims, might be consti-tutionally required in order to protect the liberty interests of the patient. How does O'Connor argue for this position? How would Rehnquist and Scalia respond to O'Connor? What ethical obliga-tions does a state have in respecting the wishes of surrogate deci-sion-makers?

10.   Justice Scalia asserts that nine people picked at random from the Kansas City telephone directory would have no better understanding or knowledge of when life becomes worthless or at what point the means necessary to preserve life are extraordinary than nine justices of the Supreme Court would. Do you agree with Justice Scalia on this? Would bioethics scholars, or philosophers engaged in clinical ethics consulting, or physicians, or students enrolled in undergraduate medial ethics courses possess more in-depth knowledge about quality of life determinations or the differences between extraordinary and ordinary treatments than people picked at random from the telephone directory?

11.   The Cruzans give three reasons for distinguishing withdrawal of artificial nutrition and hydration from suicide. Justice Scalia dismisses all three. Briefly explain each of his responses to the Cruzans. How persuasive is Justice Scalia? Does he really think that honoring the parents' request is equivalent to assisting in a suicide?

12.   Justice Brennan, in one part of his dissenting opinion (not included in the excerpt below), quotes from the President's Commission for the Study of Ethical Problems in Medicine and Biomedical and Behavioral Research:

> [T]reatment ordinarily aims to benefit a patient through preserving life, relieving pain and suffering, protecting against disability, and returning maximally effective functioning. If a prognosis of permanent unconsciousness is correct, however, continued treatment cannot confer such benefits. Pain and suffering are absent, as are joy, satisfaction, and pleasure. Disability is total, and no return to an even minimal level of social or human functioning is possible.

How would Justice Scalia respond to this argument? What moral arguments might Scalia provide?

13.   Justice Brennan believes that Nancy Cruzan possesses both moral and constitutional rights that the state is obligated to respect. Even the majority believes Cruzan has rights. (See *Youngberg v. Romeo* in the previous chapter for an interesting parallel.) But one commentator has argued that Cruzan possesses no constitutional rights, hence there are no rights to violate.[12] Such a claim rests on assertions that Cruzan is comatose, that she has no interests that can be harmed, and that she has left behind no advance directive requesting removal of treatment in such circumstances. What rights, if any, do you think Cruzan possesses? This is an excellent opportunity to examine the distinction between moral rights and constitutional rights. Read Brennan's opinion for help here.

CHIEF JUSTICE REHNQUIST:

...We granted certiorari to consider the question of whether Cruzan has a right under the United States Constitution which would require the hospital to withdraw life-sustaining treatment from her under these circumstances.

At common law, even the touching of one person by another without consent and without legal justification was a battery. Before the turn of the century, this Court observed that "[n]o right is held more sacred, or is more carefully guarded by the common law, than the right of every individual to the possession and control of his own person, free from all restraint or interference of others, unless by clear and unquestionable authority of law." This notion of bodily integrity has been embodied in the requirement that informed consent is generally required for medical treatment. Justice Cardozo, while on the Court of Appeals of New York, aptly described this doctrine: "Every human being of adult years and sound mind has a right to determine what shall be done with his own body, and a surgeon who performs an operation without his patient's consent commits an assault, for which he is liable in damages." The informed consent doctrine has become firmly entrenched in American tort law.

The logical corollary of the doctrine of informed consent is that the patient generally possesses the right not to consent, that is, to refuse treatment. Until about 15 years ago and the seminal decision in *In re Quinlan*, the number of right-to-refuse-treatment decisions were relatively few. Most of the earlier cases involved patients who refused medical treatment forbidden by their religious beliefs, thus implicating First Amendment rights as well as common law rights of self-determination. More recently, however, with the advance of medical technology capable of sustaining life well past the point where natural forces would have brought certain death in earlier times, cases involving the right to refuse life-sustaining treatment have burgeoned.

In the *Quinlan* case, young Karen Quinlan suffered severe brain damage as the result of anoxia, and entered a persistent vegetative state. Karen's father sought judicial approval to disconnect his daughter's respirator. The New Jersey Supreme Court granted the relief, holding that Karen had a right of privacy grounded in the Federal Constitution to terminate treatment. Recognizing that this right was not absolute, however, the court balanced it against asserted state interests. Noting that the State's interest "weakens and the individual's right to privacy grows as the degree of bodily invasion increases and the prognosis dims," the court concluded that the state interests had to give way in that case. The court also concluded that the "only practical way" to prevent the loss of Karen's privacy right due to her incompetence was to allow her guardian and family to decide "whether she would exercise it in these circumstances."

After *Quinlan*, however, most courts have based a right to refuse treatment either solely on the common law right to informed consent or on both the common law right and a constitutional privacy right. In *Superintendent of Belchertown State School v. Saikewicz* (1977), the Supreme Judicial Court of Massachusetts relied on both the right of privacy and the right of informed consent to permit the withholding of chemotherapy from a profoundly-retarded 67-year-old man suffering from leukemia. Reasoning that an incompetent person retains the same rights as a competent individual "because the value of human dignity extends to both," the court adopted a "substituted judgment" standard whereby courts were to determine what an incompetent individual's decision would have been under the circumstances. Distilling certain state interests from prior case law—the preservation of life, the protection of the interests of innocent third parties, the prevention of suicide, and the maintenance of the ethical integrity of the medical profession—the court recognized the first interest as paramount and noted it was greatest when an affliction was curable, "as opposed to the State interest where, as here, the issue is not whether, but when, for how long, and at what cost to the individual [a] life may be briefly extended."

In *In re Storar* (1981), the New York Court of Appeals declined to base a right to refuse treatment on a constitutional privacy right. Instead, it found such a right "adequately supported" by the informed consent doctrine. In *In re Eichner* (decided with *In re Storar*), an 83-year-old man who had suffered brain damage from anoxia entered a vegetative state and was thus incompetent to consent to the removal of his respirator. The court, however, found it unnecessary to reach the question of whether his rights could be exercised by others, since it found the evidence clear and convincing from statements made by the patient when competent that he "did not want to be maintained in a vegetative coma by use of a respirator." In the companion *Storar* case, a 52-year-old man suffering from bladder cancer had been profoundly retarded during most of his life. Implicitly rejecting the approach taken in *Saikewicz*, the court reasoned that, due to such life-long incompetency, "it is unrealistic to attempt to determine whether he would want to continue potentially life-prolonging treatment if he were competent." As the evidence showed that the patient's required blood transfusions did not involve excessive pain and, without them, his mental and physical abilities would deteriorate, the court concluded that it should not "allow an incompetent patient to bleed to death because someone, even someone as close as a parent or sibling, feels that this is best for one with an incurable disease."...

As these cases [and others the Court describes] demonstrate, the common law doctrine of informed consent is viewed as generally encompassing the right of a competent individual to refuse medical treatment. Beyond that, these decisions demonstrate both similarity and diversity in their approach to a decision of what all agree is a perplexing question with unusually strong moral and ethical overtones. State courts have available to them for decision a number of sources—state constitutions, statutes, and common law—which are not available to us. In this Court, the question is simply and starkly whether the United States Constitution prohibits Missouri from choosing the rule of decision which it did. This is the first case in which we have been squarely presented with the issue of whether the United States Constitution grants what is in common parlance referred to as a "right to die."...

The Fourteenth Amendment provides that no State shall "deprive any person of life, liberty, or property, without due process of law." The principle that a competent person has a constitutionally protected liberty interest in refusing unwanted medical treatment may be inferred from our prior decisions.

[The Court briefly discusses *Jacobson v. Massachusetts, Washington v. Harper,* and *Youngberg v. Romeo.*]

[The Cruzans] insist that, under the general holdings of our cases, the forced administration of life-sustaining medical treatment, and even of artificially-delivered food and water essential to life, would implicate a competent person's liberty interest. Although we think the logic of the cases discussed above would embrace such a liberty interest, the dramatic consequences involved in refusal of such treatment would inform the inquiry as to whether the deprivation of that interest is constitutionally permissible. But for purposes of this case, we assume that the United States Constitution would grant a competent person a constitutionally protected right to refuse lifesaving hydration and nutrition.

[The Cruzans] go on to assert that an incompetent person should possess the same right in this respect as is possessed by a competent person....The difficulty with [the Cruzan's] claim is that, in a sense, it begs the question: an incompetent person is not able to make an informed and voluntary choice to exercise a hypothetical right to refuse treatment or any other right. Such a "right" must be exercised for her, if at all, by some sort of surrogate. Here, Missouri has in effect recognized that, under certain circumstances, a surrogate may act for the patient in electing to have hydration and nutrition withdrawn in such a way as to cause death, but it has established a procedural safeguard to assure that the action of the surrogate conforms as best it may to the wishes expressed by the patient while competent. Missouri requires that evidence of the incompetent's wishes as to the withdrawal of treatment be proved by clear and convincing evidence. The question, then, is whether the United States Constitution forbids the establishment of this procedural requirement by the State. We hold that it does not....

Missouri relies on its interest in the protection and preservation of human life, and there can be no gainsaying this interest. As a general matter, the States—indeed, all civilized nations—demonstrate their commitment to life by treating homicide as a serious crime. Moreover, the majority of States in this country have laws imposing criminal penalties on one who assists another to commit suicide. We do not think a State is required to remain neutral in the face of an informed and voluntary decision by a physically able adult to starve to death.

But in the context presented here, a State has more particular interests at stake. The choice between life and death is a deeply personal decision of obvious and overwhelming finality. We believe Missouri may legitimately seek to safeguard the personal element of this choice through the imposition of heightened evidentiary requirements. It cannot be disputed that the Due Process Clause protects an interest in life as well as an interest in refusing life-sustaining medical treatment. Not all incompetent patients will have loved ones available to serve as surrogate decisionmakers. And even where family members are present, "[t]here will, of course, be some unfortunate situations in which family members will not act to protect a patient." A State is entitled to guard against potential abuses in such situations. Similarly, a State is entitled to consider that a judicial proceeding to make a determination regarding an incompetent's wishes may very well not be an adversarial one, with the added guarantee of accurate factfinding that the adversary process brings with it. Finally, we think a State may properly decline to make judgments about the "quality" of life that a particular individual may enjoy, and simply assert an unqualified interest in the preservation of human life to be weighed against the constitutionally protected interests of the individual.

In our view, Missouri has permissibly sought to advance these interests through the adoption of a "clear and convincing" standard of proof to govern such proceedings....

We think it self-evident that the interests at stake in the instant proceedings are more substantial, both on an individual and societal level, than those involved in a run-of-the-mine civil dispute. But not only does the standard of proof reflect the importance of a particular adjudication, it also serves as "a societal judgment about how the risk of error should be distributed between the litigants." The more stringent the burden of proof a party must bear, the more that party bears the risk of an erroneous decision. We believe that Missouri may permissibly place an increased risk of an erroneous decision on those seeking to terminate an incompetent individual's life-sustaining treatment. An erroneous decision not to terminate results in a maintenance of the status quo; the possibility of subsequent developments such as advancements in medical science, the discovery of new evidence regarding the patient's intent, changes in the law, or simply the unexpected death of the patient despite the administration of life-sustaining treatment, at least create the potential that a wrong decision will eventually be corrected or its impact mitigated. An erroneous decision to withdraw life-sustaining treatment, however, is not susceptible of correction....

No doubt is engendered by anything in this record but that Nancy Cruzan's mother and father are loving and caring parents. If the State were required by the United States Constitution to repose a right of "substituted judgment" with anyone, the Cruzans would surely qualify. But we do not think the Due Process Clause requires the State to repose judgment on these matters with anyone but the patient herself. Close family members may have a strong feeling—a feeling not at all ignoble or unworthy, but not entirely disinterested, either—that they do not wish to witness the continuation of the life of a loved one which they regard as hopeless, meaningless, and even degrading. But there is no automatic assurance that the view of close family members will necessarily be the same as the patient's would have been had she been confronted with the prospect of her situation while competent. All of the reasons previously discussed for allowing Missouri to require clear and convincing evidence of the patient's wishes lead us to conclude that the State may choose to defer only to those wishes, rather than confide the decision to close family members.

The judgment of the Supreme Court of Missouri is affirmed.

Justice O'Connor:

I agree that a protected liberty interest in refusing unwanted medical treatment may be inferred from our prior decisions, and that the refusal of artificially delivered food and water is encompassed within that liberty interest. I write separately to clarify why I believe this to be so....

Artificial feeding cannot readily be distinguished from other forms of medical treatment. Whether or not the techniques used to pass food and water into the patient's alimentary tract are termed "medical treatment," it is clear they all involve some degree of intrusion and restraint.

Feeding a patient by means of a nasogastric tube requires a physician to pass a long flexible tube through the patient's nose, throat and esophagus and into the stomach. Because of the discomfort such a tube causes, "[m]any patients need to be restrained forcibly, and their hands put into large mittens to prevent them from removing the tube." A gastrostomy tube (as was used to provide food and water to Nancy Cruzan), or jejunostomy tube must be surgically implanted into the stomach or small intestine. Requiring a competent adult to endure such procedures against her will burdens the patient's liberty, dignity, and freedom to determine the course of her own treatment. Accordingly, the liberty guaranteed by the Due Process Clause must protect, if it protects anything, an individual's deeply personal decision to reject medical treatment, including the artificial delivery of food and water.

I also write separately to emphasize that the Court does not today decide the issue whether a State must also give effect to the decisions of a surrogate decisionmaker. In my view, such a duty may well be constitutionally required to protect the patient's liberty interest in refusing medical treatment. Few individuals provide explicit oral or written instructions regarding their intent to refuse medical treatment should they become incompetent. States which decline to consider any evidence other than such instructions may frequently fail to honor a patient's intent. Such failures might be avoided if the State considered an equally probative source of evidence: the patient's appointment of a proxy to make health care decisions on her behalf. Delegating the authority to make medical decisions to a family member or friend is becoming a common method of planning for the future. Several States have recognized the practical wisdom of such a procedure by enacting durable power of attorney statutes that specifically authorize an individual to appoint a surrogate to make medical treatment decisions. Some state courts have suggested that an agent appointed pursuant to a general durable power of attorney statute would also be empowered to make health care decisions on behalf of the patient. Other States allow an individual to designate a proxy to carry out the intent of a living will. These procedures for surrogate decisionmaking, which appear to be rapidly gaining in acceptance, may be a valuable additional safeguard of the patient's interest in directing his medical care. Moreover, as patients are likely to select a family member as a surrogate, giving effect to a proxy's decisions may also protect the "freedom of personal choice in matters of...family life."

Today's decision, holding only that the Constitution permits a State to require clear and convincing evidence of Nancy Cruzan's desire to have artificial hydration and nutrition withdrawn, does not preclude a future determination that the Constitution requires the States to implement the decisions of a patient's duly appointed surrogate. Nor does it prevent States from developing other approaches for protecting an incompetent individual's liberty interest in refusing medical treatment. As is evident from the Court's survey of state court decisions, no national consensus has yet emerged on the best solution for this difficult and sensitive problem. Today we decide only that one State's practice does not violate the Constitution....

JUSTICE SCALIA:

...While I agree with the Court's analysis today, and therefore join in its opinion, I would have preferred that we announce, clearly and promptly, that the federal courts have no business in this field; that American law has always accorded the State the power to prevent, by force if necessary, suicide—including suicide by refusing to take appropriate measures necessary to preserve one's life; that the point at which life becomes "worthless," and the point at which the means necessary to preserve it become "extraordinary" or "inappropriate," are neither set forth in the Constitution nor known to the nine Justices of this Court any better than they are known to nine people picked at random from the Kansas City telephone directory; and hence, that even when it is demonstrated by clear and convincing evidence that a patient no longer wishes certain measures to be taken to preserve her life, it is up to the citizens of Missouri to decide, through their elected representatives, whether that wish will be honored....

The text of the Due Process Clause does not protect individuals against deprivations of liberty simpliciter. It protects them against deprivations of liberty "without due process of law." To determine that such a deprivation would not occur if Nancy Cruzan were forced to take nourishment against her will, it is unnecessary to reopen the historically recurrent debate over whether "due process" includes substantive restrictions. It is at least true that no "substantive due process" claim can be maintained unless the claimant demonstrates that the State has deprived him of a right historically and traditionally protected against State interference. That cannot possibly be established here....

[The Cruzans] rely on three distinctions to separate Nancy Cruzan's case from ordinary suicide: (1) that she is permanently incapacitated and in pain; (2) that she would bring on her death not by any affirmative act but by merely declining treatment that provides nourishment; and (3) that preventing her from effectuating her presumed wish to die requires violation of her bodily integrity. None of these suffices. Suicide was not excused even when committed "to avoid those ills which [persons] had not the fortitude to endure." "The life of those to whom life has become a burden—of those who are hopelessly diseased or fatally wounded—nay, even the lives of criminals condemned to death, are under the protection of the law, equally as the lives of those who are in the full tide of life's enjoyment, and anxious to continue to live." Thus, a man who prepared a poison, and placed it within reach of his wife, "to put an end to her suffering" from a terminal illness was convicted of murder, the "incurable suffering of the suicide, as a legal question, could hardly affect the degree of criminality...." Nor would the imminence of the patient's death have affected liability. "The lives of all are equally under the protection of the law, and under that protection to their last moment.... [Assisted suicide] is declared by the law to be murder, irrespective of the wishes or the condition of the party to whom the poison is administered...."

The second asserted distinction...relies on the dichotomy between action and inaction. Suicide, it is said, consists of an affirmative act to end one's life; refusing treatment is not an affirmative act "causing" death, but merely a passive acceptance of the natural process of dying. I readily acknowledge that the distinction between action and inaction has some bearing upon the legislative judgment of what ought to be prevented as suicide—though even there it would seem to me unreasonable to draw the line precisely between action and inaction, rather than between various forms of inaction. It would not make much sense to say that one may not kill oneself by walking into the sea, but may sit on the beach until submerged by the incoming tide; or that one may not intentionally lock oneself into a cold storage locker, but may refrain from coming indoors when the temperature drops below freezing. Even as a legislative matter, in other words, the intelligent line does not fall between action and inaction, but between those forms of inaction that consist of abstaining from "ordinary" care and those that consist of abstaining from "excessive" or "heroic" measures. Unlike action vs. inaction, that is not a line to be discerned by logic or legal analysis, and we should not pretend that it is.

But to return to the principal point for present purposes: the irrelevance of the action-inaction distinction. Starving oneself to death is no different from putting a gun to one's temple as far as the common law definition of suicide is concerned; the cause of death in both cases is the suicide's conscious decision to "pu[t] an end to his own existence."

The third asserted basis of distinction—that frustrating Nancy Cruzan's wish to die in the present case requires interference with her bodily integrity—is likewise inadequate, because such interference is impermissible only if one begs the question whether her refusal to undergo the treatment on her own is suicide. It has always been lawful not only for the State, but even for private citizens, to interfere with bodily integrity to prevent a felony. That general rule has of course been applied to suicide. At common law, even a private person's use of force to prevent suicide was privileged. It is not even reasonable, much less required by the Constitution, to maintain that, although the State has the right to prevent a person from slashing his wrists, it does not have the power to apply physical force to prevent him from doing so, nor the power, should he succeed, to apply, coercively if necessary, medical measures to stop the flow of blood....

What I have said above is not meant to suggest that I would think it desirable, if we were sure that Nancy Cruzan wanted to die, to keep her alive by the means at issue here. I assert only that the Constitution has nothing to say about the subject....

JUSTICE BRENNAN:

...Because I believe that Nancy Cruzan has a fundamental right to be free of unwanted artificial nutrition and hydration, which right is not outweighed by any interests of the State, and because I find that the improperly biased procedural obstacles imposed by the Missouri Supreme Court impermissibly burden that right, I respectfully dissent. Nancy Cruzan is entitled to choose to die with dignity....

That there may be serious consequences involved in

refusal of the medical treatment at issue here does not viti-
ate the right under our common law tradition of medical
self-determination. It is "a well-established rule of general
law…that it is the patient, not the physician, who ultimately
decides if treatment—any treatment—is to be given at
all….The rule has never been qualified in its application by
either the nature or purpose of the treatment, or the gravity
of the consequences of acceding to or forgoing it." ("The
rationale of this rule lies in the fact that every competent
adult has the right to forgo treatment, or even cure, if it
entails what for him are intolerable consequences or risks,
however unwise his sense of values may be to others.")….

The right to be free from unwanted medical attention is
a right to evaluate the potential benefit of treatment and its
possible consequences according to one's own values and to
make a personal decision whether to subject oneself to the
intrusion. For a patient like Nancy Cruzan, the sole benefit of medical treatment is being kept metabolically alive.
Neither artificial nutrition nor any other form of medical
treatment available today can cure or in any way ameliorate
her condition. Irreversibly vegetative patients are devoid of
thought, emotion and sensation; they are permanently and
completely unconscious….

There are also affirmative reasons why someone like
Nancy might choose to forgo artificial nutrition and hydration under these circumstances. Dying is personal. And it is
profound. For many, the thought of an ignoble end, steeped
in decay, is abhorrent. A quiet, proud death, bodily integrity
intact, is a matter of extreme consequence….

Although the right to be free of unwanted medical intervention, like other constitutionally protected interests,
may not be absolute, no State interest could outweigh the
rights of an individual in Nancy Cruzan's position. Whatever a State's possible interests in mandating life-support
treatment under other circumstances, there is no good to be

obtained here by Missouri's insistence that Nancy Cruzan remain on life-support systems if it is indeed her wish not to do so. Missouri does not claim, nor could it, that society as a whole will be benefited by Nancy's receiving medical treatment. No third party's situation will be improved, and no harm to others will be averted.

The only state interest asserted here is a general interest in the preservation of life. But the state has no legitimate general interest in someone's life, completely abstracted from the interest of the person living that life, that could outweigh the person's choice to avoid medical treatment. [As Justice Stevens has said in a previous case,] "The regulation of constitutionally protected decisions...must be predicated on legitimate state concerns other than disagreement with the choice the individual has made....Otherwise, the interest in liberty protected by the Due Process Clause would be a nullity."...

Moreover, there may be considerable danger that Missouri's rule of decision would impair rather than serve any interest the State does have in sustaining life. Current medical practice recommends use of heroic measures if there is a scintilla of a chance that the patient will recover, on the assumption that the measures will be discontinued should the patient improve. When the President's Commission in 1982 approved the withdrawal of life support equipment from irreversibly vegetative patients, it explained that "[a]n even more troubling wrong occurs when a treatment that might save life or improve health is not started because the health care personnel are afraid that they will find it very difficult to stop the treatment if, as is fairly likely, it proves to be of little benefit and greatly burdens the patient." A New Jersey court recognized that families as well as doctors might be discouraged by an inability to stop life-support measures from "even attempting certain types of care [which] could thereby force them into hasty and premature decisions to allow a patient to die."

[Justice Brennan then notes that Missouri may have legitimate interests in ensuring that the Cruzan's request for withdrawal of life-sustaining treatment is as accurate as possible. He next analyzes several justifications the majority offered in support of Missouri.]

The majority claims that the allocation of the risk of error is justified because it is more important not to terminate life-support for someone who would wish it continued than to honor the wishes of someone who would not. An erroneous decision to terminate life-support is irrevocable, says the majority, while an erroneous decision not to terminate "results in a maintenance of the status quo." But, from the point of view of the patient, an erroneous decision in either direction is irrevocable. An erroneous decision to terminate artificial nutrition and hydration, to be sure, will lead to failure of that last remnant of physiological life, the brain stem, and result in complete brain death. An erroneous decision not to terminate life-support, however, robs a patient of the very qualities protected by the right to avoid unwanted medical treatment. His own degraded existence is perpetuated; his family's suffering is protracted; the memory he leaves behind becomes more and more distorted.

Even a later decision to grant him his wish cannot undo the intervening harm. But a later decision is unlikely in any event. "[T]he discovery of new evidence," to which the majority refers, is more hypothetical than plausible. The majority also misconceives the relevance of the possibility of "advancements in medical science," by treating it as a reason to force someone to continue medical treatment against his will. The possibility of a medical miracle is indeed part of the calculus, but it is a part of the patient's calculus. If current research suggests that some hope for cure or even moderate improvement is possible within the life-span projected, this is a factor that should be and would be accorded significant weight in assessing what the patient himself would choose....

Too few people execute living wills or equivalently formal directives for [Missouri's standard] to ensure adequately that the wishes of incompetent persons will be honored. While it might be a wise social policy to encourage people to furnish such instructions, no general conclusion about a patient's choice can be drawn from the absence of formalities. The probability of becoming irreversibly vegetative is so low that many people may not feel an urgency to marshal formal evidence of their preferences. Some may not wish to dwell on their own physical deterioration and mortality. Even someone with a resolute determination to avoid life-support under circumstances such as Nancy's would still need to know that such things as living wills exist and how to execute one. Often legal help would be necessary, especially given the majority's apparent willingness to permit States to insist that a person's wishes are not truly known unless the particular medical treatment is specified....

Missouri and this Court have displaced Nancy's own assessment of the processes associated with dying. They have discarded evidence of her will, ignored her values, and deprived her of the right to a decision as closely approximating her own choice as humanly possible. They have done so disingenuously in her name, and openly in Missouri's own. That Missouri and this Court may truly be motivated only by concern for incompetent patients makes no matter. As one of our most prominent jurists warned us decades ago: "Experience should teach us to be most on our guard to protect liberty when the government's purposes are beneficent.... The greatest dangers to liberty lurk in insidious encroachment by men of zeal, well meaning but without understanding."

Washington v. Glucksberg
521 U.S. 702 (1997)

Chief Justice Rehnquist delivered the opinion of the Court, in which Justices O'Connor, Scalia, Kennedy, and Thomas joined.

Justice O'Connor filed a concurring opinion, in which Justices Ginsburg and Breyer joined in part. Justices Stevens, Souter, Ginsburg, and Breyer filed opinions concurring in the judgment.

Areas for Discussion and Ethical Reflection

1.   Before reading the excerpts in *Glucksberg* and *Vacco*, you might try formulating a definition of "suicide." This exercise is much more difficult than it might first appear. A definition of suicide should not be too broad, such that you are forced to categorize acts as suicides that would diminish the usefulness of the concept. For example, defining suicide simply as "killing oneself" would include such acts as smoking cigarettes, hang gliding, and driving under the influence of alcohol whenever death results. A definition of suicide should not have moral evaluation included, such that by categorizing an act as suicide you short circuit all debate on the moral permissibility of the act. For example, defining suicide as "heroically taking one's life in the face of great adversity" would tend to unfairly skew the discussion toward judging the act morally permissible. One commentator recommends that the presence of three features in an action make that action more likely to be called a suicide.[13] These features are: 1) death is intended by the agent; 2) an active cause of death is arranged by the agent; and 3) no terminal condition or mortal injury exists. Obviously, once you have formulated your own definition of suicide you will want to apply it to the case of Nancy Beth Cruzan and to the patients in *Glucksberg* and *Quill*.

2.   Chief Justice Rehnquist finds that the Due Process Clause is not violated by allowing a state to prohibit physicians from assisting their terminally ill patients to hasten death. Outline his arguments for this position. Which of these arguments are ethical in nature?

3.   Chief Justice Rehnquist asserts, "The decision to commit suicide with the assistance of another may be just as personal and profound as the decision to refuse unwanted medical treatment,

but it has never enjoyed similar legal protection." We might all agree that Rehnquist is correct on both points, but what has this observation to do with the case at hand? What ethical concerns does Rehnquist's assertion raise?

4.   What are the four interests the state claims it has in prohibiting suicide or assistance in suicide? What are the ethical foundations of these interests?

5.   If physician-assisted suicide were constitutional, would certain groups—the poor, the elderly, the disabled—be in danger of having their lives shortened against their will? If PAS were generally accepted as morally permissible, would these disadvantaged groups be in danger?

6.   What argument does Justice O'Connor give for claiming there is no need to address the constitutional status of a right of terminally ill patients to request assistance from their physicians in hastening death? Evaluate her argument.

7.   Justice Stevens admits that the state has an interest in individuals and the contributions they might make to society. However, in the matter of a terminally ill patient who is faced not with the choice of whether to live, but only with the choice of how to die, Justice Stevens believes the state's interest is diminished. What ethical arguments does he provide for this position? Does the chief justice address his concerns?

8.   Justice Stevens observes that tension exists between traditional perceptions that many people (including legislators and judges) hold regarding a physician's role at the end of life and the reality of clinical practice whereby hastening death, by omission or commission, is common. Anyone who has even passing familiarity with clinical medicine would probably agree. What should be done to ease this tension? Would educating students and the lay public on the realities of dying in America help resolve the tension?

9.   How seriously do you think the justices consider the ethical, medical, and social problems raised by patients who experi-

ence intractable pain and suffering? Are *you* able to articulate
the ethical, medical, and social problems raised by such patients?
Do some justices seem more bothered by suffering patients than
other justices? You might return to chapter 7 and look again at
item 6 under *Rutherford*.

CHIEF JUSTICE REHNQUIST:

> The question presented in this case is whether Washington's
> prohibition against "caus[ing]" or "aid[ing]" a suicide of-
> fends the Fourteenth Amendment to the United States
> Constitution. We hold that it does not....
>
> We begin, as we do in all due process cases, by exam-
> ining our Nation's history, legal traditions, and practices.
> In almost every State—indeed, in almost every western
> democracy—it is a crime to assist a suicide. The States'
> assisted suicide bans are not innovations. Rather, they
> are longstanding expressions of the States' commitment
> to the protection and preservation of all human life. The
> States—indeed, all civilized nations—demonstrate their
> commitment to life by treating homicide as a serious crime.
> Moreover, the majority of States in this country have laws
> imposing criminal penalties on one who assists another to
> commit suicide; ("[T]he primary and most reliable indica-
> tion of [a national] consensus is...the pattern of enacted
> laws"). Indeed, opposition to and condemnation of sui-
> cide—and, therefore, of assisting suicide—are consistent
> and enduring themes of our philosophical, legal, and cul-
> tural heritages.
>
> [The Court briefly discusses the seven-hundred-year
> history of laws and customs prohibiting suicide and assis-
> tance in suicide, including early American statutes.]
>
> Though deeply rooted, the States' assisted suicide bans
> have in recent years been reexamined and, generally, reaf-
> firmed. Because of advances in medicine and technology,

Americans today are increasingly likely to die in institutions, from chronic illnesses. Public concern and democratic action are therefore sharply focused on how best to protect dignity and independence at the end of life, with the result that there have been many significant changes in state laws and in the attitudes these laws reflect. Many States, for example, now permit "living wills," surrogate health care decisionmaking, and the withdrawal or refusal of life sustaining medical treatment. At the same time, however, voters and legislators continue for the most part to reaffirm their States' prohibitions on assisting suicide.

The Washington statute at issue in this case was enacted in 1975 as part of a revision of that State's criminal code. Four years later, Washington passed its Natural Death Act, which specifically stated that the "withholding or withdrawal of life sustaining treatment...shall not, for any purpose, constitute a suicide" and that "[n]othing in this chapter shall be construed to condone, authorize, or approve mercy killing...." In 1991, Washington voters rejected a ballot initiative which, had it passed, would have permitted a form of physician assisted suicide. Washington then added a provision to the Natural Death Act expressly excluding physician assisted suicide.

[The Court discusses assisted suicide laws and initiatives in several other states, and asserts that states are engaged in thoughtful debate regarding physician-assisted death.]

The Due Process Clause guarantees more than fair process, and the "liberty" it protects includes more than the absence of physical restraint. The Clause also provides heightened protection against government interference with certain fundamental rights and liberty interests. In a long line of cases, we have held that, in addition to the specific freedoms protected by the Bill of Rights, the "liberty" specially protected by the Due Process Clause includes the rights to marry, to have children, to direct the education and upbringing of one's children, to marital privacy, to use contraception, to bodily integrity, and to abortion. We have also assumed, and strongly suggested, that the Due Process Clause protects the traditional right to refuse unwanted lifesaving medical treatment.

[The Court briefly discusses the nature of fundamental rights and the problems with expanding substantive due process.]

Turning to the claim at issue here, the Court of Appeals stated that "[p]roperly analyzed, the first issue to be resolved is whether there is a liberty interest in determining the time and manner of one's death," or, in other words, "[i]s there a right to die?" Similarly, respondents assert a "liberty to choose how to die" and a right to "control of one's final days," and describe the asserted liberty as "the right to choose a humane, dignified death," and "the liberty to shape death." As noted above, we have a tradition of carefully formulating the interest at stake in substantive due process cases. For example, although *Cruzan* is often described as a "right to die" case. (Cruzan recognized "the more specific interest in making decisions about how to confront an imminent death"), we were, in fact, more precise: we assumed that the Constitution granted competent persons a "constitutionally protected right to refuse lifesaving hydration and nutrition." The Washington statute at issue in this case prohibits "aid[ing] another person to attempt suicide," and, thus, the question before us is whether the "liberty" specially protected by the Due Process Clause includes a right to commit suicide which itself includes a right to assistance in doing so.

We now inquire whether this asserted right has any place in our Nation's traditions. Here, we are confronted with a consistent and almost universal tradition that has long rejected the asserted right, and continues explicitly to reject it today, even for terminally ill, mentally competent adults. To hold for respondents, we would have to reverse centuries of legal doctrine and practice, and strike down the considered policy choice of almost every State.

Respondents contend, however, that the liberty interest they assert is consistent with this Court's substantive due process line of cases, if not with this Nation's history and practice. Pointing to *Casey* and *Cruzan*, respondents read our jurisprudence in this area as reflecting a general tradition of "self sovereignty," and as teaching that the "liberty" protected by the Due Process Clause includes "basic and intimate exercises of personal autonomy." ("It is a promise of the Constitution that there is a realm of personal liberty which the government may not enter.") According to respondents, our liberty jurisprudence, and the broad, individualistic principles it reflects, protects the "liberty of competent, terminally ill adults to make end of life decisions free of undue government interference." The question presented in this case, however, is whether the protections of the Due Process Clause include a right to commit suicide with another's assistance. With this "careful description" of respondents' claim in mind, we turn to *Casey* and *Cruzan*....

Respondents contend that in *Cruzan* we "acknowledged that competent, dying persons have the right to direct the removal of life sustaining medical treatment and thus hasten death," and that "the constitutional principle behind recognizing the patient's liberty to direct the withdrawal of artificial life support applies at least as strongly to the choice to hasten impending death by consuming lethal medication."...

The right assumed in *Cruzan*, however, was not simply deduced from abstract concepts of personal autonomy. Given the common law rule that forced medication was a battery, and the long legal tradition protecting the decision to refuse unwanted medical treatment, our assumption was entirely consistent with this Nation's history and constitu-

tional traditions. The decision to commit suicide with the
assistance of another may be just as personal and profound
as the decision to refuse unwanted medical treatment, but it
has never enjoyed similar legal protection. Indeed, the two
acts are widely and reasonably regarded as quite distinct. In
Cruzan itself, we recognized that most States outlawed assisted suicide—and even more do today—and we certainly
gave no intimation that the right to refuse unwanted medical treatment could be somehow transmuted into a right to
assistance in committing suicide.

Respondents also rely on *Casey*. There, the Court's
opinion concluded that "the essential holding of *Roe v.
Wade* should be retained and once again reaffirmed." We
held, first, that a woman has a right, before her fetus is viable, to an abortion "without undue interference from the
State"; second, that States may restrict post-viability abortions, so long as exceptions are made to protect a woman's
life and health; and third, that the State has legitimate interests throughout a pregnancy in protecting the health of
the woman and the life of the unborn child. In reaching
this conclusion, the opinion discussed in some detail this
Court's substantive due process tradition of interpreting
the Due Process Clause to protect certain fundamental
rights and "personal decisions relating to marriage, procreation, contraception, family relationships, child rearing,
and education," and noted that many of those rights and
liberties "involv[e] the most intimate and personal choices
a person may make in a lifetime."...

Similarly, respondents emphasize the statement in
Casey that: "At the heart of liberty is the right to define one's
own concept of existence, of meaning, of the universe, and
of the mystery of human life. Beliefs about these matters
could not define the attributes of personhood were they
formed under compulsion of the State."

By choosing this language, the Court's opinion in *Casey*

described, in a general way and in light of our prior cases, those personal activities and decisions that this Court has identified as so deeply rooted in our history and traditions, or so fundamental to our concept of constitutionally ordered liberty, that they are protected by the Fourteenth Amendment. The opinion moved from the recognition that liberty necessarily includes freedom of conscience and belief about ultimate considerations to the observation that "though the abortion decision may originate within the zone of conscience and belief, it is more than a philosophic exercise." That many of the rights and liberties protected by the Due Process Clause sound in personal autonomy does not warrant the sweeping conclusion that any and all important, intimate, and personal decisions are so protected, and *Casey* did not suggest otherwise.

The history of the law's treatment of assisted suicide in this country has been and continues to be one of the rejection of nearly all efforts to permit it. That being the case, our decisions lead us to conclude that the asserted "right" to assistance in committing suicide is not a fundamental liberty interest protected by the Due Process Clause. The Constitution also requires, however, that Washington's assisted suicide ban be rationally related to legitimate government interests. This requirement is unquestionably met here. Washington's assisted suicide ban implicates a number of state interests.

First, Washington has an "unqualified interest in the preservation of human life." The State's prohibition on assisted suicide, like all homicide laws, both reflects and advances its commitment to this interest....This interest is symbolic and aspirational as well as practical...

Respondents admit that "[t]he State has a real interest in preserving the lives of those who can still contribute to society and enjoy life."...Washington, however, has rejected this sliding scale approach and, through its assisted suicide ban, insists that all persons' lives, from beginning to end, regardless of physical or mental condition, are under the full protection of the law. "As we have previously affirmed, the States "may properly decline to make judgments about the 'quality' of life that a particular individual may enjoy." This remains true, as *Cruzan* makes clear, even for those who are near death. Relatedly, all admit that suicide is a serious public health problem, especially among persons in otherwise vulnerable groups. The State has an interest in preventing suicide, and in studying, identifying, and treating its causes.

Those who attempt suicide—terminally ill or not—often suffer from depression or other mental disorders. Research indicates, however, that many people who request physician-assisted suicide withdraw that request if their depression and pain are treated. The New York Task Force, however, expressed its concern that, because depression is difficult to diagnose, physicians and medical professionals often fail to respond adequately to seriously ill patients' needs. Thus, legal physician assisted suicide could make it more difficult for the State to protect depressed or mentally ill persons, or those who are suffering from untreated pain, from suicidal impulses.

The State also has an interest in protecting the integrity and ethics of the medical profession...[T]he American Medical Association, like many other medical and physicians' groups, has concluded that "[p]hysician assisted suicide is fundamentally incompatible with the physician's role as healer." And physician assisted suicide could, it is argued, undermine the trust that is essential to the doctor patient relationship by blurring the time honored line between healing and harming....

Next, the State has an interest in protecting vulnerable groups—including the poor, the elderly, and disabled persons—from abuse, neglect, and mistakes...We have recognized... the real risk of subtle coercion and undue influence in end of life situations. Similarly, the New York Task Force warned that "[l]egalizing physician assisted suicide would pose profound risks to many individuals who are ill and vulnerable.... The risk of harm is greatest for the many individuals in our society whose autonomy and well being are already compromised by poverty, lack of access to good medical care, advanced age, or membership in a stigmatized social group." If physician assisted suicide were permitted, many might resort to it to spare their families the substantial financial burden of end of life health care costs. The State's interest here goes beyond protecting the vulnerable from coercion; it extends to protecting disabled and terminally ill people from prejudice, negative and inaccurate stereotypes, and "societal indifference." The State's assisted suicide ban reflects and reinforces its policy that the lives of terminally ill, disabled, and elderly people must be no less valued than the lives of the young and healthy, and that a seriously disabled person's suicidal impulses should be interpreted and treated the same way as anyone else's.

Finally, the State may fear that permitting assisted suicide will start it down the path to voluntary and perhaps even involuntary euthanasia. The Court of Appeals struck down Washington's assisted suicide ban only "as applied to competent, terminally ill adults who wish to hasten their deaths by obtaining medication prescribed by their doctors." Washington insists, however, that the impact of the court's decision will not and cannot be so limited. If suicide is protected as a matter of constitutional right, it is argued, "every man and woman in the United States must enjoy it."...Thus, it turns out that what is couched as a limited right to "physician assisted suicide" is likely, in effect, a much broader license, which could prove extremely difficult to police and contain. Washington's ban on assisting suicide prevents such erosion....

Throughout the Nation, Americans are engaged in an

earnest and profound debate about the morality, legality, and practicality of physician assisted suicide. Our holding permits this debate to continue, as it should in a democratic society. The decision of the en banc Court of Appeals is reversed…It is so ordered.

JUSTICE O'CONNOR:

Death will be different for each of us. For many, the last days will be spent in physical pain and perhaps the despair that accompanies physical deterioration and a loss of control of basic bodily and mental functions. Some will seek medication to alleviate that pain and other symptoms….

I agree that there is no generalized right to "commit suicide." But respondents urge us to address the narrower question whether a mentally competent person who is experiencing great suffering has a constitutionally cognizable interest in controlling the circumstances of his or her imminent death. I see no need to reach that question in the context of the facial challenges to the New York and Washington laws at issue here. The parties and amici agree that in these States a patient who is suffering from a terminal illness and who is experiencing great pain has no legal barriers to obtaining medication, from qualified physicians, to alleviate that suffering, even to the point of causing unconsciousness and hastening death. In this light, even assuming that we would recognize such an interest, I agree that the State's interests in protecting those who are not truly competent or facing imminent death, or those whose decisions to hasten death would not truly be voluntary, are sufficiently weighty to justify a prohibition against physician assisted suicide.

Every one of us at some point may be affected by our own or a family member's terminal illness. There is no reason to think the democratic process will not strike the proper balance between the interests of terminally ill, mentally competent individuals who would seek to end their suffering and the State's interests in protecting those who might seek to end life mistakenly or under pressure....

In sum, there is no need to address the question whether suffering patients have a constitutionally cognizable interest in obtaining relief from the suffering that they may experience in the last days of their lives. There is no dispute that dying patients in Washington and New York can obtain palliative care, even when doing so would hasten their deaths. The difficulty in defining terminal illness and the risk that a dying patient's request for assistance in ending his or her life might not be truly voluntary justifies the prohibitions on assisted suicide we uphold here.

JUSTICE STEVENS:

The Court ends its opinion with the important observation that our holding today is fully consistent with a continuation of the vigorous debate about the "morality, legality, and practicality of physician assisted suicide" in a democratic society. I write separately to make it clear that there is also room for further debate about the limits that the Constitution places on the power of the States to punish the practice.

[Justice Stevens discusses the continuing debate over the constitutionality of the death penalty and the distinction between facial and as applied challenges to the Washington statute.]

But just as our conclusion that capital punishment is not always unconstitutional did not preclude later decisions holding that it is sometimes impermissibly cruel, so is it equally clear that a decision upholding a general statutory prohibition of assisted suicide does not mean that every possible application of the statute would be valid. A State, like Washington, that has authorized the death penalty and thereby has concluded that the sanctity of human life does not require that it always be preserved, must acknowledge that there are situations in which an interest in hastening death is legitimate. Indeed, not only is that interest sometimes legitimate, I am also convinced that there are times when it is entitled to constitutional protection.

[Justice Stevens discusses the similarities and differences between *Cruzan* and the two present cases.]

The state interests supporting a general rule banning the practice of physician assisted suicide do not have the same force in all cases. First and foremost of these interests is the " 'unqualified interest in the preservation of human life,' " which is equated with " 'the sanctity of life,' " That interest not only justifies—it commands—maximum protection of every individual's interest in remaining alive, which in turn commands the same protection for decisions about whether to commence or to terminate life support systems or to administer pain medication that may hasten death. Properly viewed, however, this interest is not a collective interest that should always outweigh the interests of a person who because of pain, incapacity, or sedation finds her life intolerable, but rather, an aspect of individual freedom.

Many terminally ill people find their lives meaningful even if filled with pain or dependence on others. Some find value in living through suffering; some have an abiding desire to witness particular events in their families' lives; many believe it a sin to hasten death. Individuals of different religious faiths make different judgments and choices about whether to live on under such circumstances. There are those who will want to continue aggressive treatment; those who would prefer terminal sedation; and those who will seek withdrawal from life support systems and death by gradual starvation and dehydration. Although as a general matter the State's interest in the contributions each person may make to society outweighs the person's interest in ending her life, this interest does not have the same force for a terminally ill patient faced not with the choice of whether to live, only of how to die. Allowing the individual, rather than the State, to make judgments " 'about the "quality" of life that a particular individual may enjoy' " does not mean that the lives of terminally ill, disabled people have less value than the lives of those who are healthy. Rather, it gives proper recognition to the individual's interest in choosing a final chapter that accords with her life story, rather than one that demeans her values and poisons memories of her.

Similarly, the State's legitimate interests in preventing suicide, protecting the vulnerable from coercion and abuse, and preventing euthanasia are less significant in this context. I agree that the State has a compelling interest in preventing persons from committing suicide because of depression, or coercion by third parties. But the State's legitimate interest in preventing abuse does not apply to an individual who is not victimized by abuse, who is not suffering from depression, and who makes a rational and voluntary decision to seek assistance in dying. Although, as the New York Task Force report discusses, diagnosing depression and other mental illness is not always easy, mental health workers and other professionals expert in working with dying patients can help patients cope with depression and pain, and help patients assess their options....

The final major interest asserted by the State is its interest in preserving the traditional integrity of the medical profession. The fear is that a rule permitting physicians to assist in suicide is inconsistent with the perception that they serve their patients solely as healers. But for some patients, it would be a physician's refusal to dispense medication to ease their suffering and make their death tolerable and dignified that would be inconsistent with the healing role. For doctors who have long-standing relationships with their patients, who have given their patients advice on alternative treatments, who are attentive to their patient's individualized needs, and who are knowledgeable about pain symptom management and palliative care options, heeding a patient's desire to assist in her suicide would not serve to harm the physician patient relationship. Furthermore, because physicians are already involved in making decisions that hasten the death of terminally ill patients—through termination of life support, withholding of medical treatment, and terminal sedation—there is in fact significant tension between the traditional view of the physician's role and the actual practice in a growing number of cases....

In New York, a doctor must respect a competent person's decision to refuse or to discontinue medical treatment even though death will thereby ensue, but the same doctor would be guilty of a felony if she provided her patient assistance in committing suicide. Today we hold that the Equal Protection Clause is not violated by the resulting disparate treatment of two classes of terminally ill people who may have the same interest in hastening death. I agree that the distinction between permitting death to ensue from an underlying fatal disease and causing it to occur by the administration of medication or other means provides a constitutionally sufficient basis for the State's classification. Unlike the Court, however, I am not persuaded that in all cases there will in fact be a significant difference between the intent of the physicians, the patients or the families in the two situations.

There may be little distinction between the intent of a terminally ill patient who decides to remove her life support and one who seeks the assistance of a doctor in ending her life; in both situations, the patient is seeking to hasten a certain, impending death. The doctor's intent might also be the same in prescribing lethal medication as it is in terminating life support. A doctor who fails to administer medical treatment to one who is dying from a disease could be doing so with an intent to harm or kill that patient. Conversely, a doctor who prescribes lethal medication does not necessarily intend the patient's death—rather that doctor may seek simply to ease the patient's suffering and to comply with her wishes. The illusory character of any differences in intent or causation is confirmed by the fact that the American Medical Association unequivocally endorses the practice of terminal sedation—the administration of sufficient dosages of pain killing medication to terminally ill patients to protect them from excruciating pain even when it is clear that the time of death will be advanced. The purpose of terminal sedation is to ease the suffering of the patient and comply with her wishes, and the actual cause of death is the administration of heavy doses of lethal sedatives. This same intent and causation may exist when a doctor complies with a patient's request for lethal medication to hasten her death.

There remains room for vigorous debate about the outcome of particular cases that are not necessarily resolved by the opinions announced today. How such cases may be decided will depend on their specific facts. In my judgment, however, it is clear that the so called "unqualified interest in the preservation of human life," is not itself sufficient to outweigh the interest in liberty that may justify the only possible means of preserving a dying patient's dignity and alleviating her intolerable suffering.

Vacco v. Quill
521 U.S. 793 (1997)

Chief Justice Rehnquist delivered the opinion of the Court, in which Justices O'Connor, Scalia, Kennedy, and Thomas joined. Justice O'Connor filed a concurring opinion, in which Justices Ginsburg and Breyer joined in part. Justices Stevens, Souter, Ginsburg, and Breyer filed opinions concurring in the judgment.

Areas for Discussion and Ethical Reflection

1. The State of New York and the U.S. Supreme Court maintain that a rational, logical, and ethically defensible distinction

exists between patients who wish to hasten their deaths by refusing life-sustaining treatment and patients who wish to hasten death by requesting assistance from a physician. It is entirely consistent then for the state to at once allow physicians to grant requests for the withholding or withdrawal of life-prolonging treatment and to prohibit through criminal statute a physician prescribing a lethal dose of medication to a terminally ill patient who requests it. Patients who happen to require a life-prolonging therapy such as ventilation or dialysis may hasten death by asking that the treatment be withdrawn. A patient who is terminally ill and suffering, but who happens not to need such treatments, is prohibited from receiving help in dying from her/his physician. Are you persuaded that this distinction and the laws that follow are rational, logical, and ethically defensible?

2.   Chief Justice Rehnquist defends the New York law against the charge that it violates the Equal Protection Clause by asserting: "Everyone, regardless of physical condition, is entitled, if competent, to refuse unwanted lifesaving medical treatment; no one is permitted to assist a suicide." Is Rehnquist correct? Does anything about his assertion bother you from an ethical perspective?

3.   Many commentators in medical ethics have discussed and evaluated the ethical arguments in support of (and against) making a moral distinction between refusal of life-saving therapy and requesting assistance from a physician to hasten death. List and discuss three arguments for asserting a morally relevant distinction and three against the distinction. How many of these arguments of either kind do you find in Justice Rehnquist's ruling?

4.   The concept of causation plays an important role in Chief Justice Rehnquist's decision. He asserts that, "…when a patient refuses life sustaining medical treatment, he dies from an underlying fatal disease or pathology; but if a patient ingests lethal medication prescribed by a physician, he is killed by that medication." There are several problems with this understanding of causation. Can we really not say that a physician causes death when honoring a request to withdraw or refuse life-sustaining

treatment? Honoring the request may be morally justifiable, even obligatory, but the physician still causes (at least in one sense of that word) death. Is it possible that those, like the chief justice, who wish to support the distinction between allowing to die and PAS, cling to a meaning of causation for the sake of convenience? How would you defend the chief justice?

5.   Evaluate Chief Justice Rehnquist's use of the principle of double effect in supporting New York's ban on PAS. Explain the distinction between foreseeing and intending.

6.   Once you have read the three cases in this chapter and had an opportunity to consider the constitutional and ethical arguments surrounding refusal of life-sustaining treatment for incompetent patients and PAS, consider for a moment what might be the circumstances of your own death. You will remember that, early in his opinion for the Court in *Washington v. Glucksberg*, Justice Rehnquist observes, "Because of advances in medicine and technology, Americans today are increasingly likely to die in institutions, from chronic illnesses." The chances are high indeed that you will die in the intensive care unit of a hospital or a long-term care facility. How do you envision your death? Will it be peaceful? Will your dignity remain intact during your last hours? Will you be surrounded by family and caring health care professionals? Given the stark realities of dying in America—dying does not come easy—are the imagined circumstances of your death realistic? Do you think Chief Justice Rehnquist has a realistic conception of what death in the modern American health care system entails? What about Justice O'Connor in her opinion in *Glucksberg*? Or Justice Stevens's opinion in the same case? How relevant to the arguments supporting PAS are the facts of dying?

CHIEF JUSTICE REHNQUIST:

In New York, as in most States, it is a crime to aid another to commit or attempt suicide, but patients may refuse even lifesaving medical treatment. The question presented by this case is whether New York's prohibition on assisting suicide therefore violates the Equal Protection Clause of the Fourteenth Amendment. We hold that it does not....

The Equal Protection Clause commands that no State shall "deny to any person within its jurisdiction the equal protection of the laws."... New York's statutes outlawing assisting suicide affect and address matters of profound significance to all New Yorkers alike. They neither infringe fundamental rights nor involve suspect classifications....

On their faces, neither New York's ban on assisting suicide nor its statutes permitting patients to refuse medical treatment treat anyone differently than anyone else or draw any distinctions between persons. Everyone, regardless of physical condition, is entitled, if competent, to refuse unwanted lifesaving medical treatment; no one is permitted to assist a suicide. Generally speaking, laws that apply evenhandedly to all "unquestionably comply" with the Equal Protection Clause.

The Court of Appeals, however, concluded that some terminally ill people—those who are on life support systems—are treated differently than those who are not, in that the former may "hasten death" by ending treatment, but the latter may not "hasten death" through physician assisted suicide. This conclusion depends on the submission that ending or refusing lifesaving medical treatment "is nothing more nor less than assisted suicide." Unlike the Court of Appeals, we think the distinction between assisting suicide and withdrawing life sustaining treatment, a distinction widely recognized and endorsed in the medical profession and in our legal traditions, is both important and logical; it is certainly rational.

The distinction comports with fundamental legal principles of causation and intent. First, when a patient refuses life sustaining medical treatment, he dies from an underlying fatal disease or pathology; but if a patient ingests lethal medication prescribed by a physician, he is killed by that medication.

Furthermore, a physician who withdraws, or honors a patient's refusal to begin, life sustaining medical treatment purposefully intends, or may so intend, only to respect his patient's wishes and "to cease doing useless and futile or degrading things to the patient when [the patient] no longer stands to benefit from them." The same is true when a doctor provides aggressive palliative care; in some cases, painkilling drugs may hasten a patient's death, but the physician's purpose and intent is, or maybe, only to ease his patient's pain. A doctor who assists a suicide, however, "must, necessarily and indubitably, intend primarily that the patient be made dead." Similarly, a patient who commits suicide with a doctor's aid necessarily has the specific intent to end his or her own life, while a patient who refuses or discontinues treatment might not.

The law has long used actors' intent or purpose to distinguish between two acts that may have the same result. Put differently, the law distinguishes actions taken "because of" a given end from actions taken "in spite of" their unintended but foreseen consequences. ("When General Eisenhower ordered American soldiers onto the beaches of Normandy, he knew that he was sending many American soldiers to certain death.... His purpose, though, was to...liberate Europe from the Nazis")....

Similarly, the overwhelming majority of state legislatures have drawn a clear line between assisting suicide and withdrawing or permitting the refusal of unwanted lifesaving medical treatment by prohibiting the former and permitting the latter. And "nearly all states expressly disapprove of suicide and assisted suicide either in statutes dealing with durable powers of attorney in health care situations, or in 'living will' statutes." Thus, even as the States move to protect and promote patients' dignity at the end of life, they remain opposed to physician assisted suicide.

This Court has also recognized, at least implicitly, the distinction between letting a patient die and making that patient die. In *Cruzan*, we concluded that "[t]he principle that a competent person has a constitutionally protected liberty interest in refusing unwanted medical treatment may be inferred from our prior decisions," and we assumed the existence of such a right for purposes of that case. But our assumption of a right to refuse treatment was grounded not, as the Court of Appeals supposed, on the proposition that patients have a general and abstract "right to hasten death," but on well established, traditional rights to bodily integrity and freedom from unwanted touching. In fact, we observed that "the majority of States in this country have laws imposing criminal penalties on one who assists another to commit suicide." *Cruzan* therefore provides no support for the notion that refusing life sustaining medical treatment is "nothing more nor less than suicide."

For all these reasons, we disagree with respondents' claim that the distinction between refusing lifesaving medical treatment and assisted suicide is "arbitrary" and "irrational." Granted, in some cases, the line between the two may not be clear, but certainty is not required, even were it possible. Logic and contemporary practice support New York's judgment that the two acts are different, and New York may therefore, consistent with the Constitution, treat them differently. By permitting everyone to refuse unwanted medical treatment while prohibiting anyone from assisting a suicide, New York law follows a longstanding and rational distinction.

New York's reasons for recognizing and acting on this distinction—including prohibiting intentional killing and preserving life; preventing suicide; maintaining physicians' role as their patients' healers; protecting vulnerable people from indifference, prejudice, and psychological and financial pressure to end their lives; and avoiding a possible slide towards euthanasia—are discussed in greater detail in our opinion in

Glucksberg. These valid and important public interests easily satisfy the constitutional requirement that a legislative classification bear a rational relation to some legitimate end.

The judgment of the Court of Appeals is reversed. It is so ordered.

Notes

1.   Thomas A. Mappes, "Persistent Vegetative State, Prospective Thinking, and Advance Directives," *Kennedy Institute of Ethics Journal* 13 (2003): 119.

2.   John A. Robertson, "*Cruzan*: No Rights Violated," in *Ethical Issues in Death and Dying*, 2nd ed., edited by Tom L. Beauchamp and Robert M. Veatch (Upper Saddle River, NJ: Prentice Hall, 1996), p. 299.

3.   Ronald Dworkin, *Life's Dominion: An Argument about Abortion, Euthanasia, and Individual Freedom* (New York: Knopf, 1993), pp. 201–13.

4.   Robertson, "*Cruzan*: No Rights Violated," p. 300.

5.   Larry Gostin, "Life and Death Choices after *Cruzan*," in *Ethical Issues in Death and Dying*, p. 295.

6.   Ibid.

7.   C. E. Harris, Jr., *Applying Moral Theories*, 3rd ed. (Belmont, CA: Wadsworth, 1997), pp. 104–5.

8.   Rebecca Dresser, "The Supreme Court and End-of-Life-Care: Principled Distinctions or Slippery Slope?" in *Law at the End of Life: The Supreme Court and Assisted Suicide*, edited by Carl E. Schneider (Ann Arbor: University of Michigan Press, 2000), pp. 89–92.

9.   Gregory E. Pence, *Classic Issues in Medical Ethics: Accounts of Cases that Have Shaped Medical Ethics with Philosophical, Legal, and Historical Backgrounds*, 2nd ed. (New York: McGraw-Hill, 1995), p. 20.

10.   Ronald Dworkin, *Life's Dominion: An Argument about Abortion, Euthanasia, and Individual Freedom* (New York: Knopf, 1993), p. 194.

11.   Jerry Menikoff, *Law and Bioethics: An Introduction* (Washington, DC: Georgetown University Press, 2001), p. 323.

12.   Robertson, "*Cruzan*: No Rights Violated," pp. 299.

13.   Tom L. Beauchamp, "The Problem of Defining Suicide," in *Ethical Issues in Death and Dying*, p. 115.

For Further Reading

Angell, Marcia. "The Supreme Court and Physician-Assisted Suicide—The Ultimate Right." *New England Journal of Medicine* 336 (1997): 50–53.

Brock, Dan. "Cause of Death." In *Ethical Issues in Death and Dying*, 2nd edition, Tom Beauchamp and Robert Veatch, eds. Upper Saddle River, NJ: Prentice Hall, 1996.

Capron, Alexander Morgan. "Constitutionalizing Death." *Hastings Center Report* 25 (1995): 23–24.

Coope, Christopher Miles. "Death with Dignity." *Hastings Center Report* 27 (1997): 37–38.

Dworkin, Ronald. *Life's Dominion: An Argument about Abortion, Euthanasia, and Individual Freedom*. New York: Knopf, 1993.

Dworkin, Ronald, Thomas Nagel, Robert Nozick, John Rawls, Thomas Scanlon, and Judith Jarvis Thompson. "The Philosophers' Brief." In *Ethical Issues in Modern Medicine*, 6th edition, Bonnie Steinbock et al., eds. New York: McGraw-Hill, 2003.

Foley, Kathleen. "Competent Care for the Dying Instead of Physician-Assisted Suicide." *New England Journal of Medicine* 336 (1997): 54–58.

Menikoff, Jerry. *Law and Bioethics: An Introduction*. Washington, DC: Georgetown University Press, 2001.

Orentlicher, David. *Matters of Life and Death: Making Moral Theory Work in Medical Ethics and the Law*. Princeton: Princeton University Press, 2001.

Pence, Gregory E. *Classic Issues in Medical Ethics: Accounts of Cases that Have Shaped Medical Ethics, with Philosophical, Legal, and Historical Backgrounds*, 2nd edition. New York: McGraw-Hill, 1995.

Quill, Timothy E. "Death and Dignity: A Case of Individualized Decision Making." In *Ethical Issues in Death and Dying*.

Rachels, James. "Active and Passive Euthanasia." In *Intervention and Reflection: Basic Issues in Medical Ethics*, 6th edition, Ronald Munson, ed. Belmont, CA: Wadsworth, 2000.

Robertson, John A. "*Cruzan*: No Rights Violated." In *Ethical Issues in Death and Dying*.

Schneider, Carl E., ed. *Law at the End of Life: The Supreme Court and Assisted Suicide*. Ann Arbor: University of Michigan Press, 2000.

CHAPTER TEN

THE RIGHT TO HEALTH CARE AND HMO CASES

*As difficult as the health-care delivery and health policy prob-
lems are to solve on their own terms, the prospect of extensive
legal intervention in health care further complicates their
resolution. Law and health care intersect at various points. At
both the state and federal levels, all three branches of the legal
system—the legislatures, regulatory agencies, and courts—
have been persistently involved in setting health-care policy
and monitoring health-care delivery since the mid-1960s....
The relationship between law and health care has never been
more visible, intertwined, or manifest than it is today.*

—Peter D. Jacobson, *Strangers in the Night: Law and Medicine
in the Managed Care Era*

Everyone agrees that receiving health care in America has become much more complex and burdensome than it once was.
From various perspectives—the health care professions, the political arena, the law, public policy, and ethics—modern health
care is in crisis. Problems include the increasing costs of medical care, the rising number of Americans who are uninsured or
underinsured, patients experiencing delayed or denied medical
care, the growing sense among health care professionals that
they have lost their professional autonomy, and the noticeable
lack of trust between all the parties involved. As intractable as the
problems appear, legislators, businesspeople, ethicists, judges,
consumer advocates, and patients themselves are increasingly
aware that they will have to work together to develop solutions.

These solutions must not only pass constitutional scrutiny, they must be morally defensible as well. Two excellent examples of the influence constitutional law and medical ethics have had on one another and that each has had on the challenges presented by the current health care crisis are highlighted in this chapter. Through the justices' deliberations and arguments, we have an opportunity to consider the extent to which society has an obligation to provide for the medical needs of poor citizens as well as to examine various problems associated with managed care, such as rising costs, lack of trust on the part of patients toward their physicians, rationing of services, and conflicts of interest. An underlying theme in much of this discussion is the meaning and justification of a right to health care.

Constitutional Issues and Background

At issue in our first case, *Harris v. McRae*, was the Hyde Amendment and its restrictions on Medicaid reimbursement of abortions for poor women. The Medicaid program was designed to provide federal and state funds to poor people for medically necessary treatment. The Hyde Amendment not only eliminated federal money for almost all abortions, it also allowed the states to refuse to pay for abortions, even medically necessary ones. Various groups (indigent pregnant women, the New York City Health and Hospitals Corp., and the Women's Division of the Board of Global Ministries of the United Methodist Church) brought suit in federal district court charging that the Hyde Amendment violated the Due Process Clause of the Fifth Amendment and the Religion Clauses of the First Amendment. These groups also claimed that even if the Hyde Amendment was constitutional, the states still had an obligation to pay for medically necessary abortions for poor women. The federal district court ruled that states had no such obligation, but the court also concluded that the Hyde Amendment was unconstitutional.

On the surface, the Supreme Court was faced with examining statutory and constitutional questions surrounding public funding of abortions for indigent women. But in reality the Court was struggling with a much more important issue: determining the role of the High Court in protecting the ability of indigent people to exercise fundamental rights. As you read the excerpts, you will notice the extreme disagreement on this point between the majority and those in dissent. When the states or federal government pass legislation that burdens poor people as a class, either under equal protection or due process guarantee, the Supreme Court will assess whether the legislation serves a rational goal of government and is a rational means to achieving that goal.[1] The Supreme Court has historically been very reluctant to strike down legislation based on individual wealth. Only where fundamental rights are implicated will the Court strike down legislation that discriminates based on economic status. As you will see, a majority of the Justices in *Harris* found no fundamental rights implicated. The vigorous dissents excerpted below speak not only to the issue of abortion funding but also to the government's treatment of poor persons generally.

The other case in this chapter, the most influential decision dealing with managed health care handed down by the High Court so far, examines the financial arrangements health maintenance organizations put in place to control costs. These financial arrangements interfere with fiduciary duties that physicians have toward their patients in managed care plans. The patient in the present case, Cynthia Herdrich, was suffering severe pain in her groin when she went to Carle Clinic, her health maintenance organization. She was seen by Dr. Lorie Pegram, who discovered an inflamed mass in Herdrich's abdomen, but required Herdrich to wait eight days for an ultrasound. She scheduled the test in another of Carle's facilities fifty miles away. Before the ultrasound could be performed, Herdrich's appendix burst. Herdrich won a malpractice award of thirty-five thousand dollars against the physician, but she lost her claim in district court that Carle breached its fiduciary duty toward her and other plan beneficiaries when it delayed medically appropriate treatment. Herdrich discovered that Carle rewarded its physicians with year-end bonuses if they saved Carle money, and that saving money typically entailed delaying or denying medical treatment to plan participants. The Seventh Circuit reversed the lower court and found that indeed Carle and its physicians did have specific duties and obligations toward plan beneficiaries and that these duties were breached in this case.

The focus of concern in this case, as in almost all cases involving managed care that came before the Supreme Court in the 1980s and 90s, was the Employee Retirement Income Security Act (ERISA). ERISA is a federal statute passed by Congress in 1974 as an instrument intended to regulate employee pensions and as a response to widespread mismanagement and fraud of employee benefit plans.[2] Moreover, ERISA applies to employee welfare benefit plans, which include employer-provided health insurance. The primary effect of ERISA on employer-provided health insurance has been to deregulate such plans, with the result that few requirements are imposed on the plans and few remedies for harms caused by the plans are available to employees. In effect, ERISA allows managed care organizations to behave the way they do. Most notably, it is ERISA that prohibits patients from suing their HMO in state courts where, if patients won, they might receive huge money damages. In *Pegram*, the Supreme Court was examining ERISA to determine if the statute could be interpreted to impose duties on managed care organizations and their physicians to act in the best interests of patients. Herdrich was claiming that physicians in their role as both administrators and clinicians had fiduciary duties toward plan beneficiaries. As you will see, the Court refuses to grant Herdrich's claim that Carle's financial incentives violate fiduciary duties under ERISA. The ethical implications of this decision are impossible to overestimate.

Ethical Issues and Background

Now that we have arrived at our final chapter and our last two Supreme Court cases, reemphasizing one of the most important claims of this book will be helpful. Examining arguments and decisions of the justices provides us with an opportunity not only to explore the relationship between constitutional law and medical ethics but also to enrich our understanding and appreciation of relevant arguments, concepts, and dilemmas in medical ethics. In this chapter we read and evaluate two Supreme Court cases in order that we might better understand ethical and public policy concerns surrounding a right to health care and the rise of health maintenance organizations. Addressing concerns associated with the claim to a right to health care and with the unique ethical challenges posed by managed care has preoccupied medical ethicists as well as physicians' groups, politicians, consumers, and the courts. The extent to which the justices incorporate these concerns into their application of the Constitution to specific laws and acts of Congress is made clearer by reading these two Court decisions.

You will recall that this chapter opens with the claim that the American health care system is in crisis. Ronald Munson contributes specificity and moral force to this observation.

> A crisis exists in a social institution when factors are present that tend to destroy it or render it ineffective in achieving its goals. Two major factors are present in the American health care system that put it in a state of crisis: the increasing cost to the society of health care (despite the advent of cost-control policies) and the failure to deliver at least a decent minimum of health care to everyone who needs it.[3]

Can the U.S. Constitution in conjunction with conceptual and theoretical analysis from medical ethics help institutions and government resolve current problems in health care? How has the U.S. Supreme Court understood the current crisis in American health care? Can, or should, the Court do anything about this crisis? Below we briefly outline some important ethical issues and considerations surrounding a right to health care. We will focus most of our attention on ethical problems surrounding managed care.

Our first case, *Harris v. McRae*, is an abortion funding case. In *Harris*, a majority of the justices ruled that the Federal Constitution permits the states and federal government to deny funding for abortions to pregnant poor women in need of abortions for health reasons. From a moral and health policy perspective, however, *Harris* is more than an abortion funding case. Viewed within the context of concerns over a right to health care, the case assumes special significance. Justice Brennan, in footnote 4 of his dissenting opinion, recognizes the broader impact of *Harris* when he observes, "Antipathy to abortion has been permitted not only to ride roughshod over a woman's constitutional right to terminate her pregnancy in the fashion she chooses, but also to distort our nation's health-care programs."

Implications of *Harris* not only for specific health care programs but also for any type of constitutionally recognized right to health care could be significant. Issues surrounding the steps government may legitimately take to limit access by a specific group of people to a medical procedure enjoying constitutional protection are at the heart of *Harris*. By refusing to require the government to fund medically necessary abortions to indigent women, the Court is in effect saying that government may decide who does and who does not enjoy a specific constitutionally protected right. The majority opinion also sheds light on how sympathetic the Court would be toward a claim that the Constitution recognizes a generalized right to health care for all Americans. If the Court is unwilling to strike down government erected barriers to one type of health care for a group that is least likely to have access, then the Court is unlikely to recognize a broader right to medical care. As you read the various opinions in *Harris*, and as you read the brief outline of conceptual and ethical issues surrounding a right to health care provided below, the relevance of *Harris* will become much clearer.

Before discussing the right to health care in more detail, it might be helpful to articulate why health care in and of itself is so special. The President's Commission for the Study of Ethical

Problems in Medicine and Biomedical and Behavioral Research describes powerfully the special nature of health care.

> Health care can relieve pain and suffering, restore functioning, and prevent death; it can enhance good health and improve an individual's opportunity to pursue a life plan; and it can provide valuable information about a person's overall health. Beyond its practical importance, the involvement of health care with the most significant and awesome events of life—birth, illness, and death—adds a symbolic aspect to health care: it is special because it signifies not only mutual empathy and caring but the mysterious aspects of curing and healing.[4]

Realizing and appreciating the special nature of health care makes discussions of a right to health care much more relevant and meaningful.

Wide disagreement exists over the meaning of a right to health care as well as over what the right should include. Most discussions of a right to health care are couched in terms of equitable access. Using equitable access as a starting point, we can list various definitions of the right.[5] A right to health care might mean: 1) equitable access to all medical care needed, 2) equitable access to all medical care that is beneficial, 3) equitable access to all the medical care everyone else is receiving, and 4) equitable access to an adequate or decent level of medical care. Obviously each of these meanings stands in need of elaboration and argumentation, and the reader is encouraged to explore each in more detail. Further exploration, for example, of 2)—receiving all medical care that is beneficial—yields the conclusion that any national health policy based on access to beneficial care is probably unworkable. Even if we could agree on what constitutes "beneficial care," no government could afford the cost required to provide everyone with all the medical care that would benefit them. Most medical ethicists and health policy analysts, it is probably fair to say, subscribe to the position that a right to health care encompasses some variation on equitable access to an adequate or decent level of medical care. The burden falls upon advocates of this definition to explain and defend what is meant by "adequate" or "decent" level of medical care.

These brief remarks on the importance of health care as well as on the right to health care provide you with background for assessing how the justices in *Harris* and *Pegram* view obligations and responsibilities of government and other parties that pay for health care services. Keep in mind that even if we could establish a moral right to health care, it would not necessarily follow that people would have a legal right to such care. These remarks also serve as appropriate introduction to a discussion of some of the ethical concerns surrounding managed health care. We begin with a brief description of managed care before turning to ethical concerns.

A host of definitions of managed care exists. This abundance of meanings is due in part to the complexity of these relatively new health care arrangements. At its simplest, managed care means, "…a system of health care delivery that tries to manage the cost of health care, the quality of that health care, and access to that care."[6] Understanding the exact nature of managed care requires a grasp of its cost-containment strategies. Allen Buchanan provides a convenient list:

> 1. payment limits (e.g., diagnosis-related groups for Medicare hospital fees); 2. requirement of preauthorization for certain services (e.g., surgeries); 3. the use of primary care physicians as gatekeepers to control referral to specialists; 4. so-called de-skilling (using less highly trained providers for certain services than was customary during the pre–managed care era); and 5. financial incentives for physicians to limit utilization of care (e.g., year-end bonuses or holdbacks of payments that physicians receive only if they do not exceed specified utilization limits).[7]

Not only does this list of cost-containment techniques facilitate our understanding of managed care, it also suggests the kinds of ethical problems with managed care that patients, politicians, and the courts are facing.

All managed care plans, including those plans categorized as health maintenance organizations (HMOs) under discussion in *Pegram*, integrate the financing of medical care with the delivery of medical care. This system stands in stark contrast to how medical care was paid for and delivered in the United States in the past. Until the 1980s, the dominant model was fee-for-service indemnity insurance. In this model, insurance companies paid for all medical services physicians deemed appropriate for their patients; little incentive existed for physicians and patients to care about the cost of medical care. As costs dramatically increased, government, employers, and other payers of health insurance searched for ways to cut costs. A plan that directly linked cost with care seemed to be the answer, and managed care arrangements quickly began to dominate the American health care system. In theory, at least, managed care holds the promise of controlling costs while at the same time providing quality health care to its members. Many people worry, however, that controlling cost is incompatible with the provision of quality care.

As the public, legislators, politicians, and ethicists have become concerned about managed care arrangements, the area receiving the most ethical scrutiny is conflict of interest. Consciousness of the cost of providing services has translated often into managed care organizations (MCOs) requiring their physicians to deny or delay care to plan members. The fewer tests ordered, the fewer surgeries performed, and the fewer treatments provided, the lower the cost will be. In addition, physicians are offered incentives—for example, year-end bonuses—to deny or delay care. Moral principles of beneficence and nonmaleficence require, however, that physicians practice in the best interest of their patients. The popular press and the ethics literature are filled with accounts of physicians performing in ways that actually harm patients. Because of the way MCOs are structured, physicians face responsibilities to the plan to save money at the same time they have obligations to provide beneficial care toward their patients.

Lawrence Gostin discusses in detail both how managed care imposes conflict of interests on physicians and the kinds of problems these conflicts can cause.[8] The first problem involves treatment decisions by physicians and is especially acute in managed care plans owned and operated by physicians themselves. MCOs provide incentives to deny care both at the point of entry and at the point of delivery. Thus, physicians in such plans make two types of decisions, coverage decisions and treatment decisions. That is, a physician may be responsible for determining what medical conditions the plan will cover or pay for and at the same time be responsible for making treatment decisions of individual patients. Determinations of what conditions are "medically necessary" and determinations of how to treat are influenced by cost consciousness. As Gostin observes, "Those directly responsible for determining coverage and recommending treatment have a clear economic incentive to do less."[9]

The second problem stemming from a conflict of interest (that Gostin notes) is that physicians will distort the medical advice they give to patients. If physicians are provided with economic incentives to withhold or delay care, then it reasonably follows that physicians will not be as complete or as truthful in their conversations with patients.[10] One particularly troubling manifestation of managed care's drive to cut cost is the gag clause, in which physicians are not allowed to discuss with patients the plan's incentive package for physicians. On occasion, gag clauses have even prohibited physicians from discussing alternative treatments that may be appropriate for particular patients. When physicians have economic incentives not to be truthful with patients, patients and the public will no longer trust physicians. A breakdown in trust obviously will negatively impact the entire health care system.

Much of the ethical relevance of *Pegram v. Herdrich* can be found in the candor of Justice Souter's opinion. Two commentators have even commented that the decision was "an exercise in moral honesty."[11] These same commentators go on to note that the justices said bluntly that "…HMOs control costs by rationing care, that Congress approved of this when it passed the 1973 HMO Act, and that physicians paid to practice parsimoniously wear 2 hats, as coverage decision makers and clinical caretakers."[12] As you read *Pegram*, you have an opportunity not only to assess the moral commitments of the Court, but also to examine and analyze moral concerns surrounding one of the most ethically, legally, and politically troubling forces in medicine—managed health care.

Harris v. McRae
448 U.S. 297 (1980)

Justice Stewart delivered the opinion of the Court, in which Chief Justice Burger and Justices White, Powell, and Rehnquist joined. Justice White filed a concurring opinion. Justice Brennan filed a dissenting opinion, in which Justices Marshall and Blackmun joined. Justices Marshall, Blackmun, and Stevens each filed dissenting opinions.

Areas for Discussion and Ethical Reflection

1.   As you read Justice Stewart's majority opinion, try to determine how he characterizes the freedom to terminate a pregnancy. You might wish to reread *Roe v. Wade* in chapter 3 to help you describe Justice Stewart's conception of the freedom. Does Justice Stewart properly understand the ruling in *Roe*? Be sure to read Justice Brennan's dissenting opinion before answering this question.

2.   As you well know by now, justices love to use analogies to support their decisions. In ruling that the state has no obligation to fund medically necessary abortions for poor women, Justice Stewart uses two analogies. First, although the government may not prohibit the use of contraceptives, it does not follow that government has an obligation to provide contraceptives to poor

people. Second, no obligation on the part of government to send every child who wishes to a private school follows from the fact that parents have a constitutional right to send their children to private schools. Do you find these two analogies convincing?

3.   How does Justice Stewart argue that the Hyde Amendment does not violate the equal protection component of the Fifth Amendment? What ethical concerns does Justice Stewart's argument raise?

4.   At the end of his majority opinion, Justice Stewart asserts that Congress may authorize federal reimbursement for medically necessary services, excluding abortion, for women receiving Medicaid on the grounds that "[a]bortion is inherently different from other medical procedures, because no other procedure involves the purposeful termination of a potential life." From an ethical perspective, is Justice Stewart correct in his use of the phrase "purposeful termination?" Is there a sense in which we might say that women who seek abortions for medical reasons do not purposely intend to kill their fetuses? You might review the discussion of double effect in the previous chapter.

5.   Justice Brennan views the Hyde Amendment as "a transparent attempt by the Legislative Branch to impose the political majority's judgment of the morally acceptable and socially desirable preference on a sensitive and intimate decision that the Constitution entrusts to the individual." Do you agree with Justice Brennan's appraisal? If you do agree, what are the ethical concerns that could be raised against you and Justice Brennan?

6.   In footnote 4 to his dissenting opinion, Justice Brennan remarks that Congress's decision not to fund medically necessary abortions should be put in "human terms." From a public policy perspective and from that of medical ethics, what would it mean to discuss the importance of the Hyde Amendment in human terms? If you broaden the discussion to include a right to health care for all citizens, what would it mean to couch that discussion in human terms?

7.   The brief excerpt from Justice Marshall's dissenting opinion in *Harris* is very powerful. He leaves little doubt as to which moral theory he employs in criticizing the majority opinion. What moral theory is Justice Marshall employing? How might you employ the same moral theory as justification for the majority opinion? Could a Kantian support Justice Marshall's reasoning and conclusion?

8.   Before leaving Justice Marshall's comments, note that he makes a claim that is at best unfair and at worse false. What is this claim?

9.   Justice Stevens calls the Court's equal protection analysis "sterile." What does he mean? Can a moral analysis of a dilemma be sterile?

10.   Justice Stevens observes that "…the cost of an abortion is only a small fraction of the costs associated with childbirth." That is, by discriminating against poor women who need abortions, the government is actually harming all poor people by making less money available to the entire class. What is the ethical import of this argument? The implications of Justice Stevens's observations for many kinds of federal tax, social welfare, and health policies are quite interesting. What are some of these implications?

11.   Over the years a majority of the justices has consistently refused to view poverty or lack of adequate economic resources as a suspect classification. As long as no infringement of a fundamental right is involved, the Court has consistently upheld legislation that burdens economically disadvantaged people as long as the government can show a rational basis for the legislation. What ethical justifications can you provide in support of this approach? Are there one or more ethical theories that would be sympathetic to this approach? Read Justice Stewart's decision carefully for guidance on these questions.

12.   How do the opinions and arguments of the justices in this case relate to a right to health care? Does the observation from

Robert Veatch introducing the discussion of various models of the physician-patient relationship quoted in chapter 6 contribute anything to your assessment of *Harris v. McRae*? Please explain and defend, in detail, your answer.

JUSTICE STEWART:

...[B]efore turning to the equal protection issue in this case, we examine whether the Hyde Amendment violates any substantive rights secured by the Constitution....In the *Wade* case, this Court held unconstitutional a Texas statute making it a crime to procure or attempt an abortion except on medical advice for the purpose of saving the mother's life. The constitutional underpinning of *Wade* was a recognition that the "liberty" protected by the Due Process Clause of the Fourteenth Amendment includes not only the freedoms explicitly mentioned in the Bill of Rights, but also a freedom of personal choice in certain matters of marriage and family life. This implicit constitutional liberty, the Court in *Wade* held, includes the freedom of a woman to decide whether to terminate a pregnancy.

But the Court in *Wade* also recognized that a State has legitimate interests during a pregnancy in both ensuring the health of the mother and protecting potential human life. These state interests, which were found to be "separate and distinct" and to "gro[w] in substantiality as the woman approaches term," pose a conflict with a woman's untrammeled freedom of choice. In resolving this conflict, the Court held that before the end of the first trimester of pregnancy, neither state interest is sufficiently substantial to justify any intrusion on the woman's freedom of choice. In the second trimester, the state interest in maternal health was found to be sufficiently substantial to justify regulation reasonably related to that concern. And at viability, usually in the third trimester, the state interest in protecting the potential life of the fetus was found to justify a criminal prohibition against abortions, except where necessary for the preservation of the life or health of the mother. Thus, inasmuch as the Texas criminal statute allowed abortions only where necessary to save the life of the mother and without regard to the stage of the pregnancy, the Court held in *Wade* that the statute violated the Due Process Clause of the Fourteenth Amendment.

In *Maher v. Roe*, [we were] presented with the question whether the scope of personal constitutional freedom recognized in *Roe v. Wade* included an entitlement to Medicaid payments for abortions that are not medically necessary. At issue in *Maher* was a Connecticut welfare regulation under which Medicaid recipients received payments for medical services incident to childbirth, but not for medical services incident to nontherapeutic abortions. The District Court held that the regulation violated the Equal Protection Clause of the Fourteenth Amendment because the unequal subsidization of childbirth and abortion impinged on the "fundamental right to abortion" recognized in *Wade* and its progeny.

It was the view of this Court that "the District Court misconceived the nature and scope of the fundamental right recognized in *Roe*." The doctrine of *Roe v. Wade*, the Court held in *Maher*, "protects the woman from unduly burdensome interference with her freedom to decide whether to terminate her pregnancy," such as the severe criminal sanctions at issue in *Roe v. Wade*, or the absolute requirement of spousal consent for an abortion challenged in *Danforth*.

But the constitutional freedom recognized in *Wade* and its progeny, the *Maher* Court explained, did not prevent Connecticut from making "a value judgment favoring childbirth over abortion, and…implement[ing] that judgment by the allocation of public funds."…

[The Court explains that in its *Maher* decision the

Connecticut statute was upheld because the statute "places no obstacles—absolute or otherwise—in the pregnant woman's path to an abortion." "Indigent women continue to be dependent on private sources for the funds she needs to obtain what she desires."

The Hyde Amendment, like the Connecticut welfare regulation at issue in *Maher*, places no governmental obstacle in the path of a woman who chooses to terminate her pregnancy, but rather, by means of unequal subsidization of abortion and other medical services, encourages alternative activity deemed in the public interest. The present case does differ factually from *Maher* insofar as that case involved a failure to fund nontherapeutic abortions, whereas the Hyde Amendment withholds funding of certain medically necessary abortions. Accordingly, the appellees argue that because the Hyde Amendment affects a significant interest not present or asserted in *Maher*—the interest of a woman in protecting her health during pregnancy—and because that interest lies at the core of the personal constitutional freedom recognized in *Wade*, the present case is constitutionally different from *Maher*. It is the appellees' view that to the extent that the Hyde Amendment withholds funding for certain medically necessary abortions, it clearly impinges on the constitutional principle recognized in *Wade*.

It is evident that a woman's interest in protecting her health was an important theme in *Wade*. In concluding that the freedom of a woman to decide whether to terminate her pregnancy falls within the personal liberty protected by the Due Process Clause, the Court in *Wade* emphasized the fact that the woman's decision carries with it significant personal health implications—both physical and psychological. In fact, although the Court in *Wade* recognized that the state interest in protecting potential life becomes sufficiently compelling in the period after fetal viability to justify an absolute criminal prohibition of nontherapeutic abortions, the Court held that even after fetal viability a State may not prohibit abortions "necessary to preserve the life or health of the mother." Because even the compelling interest of the State in protecting potential life after fetal viability was held to be insufficient to outweigh a woman's decision to protect her life or health, it could be argued that the freedom of a woman to decide whether to terminate her pregnancy for health reasons does in fact lie at the core of the constitutional liberty identified in *Wade*.

But, regardless of whether the freedom of a woman to choose to terminate her pregnancy for health reasons lies at the core or the periphery of the due process liberty recognized in *Wade*, it simply does not follow that a woman's freedom of choice carries with it a constitutional entitlement to the financial resources to avail herself of the full range of protected choices. The reason why was explained in *Maher*: although government may not place obstacles in the path of a woman's exercise of her freedom of choice, it need not remove those not of its own creation. Indigency falls in the latter category. The financial constraints that restrict an indigent woman's ability to enjoy the full range of constitutionally protected freedom of choice are the product not of governmental restrictions on access to abortions, but rather of her indigency. Although Congress has opted to subsidize medically necessary services generally, but not certain medically necessary abortions, the fact remains that the Hyde Amendment leaves an indigent woman with at least the same range of choice in deciding whether to obtain a medically necessary abortion as she would have had if Congress had chosen to subsidize no health care costs at all. We are thus not persuaded that the Hyde Amendment impinges on the constitutionally protected freedom of choice recognized in *Wade*.

Although the liberty protected by the Due Process Clause affords protection against unwarranted government interference with freedom of choice in the context of certain personal decisions, it does not confer an entitlement to such funds as may be necessary to realize all the advantages of that freedom. To hold otherwise would mark a drastic change in our understanding of the Constitution. It cannot be that because government may not prohibit the use of contraceptives, or prevent parents from sending their child to a private school, government, therefore, has an affirmative constitutional obligation to ensure that all persons have the financial resources to obtain contraceptives or send their children to private schools. To translate the limitation on governmental power implicit in the Due Process Clause into an affirmative funding obligation would require Congress to subsidize the medically necessary abortion of an indigent woman even if Congress had not enacted a Medicaid program to subsidize other medically necessary services. Nothing in the Due Process Clause supports such an extraordinary result. Whether freedom of choice that is constitutionally protected warrants federal subsidization is a question for Congress to answer, not a matter of constitutional entitlement....

[The Court then briefly considers and dismisses claims that the Hyde Amendment violates rights guaranteed by the Religion Clauses of the First Amendment.]

It remains to be determined whether the Hyde Amendment violates the equal protection component of the Fifth Amendment. This challenge is premised on the fact that, although federal reimbursement is available under Medicaid for medically necessary services generally, the Hyde Amendment does not permit federal reimbursement of all medically necessary abortions....

The guarantee of equal protection under the Fifth Amendment is not a source of substantive rights or liberties, but rather a right to be free from invidious discrimination in statutory classifications and other governmental activity. It is well settled that where a statutory classification does not itself impinge on a right or liberty protected by the

Constitution, the validity of classification must be sustained unless "the classification rests on grounds wholly irrelevant to the achievement of [any legitimate governmental] objective." This presumption of constitutional validity, however, disappears if a statutory classification is predicated on criteria that are, in a constitutional sense, "suspect," the principal example of which is a classification based on race.

For the reasons stated above, we have already concluded that the Hyde Amendment violates no constitutionally protected substantive rights. We now conclude as well that it is not predicated on a constitutionally suspect classification....

The remaining question then is whether the Hyde Amendment is rationally related to a legitimate governmental objective. It is the Government's position that the Hyde Amendment bears a rational relationship to its legitimate interest in protecting the potential life of the fetus. We agree.

...[T]he Hyde Amendment, by encouraging childbirth except in the most urgent circumstances, is rationally related to the legitimate governmental objective of protecting potential life. By subsidizing the medical expenses of indigent women who carry their pregnancies to term while not subsidizing the comparable expenses of women who undergo abortions (except those whose lives are threatened), Congress has established incentives that make childbirth a more attractive alternative than abortion for persons eligible for Medicaid. These incentives bear a direct relationship to the legitimate congressional interest in protecting potential life. Nor is it irrational that Congress has authorized federal reimbursement for medically necessary services generally, but not for certain medically necessary abortions. Abortion is inherently different from other medical procedures, because no other procedure involves the purposeful termination of a potential life....

For the reasons stated in this opinion, we hold that a State that participates in the Medicaid program is not obligated under Title XIX to continue to fund those medically necessary abortions for which federal reimbursement is unavailable under the Hyde Amendment. We further hold that the funding restrictions of the Hyde Amendment violate neither the Fifth Amendment nor the Establishment Clause of the First Amendment. It is also our view that...the Free Exercise Clause of the First Amendment [is not at issue here.]...

It is so ordered.

JUSTICE BRENNAN:

I write separately to express my continuing disagreement with the Court's mischaracterization of the nature of the fundamental right recognized in *Roe*, and its misconception of the manner in which that right is infringed by federal and state legislation withdrawing all funding for medically necessary abortions....

When viewed in the context of the Medicaid program to which it is appended, it is obvious that the Hyde Amendment is nothing less than an attempt by Congress to circumvent the dictates of the Constitution and achieve indirectly what *Roe v. Wade* said it could not do directly. Under Title XIX of the Social Security Act, the Federal Government reimburses participating States for virtually all medically necessary services it provides to the categorically needy. The sole limitation of any significance is the Hyde Amendment's prohibition against the use of any federal funds to pay for the costs of abortions (except where the life of the mother would be endangered if the fetus were carried to term)...[T]he Hyde Amendment is a transparent attempt by the Legislative Branch to impose the political majority's judgment of the morally acceptable and socially desirable preference on a sensitive and intimate decision that the Constitution entrusts to the individual. Worse yet, the Hyde Amendment does not foist that majoritarian viewpoint with equal measure upon everyone in our Nation, rich and poor alike; rather, it imposes that viewpoint only upon that segment of our society which, because of its position of political powerlessness, is least able to defend its privacy rights from the encroachments of state-mandated morality. The instant legislation thus calls for more exacting judicial review than in most other cases.... Though it may not be this Court's mission "to decide whether the balance of competing interests reflected in the Hyde Amendment is wise social policy," it most assuredly is our responsibility to vindicate the pregnant woman's constitutional right to decide whether to bear children free from governmental intrusion....

JUSTICE MARSHALL:

...The consequences of today's opinion—consequences to which the Court seems oblivious—are not difficult to predict. Pregnant women denied the funding necessary to procure abortions will be restricted to two alternatives. First, they can carry the fetus to term—even though that route may result in severe injury or death to the mother, the fetus, or both. If that course appears intolerable, they can resort to self-induced abortions or attempt to attain illegal abortions—not because bearing a child would be inconvenient, but because it is necessary in order to protect their health. The result will not be to protect what the Court describes as "the legitimate governmental objective of protecting potential life, but to ensure the destruction of both fetal and maternal life." "There is another world 'out there,' the existence of which the Court...either chooses to ignore or fears to recognize." In my view, it is only by blinding itself to that other world that the Court can reach the result it announces today....

JUSTICE STEVENS:

...[This case] involves a special exclusion of women who, by definition, are confronted with a choice between two serious harms: serious health damage to themselves on the one hand and abortion on the other. The competing interests are the interest in maternal health and the interest in protecting potential human life. It is now part of our law that the pregnant woman's decision as to which of these conflicting interests shall prevail is entitled to constitutional protection.

If a woman has a constitutional right to place a higher value on avoiding either serious harm to her own health or perhaps an abnormal childbirth than on protecting potential life, the exercise of that right cannot provide the basis for the denial of a benefit to which she would otherwise be entitled. The Court's sterile equal protection analysis evades this critical though simple point. The Court focuses exclusively on the "legitimate interest in protecting the potential life of the fetus." It concludes that since the Hyde Amendments further that interest, the exclusion they create is rational and therefore constitutional. But it is misleading to speak of the Government's legitimate interest in the fetus without reference to the context in which that interest was held to be legitimate. It is thus perfectly clear that neither the Federal Government nor the States may exclude a woman from medical benefits to which she would otherwise be entitled solely to further an interest in potential life when a physician, "in appropriate medical judgment," certifies that an abortion is necessary "for the preservation of the life or health of the mother." The Court totally fails to explain why this reasoning is not dispositive here....

It cannot be denied that the harm inflicted upon women in the excluded class is grievous....Nor can it be argued that the exclusion of this type of medically necessary treatment of the indigent can be justified on fiscal grounds.

There are some especially costly forms of treatment that may reasonably be excluded from the program in order to preserve the assets in the pool and extend its benefits to the maximum number of needy persons. Fiscal considerations may compel certain difficult choices in order to improve the protection afforded to the entire benefited class. But, ironically, the exclusion of medically necessary abortions harms the entire class as well as its specific victims. For the records in [prior cases] demonstrate that the cost of an abortion is only a small fraction of the costs associated with childbirth. Thus, the decision to tolerate harm to indigent persons who need an abortion in order to avoid "serious and long-lasting health damage" is one that is financed by draining money out of the pool that is used to fund all other necessary medical procedures. Unlike most invidious classifications, this discrimination harms not only its direct victims but also the remainder of the class of needy persons that the pool was designed to benefit....

Pegram et al. v. Herdrich
530 U.S. 211 (2000)

Justice Souter delivered the opinion for a unanimous Court.

Areas for Discussion and Ethical Reflection

1.   The constitutional and ethical problems presented by managed care are complex and often frustrating for those considering the issues for the first time. However, a little time and effort can dissolve much of this complexity and frustration; given what is at stake for individual patients, the public, and the health care professions, expending some time and effort will prove quite rewarding. Express in your own words your understanding of some of the moral dilemmas raised by managed care.

2.   By now you should be familiar with many of the theories, principles, concepts, and approaches central to medical ethics. After reading Justice Souter's opinion, morally assess the events surrounding Lori Pegram's behavior and actions toward Cynthia Herdrich. What ethical justifications can you provide for finding Dr. Pegram's actions immoral? Do you think Justice Souter adequately appreciates the special nature of health care? Is it at all relevant whether he understands the important role of health care for individuals and society?

3.   Now take and defend the position that Dr. Pegram's actions were morally appropriate. Who is likely to find the policies and actions of Carle Clinic and Dr. Pegram morally appropriate? Suppose for a moment that you work for an employer who contracts with Carle (Herdrich's HMO) to provide you and your family with health care services. Unfortunately, health care costs, both for you and your employer, continue to rise. Evaluate Dr. Pegram's actions from this perspective. Where in Justice Souter's opinion does he do this for you?

4.   The Court rules in *Pegram* that treatment decisions made by physicians in the employ of health maintenance organizations are not fiduciary acts. What does it mean for one person to have a fiduciary duty toward another? Can institutions or organizations have fiduciary duties toward individuals?

5.   Many passages in Justice Souter's decision are technical; this is unavoidable given that the Court has to analyze both ERISA regulations and Congress's intent in crafting those regulations. Are there passages, however, where you detect the influence of medical ethics? If so, mark those and determine to what degree Justice Souter is thorough and fair.

6.   Justice Souter seems to believe that conflicts of interest are no worse in managed care than in traditional fee-for-service arrangements. In the former, physicians are rewarded for not providing needed care and in the latter physicians are rewarded for providing unnecessary care; either way, the patient "loses." But

is this really the case? Justice Souter's contention appears to call into doubt the following observation: "The patient is in a different position when the physician has incentives to *restrict* needed treatment than when the physician has incentives to provide *unnecessary* treatment. In the latter situation, patients can obtain another opinion. In the former situation, patients may not be aware of a needed treatment."[13] How do you think Justice Souter would respond to this observation?

7.   Justice Souter maintains that courts, including the U.S. Supreme Court, are not in a position to distinguish "good" from "bad" HMOs. What do you think Justice Souter means by the terms "good" and "bad"? Is he speaking morally? Constitutionally? What are Justice Souter's arguments for courts not playing a role?

8.   Since its decision in *Pegram* in June 2000, the Supreme Court has handed down two very significant decisions relating to managed care. The first was *Rush Prudential HMO, Inc. v. Moran*, 536 U.S. 355 (2002). At issue in this case was the meaning of medical necessity and a state's law requiring independent review of any HMO's denial of coverage to a patient on the grounds that the treatment was not medically necessary. Debra Moran was denied payment for surgery by her HMO, Rush Prudential. Only one part of the procedure was not considered standard care, but it was this part that Moran's primary physician recommended and Moran wanted. Rush claimed the procedure was not medically necessary. Illinois law required that HMOs provide review of denied benefits by an independent physician and that the HMO must cover the procedure if the independent reviewer found the procedure medically necessary. When Rush refused Moran's request for a review, she challenged the decision in state court. The court ordered the review, which in turn found the surgery necessary. Again, however, Rush refused to cover the procedure. In the meantime Moran had the surgery and then made the additional claim that Rush should reimburse her. Rush Prudential then had the case removed to federal court claim-

ing that Moran was now making an ERISA claim. The Seventh Circuit ruled that ERISA does not preempt or ban the state law from requiring the review. In a 5-4 decision, the Supreme Court agreed and upheld Moran's claim and found that Illinois could require HMOs to submit their denials of care to outside review. To what extent HMOs will alter their practices with regard to treatment refusals on grounds of medical necessity is yet to be determined.

9.   The Court's second major decision regarding managed care came in April, 2003, in *Kentucky Association of Health Plans, Inc, et al. v. Miller*, 538 U.S. ___ (2003). At issue in this case was Kentucky's Any Willing Provider (AWP) law, which prohibited any health insurer from discriminating against any physician who is willing to meet the conditions for participation established by the insurer. The state's managed care organizations filed suit asserting that Kentucky's AWP law was forbidden under ERISA. The HMOs argued that in order to control costs and assure quality patient care they must be allowed to create exclusive provider networks. By limiting the number of physicians in a network a high patient volume is assured, which in turn compensates for the discounted rates the HMOs pay physicians. The district court upheld Kentucky's AWP law against ERISA preemption, and the Sixth Circuit affirmed. In a unanimous opinion, the Supreme Court agreed with the lower courts and indicated that it was unwilling to weaken state regulations of managed care in support of ERISA. Much discussion accompanied the ruling in this case. Representatives of the managed care industry argued that premiums would rise and quality of care would suffer. Patient advocates claimed the Court's ruling would translate into more accountability on the part of managed care. As of this writing it is too early to tell what effect if any the decision will have on patient care.

10.   On January 1, 2003, California enacted into law the Health Care Providers' Bill of Rights. This legislation is an attempt to address some of the problems physicians are facing with MCOs.[14]

Problems include MCOs forcing doctors to treat an excessive number of patients and MCOs changing the terms of physicians' contracts without input from physicians. Physicians in California had worried that they no longer had power and autonomy to practice medicine in the way they deemed proper. Governor Davis praised the legislation, stating that "...in order to provide patients with world-class care, we must ensure that our doctors have world-class rights."[15] Managed care organizations argued that the legislation would raise health care costs and would cause even more people to become uninsured. As you read *Pegram v. Herdrich*, consider the moral responsibilities of physicians, MCO's, and patients to develop and implement a health care system that provides as much coverage and access as possible.

Justice Souter:

The question in this case is whether treatment decisions made by a health maintenance organization, acting through its physician employees, are fiduciary acts within the meaning of the Employee Retirement Income Security Act of 1974 (ERISA). We hold that they are not.

[The Court notes: Cynthia Herdrich charged that her physician, Lori Pegram, and Pegram's HMO, Carle Clinic, made treatment decisions that were in their self-interest. Herdrich charged that such treatment was a violation of the fiduciary duty Dr. Pegram and Carle owed to Herdrich and other plan beneficiaries. When Carle Clinic moved to have the claim dismissed, the District Court agreed. But the Court of Appeals for the Seventh Circuit reversed stating: "Our decision does not stand for the proposition that the existence of incentives *automatically* gives rise to a breach of fiduciary duty. Rather, we hold that incentives can *rise* to the level of a breach where, as pleaded here, the fiduciary trust between plan participants and plan fiduciaries no longer exists (i.e., where physicians delay providing necessary treatment to, or withhold administering proper care to, plan beneficiaries for the sole purpose of increasing their bonuses).]

We granted certiorari and now reverse the Court of Appeals.

Whether Carle is a fiduciary when it acts through its physician owners as pleaded in the ERISA count depends on some background of fact and law about HMO organizations, medical benefit plans, fiduciary obligation, and the meaning of Herdrich's allegations.

Traditionally, medical care in the United States has been provided on a "fee-for-service" basis. A physician charges so much for a general physical exam, a vaccination, a tonsillectomy, and so on. The physician bills the patient for services provided or, if there is insurance and the doctor is willing, submits the bill for the patient's care to the insurer, for payment subject to the terms of the insurance agreement. In a fee-for-service system, a physician's financial incentive is to provide more care, not less, so long as payment is forthcoming. The check on this incentive is a physician's obligation to exercise reasonable medical skill and judgment in the patient's interest.

Beginning in the late 1960s, insurers and others developed new models for health care delivery, including HMOs. The defining feature of an HMO is receipt of a fixed fee for each patient enrolled under the terms of a contract to provide specified health care if needed. The HMO thus assumes the financial risk of providing the benefits promised: if a participant never gets sick, the HMO keeps the money regardless, and if a participant becomes expensively ill, the HMO is responsible for the treatment agreed upon even if its cost exceeds the participant's premiums.

Like other risk-bearing organizations, HMOs take steps to control costs. At the least, HMOs, like traditional insurers, will in some fashion make coverage determinations, scrutinizing requested services against the contractual provisions to make sure that a request for care falls within the scope of covered circumstances (pregnancy, for example), or that a given treatment falls within the scope of the care promised (surgery, for instance). They customarily issue general guidelines for their physicians about appropriate levels of care. And they commonly require utilization review (in which specific treatment decisions are reviewed by a decisionmaker other than the treating physician) and approval in advance (precertification) for many types of care, keyed to standards of medical necessity or the reasonableness of the proposed treatment. These cost-controlling measures are commonly complemented by specific financial incentives to physicians, rewarding them for decreasing utilization of health-care services, and penalizing them for what may be found to be excessive treatment. Hence, in an HMO system, a physician's financial interest lies in providing less care, not more. The check on this influence (like that on the converse, fee-for-service incentive) is the professional obligation to provide covered services with a reasonable degree of skill and judgment in the patient's interest.

The adequacy of professional obligation to counter financial self-interest has been challenged no matter what the form of medical organization. HMOs became popular because fee-for-service physicians were thought to be providing unnecessary or useless services; today, many doctors and other observers argue that HMOs often ignore the individual needs of a patient in order to improve the HMOs' bottom lines. In this case, for instance, one could argue that Pegram's decision to wait before getting an ultrasound for Herdrich, and her insistence that the ultrasound be done at a distant facility owned by Carle, reflected an interest in limiting the HMO's expenses, which blinded her to the need for immediate diagnosis and treatment.

Herdrich focuses on the Carle scheme's provision for a "year-end distribution," to the HMO's physician owners.

She argues that this particular incentive device of annually paying physician owners the profit resulting from their own decisions rationing care can distinguish Carle's organization from HMOs generally, so that reviewing Carle's decisions under a fiduciary standard as pleaded in Herdrich's complaint would not open the door to like claims about other HMO structures. While the Court of Appeals agreed, we think otherwise, under the law as now written.

Although it is true that the relationship between sparing medical treatment and physician reward is not a subtle one under the Carle scheme, no HMO organization could survive without some incentive connecting physician reward with treatment rationing. The essence of an HMO is that salaries and profits are limited by the HMO's fixed membership fees. This is not to suggest that the Carle provisions are as socially desirable as some other HMO organizational schemes; they may not be. But whatever the HMO, there must be rationing and inducement to ration.

Since inducement to ration care goes to the very point of any HMO scheme, and rationing necessarily raises some risks while reducing others (ruptured appendixes are more likely; unnecessary appendectomies are less so), any legal principle purporting to draw a line between good and bad HMOs would embody, in effect, a judgment about socially acceptable medical risk. A valid conclusion of this sort would, however, necessarily turn on facts to which courts would probably not have ready access: correlations between malpractice rates and various HMO models, similar correlations involving fee-for-service models, and so on. And, of course, assuming such material could be obtained by courts in litigation like this, any standard defining the unacceptably risky HMO structure (and consequent vulnerability to claims like Herdrich's) would depend on a judgment about the appropriate level of expenditure for health care in light of the associated malpractice risk. But such complicated factfinding and such a debatable social judgment are not wisely required of courts unless for some reason resort cannot be had to the legislative process, with its preferable forum for comprehensive investigations and judgments of social value, such as optimum treatment levels and health care expenditure. [As was stated in a prior case] "The relevant policy considerations do not invariably point in one direction, and there is vehement disagreement over the validity of the assumptions underlying many of them. The very difficulty of these policy considerations, and Congress' superior institutional competence to pursue this debate, suggest that legislative not judicial solutions are preferable."

We think, then, that courts are not in a position to derive a sound legal principle to differentiate an HMO like Carle from other HMOs. For that reason, we proceed on the assumption that the decisions listed in Herdrich's complaint cannot be subject to a claim that they violate fiduciary standards unless all such decisions by all HMOs acting through their owner or employee physicians are to be judged by the same standards and subject to the same claims....

[The Court next spends some time discussing technical requirements of ERISA and what it means to be a fiduciary within the meaning of ERISA. A fiduciary is someone "acting in the capacity of manager, administrator, or financial advisor to a plan." The Court then notes that HMOs, such as Carle Clinic, have both fiduciary and nonfiduciary obligations. A physician such as Dr. Pegram is not acting as an ERISA fiduciary when treating patients, but would be acting as a fiduciary when managing or making eligibility decisions for the plan.]

These decisions are often practically inextricable from one another. This is so not merely because, under a scheme like Carle's, treatment and eligibility decisions are made by the same person, the treating physician. It is so because a great many and possibly most coverage questions are not simple yes-or-no questions, like whether appendicitis is a covered condition (when there is no dispute that a patient has appendicitis), or whether acupuncture is a covered procedure for pain relief (when the claim of pain is unchallenged). The more common coverage question is a when-and-how question. Although coverage for many conditions will be clear and various treatment options will be indisputably compensable, physicians still must decide what to do in particular cases. The issue may be, say, whether one treatment option is so superior to another under the circumstances, and needed so promptly, that a decision to proceed with it would meet the medical necessity requirement that conditions the HMO's obligation to provide or pay for that particular procedure at that time in that case. The Government in its brief alludes to a similar example when it discusses an HMO's refusal to pay for emergency care on the ground that the situation giving rise to the need for care was not an emergency. In practical terms, these eligibility decisions cannot be untangled from physicians' judgments about reasonable medical treatment, and in the case before us, Dr. Pegram's decision was one of that sort. She decided (wrongly, as it turned out) that Herdrich's condition did not warrant immediate action; the consequence of that medical determination was that Carle would not cover immediate care, whereas it would have done so if Dr. Pegram had made the proper diagnosis and judgment to treat. The eligibility decision and the treatment decision were inextricably mixed, as they are in countless medical administrative decisions every day.

The kinds of decisions mentioned in Herdrich's ERISA count and claimed to be fiduciary in character are just such mixed eligibility and treatment decisions: physicians' conclusions about when to use diagnostic tests; about seeking consultations and making referrals to physicians and facilities other than Carle's; about proper standards of care, the experimental character of a proposed course of treatment, the reasonableness of a certain treatment, and the emergency character of a medical condition....

Our doubt that Congress intended the category of fiduciary administrative functions to encompass the mixed determinations at issue here hardens into conviction when we consider the consequences that would follow from Herdrich's contrary view....

First, we need to ask how this fiduciary standard would affect HMOs if it applied as Herdrich claims it should be applied, not directed against any particular mixed decision that injured a patient, but against HMOs that make mixed decisions in the course of providing medical care for profit. Recovery would be warranted simply upon showing that the profit incentive to ration care would generally affect mixed decisions, in derogation of the fiduciary standard to act solely in the interest of the patient without possibility of conflict. Although Herdrich is vague about the mechanics of relief, the one point that seems clear is that she seeks the return of profit from the pockets of the Carle HMO's owners, with the money to be given to the plan for the benefit of the participants. Since the provision for profit is what makes the HMO a proprietary organization, her remedy in effect would be nothing less than elimination of the for-profit HMO. Her remedy might entail even more than that, although we are in no position to tell whether and to what extent nonprofit HMO schemes would ultimately survive the recognition of Herdrich's theory. It is enough to recognize that the Judiciary has no warrant to precipitate the upheaval that would follow a refusal to dismiss Herdrich's ERISA claim....

The fiduciary is, of course, obliged to act exclusively in the interest of the beneficiary, but this translates into no rule readily applicable to HMO decisions or those of any other variety of medical practice. While the incentive of the HMO physician is to give treatment sparingly, imposing a fiduciary obligation upon him would not lead to a simple default rule, say, that whenever it is reasonably possible to disagree about treatment options, the physician should treat aggressively. After all, HMOs came into being because some groups of physicians consistently provided more aggressive treatment than others in similar circumstances, with results not perceived as justified by the marginal expense and risk associated with intervention; excessive surgery is not in the patient's best interest, whether provided by fee-for-service surgeons or HMO surgeons subject to a default rule urging them to operate. Nor would it be possible to translate fiduciary duty into a standard that would allow recovery from an HMO whenever a mixed decision influenced by the HMO's financial incentive resulted in a bad outcome for the patient. It would be so easy to allege, and to find, an economic influence when sparing care did not lead to a well patient, that any such standard in practice would allow a factfinder to convert an HMO into a guarantor of recovery....

We hold that mixed eligibility decisions by HMO physicians are not fiduciary decisions under ERISA. Herdrich's ERISA count fails to state an ERISA claim, and the judgment of the Court of Appeals is reversed. It is so ordered.

Notes

1.   John E. Nowak and Ronald D. Rotunda, *Constitutional Law*, 6th ed. (St. Paul, MN: West Group, 2000), pp. 848–50.

2.   Barry R. Furrow et al., *Health Law*, 2nd ed. (St. Paul, MN: West Group, 2000), pp. 418–19.

3.   Ronald Munson, "Social Context: The Crisis Isn't Over," in *Intervention and Reflection: Basic Issues in Medical Ethics*, 6th ed., edited by Ronald Munson (Belmont, CA: Wadsworth, 2000), p. 805.

4.   President's Commission for the Study of Ethical Problems in Medicine and Biomedical and Behavioral Research, "An Ethical Framework for Access to Health Care," in *Intervention and Reflection*, p. 831.

5.   Ibid., pp. 832–33.

6.   John P. Little, "Managed Care Contracts of Adhesion: Terminating the Doctor-Patient Relationship and Endangering Patient Health," *Rutgers Law Review* 49 (1997): 1398.

7.   Allen Buchanan, "Managed Care: Rationing without Justice, but Not Unjustly," *Journal of Health Politics, Policy and Law* 23 (1998): 619.

8.   Lawrence O. Gostin, "Managed Care, Conflicts of Interest, and Quality," *Hastings Center Report* 30 (2000): 27–28.

9.   Ibid., 27.

10.   Ibid., 28.

11.   M. Greg Bloche and Peter D. Jacobson, "The Supreme Court and Bedside Rationing," *Journal of the American Medical Association* 284 (2000): 2779.

12.   Ibid.

13.   Tom L. Beauchamp and James F. Childress, *Principles of Biomedical Ethics*, 5th edition (New York: Oxford University Press, 2001), p. 318.

14.   Bryan Lee, "Managed Care: Health Providers' Bill of Rights Now Law in California," *Journal of Law, Medicine & Ethics* 31 (2003): 157–59.

15.   Ibid., p. 157.

For Further Reading

Beauchamp, Tom L., and James F. Childress. *Principles of Biomedical Ethics*, 5th edition. New York: Oxford University Press, 2001.

Bloche, M. Gregg, and Peter D. Jacobson. "The Supreme Court and Bedside Rationing." *Journal of the American Medical Association* 284 (2000): 2776–79.

Buchanan, Allen. "Managed Care: Rationing without Justice, but Not Unjustly." *Journal of Health Politics, Policy and Law* 23 (1998): 617–34.

Cahill, Michael T., and Peter D. Jacobson. "*Pegram's* Regress: A Missed Chance for Sensible Judicial Review of Managed Care Decisions." *American Journal of Law & Medicine* 27 (2001): 421–38.

Emanuel, Ezekiel, and Lee Goldman. "Protecting Patient Welfare in Managed Care: Six Safeguards." *Journal of Health Politics, Policy and Law* 23 (1998): 635–59.

Gervais, Karen G. et al., eds. *Ethical Challenges in Managed Care.* Washington, DC: Georgetown University Press, 1999.

Gostin, Lawrence O. "Managed Care, Conflicts of Interest, and Quality." *Hastings Center Report* 30 (2000): 27–28.

Jacobson, Peter D. *Strangers in the Night: Law and Medicine in the Managed Care Era.* New York: Oxford University Press, 2002.

Lee, Bryan. "Managed Care: Health Providers' Bill of Rights Now Law in California." *Journal of Law, Medicine & Ethics* 31 (2003): 157–59.

Little, John P. "Managed Care Contracts of Adhesion: Terminating the Doctor-Patient Relationship and Endangering Patient Health." *Rutgers Law Review* 49 (1997): 1397–1444.

BIBLIOGRAPHY

Angell, Marcia. "The Supreme Court and Physician-Assisted Suicide—The Ultimate Right." *New England Journal of Medicine* 336 (1997): 50–53.

Annas, George J. *Standard of Care: The Law of American Bioethics.* New York: Oxford University Press, 1993.

———. "*Roe v. Wade* Reaffirmed Again." *Hastings Center Report* 16 (1986): 26–27.

Arthur, John, and William Shaw, eds. *Readings in the Philosophy of Law*, 3rd edition. Upper Saddle River, NJ: Prentice Hall, 2001.

Beauchamp, Tom L., and James F. Childress. *Principles of Biomedical Ethics*, 5th edition. New York: Oxford University Press, 2001.

Beauchamp, Tom L., and Robert M. Veatch, eds. *Ethical Issues in Death and Dying*, 2nd edition. Upper Saddle River, NJ: Prentice Hall, 1996.

Beauchamp, Tom L., and LeRoy Walters, eds. *Contemporary Issues in Bioethics*, 4th edition. Belmont, CA: Wadsworth, 1994.

Bickel, Alexander M. *The Least Dangerous Branch: The Supreme Court at the Bar of Politics*, 2nd edition. New Haven: Yale University Press, 1986.

Bloche, M. Gregg, and Peter D. Jacobson. "The Supreme Court and Bedside Rationing." *Journal of the American Medical Association* 284 (2000): 2776–79.

Buchanan, Allen. "Managed Care: Rationing without Justice, but Not Unjustly." *Journal of Health Politics, Policy and Law* 23 (1998): 617–34.

Burtt, Edwin A., ed. *The English Philosophers from Bacon to Mill.* New York: Modern Library, 1967.

Cahill, Michael T., and Peter D. Jacobson. "*Pegram's* Regress: A Missed Chance for Sensible Judicial Review of Managed Care Decisions." *American Journal of Law & Medicine* 27 (2001): 421–38.

Capron, Alexander Morgan. "Punishing Mothers." *Hastings Center Report* 28 (1998): 31–33.

———. "Morality and the State, Law and Legalism." *Hastings Center Report* 26 (1996): 35–37.

————. "Constitutionalizing Death." *Hastings Center Report* 25 (1995): 23–24.

Coope, Christopher Miles. "Death with Dignity." *Hastings Center Report* 27 (1997): 37–38.

Dresser, Rebecca. "Procreation and Punishment." *Hastings Center Report* 31 (2001): 8–9.

Dworkin, Ronald. *Life's Dominion: An Argument about Abortion, Euthanasia, and Individual Freedom.* New York: Knopf, 1993.

Edwards, Rem B., and Glenn C. Graber, eds. *Bio-Ethics.* San Diego: Harcourt Brace Jovanovich, 1988.

Emanuel, Ezekiel, and Lee Goldman. "Protecting Patient Welfare in Managed Care: Six Safeguards." *Journal of Health Politics, Policy and Law* 23 (1998): 635-659.

Epstein, Lee, and Joseph Kobylka. *The Supreme Court and Legal Change: Abortion and the Death Penalty.* Chapel Hill: The University of North Carolina Press, 1992.

Etzioni, Amitai. "Medical Records: Enhancing Privacy, Preserving the Common Good." *Hastings Center Report* 29 (1999): 14–23.

Foley, Kathleen. "Competent Care for the Dying Instead of Physician-Assisted Suicide." *New England Journal of Medicine* 336 (1997): 54–58.

Furrow, Barry R., et al. *Bioethics: Health Care Law and Ethics*, 4th edition. St. Paul, MN: West Group, 2001.

————. *Health Law*, 2nd edition. St. Paul, MN: West Group, 2000.

Gervais, Karen G., et al., eds. *Ethical Challenges in Managed Care.* Washington, DC: Georgetown University Press, 1999.

Gostin, Lawrence O., ed. *Public Health Law and Ethics.* Berkeley: University of California Press, 2002.

————. "The Rights of Pregnant Women: The Supreme Court and Drug Testing." *Hastings Center Report* 31 (2001): 8–9.

————. "Managed Care, Conflicts of Interest, and Quality." *Hastings Center Report* 30 (2000): 27–28.

Gottlieb, Stephen E. *Morality Imposed: The Rehnquist Court and Liberty in America.* New York: New York University Press, 2000.

Gray, Jennifer. "Public Health: Bush's Smallpox Vaccination Plan." *Journal of Law, Medicine & Ethics* 31 (2003): 312–14.

Hall, Kermit L., ed. *The Oxford Companion to the Supreme Court of the United States*. New York: Oxford University Press, 1992.

Halper, Thomas. "Privacy and Autonomy: From Warren and Brandeis to *Roe* and *Cruzan*." *Journal of Medicine and Philosophy* 21 (1996): 121–35.

Halpern, Aviva. "Pain: No Medical Necessity Defense for Marijuana to Controlled Substances Act." *Journal of Law, Medicine & Ethics* 29 (2001): 410–11.

Harris, Jr., C. E. *Applying Moral Theories*, 3rd edition. Belmont, CA: Wadsworth, 1997.

Hinman, Lawrence M., ed. *Contemporary Moral Issues: Diversity and Consensus*, 2nd edition. Upper Saddle River, NJ: Prentice Hall, 2000.

Irons, Peter. *A People's History of the Supreme Court*. New York: Penguin Books, 2000.

Jacobson, Peter D. *Strangers in the Night: Law and Medicine in the Managed Care Era*. New York: Oxford University Press, 2002.

Jonsen, Albert R., Mark Siegler, and William J. Winslade. *Clinical Ethics: A Practical Approach to Ethical Decisions in Clinical Medicine*, 4th edition. New York: McGraw-Hill, 1998.

Lazarus, Edward. *Closed Chambers: The Rise, Fall, and Future of the Modern Supreme Court*. New York: Penguin Books, 1999.

Lee, Bryan. "Managed Care: Health Providers' Bill of Rights Now Law in California." *The Journal of Law, Medicine & Ethics* 31 (2003): 157–59.

Little, John P. "Managed Care Contracts of Adhesion: Terminating the Doctor-Patient Relationship and Endangering Patient Health." *Rutgers Law Review* 49 (1997): 1397–1444.

Lombardo, Paul A. "Facing Carrie Buck." *Hastings Center Report* 33 (2003): 14–17.

Mappes, Thomas A. "Persistent Vegetative State, Prospective Thinking, and Advance Directives." *Kennedy Institute of Ethics Journal* 13 (2003): 119–39.

McKinlay, John B., ed. *Law and Ethics in Health Care*. Cambridge: MIT Press, 1982.

Meilaender, Gilbert. "Less Law? Or Different Law?" *Hastings Center Report* 26 (1996): 39–40.

Menikoff, Jerry. *Law and Bioethics: An Introduction*. Washington, DC: Georgetown University Press, 2001.

Morreim, E. Haavi. *Holding Health Care Accountable: Law and the New Medical Marketplace*. New York: Oxford University Press, 2001.

Munson, Ronald. *Intervention and Reflection: Basic Issues in Medical Ethics*, 6th edition. Belmont, CA: Wadsworth, 2000.

National Association of Social Workers. *NASW Code of Ethics*. 1997.

Nowak, John E., and Ronald D. Rotunda. *Constitutional Law*, 6th edition. St. Paul, MN: West Group, 2000.

Orentlicher, David. *Matters of Life and Death: Making Moral Theory Work in Medical Ethics and the Law*. Princeton: Princeton University Press, 2001.

Peltason, J. W., and Sue Davis. *Understanding the Constitution*, 15th edition. Belmont, CA: Wadsworth, 2000.

Pence, Gregory E. *Classic Issues in Medical Ethics: Accounts of Cases that Have Shaped Medical Ethics, with Philosophical, Legal, and Historical Backgrounds*, 2nd edition. New York: McGraw-Hill, 1995.

Reich, Warren T., ed. *Encyclopedia of Bioethics*, 2nd edition. New York: Simon & Schuster and Macmillan, 1995.

Rich, Ben A. "*Oregon v. Ashcroft*: The Battle over the Soul of Medicine." *Cambridge Quarterly of Health Care Ethics* 12 (2003): 310–21.

Rosen, Jeffrey. "Kennedy Curse: On Sodomy, the Court Overreaches." *New Republic*, July 21, 2003, 15–18.

Schneider, Carl E., ed. *Law at the End of Life: The Supreme Court and Assisted Suicide*. Ann Arbor: University of Michigan Press, 2000.

———. "Justification by Faith." *Hastings Center Report* 29 (1999): 24–25.

———. "Moral Discourse, Bioethics, and the Law." *Hastings Center Report* 26 (1996): 37–39.

Shapiro, Michael H., Roy G. Spece, Jr., Rebecca Dresser, and Ellen Wright Clayton. *Bioethics and Law: Cases, Materials and Problems*, 2nd edition. St. Paul, MN: West Publishing Company, 2003.

Sullivan, Andrew. "Unnatural Law: What Sodomy Laws Really Mean."

New Republic, March 24, 2003, 18–23.

———. "Citizens: On Sodomy, the Court Gets It Right." *New Republic*, July 21, 2003, 18–19.

Tribe, Laurence H., and Michael C. Dorf. *On Reading the Constitution*. Cambridge: Harvard University Press, 1991.

Turkington, Richard C., George B. Trubow, and Anita L. Allen, eds. *Privacy: Cases and Materials*. Houston, TX: John Marshall Publishing Co., 1992.

Veatch, Robert M. *The Basics of Bioethics*. Upper Saddle River, NJ: Prentice Hall, 2000.

———. *A Theory of Medical Ethics*. New York: Basic Books, 1981.

———, ed. *Medical Ethics*, 2nd edition. Boston: Jones and Bartlett, 1997.

Warren, Samuel, and Louis Brandeis. "The Right to Privacy." *Harvard Law Review* (1890): 193–220.

Wiley, Lindsay F. "Assisted Suicide: Court Strikes Down Ashcroft Directive." *Journal of Law, Medicine & Ethics* 30 (2002): 459–60.

Wolf, Susan M., ed. *Feminism and Bioethics: Beyond Reproduction*. New York: Oxford University Press, 1996.

Zimmerman, Sacha. "Fetal Position: The Real Threat to *Roe v. Wade*." *New Republic*, August 18 and 25, 2003, 14–17.

INDEX

abortion, 109-181; constitutional issues surrounding, 110-112, 119-130, 133-140, 144-146, 151-163, 168, 181; ethical issues surrounding, 112-116; 131-133; medically necessary, 390-399; sacredness of life, 115-116, 126-128; right to, 110-111, 116-130; self-determination, 146-149; state regulation of, 111-112, 128-129, 133-140, 144-181

American Academy of Pediatrics Committee on Bioethics, 190

Annas, George J., 226, 249

Any Willing Provider law, 402

artificial hydration and nutrition, 325, 328-330, 335, 338-353

artificial womb, 132-133

Ashcroft, John, 279-280

assisted reproductive technologies, 77, 132-133

assisted suicide. *See* physician-assisted suicide.

Atkins v. Virginia, 302

autonomy, defined, 19-20, 34-35; reproductive rights for women, 109-130, 143-149, 164-181;

sexual freedom, 29-68; treatment of mental illness, 290-291, 294-295, 310-321

Bellotti v. Baird, 167

beneficence, principle of, 20-21

best interests standard, 252-253, 287-297

Bickel, Alexander, 9-10

bioethics and law. *See* medical ethics and law.

Brandeis, Justice Louis, 287, 311

Buchanan, Allen, 384-385

Capron, Alexander M., 8

Carey v. Population Services International, 49

children, access to abortion, 167; organ donation, 39; parental control over medical decisions regarding, 200-206; withholding medical care from, 185-186, 189-191, 199-206

City of Akron v. Akron Center for Reproductive Health, 167

clear and convincing evidence standard, 324-325, 342-353